Everyman, I will go with thee,
and be thy guide

ITALIAN TALES FROM THE AGE OF SHAKESPEARE

Edited by
PAMELA JOSEPH BENSON
Rhode Island College

EVERYMAN
J. M. DENT · LONDON
CHARLES E. TUTTLE
VERMONT

Consultant Editor for this Series
ROBIN KIRKPATRICK
University of Cambridge

First published by Everyman Paperbacks in 1996
Introduction and other critical apparatus © J. M. Dent 1996

J. M. Dent
Orion Publishing Group
Orion House
5 Upper St Martin's Lane
London WC2H 9EA
and
Charles E. Tuttle Co. Inc.
28 South Main Street
Rutland, Vermont 05701, USA

Typeset in Sabon by CentraCet Ltd, Cambridge
Printed in Great Britain by
The Guernsey Press Co. Ltd, Guernsey, C. I.

British Library Cataloguing-in-Publication Data is
available upon request.

ISBN 0 460 87551 5

CONTENTS

Note on the English Authors and the Editor vii
Chronology of the Authors' Lives xi
Chronology of the Authors' Times xiv
Introduction xxi
Note on the Text xxxiv

A Tale from Sir Thomas Elyot's *The Governour*
  Titus and Gisippus 1

Nine Tales from William Painter's *The Palace of Pleasure*
  Melchisedech's Tale of Three Kings 25
  Ermino Grimaldi 28
  Andreuccio of Perugia 31
  Giletta of Narbona 44
  Philenio Sisterno 53
  King Massinissa and Queen Sophonisba 63
  The Duchess of Malfi 79
  Two Gentlewomen of Venice 118
  The Lady of Boeme 149

A Tale from *The Sack-Full of Newes*
  The Old Man and His Young Wife 177

A Tale from *The Forrest of Fancy*
  Seigneor Vergelis and His Wife 181

Three Tales from Barnabe Riche's *His Farewell to Militarie
Profession*
  Of Apolonius and Silla 189

Of Two Brethren and Their Wives   210
Of Gonsales and His Vertuous Wife Agatha   236

Two Tales from Whetstone's *An Heptameron of Civill
Discourses*
Friar Inganno   255
Promos and Cassandra   259

Four Tales from *Tarlton's Newes out of Purgatorie*
Friar Onion   273
Why the Cook Sat in Purgatory   279
The Gentlewoman of Lyons   283
The Two Lovers of Pisa   287

Notes   297
Glossary   328
Anthology of Criticism   346
Suggestions for Further Reading   355
Acknowledgements   357

NOTE ON THE ENGLISH AUTHORS
AND THE EDITOR

SIR THOMAS ELYOT (1490?–1546) was active at the court of
Henry VIII. He was well educated; some have claimed he went
to university, but in the preface to his *Castell of Helth* (1534) he
says that he was his own tutor from the age of twelve in all
subjects but medicine. His father was justice of assize (circuit
court) and from 1511 until 1528 Elyot was clerk to the assize.
In 1531 he published *The Boke named The Governour* and
dedicated it to King Henry. The king received it favourably and
sent him as ambassador to the court of the Holy Roman
Emperor Charles V to try to induce him to take a more
favourable view of Henry's intention to divorce Catherine of
Aragon, but Elyot's efforts seem to have been only half-hearted;
he was again sent as ambassador to Charles in 1534–6. Elyot
was a well-respected author. His works include a Latin–English
dictionary (1531), *The Knowledge which maketh a Wise Man*
and *Pasquyll the Playne* (1533), and *The Defence of Good
Women* (1545). *The Boke named The Governour* is a practical
treatise on the education of youths who 'will have authority in
a weal public', that is, members of the nobility and upper class.
In it Elyot stresses the connection between learning and morals.
'Titus and Gisippus', which is included in the present volume, is
the only story in *The Governour*; Elyot describes it as 'an
example of friendship'.

WILLIAM PAINTER (1540?–94) was educated at St John's College, Cambridge, although he may not have taken a degree. He
was headmaster of a school and, later, the clerk of the ordnance
in the Tower of London, where he seems to have abused his
position by fraudulent appropriation of large sums of money.
His *Palace of Pleasure* (volume I, 1566; complete edition 1575)
is an anthology of his translations of 101 stories by Roman,
Italian and French authors; it gave English readers their first
opportunity to read a large number of continental stories.

Painter did not create a frame story for his collection, but his voice is frequently heard in the many moralizing comments he added to the tales. The dedicatory letters explain that he believes that reading his translations is good for both moral and physical health because they teach good behaviour and they discharge bad humours. *The Palace* was very popular; many playwrights drew their plots and sub-plots from stories in Painter's collection. A majority of the tales in the present volume are from *The Palace*.

GEORGE WHETSTONE (1551–87) was the son of a rich London haberdasher. His father died when he was a small child and, according to his account in *Rocke of Regard* (1576), he mishandled his inheritance by spending a profligate youth in London. His works show that he had a humanist education, but there is no record of his having matriculated from one of the universities, as two of his brothers did. He lived near the Inns of Court and had friends who were studying law, so he may have been a law student, although there is no record of it. He probably travelled to France in 1577 and to Italy in 1580. At Burghley's instigation, he was sent as civilian commissary of musters (troops) under Thomas Digges in the Netherlands. There he was killed in a duel; in a letter written after his death, Digges praised his honesty and suggested that he duelled because he could not be corrupted. Whetstone published fourteen works. The *Heptameron* (1582) purports to be the record of formal conversations about marriage in which he participated during seven days at Christmas time in a country house near Ravenna, Italy during his travels in 1580. The dialogue is Italianate in its structure and in the social customs it represents; it resembles Castiglione's *Il Cortegiano*, although Whetstone's characters have allegorical names. Seven stories are told in the dialogue; two from the fourth day are included in this volume.

BARNABE RICHE (1542–1617) was a professional soldier and a professional writer. His military career was hard. He served at Le Havre during 1562–3 in a campaign in which the English lost three-quarters of their men to typhus. In 1570–82 he served primarily in Ireland, although he also was in the Netherlands. In 1582, he returned to England from Ireland, having survived the starvation and illness rampant in the troops after Queen

Elizabeth's sudden discharge of them following the suppression of Desmond's rebellion in 1581. He later returned to military service in Ireland and was granted a pension by the queen, although he complains that it was difficult to collect. Riche's private life was tumultuous. He was imprisoned for debt and arrested by the Star Chamber, probably for slander. His first published work was *A Right Pleasant Dialogue between Mercury and an English Soldier*, and many of his other works have to do with military matters. *His Farewell to Militarie Profession* (1581) consists of three dedicatory epistles: one to the 'Gentlewomen both of England and Ireland', another to the noble soldiers of the same countries, and a third 'to the readers in general'. There are two poems in praise of the author, one poem from the printer, eight stories, and a conclusion which includes another story. Five of the stories are pastiches of several Italian tales; three of them are translations of single stories. Riche was a prolific author, although his claim to have written twenty-six works has been challenged because he borrowed so heavily from other authors' works. Three stories from *His Farewell* are included in the present volume.

The Sack-Full of Newes (before 1575) is a twelve-page-long collection of twenty-two very brief, untitled stories that are not connected by any sort of framework. The stories are translations and retellings of stories that appear elsewhere. *The Sack-Full* is referred to by critics as a 'jest book' because the stories are reduced to their bare essentials. The story included in this volume is one of the longer stories in *The Sack-Full*.

The author of *The Forrest of Fancy* (1579) is identified only as H. C. Despite much speculation, he has not been identified. The book includes a great variety of fictional materials, among them prose letters from various sorts of lovers trying to persuade ladies to love them, a letter from Oedipus' son Eteocles to his brother Polyneices, and poems on many subjects. Four translated stories conclude the volume; one of these is included here.

RICHARD TARLTON (d. 1588), of the acting troop the Queen's Men, was Queen Elizabeth's favourite clown. His clowning combined verbal wit, song and dance; his technique was ad lib, and Hamlet's advice to the players (III.ii.42–50), in which he requests that they make the clowns 'speak no more than is set down for them', may have been a response to the method he established. Tarlton was famed for his jigs (farces in rhyme that were sung and danced); he played a tabor (a small drum) and a pipe. After his death in 1588 several books and pamphlets were issued purporting to record his jests or even to have been written by him. *Tarltons Newes out of Purgatorie* (1590) is one of these. The anonymous author of this work explains that he fell asleep and was visited by the spirit of Dick Tarlton with 'newes'. The news consists of a comical description of Purgatory and a collection of translated stories which are used to explain the presence of some of the inhabitants and their punishments. The stories included in the present volume are accompanied with excerpts from the frame.

PAMELA JOSEPH BENSON was educated at the University of California, Berkeley, the University of Florence and Columbia University. She has taught at Yale University and Harvard University and is currently Professor of English at Rhode Island College. She has contributed to *The Spenser Encyclopedia*, the *Dante Encyclopedia*, *Spenser Studies*, *English Literary Renaissance*, *Italica* and other journals. Her widely-reviewed *The Invention of the Renaissance Woman: The Challenge of Female Independence in the Literature and Thought of Italy and England* was published in 1992. She is at work on *Gualdrada and the Emperor's Kiss: Politics, Narrative and Art in a Florentine Legend*.

CHRONOLOGY OF THE AUTHORS' LIVES

Year   Life

1490   Sir Thomas Elyot born
1511   Elyot clerk to the assize, western circuit (through 1528)
1531   Elyot, *The Boke named The Governour*
       Elyot represents Henry VIII at the court of the Emperor Charles V
       (through 1532)
1533   Elyot, *The Knowledge which maketh a Wise Man*, *Pasquyll the
       Playne*
1534   Elyot swears to the Oath of Supremacy
1535   Elyot represents Henry VIII at the court of the Emperor Charles V
1540   William Painter born
       Elyot, translation of Eucolpius, *Image of Governance*
1542   Barnaby Riche born?
1544   George Whetstone born?
1545   Elyot, *The Defence of Good Women*
1546   Sir Thomas Elyot dies
1550   Straparola, *Le piacevoli notti*
1551   Whetstone born?
1554   Bandello, *Novelle* I–III
1557   *Sackfull of Newes* entered in Stationer's Register
       (possibly not the novella collection)
1558   Painter, *Murder of Solyman*
1559   Belleforest, *Histoires tragiques*, volume I
1560   Painter master of Sevenoaks School
1561   Painter appointed clerk of the ordnance in the Tower, 9 February
1562   Riche serves under the earl of Warwick at Le Havre (through
       1563)
       Bandello dies
1565   Riche borrows money to equip a privateering enterprise
       Giraldi Cinthio, *Hecatommithi*
       Painter marries Dorothy Bonham of Cowling (approximate date)
1566   Painter, *Palace of Pleasure*, volume I
1567   Painter, *Second Tome of the Palace of Pleasure*
1569   Painter, second edition of *Palace of Pleasure*, volume I

Year Life

1570   Riche imprisoned and released on bond for debt incurred by loss in
       privateering
       Riche's service in Ireland begins
1572   Riche repays bond
       Riche and Whetstone serve in the Netherlands
1573   Bandello, *Novelle* IV
       Riche begins service in Ireland that continues, with interruptions
       until 1582
1574   Riche, *A Right Pleasant Dialogue between Mercury and an English
       Soldier*
1575   Before this date an edition of *The Sack-Full of Newes* had been
       published
       Painter, *Palace of Pleasure*, 2 volumes
1576   Whetstone, *Rocke of Regard*
       Whetstone may have been a student at the Inns of Court, near
       which he was living
1577   Whetstone may have travelled in France
1578   Whetstone sails on expedition with Sir Humphrey Gilbert
1579   *The Forrest of Fancy*
1580   Whetstone travels in Italy
1581   Riche, *His Farewell to Militarie Profession* and *Strange and
       Wonderful Adventures of Don Simonides*
1582   Whetstone, *Heptameron of Civill Discourses*
       Riche returns to England
       Belleforest, *Histoires tragiques*, seventh and last volume
1584   Riche, *Seconde Tome of Don Simonides*
       Whetstone, *Mirror for Magistrates of Cities* and *Touchstone for
       the Time*
1585   Whetstone, *Enemy to Unthriftiness* (second edition of *Mirror for
       Magistrates*) and *Mirror of True Honor*
1586   Whetstone, *English Mirror*
       Whetstone serves in Leicester's campaign in the Low Countries;
       present at Sidney's death ??
       Riche marries Katherine Aston, daughter of Sir Edward Aston,
       knight
1587   Riche receives a small life pension from the queen for his service in
       Ireland
       Whetstone appointed a commissary of musters
       Whetstone dies
1588   Death of Richard Tarlton
1590   Publication of *Tarlton's Newes out of Purgatorie*
1592   Riche, *Adventures of Brusanus*

Year *Life*

1593 Riche arrested, probably for slander, by warrant of the Star
      Chamber
      Whetstone, *Aurelia* (new edition of *Heptameron*)
1594 Painter dies
1614 Riche, *The Honesty of this Age*
1617 Riche dies

Year	Historical Event
1527	Sack of Rome
1528	Italian edition of Castiglione's *Cortegiano*
1529	France renounces her claims on Italy
	More becomes chancellor
1530	English clergy call Henry 'Supreme Head of the Church, as far as the law allows'
	Thomas Hoby born
1531	Act against Vagabonds
1532	Henry divorces Catherine of Aragon
	Thomas More resigns
	Third edition of Ariosto's *Orlando Furioso*
1533	Cranmer archbishop of Canterbury
	Henry excommunicated
	Henry marries Anne Boleyn
1534	Paul III pope
	Acts of Succession and Supremacy
1535	Henry 'supreme head on earth' of the English Church
	Cromwell's visitation of monasteries
	More and Fisher executed
	Coverdale Bible
1536	Anne Boleyn executed
	Henry marries Jane Seymour
	New Act of Succession
	Act against Vagabonds
	Thomas Wyatt active as poet
1537	The pope condemns slavery
1538	English Bible required in every church
	Breaking of images
1539	Great Bible
	Greater abbeys suppressed
1540	Jesuit order founded
	Fall and execution of Cromwell
	Henry marries Anne of Cleves; marriage annulled
	Henry marries Catherine Howard

Year   Historical Event

1541   Henry assumes titles 'King of Ireland' and 'Head of the Church in
       Ireland'
1542   Catherine Howard executed
       English troops rout the Scots at the battle of Solway Moss
       Act against Vagabonds
       Mary becomes queen of Scotland
       Wyatt dies
1543   Surrey active as poet
1544   War with France; capture of Boulogne
1545   Council of Trent opens
       Confiscation of chantries
1546   Peace with France
       Luther dies
1547   Death of Henry VIII; accession of Edward VI
       Execution of Surrey
       Penal slavery for some types of vagabond
1549   *Book of Common Prayer*
       William Thomas, *The Historie of Italie*
       War with France
1550   First edition of Vasari's *Lives of the most excellent Italian
       Architects, Painters and Sculptors*
       William Thomas, *The Principal Rules of the Italian Grammar*
       Julius III pope
       Roman Catholic bishops removed
       Burning of books at Oxford
1552   Edmund Spenser born
       Walter Ralegh born?
1553   Death of Edward VI; accession of Mary I
       Thomas Wilson, *Art of Rhetoric*
1554   Philip Sidney born
       Richard Hooker born
       Rebellion of Sir Thomas Wyatt
       Execution of Lady Jane Grey
       Mary marries Philip of Spain
       England reconciled with Rome
1555   *Mirror for Magistrates*
       Paul IV pope
       Persecution of Protestants: Latimer and Ridley burned
1556   Philip II king of Spain, the Indies, Netherlands, Naples
       Philip II excommunicated
       Cranmer burned

Year	Historical Event
1557	Tottel's *Miscellany*
	More, *English Works*
	Henry Howard, earl of Surrey, *Aeneis*
	War with France
1558	John Knox, *First Blast of the Trumpet* . . .
	Death of Mary; accession of Elizabeth I
	Loss of Calais
1559	Peace with France
	Pius IV pope
	Mary of Scotland marries the dauphin
	Revolution in Scotland assisted by Elizabeth
	Acts of Uniformity (fine for not attending church) and Supremacy
	Popular iconoclasm and looting of churches
1560	Geneva Bible
	Peace with Scotland
	Statute against the destruction of church monuments
1561	Publication of Thomas Hoby's translation of *The Courtier*
	English occupation of Le Havre
	O'Neill's rebellion in Ireland
1562	French civil war
	Arthur Brooke, *Romeus and Juliet* (translated from Bandello)
1563	John Foxe, *Book of Martyrs*
	Council of Trent ends
	Act forbidding conversion of arable land to pasture
	Elizabeth's first Poor Law
1564	Calvin dies
	Michelangelo dies
	Galileo born
	William Shakespeare born
	Christopher Marlowe born
1565	Arthur Golding, translation of Ovid's *Metamorphoses* I–IV
1566	Pius V pope
	James (afterwards VI of Scotland and I of England) born
	Hoby dies
1567	Golding, *Metamorphoses*, I–XV
	Fenton, *Certain Tragical Discourses*
	Revolt of the Netherlands
	Thomas Nashe born
1568	Mary Queen of Scots flies to England
	Growing tension with Spain
	Ascham dies
1569	Unsuccessful rebellion of Norfolk and northern earls

Year	Historical Event
1570	Queen Elizabeth excommunicated
	Ascham, *The Schoolmaster*
1571	Battle of Lepanto
	Ridolfi plot
	Diplomatic relations with Spain broken off
	Thirty-nine Articles enforced
1572	St Bartholomew Day massacre in France
	Gregory XIII pope
	Treaty of Blois
	John Donne born
	Ben Jonson born
	Unpatronized troops of actors declared rogues and vagabonds
1573	Diplomatic relations with Spain resumed
	Giraldi Cinthio dies
1574	Persecution of Roman Catholics
1575	Burning of Anabaptists
	John Marston born?
	Thomas Heywood born?
	George Pettie, *The Petite Palace of Pettie his Pleasure*
1576	James Burbage builds the Theatre in London
	Sack of Antwerp
	Frobisher's voyage begins
	Priests from Douai arrive
1577	Raphael Holinshed, *Chronicle*
	Francis Drake sets out to voyage around the world
	Curtain Theatre opens
	Blackfriars Theatre opens
1578	John Lyly, *Euphues*
1579	Spenser, *The Shepheardes' Calender*
	Sidney, *Arcadia*, *Astrophil and Stella*, *Defence of Poesy*
	Fenton, translation of Guicciardini's *History*
	Margaret Tyler, *The Mirrour of Knighthood*, translation
	Negotiations for marriage between Elizabeth and Alençon, duke of Anjou
	Organization of Jesuit mission to England
1580	Letter of cardinal of Como pronouncing the assassination of Elizabeth lawful and worthy of merit
	John Webster born
1581	Torquato Tasso, *Gerusalemme liberata*
	Pettie, translation of Guazzo, *Civil Conversation*
	Alençon in England
	Execution of Campion
1582	Richard Hakluyt, *Voyages*

Year	Historical Event
1583	Philip Stubbs, *Anatomy of Abuses*
	Irish rebellion defeated
	Queen's Players formed
	Whitgift archbishop of Canterbury
1584	Ralegh's failure in Virginia
1585	Sixtus V pope
	Expedition to Netherlands under Leicester
1586	Thomas Kyd's *Spanish Tragedy* acted?
	Sidney dies after battle of Zutphen
	Babington Plot
	Trial of Mary Queen of Scots
1587	Marlowe, *Tamburlaine*, I
	Mary Queen of Scots beheaded
	Pope proclaims a crusade against England
1588	Montaigne, *Essais*
	Lyly's *Galathea*? and *Endimion* acted
	Stapleton, *Vita Thomae Mori*
	Defeat of the Spanish Armada
1589	Marlowe, *The Jew of Malta* and *Dr Faustus* acted
	George Puttenham, *Art of English Poetry*
1590	Spenser, *The Faerie Queene*, I–III
	Thomas Lodge, *Rosalynde*
	Shakespeare, *Two Gentlemen of Verona* (earliest possible date)
	Urban VII pope
1591	Shakespeare, *Henry VI* acted
	Sir John Harington, translation of *Orlando Furioso*
	Sidney, *Astrophil and Stella* (corrupt text)
	Robert Southwell, *Mary Magdalene's Tears*
	Increased severity against recusants
1592	Robert Greene, *Friar Bacon and Friar Bungay* acted
	Marlowe, *Edward II* acted ?
	Clement VIII pope
	Rose Theatre opens
1593	Richard Hooker, *Laws of Ecclesiastical Polity*, I–IV
	Plague closes theatres
	Marlowe dies
	Henry IV of France changes his religion
	Increased severity against recusants
1594	Thomas Nashe, *Unfortunate Traveller*

Year   *Historical Event*

1595   Spenser, *Amoretti*, 'Epithalamium'
        Shakespeare, *Midsummer Night's Dream, Romeo and Juliet* acted
        Thomas Beddingfield, translation of Machiavelli's *Florentine Histories*
        Execution of Southwell
        Ralegh's voyage to Guiana
        Drake and Hawkins die on unsuccessful voyage to West Indies

1596   Shakespeare, *Richard II, Merchant of Venice* acted
        Spenser, *Faerie Queene*, IV–VI, *Four Hymns*
        Shakespeare, *Merchant of Venice* acted
        Calais captured by Spanish
        Essex storms Cadiz
        Spanish aid the Irish

1597   Francis Bacon, *Essays*
        Nashe, *Isle of Dogs*
        Shakespeare, *Henry IV* acted
        Thomas Morley, *Plain Introduction to Practical Music*
        John Dowland, *Songs of Four Parts*
        James VI and I, *Demonology*
        Unsuccessful expedition against the Spanish under Essex, Munsard and Vere

1598   Jonson, *Everyman in his Humour*
        Sidney, *Arcadia* with *Lady of May*, *Certain Sonnets*, and improved text of *Astrophil*
        Thomas Speght's first edition of Chaucer
        Philip II dies
        End of French civil war; Edict of Nantes
        New Poor Law
        Burghley dies

1599   Shakespeare, *Much Ado about Nothing, As You Like It, Julius Caesar, Henry V* acted
        Jonson, *Everyman out of his Humour*
        Essex imprisoned
        Globe Playhouse opened
        Spanish fleet sent in aid of Irish dissipated by bad weather
        Essex sent to Ireland as lord deputy; his unauthorized return and imprisonment
        Spenser dies
        Oliver Cromwell born

Year	Historical Event
1600	Shakespeare, *Merry Wives of Windsor*, *Troilus and Cressida*
	George Chapman, *Bussy d'Ambois* acted?
	Jonson, *Cynthia's Revels* acted
	Edward Fairfax, *Godfrey of Buloigne* (Tasso's *Gerusalemme liberata*)
	East India Company founded
	Future Charles I born
	Hooker dies
	Nashe dies
1601	Shakespeare, *Twelfth Night?*, *Hamlet*
	Essex rebellion and execution
1602	Galileo discovers law of falling bodies
	Bodleian Library opened
1603	Shakespeare, *All's Well that Ends Well?*
	Elizabeth I dies
	James I succeeds
	King's Men appointed
	Plague closes theatres
	Mountjoy completes conquest of Ireland

INTRODUCTION

During Shakespeare's lifetime, some of the most popular literature in England was originally written in Italian. Thomas Hoby's
translation of Castiglione's *The Book of the Courtier* (1561),
William Painter's *The Palace of Pleasure* (1566), an anthology
that included many translations of Italian stories, and Sir John
Harington's version of Ariosto's *Orlando Furioso* (1591) are
outstanding examples of sixteenth-century English translations
of celebrated Italian texts. Hoby's and Harington's works are
well known and easily available today, but Painter's *Palace* is
not well known or widely available, nor are the other collections
that followed Painter's lead and included translations from the
Italian: Barnabe Riche's *His Farewell to Militarie Profession*,
George Whetstone's *Heptameron*, and the anonymous *Tarlton's
Newes out of Purgatorie*, *The Forrest of Fancy*, and *The Sack-
Full of Newes*. Most readers know the story anthologies, if they
know them at all, only as the volumes from which Shakespeare
drew the plots of several of his plays. In assembling the
collection of stories from the above volumes to present here in
Italian Tales from the Age of Shakespeare, it has been my goal
to recover the genre for modern readers so that its pleasures
may be experienced, its characteristics understood and its role
in Elizabethan culture explored.

'Novella' (plural 'novelle'), the Italian term for these tales,
means 'news' or 'something new', and it suggests one of the
most important characteristics of the genre: no matter how old
they really are and how many times they have been told, they
are narrated as though they were fresh and new. The author
does not cite sources and heap up authorities but, rather, reports
the events and the words of the characters in the liveliest way
possible. The story being told may be a romance (an adventure
story about faraway places, in which fortunate coincidence plays
an important part) or a fabliau (a realistic and frequently bawdy
comic tale about lower-class people), but the emphasis is always

on what happened, the practical journalistic who, when, where, why and how.

Despite its name, the novella has very little to do with the classic novel and, despite its brevity, little to do with the modern short story.[1] It is not an immature stage in the development of these genres but, rather, a literary form unto itself, and reading novelle is made easier by remembering that while both novels and short stories emphasize interior life, the novella talks about actions. One cannot get to know the characters in a novella or empathize with them because in the novella the characters do not have an inner life beyond the simplest passions such as lust, fear and jealousy. What the characters in novelle do have, however, is wit: the ability to use words or deeds to manipulate events, other people and even fortune to their own advantage. The letters and speeches, the disguises and stratagems, that characters use to get what they want provide the pleasure of reading the genre. In a novella, the plot and plotting are all.

The Italian Novella

The central role of wit in the novella was established by Boccaccio in his *Decameron* (c. 1350), the most influential novella collection in Europe. It is an anthology of one hundred stories told by a group of young women and men over ten days while they are in the country to avoid the plague, and the overwhelming majority of the stories turn on the clever words or deeds that the protagonists employ to confront and even triumph over the barriers that fortune and other people put in the way of their practical or spiritual success. Boccaccio was the major prose stylist of the Italian late Middle Ages and early Renaissance, and the *Decameron* is characterized above all by the skill with which the stories are narrated, but two other characteristics, in addition to its style and the role assigned to wit, were major factors in the *Decameron*'s lasting popularity and influence. First, the variety of the tales: subject-matter, location, genre, and level of style change from tale to tale, so that readers have a sense that the whole of the contemporary world, Christian, Jewish, Moslem, courtly and peasant, urban and rural, is spread out before them. Secondly, the realism of the representation of events and everyday life in many of the tales: we smell the cesspools, know the value of jewels, hear the dialects and modes of speech of different regions and social classes. Prose, variety, verisimilitude and the confrontation between human wit and fortune, these are Boccaccio's legacy to his Italian and English successors – these and an enormous repertory of plots and characters to use and reuse.

The novella collection was one of the most popular literary forms in Italy in the late Middle Ages and the Renaissance, but, in order to provide background for the stories in this volume, the following account of the genre will discuss only works translated into English in Shakespeare's day: Matteo Bandello's *Novelle* (1554 and 1573), Giambattista Giraldi Cinthio's *Hecatommithi* (1565), Ser Giovanni Fiorentino's *Il pecorone* (*The Big Sheep*; c. 1378–1385), and Giovan Francesco Straparola's *Le piacevoli notti* (*The Delightful Nights*; 1550–3). All these authors wrote their novelle in prose. Bandello, a Dominican friar and a bishop, was the major Italian writer of stories in the sixteenth century; he was very popular with English translators. His huge four-part collection of 214 novelle has the variety of Boccaccio's and an added element: current events. Bandello prefaced each story with a dedicatory letter to a living (or recently deceased) contemporary, usually illustrious or a member of the ruling class, who he suggests will have a special interest in the content or tone of the story. He frequently claims that he just heard the story at someone's house the other night or that it happened recently in a nearby town; indeed, many of the stories are accounts of events that happened in Bandello's lifetime; they really are 'news' about sixteenth-century Italy. 'The Duchess of Malfi' is such a story.

Giambattista Giraldi Cinthio (1504–73) was at various times a professor of philosophy, literature and rhetoric and served as secretary to the dukes of Este. He was best known for his theoretical works on genre. His *Hecatommithi* (1565) contains more than one hundred stories narrated by a group of noble men and women travelling together on a ship to escape the sack of Rome in 1527; it also includes three dialogues on civil life. Cinthio explains that these stories are both delightful and useful; his goal is to prompt his readers' minds to wisdom and proper living. His narrator points out the moral teaching implied by the stories, and the nobles discuss it.

Boccaccio, Bandello and Cinthio all moved in court circles and found their primary initial audience among the upper classes and the highly educated; their novella collections show the influence of this environment in their frames and in their material and style. Nothing is known about Ser Giovanni and little about Straparola (*c.* 1480–*c.* 1557), the authors of the story anthologies from which the remaining tales in this volume are drawn, but their works themselves suggest a more popular audience. They were far less influential in Italy, and their stories are more formulaic. In Ser Giovanni's *Il pecorone* a young man in love with a nun becomes a monk and the chaplain at her convent in order to be near her; these two tell each other stories, both fictional and historical. Straparola's *Le piacevoli notti* takes place during the last days of carnival in a palace on an island in the Venetian lagoon. The group of people is gathered together by Lucrezia Sforza Gonzaga, a Milanese exile; although men are present, all the stories are narrated by women. This is the first anthology to include fairy-tales. The little that is known about the author suggests that he was a professional writer but not part of the literary elite.

Translation of the Novella in Sixteenth-Century England

In the sixteenth century the boundary between translating and imitating was not clear. Generally, translators can be said to have considered it their responsibility to provide a version of the foreign text that would please their readers by not being too foreign and their right to put their own stamp on the story rather than attempt to reproduce the original author's style.

The tales included in the present anthology provide a representative sample of the types of translations of novelle that were made, with one major restriction: I have included only prose translations. This is because, without exception, the novella was a prose form in Italian and I have taken prose to be one of the genre's essential characteristics. Nine stories from Painter's anthology form the core of the present volume because they are so good, because the *Palace* shaped the notion of what a novella was for English readers, and because it had so much influence on other story-writers and on dramatists; six of the included stories contributed plots or scenes to plays.[2] The single story from *The Sack-Full of Newes*, the one from *The Forrest of Fancy*, and the three from *Tarlton's Newes out of Purgatorie* are examples of popular renditions, whereas the two stories from Whetstone's *Heptameron* and the one from Elyot's *Governour* show what a highly educated writer might do with a novella. Riche's *Farewell to Militarie Profession* provides an example of a translation from Giraldi, rare in this period, and two samples of his method of interweaving several tales together. (Most of the story collections are divided into large units: for example, Boccaccio's *Decameron* and Cinthio's *Hecatommithi* are divided into days, and Bandello's *Novelle* and Painter's *Palace* into volumes. In all references to collections, Roman numerals refer to volume or day, while arabic numbers indicate the order in which stories appear within the volume or day.)

Painter acknowledges that his stories are translations and provides a list of the authors (mostly Italian) whose stories he has included. Some of his versions of Bandello's stories are longer than their Italian counterparts because they are not translated directly from the Italian but are based on French translations, and the French translators, Boaistuau and Belleforest, greatly increased the length of Bandello's tales; in their treatments, stories of seven to ten pages grew to twenty or thirty. The bulk of the amplification came from having the characters speak, write and recite long, rhetorically formal speeches, letters and poems; each French translator also broke into the narration of the stories to make moralizing comments in his own voice. As a result of these changes, the nature of the experience of reading a story changes: the pace is slower and the point of view is confused, since the narrator's moralizing often conflicts with a more sympathetic view of the character that remains in passages taken directly from the original. Painter translated three of his most influential stories, 'Romeo and Juliet', 'The Countess of Celant' and 'The Duchess of Malfi', from the French versions of Bandello. 'The Duchess of Malfi' is included in this volume to provide an example of the French style; 'Romeo and Juliet' is not, because Shakespeare probably worked from Arthur Brooke's verse adaptation of the French translation.

Painter translated all the other stories from the *Palace* in the present volume directly from Italian, and in these he was usually fairly faithful, although he sometimes anglicized the tales by adding details of life in England as he knew it when the Italian story gave no local information. For example, the husband in

Bandello's 'A Lady of Boeme' is reluctant to take his wife to live at court, but the narrator does not explain his reasons. The English narrator explains that providing his wife with clothes appropriate to court would drive him into debt to the draper and he would not be able to walk the streets without worrying about being arrested for debt. Such details translated the experience of the tale into something familiar to an English reader. Painter also added some moralizing passages to Bandello's stories and to no others.

All the tales in Barnabe Riche's *Farewell to Militarie Profession* are translations, rewritings and pastiches of other people's stories, especially Italian stories, although Riche does not reveal this fact until the third dedicatory letter, the one addressed 'To the Readers in General', and even then he is ambiguous. He divides his stories into two groups: 'tales that are forged only for delight', and 'Italian histories written likewise for pleasure by master L.B.'. 'Forged' is a cagey term; it does not indicate where the material that he forged came from. In fact, each of the stories in the first group interweaves material from several Italian stories. 'Apolonius and Silla' and 'Two Brethren', which are included in this volume, are typical. In writing 'Apolonius', Riche seems to have worked with Belleforest's (IV.59) French version of Bandello's romance (II.36), in combination with, among other sources, the original Italian version of Cinthio's 'Cesare Gravina' (V.8) and many stories in Painter's *Palace*, from which he took phrases and sentences verbatim. 'Two Brethren' combines four stories by Straparola (VIII.2, I.5, II.5, IV.4), although one (VIII.2) provides the framework on which the others are fastened. The final result in both cases is a variation on the original. The Italian source can still be recognized through all the added material, yet Riche does not attribute the borrowed tale or the directly quoted words and phrases to their authors. The three 'Italian histories written ... by master L.B.' are translated according to a completely different method. Each of them is a version of a single tale from Cinthio's *Hecatommithi*. 'Gonsales and his Vertuous Wife Agatha', included in this volume, is one of them.[3]

Sir Thomas Elyot and George Whetstone, the most sophisticated and ambitious authors whose works are included here, treated the original Italian stories as material for their own 'forging' and did not identify their sources. Both wrote very free adaptations of their originals; Elyot probably worked with a Latin translation of Boccaccio's tale rather than directly from the Italian novella. Both included the stories in serious didactic works whose form and content were influenced by Italian humanism, which stressed the study of the classics and the importance of the application of moral philosophy to everyday conduct and to government. *The Governour* is an exposition of Elyot's humanist theory of education; its goal is to reform the kind of education given to those who will hold positions of authority. 'Titus', the only novella in it, is directed at an audience that is interested in ethical questions. Elyot presents it as an example of friendship and suggests that it provides a moment of educative recreation. Whetstone's *An Heptameron of Civill Discourses* is a dialogue on the topic of marriage; its goal is to allow 'the better sort' to see their virtues and 'the inferior' to learn 'such rules of civil Government as wil rase out the blemish of their basenesse'. The interlocutors tell stories in order to illuminate the nature of marriage while entertaining the group. So 'Friar Inganno' and 'Promos and Cassandra', like Elyot's 'Titus', are directed at an audience that has taken the book in hand because of its interest in ethical questions.

The remaining three novelle collections, *Tarlton's Newes*, *The Forrest of Fancy* and *The Sack-Full of Newes*, differ from all the other works discussed so far because they condense the novelle rather than expanding them. *The Sack-Full of Newes* is an extreme example of this. 'The Old Man and His Young Wife', included in this volume, is a translation of a novella by Boccaccio, but the author of *Sack-Full* translated only the second half of Boccaccio's story and in doing so left out many of the details of the action, replaced the names of the characters with 'the old man', 'the wife', and 'the servant', and abbreviated the speeches. What in the *Decameron* was a brief novella that gave insight into the foolishness of old men married to young wives, in *Sack-Full* becomes a long joke at the husband's expense.

Italy and England in the Sixteenth Century

In the sixteenth century two major differences distinguished Italy and England, one political and one religious. England was a single nation governed by a monarch and her ministers and by Parliament. Although there were conspiracies against the queen,

England's major military involvements in this period were foreign; she attempted to subdue Ireland and fought Spain. Italy was not a nation, although the concept of 'Italy' existed as a desired entity and printing had hastened the growth of a single written language on the entire peninsula. In the Middle Ages Italy was made up of a large number of independent and self-governing city republics and dukedoms which frequently made war on each other; by the sixteenth century a few dukedoms and the pope, who was the ruler of a sizeable secular state, had come to dominate large sections of the peninsula. They vied with each other for power and made foreign alliances; for much of the first half of the century foreign troops made war on Italian soil. The novelle make frequent reference to the Italian city republics and dukedoms and to the wars that ravaged the peninsula; the English translations assume that the reader has a general knowledge of the Italian situation.

The other major difference between the countries was in established religion. Throughout the Middle Ages all Europe professed the Roman Catholic faith and looked to the pope and the church hierarchy for authority. Because the pope was usually resident there, Rome was the centre of European Catholicism and of a transnational administrative bureaucracy. A single ecclesiastical law, canon law, governed many aspects of people's lives. By the time all these translations, except Elyot's, were made, England had broken from Rome and had established a new national Church with the monarch as its head. Although a few of its doctrines remained close to Catholic ones, this Church was allied with the Protestant sects of Europe, and most English people thought of the pope as their great spiritual and secular enemy, sometimes even as the Antichrist. Canon law was replaced by a body of law particular to the English Church. Thus, fundamental religious beliefs and legal practices changed, and aspects of the novelle that would have been clear to a Catholic reader were obscure to the English translators, who sometimes produced vague or confusing renditions of details.

Even more important was the effect of religious prejudice. The Italian writers of novelle often satirized the clergy, especially friars, but they did so from within the institution of the Church. For example, Boccaccio's stories, such as the one that *Tarlton's Newes* translates as 'Friar Onion', and Whetstone as 'Friar

Inganno', often mocked friars and other clergy who violated
their vows, but they in no way attacked the fundamental beliefs
of Roman Catholics. Sometimes English translators of anticleri-
cal stories made them vehicles of the larger Protestant pro-
gramme of attack on Catholicism, as Whetstone does in 'Friar
Inganno'. *Tarlton's Newes out of Purgatorie* is an extreme
example. In its frame it makes use of a fundamental disagree-
ment about the nature of the afterlife in order to create comedy:
Protestants believe in Heaven and Hell but not in Purgatory, the
place where, according to Catholic belief, repentant sinners are
purged of their sins before going to Heaven; the author of
Tarlton's Newes presents Purgatory as a very silly place. In this
context, the story of Friar Onion shows the inadequacy of
Catholic teaching about the results of sin.

As this last example suggests, many patriotic English Protestant authors represented Italian social practice as being as
corrupt as its religious practice. They derided the fashion for
things Italian, mocked travellers who returned from Italy and
aped Italian manners, and inveighed against the production of
translations of Italian texts, because the reading of such texts
was likely to corrupt English morals. The novella's essential plot
– the use of wit to satisfy passion – made it particularly
vulnerable, and it seems likely that Roger Ascham's famous
diatribe against Italian texts in his *Schoolmaster* (1571) was
prompted by Painter's *Palace of Pleasure*. After attacking native
English medieval romance for its encouragement of immorality,
Ascham impugns the practice of translating Italian texts even
more harshly, because the Italian works 'open, not fond and
common ways to vice, but such subtle, cunning, new, and
diverse shiftes to cary yong willes to vanitye, and yong wittes to
mischief, to teach old bawdes new schole pointes, as the simple
head of an Englishman is not hable to invent'. (See the longer
passage from which this is drawn in 'The Anthology of Criticism' at the end of this volume.) Painter, Riche, Whetstone and
others attempted to solve the problem of the incompatibility of
Protestant morals and the world represented in the novelle by
directing readers to take the stories as cautionary examples and
by inserting moralizing passages into the novelle; however,
because they left the plots intact, their strategy resulted in
ambiguity rather than the silencing of the amoral voice to which
Ascham objected.

The Novella and the Sixteenth-Century Woman Reader

One of the characteristics of the Italian and English novella collections most commented on today is their address to women; the authors of such books frequently flirt with their female audience and cast themselves as the protectors of women or, even more often, of the individual female reader whom they protect from slander at the same time as they sling it at the rest of her sex. Riche's book includes a special dedication to women readers; Boccaccio speaks to his 'dear ladies', and he, Cinthio and Whetstone include women story-tellers; Bandello dedicated many stories to women; and Painter's narrator often speaks directly to the women in the audience.

There is much speculation about the reason for the attention that writers of novelle paid to women and about the effect of associating the genre with women. Since the subject-matter of novelle is frequently private (love, romantic intrigue and domestic discord) rather than public (war, politics and the latest intellectual questions), it has been suggested that writers thought of the material of novelle as being of particular interest to women, and thus aimed their stories at an audience that was neglected by the many books published on topics of masculine concern. But there is no evidence that women read these books more than men did; indeed, there is little evidence about women's reading-habits, so it is only possible to say with certainty that the address to women in the texts associates the books with women and at times invites male readers to read as though they were women.

Women were trained to read in a different way from men. They were less frequently educated in classical and modern languages than men and thus needed translations and retellings of texts that were accessible to men in the original. Their primary spheres of action were the home and the family; they did not practise professions and were not in the civil service, and thus did not need to be educated in the subjects that prepared for public life (although they might have enjoyed it): subjects such as history, oratory, rhetoric and political philosophy. A consequence of this education was that women in general were not expected to read texts with the same degree of sophistication as men; perhaps they genuinely were not prepared to do so. They were expected to bring less knowledge to their reading and to be less analytic. So, it may be that the novelle, associated with women by their subject-matter and by the author's direct address to women, offered men the opportunity to be less rigorous and logical than their training prepared them to be, the opportunity to read for pleasure.

The Influence of the English Novelle

The publication record of these anthologies suggests that early modern readers found the translated stories to be delightful. Painter's first volume was reprinted once on its own and again in combination with the second edition of the second volume. Whetstone's *Heptameron* was reprinted in a revised edition after his death; there were four editions of Riche's *Farewell* by 1606, and three of *Tarlton's Newes* by 1630. But the most striking testimony to the popularity of the tales is the frequency with which dramatists drew on these tales as material for entire plots and for substantial scenes in their plays. John Webster's *The Duchess of Malfi* is based on Painter's translation of Belleforest's version of Bandello's story. Philip Massinger's *The Picture* is based on Painter's 'The Lady of Boeme', which is a translation of Bandello's 'An Amazing Trick that a Gentlewoman Played on Two Hungarian Barons'. John Marston's *Wonder of Women* dramatizes Painter's *Sophonisba*, a translation of Bandello's story about the Carthaginian noblewoman, while his *The Insatiate Countess* draws on two of Painter's translations: 'Two Gentlewomen', (a translation of Bandello I.15), and 'The Countess of Celant' (which translates Belleforest's translation of Bandello's story). Ben Jonson's *The Devil Is an Ass* owes its main plot to 'Seigneor Vergelis and his Wife' in *The Forrest of Fancy*, a translation of *Decameron* III.5. All these source-stories are published in this anthology except 'The Countess of Celant', which Painter translated from the French. The notes point out still more sources and analogues.

All the above authors drew on Italian tales occasionally, but Shakespeare was the author who made the most frequent and various use of the translated novelle. Different as the results are, his procedure had some similarities to Barnabe Riche's. At times he used the whole story; at times he took advantage of the episodic structure that characterizes many of them and bor-

rowed only an incident or two; at times he drew material from
more than one story when constructing a single play. Two plays
follow their source novelle translations closely: *All's Well That
Ends Well* is based on Boccaccio's tale 'Giletta of Narbona', as
translated by Painter (included in this volume); and *Romeo and
Juliet* is based on Bandello's story as translated by Arthur
Brooke from Belleforest's translation, although some internal
evidence suggests that Shakespeare also referred to Painter's
translation of Belleforest's French version.

Many of Shakespeare's other plays bear a more complicated
relationship to the translation anthologies. The main plot of
Twelfth Night is a version of Riche's 'Apolonius and Silla',
which is an adaptation of a story by Bandello which was, in its
turn, an adaptation of an Italian play, *Gl'ingannati*. Shakespeare
seems to have consulted at least *Gl'ingannati* and 'Apolonius
and Silla' when writing it, but he may have known other Italian
dramatic versions as well. But that does not exhaust Shakespeare's use of Riche's adaptations of Italian material from the
Farewell in *Twelfth Night*. The Malvolio plot is indebted to the
fifth story, 'Two Brethren', which is an adaptation of several
stories by Straparola. In *The Merry Wives of Windsor* Shakespeare used 'Two Brethren' again, and he also used 'Philenio
Sisterno', a story from Painter's *Palace*. *Measure for Measure* is
related to Whetstone's story of 'Promos and Cassandra', but
Whetstone told the story twice, once as a play and once as a
story. Shakespeare used both versions.

Shakespeare also made use of novelle that had not yet been
translated into English. *The Merchant of Venice* is indebted to a
story from *Il pecorone*, *Cymbeline* to a story in the *Decameron*,
and *Othello* to one in Cinthio's *Hecatommithi*, although the
latter was available in a French translation. From this, one can
conclude that there were translations of stories circulating that
were never printed, or that Shakespeare must have been able to
read Italian, or that he had the stories translated for him.

It is mainly thanks to Shakespeare that interest in these stories
has remained alive over the centuries, but recent criticism, cited
at the end of this volume, has brought these stories out of his
shadow, and it is my hope that, in addition to appreciating their
utility as material for intertextual studies, the reader of this
anthology will discover and take advantage of the opportunities
for literary and cultural analysis that the stories offer. Some of

the most prominent characteristics of the novella, the interest in the surface details of everyday life, the awareness of social class and gender, even the frequent attention paid to the non-Western world, may bridge the gap in time between the sixteenth century and ours for some readers, while others may take delight in considering the very difference of the world portrayed in these stories from ours. But all, I hope, will find that they fulfil Painter's promise, that they are 'pleasuant so well abroade as at home, to avoid the griefe of Winter's night and length of Sommer's day ... Delectable they be for al sortes of men [and women], for the sad, the angry, the cholericke, the pleasaunt, the whole and sicke.'

PAMELA JOSEPH BENSON

References

1 The term 'novella' is also used to describe brief novel-like books such as Conrad's *Heart of Darkness*, but this usage has nothing to do with the sixteenth-century use of the term.

2 Two other collections of tales appeared about the same time as Painter's and contributed to the popularity of Italianate stories. Fenton's *Tragicall Discourses* translated Belleforest's *Histoires tragiques*, which was a translation of some of Bandello's tales, and thus is inappropriate to this volume of tales translated from Italian. George Turberville's *Tragical Tales* was in verse.

3 Most scholars agree that L. B. is Lodowick Bryskett, Sir Philip Sidney's companion on his grand tour of the continent, and that Riche rewrote Bryskett's translations to make their style conform with the rest of *Farewell*.

4 Kenneth Muir, *Shakespeare's Sources*, I: *Comedies and Tragedies* (London: Methuen & Co., 1957; repr. with new appendices 1961; repr. 1965), p. 70.

NOTE ON THE TEXT

During the sixteenth century in England, many words were spelled differently from the way they are now, and some letters were printed differently. In this edition the old spelling has been retained but the typography has been modernized to make the text more comfortable for a modern reader. A *y* was frequently used where we would use an *i*, and a *v* where we would use *u*, and vice versa; *I* and *i* were often used for *J* and *j*. Except in proper nouns, the use of these letters has been modernized. Printers had a version of the letter *s* now called a 'long *s*'; it has been replaced here with the modern *s*. Some typesetters used capital letters randomly throughout the texts; these have been retained only in their modern positions. Typesetters also often divided words differently from the way they are divided today; for example, 'himself' was often printed as two words. In this volume, word-division is as in modern English. In all other cases the old spelling has been retained, because other spelling changes might alter the sound of a word or prevent visual links between words. A sixteenth-century author will often spell the same word several ways, even on the same page; modern spelling gives an inaccurate appearance of uniformity to the text.

Sixteenth-century sentence and paragraph construction differed considerably from modern usage. Many authors wrote long, run-on sentences that are difficult to understand if approached from a modern sense of sentence structure. These I have divided into smaller units, although this means that some sentences start with the relative pronoun Who used as a subject. Some sixteenth-century texts are divided into paragraphs like modern texts, others are not. For ease of reading I have divided the latter stories into blocks of text resembling paragraphs, although the notion of the paragraph as a logical unit is absent, and I have set dialogue as it would be in a modern text.

All the tales are transcribed from the first extant editions, cited in the notes to each extract, except those from the *Palace of Pleasure*, which are from the first edition of the complete text.

A TALE FROM SIR THOMAS ELYOT'S

THE GOVERNOUR

The wonderfull history of Titus and Gisippus, and whereby is fully declared the figure of perfet amitye

But nowe in the middes of my labour, as it were to pause and take brethe and also to recreate the reders, which, fatigate with longe preceptes, desire varietye of mater or some newe pleasaunt fable or historye, I will reherce a right goodly example of frendship. Whiche example, studiousely radde, shall ministre to the redar's singuler pleasure and also incredible comforte to practise amitye.

There was in the citye of Rome a noble senatour named Fulvius, who sent his sone called Titus, beinge a childe, to the citye of Athenes in Greece (whiche was the fountaine of al maner of doctrine), there to lerne good letters, and caused him to be hosted with a worshipfull man of that citye called Chremes.[1] This Chremes hapned to have also a sone named Gisippus, who nat onely was equall to the said yonge Titus in yeres, but also in stature, proporcion of body, favour and colour of visage, countenaunce and speche. The two children were so like, that without moche difficultye it coulde nat be discerned of their propre parentes, whiche was Titus from Gysippus, or Gysippus from Titus. These two yonge gentilmen, as they semed to be one in fourme and personage, so, shortely after acquaintaunce, the same nature wrought in their hartes suche a mutuall affection that their willes and appetites daily more and more so confederated themselfes, that it seemed none other, whan their names were declared, but that they hadde onely chaunged their places, issuinge (as I mought saye) out of the one body and entringe in to the other. They together and at one time went to their lerninge and studye, at one time to their meales and refection; they delited bothe in one doctrine, and profited equally therein. Finally, they together so increased in doctrine that, within a fewe yeres, fewe within Athenes mought be compared unto them. At the laste died Chremes, whiche was nat only to his sone, but also to Titus, cause of moche sorowe and hevinesse.

Gysippus, by the goodes of his father, was knowen to be a man of great substaunce, wherfore there were offred to him great and riche mariages. And he than, beinge of ripe yeres and of an habile and goodly parsonage, his frendes, kinne, and alies exhorted him busely to take a wife, to the intent he mought increase his lignage and progenye. But the yonge man, havinge his hart allredy wedded to his frende Titus, and his minde fixed to the studye of philosophye, fearinge that mariage shulde be the occasion to sever him bothe from th'one and th'other, refused of longe time to be parswaded. Untill at the last, partly by the importunate callinge on of his kinnesmen, partly by the consent and advise of his dere frende Titus, therto by other desired, he assented to mary suche one as shulde like him.[2]

What shall nede many wordes? His frendes founde a yonge gentilwoman, whiche in equalitye of yeres, vertuous condicions, nobilitye of blode, beautye, and sufficient richesse, they thought was for suche a yonge man apte and convenient. And whan they and her frendes upon the covenauntes of mariage were throughly accorded, they counsailed Gysippus to repaire unto the maiden and to beholde howe her parsone contented him. And he so doinge founde her in every fourme and condicion accordinge to his expectation and appetite; wherat he moche rejoised and became of her amorouse, in so moche as many and often times

he, leavinge Titus at his studye secretely repaired
unto her.

Natwithstanding, the fervent love that he had
to his frende Titus at the last surmounted shamefastnes. Wherfore he disclosed to him his secrete
journayes, and what delectacion he toke in
beholdinge the excellent beautye of her whom he
purposed to mary, and howe, with her good
maners and swete entretainement, she had constrained him to be her lover.[3] And on a time he,
havinge with him his frende Titus, went to his
lady, of whom he was resceived moste joyously.
But Titus furthwith as he behelde so hevenly a
personage adourned with beautye inexplicable, in
whose visage was moste amiable countenaunce
mixte with maidenly shamefastnesse, and the rare
and sobre wordes, and well couched, whiche
issued out of her pratye mouthe, Titus was therat
abasshed and had the harte through perced with
the firy darte of blinde Cupide. Of the whiche
wounde the anguisshe was so excedinge and vehement that neither the study of philosophye, neither
the remembraunce of his dere frende Gysippus,
who so moche loved and trusted him, coulde
anythinge withdrawe him from that unkinde appetite, but that of force he must love inordinately
that lady whom his said frende had determined to
mary. Allbeit, with incredible paines he kepte his
thoughtes secrete untill that he and Gysippus were
retourned unto their lodginges. Than the miserable Titus, withdrawinge him as it were to his
studye, all turmented and oppressed with love,
threwe himselfe on a bedde, and there rebuking
his owne moste despitefull unkindnesse, whiche,
by the sodaine sight of a maiden, he had conspired
againe his moste dere frende Gysippus againe all
humanitye and reason, he cursed his fate or
constellation[4] and wisshed that he had never
comen to Athenes. And therewith he sent out from
the botome of his harte depe and colde sighes, in
suche plentye that it lacked but litle that his harte

ne was riven in peces.[5] In dolour and anguisshe tossed he himselfe by a certaine space, but to no man wolde he discover it. But at the last the paine became so intollerable that, wolde he or no, he was inforced to kepe his bedde, beinge, for lacke of slepe and other naturall sustenaunce, brought in suche feblenesse that his legges mought nat sustaine his body.

Gysippus, missing his dere frende Titus, was moche abasshed, and, heringe that he laye sicke in his bedde, had furthwith his harte perced with hevinesse, and with all spede came to him where he laye. And beholding the rosiall colour, which was wont to be in his visage, tourned into salowe, the residue pale, his ruddy lippes wanne, and his eyen ledy and holowe, Gysippus mought uneth kepe himselfe from wepinge, but, to th'entent he wolde nat discomfort his frende Titus, he dissimuled his hevinesse, and with a comfortable countenaunce demaunded of Titus what was the cause of his disease, blaminge him of unkindenesse that he so longe had sustained it without geving him knowlege, that he mought for him have provided some remedye, if any mought have been goten, though it were with the dispendinge of all his substaunce. With whiche wordes, the mortall sighes renewed in Titus, and the salte teares brast out of his eyen in suche habundaunce as it had ben a lande flode runninge downe of a mountaine after a storme. That beholdinge Gysippus, and beinge also resolved into teares, moste hartely desired him and (as I mought saye) conjured him that for the fervent and entier love that had ben, and yet was, betwene them, he wolde no lenger hide from him his griefe, and that there was nothing to him so dere or precious (allthough it were his owne life) that mought restore Titus to helthe, but that he shulde gladly and without grutchinge employe it.

With whiche wordes, obtestations and teares of Gysippus, Titus constrained, all blusshinge and ashamed, holdinge downe his hedde, brought furthe with great difficultye his wordes in this wise:

'My dere and moste lovinge frende, withdrawe your frendely offers, cease of your courtaisye, refraine your tears and regrettinges, take rather your knife and slee me here where I lie, or otherwise take vengeaunce on me, moste miserable and false traitour unto you, and of all other moste worthy to suffre moste shamefull dethe. For where as God of nature, like as he hath given to us similitude in all the partes of our body, so had he conjoined our willes, studies, and appetites together in one, so that betwene two men was never like concorde and love, as I suppose. And nowe natwithstandinge, onely with the loke oí a woman, those bondes of love be dissolved, reason oppressed, frendship is excluded. There auaileth no wisedome, no doctrine, no fidelitye or truste; ye, your truste is the cause that I have conspired againe you this treason. Alas, Gysippus, what envious spirite meved you to bringe me with you to her whom ye have chosen to be your wife, where I received this poison? I saye, Gysippus, where was than your wisedom, that ye remembred nat the fragilitye of our commune nature? What neded you to call me for a witnesse of your private delites? Why wolde ye have me see that whiche you youreselfe coulde nat beholde without ravisshinge of minde and carnall appetite? Alas, why forgate ye that our mindes and appetites were ever one? And that also what so ye liked was ever to me in like degree pleasaunt? What will ye more? Gysippus, I saye your trust is the cause that I am intrapped. The rayes or beames issuinge from the eyen of her whom ye have chosen, with the remembraunce of her incomparable vertues, hath thrilled throughout the middes of my hart, and in suche wise brenneth it, that above all thinges I desire to be out of this wretched and moste unkinde life, whiche is nat worthy the company of

The wordes of Titus to Gysippus.

so noble and lovinge a frende as ye be.' And therewith Titus concluded his confession with so profounde and bitter a sigh, received with teares, that it seemed that al his body shulde be dissolved and relented into salt dropes.

But Gysippus, as he were there with nothinge astonied or discontented, with an assured countenaunce and mery regarde, imbrasinge Titus and kissinge him, answered in this wise: 'Why, Titus, is this your onely sickenesse and griefe that ye so uncurtesely have so longe counceiled, and with moche more unkindnesse kept it from me than ye have conceived it? I knowlege my foly, wherwith ye have with good right imbraided me, that, in showing to you her whom I loved, I remembred nat the commune astate of our nature, ne the agreablenesse, or (as I mought saye) the unitye of our two appetites. Suerly that defaulte can be by no reason excused. Wherfore it is onely I that have offended. For who may by right prove that ye have trespased, that by the inevitable stroke of Cupide's darte are thus bitterly wounded? Thinke ye me suche a fole or ignorant persone that I knowe nat the powar of Venus where she listeth to shewe her importable violence? Have nat ye well resisted againe suche a goddesse, that for my sake ye have striven with her allmoste to the dethe? What more loyaltye or trouthe can I require of you? Am I of that vertue that I may resiste againe celestiall influence preordinate by providence divine? If I so thought, what were my wittes? Where were my studye so longe time spent in noble philosophye? I confess to you, Titus, I love that maiden as moche as any wise man mought possible, and toke in her companye more delite and pleasure than of all the treasure and landes that my father lefte to me, whiche ye knowe was right abundaunt. But nowe I perceive that the affection of love towarde her surmounteth in you above measure, what, shal I thinke it of a wanton lust or sodaine appetite in you, whome I have ever

The answere of Gysippus.

knowen of grave and sadde disposition, inclined
alway to honest doctrine, fleinge all vaine dal-
iaunce and dishonest passetime? Shall I imagine to
be in you any malice or fraude, sens from the
tendre time of our childhode I have alway founden
in you, my swete frende Titus, suche a conformitye
with all my maners, appetites, and desires that
never was sene betwene us any maner of contention? Nay, God forbede that in the frendshippe of
Gysippus and Titus shulde happen any suspition,
or that any fantasye shulde perce my hedde,
whereby that honorable love betwene us shulde be
the mountenaunce of a cromme perisshed. Nay,
nay, Titus, it is (as I have said) the onely providence of God. She was by him from the beginninge
prepared to be your lady and wife. For suche
fervent love entreth nat into the harte of a wise
man and vertuous, but by a divine disposition;
whereat if I shulde be discontented or grudge, I
shulde nat onely be injuste to you, withholdinge
that from you whiche is undoughtedly youres, but
also obstinate and repugnaunt againe the determination of God; whiche shall never be founden
in Gysippus. Therfore, gentill frende Titus, dismay
you nat at the chaunce of love, but receive it
joyously with me, that am with you nothinge
discontented, but mervailous gladde, sens it is my
happe to finde for you suche a lady, with whome
ye shall live in felicitye and receive frute to the
honour and comfort of all your linage. Here I
renounce to you clerely all my title and interest
that I nowe have or mought have in that faire
maiden. Call to you your pristinate courage,
wasshe clene your visage and eyen thus biwept,
and abandone all hevinesse.

The day appointed for our mariage approcheth;
let us consult howe without difficultye ye may
holy attaine your desires. Take hede, this is mine
advise. Ye knowe well that we two be so like that,
beinge aparte and in one apparaile, fewe men do
knowe us. Also ye do remembre that the custome

is, that, natwithstandinge any ceremony done at
the time of the spousailes, the mariage natwithstandinge is nat confirmed untill at night that the
husbande putteth a ringe on the finger of his wife
and unloseth her girdell. Therfore, I myselfe will
be present with my frendes and perfourme all the
partes of a bride.[6] And ye shall abide in a place
secrete, whee I shall appoint you, untill it be night.
And than shall ye quickely convaye yourselfe in to
the maiden's chambre, and for the similitude of
our parsonages and of our apparaile, ye shall nat
be espied of the women, whiche have with none
of us any acquaintaunce, and shortely gette you to
bedde, and put your owne ringe on the maiden's
finger, and undo her girdell of virginite, and do all
other thinge that shall be to your pleasure.

Be nowe of good chere, Titus, and comfort
yourselfe with good refections and solace, that
this wan and pale colour, and your chekes meigre
and leane, be nat the cause of your discoveringe. I
knowe well that, ye havinge your purpose, I shall
be in obloquy and derision of all men and so hated
of all my kinrede that they shall seke occasion to
expulse me out of this citye, thinking me to be a
notable reproche to al my familye. But let God
therin warke. I force nat what paine that I abide,
so that ye, my frende Titus, may be saulfe and
pleasauntly enjoy your desires to the increasinge
of your felicitye.'

With these wordes Titus began to meve, as it
were, out of a dreme, and, doughtinge whither he
harde Gysippus speke or els sawe but a vision,
laye still as a man abasshed. But whan he behelde
the tears trickelinge downe by the face of Gysippus, he than recomforted him and, thankinge him
for his incomparable kindnesse, refused the benefite that he offred, sayenge that it were better that
a hundred suche unkinde wretches as he was
shulde perisshe than so noble a man as was
Gysippus shulde sustaine reproche or damage.

But Gysippus eftsones comforted Titus, and

therewith sware and protested that with free and
glad will he wolde that this thinge shulde be in
fourme aforesaide accomplisshed, and therwith
inbraced and swetely kissed Titus. Who perceivinge the mater suer and nat fained, as a man nat
sicke but onely awaked out of his slepe, he set
himselfe up in his bedde, the quicke bloode somwhat resorted unto his visage, and, after a little
good meates and drinkes taken, he was shortly
and in a fewe dayes restored into his olde facion
and figure.

To make the tale shorte. The day of mariage
was commen. Gysippus accompanied with his
alies and frendes came to the house of the damosel, where they were honorably and joyously
fested. And betwene him and the maiden was a
swete entretainement, which to beholde all that
were present toke moche pleasure and comfort,
praisinge the beautye, goodlinesse, vertue and
curtesye whiche in those couples were excellent
above all other that they hadde ever sene. What
shall I saye more? The covenauntes were radde
and sealed, the dowar appointed, and al other
bargaines concluded, and the frendes of either
parte toke their leave and departed, the bride with
a fewe women (as was the custome) brought into
her chambre. Than (as it was before agreed) Titus
conveyed himselfe after Gysippus retourned to his
house, or parchaunce to the chambre appointed
for Titus, nothinge sorrowfull, allthough that he
hartely loved the maiden, but with a glad harte
and countenaunce, that he had so recovered his
frende from dethe, and so well brought him to the
effecte of his desire.

Nowe is Titus in bedde with the maiden, nat
knowen of her, nor of any other, but for Gysippus.
And first he swetely demaunded her, if that she
loved him and dained to take him for her husbande, forsaking all other, which she all blusshing
with an eye halfe laughinge, halfe mourninge (as
in pointe to departe from her maidenhede, but

supposinge it to be Gysippus that asked her)
affirmed. And than he eftsones asketh her, if she
in ratifienge that promise wolde receive his ringe,
whiche he hadde there all redy, wherto she con-
sentinge putteth the ringe on her finger and unloseth her girdell. What thinge els he did, they two
onely knewe it. Of one thing I am suer, that night
was to Titus more comfortable than ever was the
lengest daye of the yere, ye, and I suppose a hole
yere of dayes.

The morowe is comen. And Gysippus, thinking
it to be expedient that the trouthe shulde be
discovered, assembled all the nobilitye of the citye
at his owne house, where also by appointment
was Titus, who amonge them had these wardes
that do folowe: 'My frendes Atheniensis, there is
at this time shewed amonge you an example
allmoste incredible of the divine powar of honorable love, to the perpetuall renoume and commendation of this noble citye of Athenes, wherof ye
ought to take excellent comfort, and therfore give
due thankes to God, if there remaine amonge you
any token of the auncient wisedome of your moste
noble progenitours. For what more praise may be
given to people, than benevolence, faithfulnesse
and constaunce? Without whome all contrayes
and cities be brought unto desolation and ruine,
like as by them they become prosperous and in
moste highe felicitye.

What shall I longe tary you in conjectinge mine
intent and meaninge? Ye all knowe from whens I
came unto this citye, that of adventure I founde in
the house of Chremes his sone Gysippus, of mine
owne age and in everythinge so like to me that
neither his father nor any other man coulde discerne of us the one from the other, but by our
owne insignement or showinge, insomoche as
there were put about our neckes lacis of sondry
colours to declare our personages. What mutuall
agrement and love have ben alwaye betwene us,
duringe the eight yeres that we have ben together,

The oration
of Titus to the
Atheniensis.

ye all be witnesses that have ben beholders and
wonderars of our moste swete conversation and
consent of appetites, wherein was never any dis-
corde or variaunce. And as for my parte, after the
decease of my father, natwithstandinge that there
was discended and hapned unto me great possessions, faire houses, with abundaunce of riches;
also I beinge called home by the desirous and
importunate letters of mine alies and frendes,
whiche be of the moste noble of all the senatours,
offred the advauncement to the highest dignities
in the publike weale. I will nat remembre the
lamentations of my moste naturall mother,
expressed in her tender letters, all besprent and
blotted with abundaunce of teares, wherein she
accuseth me of unkindenesse for my longe tar-
yenge, and specially nowe in her mooste discom-
forte. But all this coulde nat remove me the breade
of my naile from my dere frende Gysippus. And
but by force coulde nat I, nor yet may, be drawen
from his swete company, but if he therto will
consent. I chosinge rather to live with him as his
companion and felowe, ye, and as his servaunt,
rather than to be consull of Rome.

Thus my kindenesse hathe he well acquited, or
(as I mought saye) redoubled, deliveryinge me
from the dethe, ye, from the moste cruell and
painefull dethe of all other. I perceive ye wonder
hereat, noble Atheniensis, and no mervaile. For
what persone shulde be so hardy to attempte any
suche thinge againe me, beinge a Romaine, and of
the noble bloode of the Romanes? Or who shulde
be thought so malicious to slee me, who (as all ye
be my juges) never trespased againe any persone
within this citye? Nay, nay, my frendes, I have
none of you all therein suspected. I perceive ye
desire and harken to knowe what he was that
presumed to do so cruell and great an enterprise.
It was love, noble Atheniensis, the same love
whiche (as youre poetes do remembre) didde
wounde the more parte of all the goddes that ye

do honoure, that constrained Juppiter to trans-
fourme himselfe in a swanne, a bulle, and divers
other likenesses; the same love that caused Hercules, the vainquissher and distroyer of monstres
and geauntes, to spinne on a rocke, sittinge
amonge maidens in a woman's apparaile; the same
love that caused to assemble all the noble princes
of Asia and Greece in the feldes of Troy;[7] the same
love, I saye, againe whose assaultes may be founde
no defence or resistence, hath sodainely and
unware striken me unto the harte with suche
vehemence and might, that I had in shorte space
died with moste fervent tourmentes, hadde nat the
incomparable frendship of Gysippus holpen me.

I se you wolde faine knowe who she is that I
loved. I will no lenger delaye you, noble Atheniensis. It is Sophronia, the lady whom Gysippus had
chosen to have to his wife, and whome he moste
intierly loved. But whan his moste gentill harte
percived that my love was in a moche higher
degree than his towarde that lady, and that it
proceded neither of wantonesse, neither of longe
conversation, nor of any other corrupte desire or
fantasye, but in an instant, by one onely loke, and
with suche fervence that immediately I was so
cruciate that I desired and, in all that I mought,
provoked deth to take me, he by his wisedome
soone perceived (as I dought nat but that ye do)
that it was the very provision of God that she
shuld be my wife and nat his. Wherto he gevinge
place, and more esteminge true frendship than the
love of a woman, where unto he was induced by
his frendes and nat by violence of Cupide constrained, as I am, hath willingly graunted to me
the interest that he had in the damosell. And it is
I, Titus, that have verely wedded her, I have put
the ringe on her finger, I have undone the girdell
of shamefastnes. What wil ye more? I have lien
with her, and confirmed the matrimonye, and
made her a wife.'

At these wordes all they that were present began

to murmure and to cast a disdainous and grevous loke upon Gysippus. Than spake againe Titus. 'Leave youre grudginges and menasinge countenaunce towarde Gysippus. He hathe done to you all honour and no dede of reproche. I tell you he hathe accomplisshed all the partes of a frende; that love which was moste certaine that he continued; he knewe that he mought finde in Greece another maiden as faire and as riche as this that he had chosen, and one perchaunce that he mought love better. But suche a frende as I was (havinge respecte to our similitude, the longe approved concorde, also mine astate and condition) he was suer to finde never none.[8] Also the damosell suffreth no dispergement in her bloode, or hinderaunce in her mariage, but is moche rather advaunced (no dispreise to my dere frende Gysippus). Also consider, noble Atheniensis, that I toke her nat my father livinge, whan ye mought have suspected that as well her riches as her beautye shulde have thereto alloured me, but soone after my father's decease, whanne I ferre exceded her in possessions and substaunce, whan the moste noble men of Rome and of Italy desired mine aliaunce.

Ye have therfore all cause to rejoise and thanke Gysippus, and nat to be angrye, and also to extolle his wonderfull kindenesse towarde me, whereby he hathe wonne me and all my bloode suche frendes to you and your citye that ye may be assured to be by us defended againe all the worlde. Whiche beinge considered, Gysippus hathe well deserved a statue or image of golde to be set on a piller in the middes of youre citye for an honorable monument in the remembraunce of our incomparable frendship and of the good that thereby may come to your citye. But if this persuasion can nat satisfye you, but that ye will imagine any thinge to the damage of my dere frende Gysippus after my departinge, I make mine avowe unto God, creatoure of all thinge, that as I shall have knowelege therof, I shall furthwith resort hither with

the invincible power of the Romanes and revenge
him in suche wise againe his enemies that all
Greece shall speke of it to their perpetuall dishonour, shame and reproche.' And therwith Titus
and Gysippus rose; but the other, for feare of
Titus, dissembled their malice, makinge semblaunt
as they had ben with all thinge contented.

Soone after, Titus, beinge sent for by the auto-
rite of the senate and people of Rome, prepared to
departe out of Athenes, and wolde faine have had
Gysippus to have gone with him, offringe to
devide with him all his substaunce and fortune.
But Gysippus, consideringe howe necessary his
counsaile shulde be to the cityde of Athenes, wolde
nat departe out of his countraye, natwithstandinge
that above all erthly thinges he moste desired the
company of Titus. Whiche abode also, for the said
consideration, Titus approved. Titus with his lady
is departed towardes the cityde of Rome, where at
their comminge they were of the mother of Titus,
his kinsemen, and of all the senate and people
joyously received. And there lived Titus with his
lady in joye inexplicable, and had by her many
faire children, and for his wisedome and lerninge
was so highly estemed that there was no dignitye
or honorable office within the cityde that he had
nat with moche favour and praise achieved and
occupied.

But nowe let us resorte to Gysippus, who
immediately upon the departinge of Titus was so
maligned at, as well by his owne kinsemen as by
the frendes of the lady, that he to their seming
shamefully abandoned, leavinge her to Titus, that
they spared nat daily to vexe him with all kindes
of reproche that they coulde devise or imagine.
And firste they excluded him out of their counsaile
and prohibited from him all honest company. And
yet nat beinge therewith satisfied, finally they
adjuged him unworthy to enjoye any possessions
or goodes lefte to him by his parentes, whome he
(as they supposed) by his undiscrete frendship had

so distained. Wherfore they dispoiled him of all
thinges, and almoste naked expelled him out of
the citye. Thus is Gysippus, late welthy and one of
the moste noble men of Athenes, for his kinde
harte banisshed his owne countraye for ever, and
as a man dismayed, wandringe hither and thither,
findeth no man that wolde socour him.

At the laste, remembring in what pleasure his
frende Titus lived with his lady, for whome he
suffred these damages, concluded that he wolde
go to Rome and declare his infortune to his said
frende Titus. What shall nede a longe tale? In
conclusion, with moche paine, colde, hunger and
thurste, he is commen to the citye of Rome, and
diligently enquiringe for the house of Titus, at the
laste he came to hit, but beholdinge it so beau-
teous, large and princely, he was ashamed to
approche nigh to it, beinge in so simple astate and
unkladde; but standeth by, that in case that Titus
came forthe out of his house he mought than
present himselfe to him. He beinge in this thought,
Titus holdinge his lady by the hande issued out
from his doore and takinge their horses to solace
themselfe, behelde Gysippus, but, beholding his
vile apparaile, regarded him nat, but passed furthe
on their waye. Wherwith Gysippus was so
wounded to the harte, thinking that Titus had
condemned his fortune, that, oppressed with mortall hevines, he fell in a sowne, but, beinge
recovered by some that stode by, thinking him to
be sicke, he furthwith departed, entendinge nat to
abide any lenger, but as a wilde beste to wandre
abrode in the worlde.

But for werinesse he was constrained to entre
into an olde berne, without the citye, where he,
castinge himself on the bare grounde, with wepinge and dolorous cryenge bewailed his fortune.
But moste of all accusinge the ingratitude of Titus
for whome he suffred all that misery, the remembraunce wherof was so intollerable that he determined no lenger to live in that anguisshe and

dolour. And therwith drewe his knife, purposinge
to have slaine himselfe. But ever wisedome
(whiche he by the studye of philosophye had
attained) withdrewe him from that desperate acte.
And in this contention betwene wisedome and
wille, fatigate with longe journayes and watche,
or as God wolde have it, he fell into a deade
sleepe, his knife (wherewith he wolde have slaine
himselfe) fallinge downe by him.

In the meanetime a commune and notable rufian
or thefe, whiche had robbed and slaine a man,
was entred into the barne where Gisippus laye, to
the intent to sojourne there all that night. And
seinge Gysippus bewept, and his visage replen-
isshed with sorowe, and also the naked knife by
him, perceived well that he was a man desperate
and supprised with hevinesse of harte, was wery
of his life. Whiche the said rufian takinge for a
good occasion to escape, toke the knife of Gysippus, and puttinge it in the wounde of him that
was slaine, put it all blody in the hande of
Gysippus, beinge fast aslepe, and so departed.

Sonne after, the dedde man beinge founde, the
officers made diligent serche for the murderar. At
the laste they entring into the barne and finding
Gysippus on slepe with a blody knife in his hande,
they awaked him, wherwith he entred againe in to
his olde sorowes, complaininge his evill fortune.
But whan the officers laide unto him the dethe of
the man, and the havinge of the blody knife, he
thereat rejoised, thankinge God that suche
occasion was hapned, wherby he shulde suffre
deth by the lawes and escape the violence of his
owne handes.[9] Wherfore he denied nothing that
was laide to his charge, desiringe the officers to
make haste that he mought be shortly out of his
life. Whereat they mervailed.

Anone reporte came to the senate that a man
was slaine and that a straunger and a Greeke
borne was founden in suche fourme as is before
mencioned. They furthwith commaunded him to

be brought unto their presence, sittinge there at that time Titus, beinge than consull or in other like dignitye. The miserable Gysippus was brought to the barre with billes and staves like a felon, of whome it was demaunded if he slewe the man that was founden dedde. He nothinge denied, but in moste sorowful maner cursed his fortune, naminge himselfe of all other most miserable.

At the last, one demaundinge him of what countray he was, he confessed to be an Atheniense, and therwith he cast his sorowfull eyen upon Titus with moche indignation and braste out into sighes and teares abundauntly. That beholdinge Titus, and espyenge by a litle signe in his visage, whiche he knewe, that it was his dere frende Gysippus, and anone consideringe that he was brought into dispaire by some misadventure, he anone rose out of his place where he sate and, fallinge on his knees before the juges, saide that he had slaine the man for olde malice that he bare towarde him and that Gysippus, beinge a straunger, was giltles, and that all men mought perceive that the other was a desperate person; wherfore, to abbreviate his sorowes, he confessed the acte, whereof he was innocent, to the intent that he wolde finisshe his sorowes with dethe. Wherfore Titus desired the juges to give sentence on him accordinge to his merites. But Gysippus perceivinge his frende Titus (contrary to his expectation) to offre himselfe to the dethe, for his saulfegarde, more importunately cried to the senate to procede in their jugement on him that was the very offendar. Titus denyed it and affirmed with reasons and argumentes that he was the murderer, and nat Gysippus. Thus they of longe time with abundaunce of teares contended whiche of them shulde die for the other. Wherat all the senate and people were wonderly abasshed, nat knowinge what it ment.

There hapned to be in the prease at that time he whiche indede was the murdrer, who, perceivinge

the mervailous contention of these two persones,
whiche were bothe innocent, and that it proceded
of an incomparable frendshippe, was vehemently
provoked to discover the trouthe. Wherfore he
brake through the prease and, comminge before
the senate, he spake in this wise: 'Noble fathers, I
am suche a persone whom ye knowe have ben a
commune baratour and thefe by a longe space of
yeres. Ye knowe also that Titus is of a noble
blode, and is aproved to be alway a man of
excellent vertue and wisedome, and never was
malicious. This other straunger semeth to be a
man full of simplicitye, and, that more is, desperate for some grevous sorowe that he hathe taken,
as it is to you evident. I say to you, fathers, they
bothe be innocent. I am that persone that slewe
him that is founden dedde by the barne and
robbed him of his money. And whan I founde in
the barne this straunger lyenge on slepe; havinge
by him a naked knife, I, the better to hide mine
offence, did put the knife into the wounde of the
dedde man, and so all blody laide it againe by this
straunger. This was my mischevous devise to
escape your jugement. Whereunto nowe I remitte
me holy, rather than this noble man Titus and this
innocent straunger shulde unworthely die.'

Hereat all the senate and people toke comfort,
and the noise of rejoising hartes filled all the court.
And whan it was further examined, Gysippus was
discovered. The frendship betwene him and Titus
was throughout the citye publisshed, extolled and
magnified. Wherfore the senate consulted of this
mater, and finally, at the instaunce of Titus and
the people, discharged the felon. Titus recognised
his negligence in forgettinge Gysippus, and Titus,
beinge advertised of the exile of Gysippus and the
dispitefull crueltye of his kindrede, he was therewith wonderfull wrathe, and havinge Gysippus
home to his house (where he was with incredible
joye received of the lady, whome sometime he
shulde have wedded), he was honorably appa-

railed, and there Titus offred to him to use all his goodes and possessions at his owne pleasure and appetite. But Gysippus desiringe to be againe in his propre countray, Titus, by the consent of the senate and people, assembled a great armye and went with Gysippus unto Athenes. Where he havinge delivered to him al those whiche were causers of banisshinge and dispoilinge of his frende Gysippus, he did on them sharpe execution, and, restoringe to Gysippus his landes and substaunce, stablisshed him in perpetuall quietenes, and so retourned to Rome.

This example in the affectes of frendshippe expresseth (if I be nat deceived) the description of frendship engendred by the similitude of age and personage, augmented by the conformitye of maners and studies, and confirmed by the longe continuance of company.

NINE TALES FROM WILLIAM PAINTER'S

THE PALACE OF PLEASURE

How Melchisedech, a Jewe, by telling a pretye tale of three kinges, saved his life

Saladine, whose valiaunce was so great that not onely the same from base estate advaunced him to be souldan of Babilon, but also thereby hee wanne divers victories over the Saracene kinges and Christians;[1] who, throughe his manifolde warres and magnificent triumphes, having expended al his treasure and for th'execution of one exploite lackinge a great summe of money, knewe not where to have the same so redily as he had occasion to imploy it. At length he called to remembraunce a rich Jewe named Melchisedech, that lent out money for interest in Alexandria, whose greedie and covetous nature was such that with his good will he would not do it, and to force him the souldan was very loth. Howbeit, compelled by necessity, he cast his wits about him to finde a meanes how the Jew might serve his tourne, and thereuppon founde out a sleight and waye by a colourable force.

Who, causing the Jew to be called before him, intertained him familiarly, making him to sit downe besides him, and said to him these words: 'Sir, I do learne by report of divers that you are verye wise and well learned in things concerning God. For which cause I would gladly know of you which of the three lawes you judge to be most sincere and true, the Jewishe law, the Saracene law or the Christian lawe.'

The Jewe, which indeede was very wise, perceived wel that Saladine went about to intrappe him in wordes, thereby to raise some quarell against him, and thought that it was not good for him to praise one of those lawes more then another, lest Saladine might take advauntage of him. Wherefore, to make a wise and discrete aunswere, that he might not be overshotte, he sharpened his wittes, and sodainly came into his remembraunce this aunswere: 'My Lorde, the question which you have proponed is excellent, and to declare unto you that which I knowe, I muste tell you a tale, the better to open my meaninge which, if it shall please you to heare, is this:

'I doe remember (if I be not deceived) that many times I have heard tell how upon a time there was a noble man, which was very rich and had amonges his other treasures a verye beautifull ringe of great price and estimation, which, for the valour and beautye, hee was very desirous perpetually to leave unto his successours. Willing and ordeining that the same sonne which should have that ring by the gift of his father after his decease should be taken and reputed for his heire and should be honoured and magnified of the reste as the chiefest. He to whom the same ring was left observed sembable order in his posteritye and did the like that his predecessor had done before him. In short time this ring succeded from hand to hand to many sucessours. And last of al it came to the hand of one that had three godly sonnes, vertuous and very obedient to their father, who loved them all indifferently and in equal maner. Which, knowing the order for the disposition of that ring, curious to be best esteemed and beloved, every of them prayed his father so well as severally they could (which then was aged) that when hee died he would give him the ring.

The good man, which loved one no better then another, knew not which of them to chose to whom he might dispose it and thought best to promise the same to every of them to satisffye all three. Secretly, he procured an excellente goldsmith to make two other rings, which accordinglye were made, so like unto the first as the owner himselfe unnethes knew one from the other. And when he was upon his death bedde, he secretly gave to every of his sonnes a ring. Who, after the death of their father, desirous to enter the inheritaunce and honour, one goinge about to displace another, every of them to declare what title he had to enjoy the same brought forth his ringe. And the ringes were founde so like that the true ring could not be knowen. Therefore, the processe for the title remained in doubt and yet continueth til this daye. And so I say unto you, my lord, of the lawes given by God the father to those three people, whereof you have made the question, every of those nations thinketh to enjoy the inheritaunce of God and to observe the true lawe and his commaundementes, but which of them hath the truest law, that remaineth in doubt like the question of the rings.'

Saladine, perceiving that Melchisedech knew right well how to avoide the snare which he had layed for him, determined therefore to open and disclose unto him his necessitye to prove if he would do him that pleasure. Which hee did, telling him his intent and meaninge, if he had not framed him that wise aunswere.

The Jewe liberally lent him the summe of money that he demaunded, which Saladine wholye repayed unto him againe, besides other very greate rewardes that he gave him, using him still for his frende, and afterwards maintained him next his person in great and honourable state.

One called Guglielmo Borsiere, with certaine wordes well placed, taunted the covetous life of Ermino Grimaldi

Longe sithes, there was a gentleman at Genova called M. Ermino Grimaldi, whoe, as all men thoughte, was the richest of possessions and ready money within that citye and therin farre excelled all other citizens which then were knowen in Italye.[1] And, as he did surpasse al other Italians in substance and wealth, so in avarice and wretchednes he surmounted beyond measure the most covetous and miserable of the worlde. For he kept his purse so close that he did not onely neglecte to do good to other, but also to himselfe, by sparinge many things necessary for his owne person. He indured much hardnes in meate and drinke because he would spend nothinge, contrary to the common custome of the Genevois, who be wonte very nobly and honourbly to maintaine themselves in apparell and fare. For which cause, his surname, Grimaldi, deservedly was taken away, and was called of every man nothing else but M. Ermino the Covetous.

It chanced in those dayes that, as he by spending nothing multiplied his goods, there arived at Genova an honest gentleman and well spoken, a courtier of good interteignement, named Guglielmo Borsiere (nothing like the courtiers in these dayes that, to their great shame, for their corrupt and rude maners would be called and reputed gentlemen, which indeede may bee counted asses, broughte uppe and noseled rather in the filthye conditions of the vilest menne then in courtesy).[2] In those days courtiers occupied themselves in treating of peace and endinge of quarelles that bredde strife and dissention amonges gentlemen, or in makinge of mariages, amities and attonementes, and with mery woordes and pleasaunt did recreate troubled mindes, and exhilarated with pastimes other courtiers, not with sharpe reprehensions but, like fathers, rebuking the lives of the wicked, and that for no gaine or reward. Where some of the courtiers of oure age do imploye their time in ill reportes one of another, and do disseminate debate and strife, utteringe a thousande unhappye and vile wordes, yea and that (which is worst of all) in common audience. Their maner is to reprove and checke one another with injuries, reproches and nipping girdes, with false and deceivable flatteries, villanously and dissemblingly to begile poore and needye gentlemen. He is also the proprest man, and best beloved of some great men of like conditions and of them is best rewarded, that can use the vilest and most abhominable talke, or can do sembable deeds which redoundeth to the great shame and dishonour of the chiefe and principall that beare the swaye in court. Proofe wherof is evident enough for that the vertues past have forsaken the presente sort, who live in the ordure and filth of vices.

But to procede in that which I have begon (although upon just occasion I have a litle more digressed then I thought) I say that the foresaid Guglielmo Borsiere, was honoured and visited of the gentlemen of Genova. Who, making his abode for a certaine time in the citye, and hearing tel of the miserye and covetousnes of M. Ermino, had great desire to see him. M. Ermino, hearing tell that this Guglielmo Borsiere was an excellente man, and therefore (although a covetous man) yet having in him some sparke of gentilitye, he received him with frendlye woords and good countenaunce, entringe into communication with him of divers and sundrye matters, and in talking brought him with certaine other citizens to one of his houses which was very faire and newe, where (after hee had shewed him his house) he said unto him: 'M. Guglielmo, you that have seene and heard many things, can you shew unto me any new devise never seene before, that I may cause the same to be painted in the hall of this my house?'

To whom M. Guglielmo (hearing his fonde demaunde) aunsweared: 'Sir, I can shewe you nothing but that which hath beene knowen before, excepte nesinges[3] or such like. But if it please you, sir, I will gladly teach you one, which I thincke you never saw.'

M. Ermino, glad to heare of that, said: 'I pray you, sir, tell mee what it is' (not thinking he would have made that aunswere).

To whom M. Guglielmo redely said: 'Cause the figure of Liberality to be painted.'[4]

At which answeare M. Ermino was so sodenlye ashamed, as he was forced to chaunge his minde in maner cleane contrarye to his accustomed use and trade of life, saying: 'M. Guglielmo, I will cause the same to be painted in such wise, as neither you nor any man else shall have occasion justly to object the same against me.'

And from that time forth (such was the force of that taunt) hee was the most liberall and bountefull gentleman that dwelte in Genova, and one that honoured straungers and citizens more then ever did any in his time.

ANDREUCCIO OF PERUGIA

Andreuccio of Perugia, being come to Naples to buy horses, was in one night surprised with three marveilous accidentes. All which havinge escaped, with one rubye, he retourned home to his house.

There was at Perugia a yong man called Andreuccio di Pietro, a horse corser, who, understanding of a horse faire at Naples, did put five hundred crownes in his pursse and, never traveling before from his owne house, went thither with certaine other marchants, who arrived at Naples upon a Sonday at night.[1] The next morninge, accordinge to the instructions given him by his host, he went to the faire, where he viewed and saw many horses, whereof divers did very well like him,[2] and demaunded their prises, but with none he could agree of price. And to shew himselfe a right well able man to paye for that he boughte, many times (like a dolte and foole as he was) hee drew out his pursse stuffed with crownes in the presence of them that passed to and fro.

It chaunced that a yonge woman of Scicilia (which was very faire, but at every man's commaundement, and that for little hire) passed by as he was shewinge his pursse, not marked or perceived by Andreuccio; who sodenlye saide to herselfe: 'What is she in all this towne that should be like unto me, if all those crownes were mine?' And so passed forth.

There was with this yong peate an old woman, a Scicilian also, who so sone as she espied Andreuccio, forsoke her companion and ran affectuouslye to imbrace him. Which the yong woman perceivinge (not speaking a word) she gave good heede to that they said. Andreuccio, tourninge himselfe to the olde woman, immediatlye knew her and rejoised muche that he had so happely met her; whom, after greate gratulacions and manye welcomes, she promised to visit at his lodginge. Which done, she departed from Andreuccio, and hee returned to buy his horsse; howbeit, that morning he bought none at all.

The yonge dame, which had first seene this pursse and marked the acquaintaunace betweene the old woman and him, to assaie by what meanes she might get that moneye, or at least some part thereof, subtelly asked the old woman what man that was, of whence, what he did there, and how he knew her. To whom the olde woman particularlye recompted her whole acquaintaunce, how she dwelt of long time in Scicilia with his father, and afterwards at Perugia. And likewise she told her when he retourned, and for what cause hee was come to Naples. This jolly wenche, wholy informed of Andreuccio his parentes, and of their names, made a plat and foundation by subtill and craftye meanes how to obtaine her purpose. And when she was come home to her house, she sent the old woman about business for that day, because she might not retourne to Andreuccio.

She had dwelling with her a pretye girle, well noseled and brought up in doing of arrantes, whom, about evening, she sent to the lodging of Andreuccio to make inquirye for him. Where by fortune she chaunced to finde him, standing alone at his hoste's doore; whom the girle did aske if he knew not an honest man of Perugia called Andreuccio di Pietro, that hosted there: 'Yes, my girle' (quoth he) 'I am the same man.'

Then she toke him aside and saide unto him: 'Sir, there is a gentlewoman of this towne that would gladly speake with you, if it were your pleasure.'

Which, when Andreuccio heard, by and by hee called to minde, and seemed to himselfe that hee was a goodly yonge man of person and that withoute doubte the same woman was in love with him, because in all Naples he thought ther was none so proper a stripling as himselfe. Whom incontinently he aunsweared that he would waite upon her, demaunding when he should come and to what place.

To whom she made answere: 'Even when it pleaseth you, sir, for my maistresse attendeth at home for you.'

Andreuccio upon that, withoute any word spoken to his hoste whither he was gone, said to the wench: 'Go thou before, and I will follow.'

And the girle did conduct him to her maistres' house, which dwelt in a streate called Marpertugio, a name shewing the honestye of the streate wher she dwelt.[3] But he, knowing and suspecting nothing, thought the place to be right honest that he went unto, and the wife likewise honest and good, and boldlye entred the house, the wenche going before. And mountinge up the staiers, this yonge gristle called her maistres, sayinge unto her that maister Andreuccio was come. Who, redye at the upper steppe, seemed as though she attended for him.

This ladye was fine and had a good face, well apparelled and trimmed after the beste maner. And seinge maister Andreuccio at hand, descended two steppes of the staiers with her armes open to imbrace him, foldinge the same aboute his necke, and paused a certaine space without speaking any word, as thoughe great love and earneste affection enforced her so to doe. Then weeping, she kissed his face, and, with a voice halfe uttered betwene howling and speaking, she said unto him: 'O Andreuccio, mine owne deare hart, most hartely welcome.'

Andreuccio, marveiling at those tender words, all amazed aunsweared: 'Gentlewoman, and you also well found out.'

Afterwards she toke him by the hand and conveyed him up into a parlour, and from thence (without further talke) into a chamber, which was all perfumed with roses, with flowers of orenges, and other sweete smelles, where he sawe a bedde well furnished, and divers sortes of apparell placed upon presses (accordinge to the maner of that countrye), and many other faire and riche ornaments. By reason whereof Andreuccio, which was but a freshewater souldiour, thought that shee had been a great ladye.

And they two sittinge together uppon a cheste, at her bed's feete, she began thus to saye unto him: 'Andreuccio, I am assured you do greatly wonder at these faire words, this curteous interteignement, and at the teares which I let fall. And no marveile, although you do not know mee, and peradventure never heard tel of me before, but I wil declare unto you a thing more straunge and marveilous then that is. And to tell you plaine, I am your owne sister, and I say unto you that, sith it hath pleased my Lord God to shew me so much grace and favour that I doe now see one of my brethren before I die (althoughe I desire to see them all), I care not when hee do call mee from this wretched world; I am so in minde comforted and releved. And where it may chaunce that you never understoode so much before this time, I will tell you the whole discourse.

So it is that Pietro, my father and yours, dwelt of long time (whereof it is possible that you have heard report) at Palermo, where, through the goodnesse and frendlye behavioure of him, there be yet some remaininge that did beare him singular goodwil and frendship. But amonges other which loved him moste, my mother (which was a gentlewoman, and then a widow) without doubt did love him best. In such wise that shee, forgetting the love of her father and of her brethren and the love of her owne honour and reputation, they dealed so together as they begat mee, and am here as you see. Afterwardes, when your father and mine had occasion to depart from Palermo, he retourned to Perugia, leaving my mother behinde, and me his yong doughter, never after that (so farre as I knowe) caringe neither for my mother or me; whereof if he were not my father, I coulde blame him very much, consideringe his ingratitude towards my mother. Albeit, he ought to use towards mee so muche affection and fatherlye love as to his owne doughter, being come of no kitchin maide, ne yet of anye base woman, for my mother, otherwise not knowinge what he was, did commit into his handes (moved of mere love) both herselfe and all that she had. But what? Thinges ill done, and so longe time past are more easye to be reprehended then amended.

Thus the matter went. He left mee a litle infante at Palermo; where when I was growen to yeares, my mother, which was riche, gave mee to wife to one of the house of Gergenti,[4] a gentleman of great honesty and reputation, who, for the love of my mother and me, retourned to dwell at Palermo, where, greatly favouringe the faction of the Guelphi, hee began to practise a certaine enterprise with oure King Charles, which being knowen to King Frederick, before the same enterprise could take effect, we were forced to flye out of Scicilia.[5] At what time, I had thought to have been the chiefest ladye that ever dwelte in that island. Wherfore, taking with us such fewe things as wee were able to carye (few I maye well call them, in respect of them we possessed) and leavinge our houses and palaces, we came unto this citye; where we found Kinge Charles so beningne towards us that he hath recompenced part of our losses which we sustened in his service. For he hath given us possessions and houses, with good provision of housholde to my husband and your brother in law, as you now see and perceive. And in this maner I do remaine here, where (sweete brother) I thancke God (and not you) that at this present I see you.' And therwithall she

toke him about the necke, weeping tenderly, and then kissed his
face againe.

Andreuccio, hearing this tale spoken in order and digested
from poinct to poinct with good utterance, wherof no word
stucke betwene her teeth or was impeached by default of tongue,
and remembring how it was true that his father dwelt at
Palermo, knowing also by himselfe the maner of yong men,
which in their youth be prompte and willinge to love, and seinge
her tender teares, her imbracinges and honeste kisses, thoughte
all that shee had spoken to be most certaine and true. And after
shee had done her tale, he answered in this wise: 'Madame, you
may not thincke unkindness if I doe marveile at this, for that in
verye deede I have no acquaintance of you, no more then if you
had never beene borne, but whether my father hath spoken of
you or of your mother at any time, truly I do not now remember.
But so much the more I do rejoice that I have founde a sister
here (as I truste) because I am here alone. And certainely I
knowe none so honourable but you may seeme agreeable unto
him so well as to mee, which am but a poore marchaunt.[6]
Howbeit, I do beseeche you to tell me how you did know that I
was in the city.'

To whom she aunsweared: 'This morning a poore women
which oftentimes repaireth my house gave mee knowledge
thereof, because of long time (as she told me) she did dwell with
your father at Palermo and at Perugia. And because I thought it
more convenient and meete to bidde you home to mine owne
house then to seke you in another man's, I thought good to send
for you.' After these words, she began in order to inquire of the
state of his parents, calling them by their proper names. Whereunto Andreuccio made aunswere that now he perceived he had
better cause to give credite unto her words then before.

Their discourse and talke of thinges being long and the
weather hot, shee called for Greke wine and comfits and made
Andreuccio to drinke. Who, after the banquet, desirous to
depart to his lodging (for it was about supper time) shee by no
meanes woulde suffer him, but making as though she were
angrye, said unto him: 'Oh God! I see now most evidently that
you do make little accompte of mee, being your owne sister
whom you never sawe before, and in her house, whereunto you
ought to resorte whensoever you come to towne. And will you
nowe forsake the same to suppe in an inne? But of trouth you

shall not chose but take part of my supper. And althoughe my husbande be not at home (whereof I am righte sorye), yet you shall knowe that his wife is able to make you some good chere.'

To whom Andreuccio, not knowing wel what to say els, made this aunsweare: 'I do love you as I oughte to love a sister, but if I goe not to mine inne, I know they will tarye for mee all this night before they go to supper, to my great reproch and shame.'

'Praised be God' (quoth she then) 'I have servauntes to advertise your host that you be here with me, to the intente hee shall not tarrye for you. But pleaseth you, sir, to do me this great curtesye that I may sende for your companions hither to beare you company, that afterwardes, if you will needes depart, ye may goe all together.' Andreuccio aunsweared that he would send for none of his company that night, but for so much as she was so importunate, he himselfe was righte well content to satisfye her request.

Then she made as thoughe shee had sent to his inn to give word that they should not tarye for him, and, after much communication, supper was placed upon the table, served in with manye devises and sondrye delicates abundantly, and she with like sleights continued the supper till it was darke night. And when they rose from the table, Andreuccio made hast to departe, but shee would not suffer him, tellinge him that Naples was a towne so straight of orders that none might walke abrode in the night, and specially straungers, and that, like as she had sent word how they should not tary for him at supper, even so she had done for his bedde. All which Andreuccio beleeving, and taking pleasure that he was with his sister (deceived though he were of his false beliefe), was wel contented to tarye. Their talke and communication after supper was of purpose dilated and protracted, and, one part of the night being spent, she left Andreuccio in his chamber going to bedde, and a litle boye to waite upon him to see that he lacked nothinge, and shee with her women went into another chamber.

The time of the yeare was very hotte, wherefore Andreuccio, being alone, striped himselfe and laid his hose and doublette under his bedde's head, and, desirous to go to the privye, he asked the boye where it was; who, pointing to the doore in a corner of the chamber, said unto him: 'Goe in there.'

Andreuccio safely wente in and chaunced by fortune to set his foote upon a borde which at both endes was loose from the joist whereupon it lay, by reason whereof the bord and he tombled downe into the jakes.[7] And God so loved him that in the fall he received no hurt, although it were of a good height, saving he was imbroined and arrayed with the dunge of the place, wherof the jakes was full. Which place (to the intent you may the better understand what is said and what shall follow) even as it was I wil describe unto you. There was in a litle straighte entrye (as manye times we see betweene two houses) certaine bordes laied uppon two joistes, betwene the one house and the other, upon which was placed the seate of the privye, one of which bordes was the same that fill downe with Andreuccio; who, now being in the bottome of the jakes, sorowfull for that sodaine chaunce, cried oute to the boye for helpe. But the boye, so soone as hee hearde that hee was fallen, wente in to tell his maistres, whoe by and by ranne into his chamber to seeke for his clothes. And when she had founde them, and in the same his money, which Andreuccio, like a foole, without mistruste, still caried about him, she now possessed the thing for which she had before laied the snare in faining her selfe to be of Palermo and the doughter of one of Perugia. And caring no longer for him, she straightway shut fast the privy doore whereat he went forth when he fell.

Andreuccio, seing that the boye would not aunswere, began to cry out aloude, but all was in vaine. Wherefore suspecting the cause and beginning somewhat to late to understande the deceipt, he lept over a litle wall which closed the place from the sight of the streat. And when he was in the open streate, he went to the dore of the house, which he knew well inough, makinge a noise, rapping hard and long at the doore, but it was in vaine. For which cause he began to complaine and lamente, like unto one that manifestly saw his misfortune, saying: 'Alas, in howe litle time have I lost five hundred crownes and a sister.' And after many other words he began againe to bounse at the doore and to crye out.

He rapped so long and cried so loude as he waked manye of the neighbours thereaboutes, who, not able to suffer that noise, rose out of their beds. And amonges others one of the maides of the house (faining herselfe to be slepye) looked out at the window and said in great rage: 'What noise is beneath?'

'Oh,' saide Andreuccio, 'do yee not know me? I am Andreuccio, the brother of madame Floredelice?'

'Thou hast droncke to much methinketh' (quoth the maide).

'Go sleepe, and come againe to morow. I know none called Andreuccio, nor yet do understand what thou meanest by those foolish words. Get thee hence good man, and let us sleepe, I pray thee.'

'Why' (quoth Andreuccio) 'doest thou not heare me what I say? Thou knowest me well inough if thou wilt, but if the Scicilian kinred be so sone forgotten, give me my clothes which I have left behinde me, and I will go hence with al my hart.'

Whereat the maide laughed and saide: 'I thincke the man is in a dreame.' And with that she tourned herselfe and shut fast the window.

Andreuccio, now sure and certaine of his losses, attached with incredible sorow, converted his anger into rage, thoughte to recover by anoiaunce that which he could not get with faire wordes. Wherefore, takinge up a bigge stone, he began againe with greater blowes to beate at the doore. Which when manye of the neighbours (that before were waked oute of their sleepe and risen) did heare, thinking that it was some troublesome felow that counterfeited those words to anoye the good wife of the house, and all they likewise troubled with the noise, loking out of the windowes, began to rate him with one voice (like a sorte of curres of one streate, which doe baule and barke at a straunge dogge that passeth by), sayinge: 'This is to much shame and villanye, to come to the houses of honest women at that time of the night and to speake such fonde wordes. Wherefore (good man) gette thee hence for God's sake, and let us sleepe. If thou have anything to do with the good wife, come againe to morrow, and disquiet us no more to night.'

With which woordes, as poore Andreuccio was somewhat appeased, one that was within the house, a ruffian (that kept the good wife) whom Andreuccio never saw nor heard before, looked out of the windowe and with a bigge and horrible voice demaunded who was beneath? Whereat Andreuccio, lifting up his head, saw one that so far as he could perceive, seemed to be a long lubber and a large, with a blacke beard and a sterne visage, looking as though he were newly risen from bedde, ful of sleepe, gaping and rubbing his eyes. Whom Andreuccio aunsweared in fearefull wise, saying: 'I am the good wive's brother of the house.'

But the ruffian, interrupting his answeare, speaking more fiercely then at the first, said: 'I know not who thou arte, but if I come downe, I will so codgel and bombast thee as thou shalte not be able to sturre thyselfe, like an asse and dronken beast as thou art, which all this night wilt not suffer us to slepe.' And, with these wordes turning himselfe aboute, he shutte the windowe.

Divers of the neighbours (which knewe better the conditions of that terrible ruffian), speakinge faire to Andreuccio, saide unto him: 'For God's sake, good man, depart hence in time, and suffer not thyselfe to be slaine.'

'Gette thee hence' (quoth another) 'and saye not but thou haddest warning.'

Whereat Andreuccio, being appalled and with the ruffian's woordes and sight amazed, moved likewise by the counsaile of the neighbours that spake to him, as he thoughte, in charitable wise, toke his waye to retourne to his inne, the sorowfulles man that ever lived, and in greatest despaire for losse of his money.

Turninge that way wherein he was guided by a litle girle the day afore and, anoyed with the stenche that he felt about him, desirous to goe to the sea side to washe him, hee declined to muche on the left hande, taking the waye up to the streat called La Ruga Catellana,[8] and, as hee was marching up to the highest parte of the citye, by chaunce he sawe twoo men before him, with a lanthorne light in one of their handes, coming towardes him. For avoiding of whom (because he feared that it was the watche, or some other ill disposed persones) he hidde himselfe in an olde house harde by. But they (as of purpose) went to the very same place; where, one of them discharging himselfe of certain instrumentes of iron whiche he bare upon his backe, both of them did vewe and surveye those irons, debating of divers thinges touching the same.

And as they were talking togethers, one of them saide: 'What meaneth this? I smel the foulest stenche that ever I felte in all my life.' And when he had said so, he lifted up the lanthorne and espied miserable Andreuccio couching behinde the wall, and, being afraide, asked who it was.

Andreuccio helde his peace. But they, approaching neare him with their lighte, demaunded what hee made there, so filthely arayed. To whom Andreuccio rehersed the whole adventure as it chaunceth. Who, considering the cause of that misfortune, said one to another: 'This no doubt was done in the house of Scarabone Butta Fuoco.'[9]

And, tourning towardes Andreuccio, one of them saide unto him: 'Good man, although thou hast lost thy money, yet thou hast great cause to praise God that it was thy chaunce to falle and not to enter againe into the house. For if thou haddest not fallen, assure thyselfe that when thou haddest bene aslepe, thy throte had bene cutte, and so with thy money shouldest have loste thy life. But what availeth it nowe to wepe and lament? For thou shalt so sone plucke the starres out of the skye as ever recover one peny of thy losse; and without doubt he will kill thee, if hee understande that thou make any wordes thereof.'

When they had sayde so, and had given him that admonition, they comforted him in this wise: 'Good felowe, we doe lament thy state. And therefore, if thou wilt joine thyself with us about an enterprise which we have in hande, we warraunt thee thou shalt get a great deale more than thou hast loste.' Andreuccio, like one in extreame dispaire, was content.

The daye before was buried one Messer Philippo Minutulo, an archebishop of Naples,[10] in riche pontificalles and orna-mentes, with a rubye upon his finger that was worth five hundred ducates of golde, whome they purposed to robbe and dispoile, telling Andreuccio the whole order of their intent. Who, more covetous then well advised, went with them.

And, going towardes the great church, Andreuccio his per-fume began to sente very strong, whereupon one of them saide: 'Is it not possible to devise a waye that this shitten beaste may washe himselfe in some place, that he stinke no more thus filthelye?'

'Yes' (quod the other) 'there is a pitte herre harde by, over whiche there hangeth a pulley and a great bucket, where we may presently washe him.'

When they were come to the pitte, they founde the rope hanging still upon the pulley, but the bucket was taken away. Wherefore they thought beste to tie him to the rope and to let him downe the pitte to washe himselfe, and that when he was washed he should wagge the rope, and they woulde hoist him up againe. Whiche they did.

But it chaunced that, whiles he was thus clensing himselfe in the pitte, the watche of the citye (because they swette and the night was very hot), being drye and thirsty came to the pitte to drinke. The other twoo, perceiving the watche at hande, left Andreuccio in the pitte and ranne awaye. The watche, whiche

ANDREUCCIO OF PERUGIA 41

was come thether to drinke, perceived not those two that were
fledde. And Andreuccio being still in the bottome, when he had
clensed himselfe, began to wagge the rope. The watche, sitting
downe by the pitte's side, caste of their clokes and laide down
their halbardes and other weapons and began to drawe up the
rope, thinking that the bucket full of water was tied to the same.
When Andreuccio was haled up to the brincke of the pitte, hee
forsoke the rope and cast himselfe with one of his handes upon
the side of the same. When the watche sawe that, they for feare
ranne away so faste as they could without speaking any worde.
Wherof Andreuccio did marveile very much and, if he had not
taken good holde, he had fallen againe downe to the bottome,
to his great hurt and, peradventure, not without peril of his life.
Notwithstanding, being out of the pitte and finding halberdes
and other weapons there, which he knew wel his fellowes
brought not with them, he then began muche more to wonder.
But betwene feare and ignoraunce of that which happened,
complaining himself of his harde fortune, without touching of
anything, he determined to go from thence and wandred he
could not tell whether.

But as he was departing from that place, he met his fellowes,
retiring backe to drawe him up. And when they perceived him
alredye haled out of the pitte, they wer wonderfully abashed
and asked who drewe him out? Andreuccio made aunswere that
he coulde not tell, rehearsing to them in order what had
chaunced and of the things he founde without. They, understanding the matter, laughed and tolde him againe the cause
wherefore they ran awaye and what they were that drewe him
up.

And, without further talke (being then about midnight), they
repaired to the great churche, into the whiche they easely entred,
and wente to the tombe, whiche was of marble, verye huge and
weightye. The cover whereof being verye great, with their
crowes of iron and other tooles they lifted up so farre as one
man was able to enter. Which doen, one asked another who
should goe in?

'Not I', quod one.

'And not I' (quod the other).

'No, nor I', quod Andreuccio.

The other twoo, hearing Andreuccio saye so, stepped unto
him, saying: 'Wilte thou not goe in? By the faithe wee owe to

God, if thou goe not in, we will so beate thee with one of these
iron barres as thou shalt never sturre againe out of this place.'

Andreuccio, being made their common riding foole, greately
fearing when he heard them saye so, went in. And when he was
in the grave, he saide unto himselfe: 'These good felowes do
make me goe in because they would deceive me. For, when I
have geven them al that is here, and I readye to come out, they
meane to runne awaye to save themselves and to leave me
behinde without any parte thereof.' Wherfore he purposed first
to take his owne porcion to himselfe. And, remembring the ring
of great valour whereof they tolde him, so sone as he was in the
grave he pulled it of from the archebishop's finger and put it
upon his own. And afterwardes taking the crosse, the miter, and
the gloves, dispoiling him even to his shirt, he gave them all,
saying that there was nothing els.

But they, pressing upon him that there was a ring behinde,
willed him throughly to make searche for it; howebeit, he still
aunswered that he could not finde it. And because he would
make them to tarye a litle longer, he fained as though he had
made a further searche. The other, so subtile and malicious as
he, bad him to seke stil, and, when they saw time, they toke
away the proppes that stayed up the tombe and ran awaye,
leaving poore Andreuccio fast shutte in the grave. Whiche when
Andreuccio perceived what chaunced to him then, eche man
may consider.

Then he assayed, sometimes with his shoulders, sometimes
with his head, to remove the cover, but all was in vaine.
Wherefore even for verye sorowe, he fell in a sownde upon the
dead bodye of the bishop. And if a man had seene them both at
that instant, it coulde not well have bene discerned whether was
the dead corps the archebishhope dead or poore Andreuccio
dying. But after he was come to himself, he began piteously to
complaine, seing hee was arrived to one of these twoo endes,
either in the tombe to die for hunger and with the stenche of the
dead bodye putrifying with wormes, if no man came to open it,
or els to be hanged as a thiefe, if hee were founde within.

And as he was in these considerations tormented with sorowe,
he heard a noise in the church of divers men, who, as he thought,
came to the like facte that he and his felowes had done before;
wherewith his feare began much more to augmente. But, after
they had opened the grave and stayed it up, it came in question

amongs them who should go in. And when they had contended a good space about the same, a priest that was in the companye saide: 'Why are ye afraide? Doe ye thinke that hee will eate you? The dead never eate men. I will go in myselfe.'

And when he had saide so, he layed him downe upon his breste at the side of the grave, and thrusting his feete in before, he went downe. Andreuccio seeing that, erected himselfe upright and caught the priest by one of the legges, making as though he would have drawen him in. Which when the priest perceived, he cried out aloude, speeding himself out so fast as he could. Wherewithal the reste, dismayed almost out of their wittes, leaving the grave open, toke their legges and ran, as though a hundred thousand devels had bene at their tailes.

Whiche seing, Andreuccio (more joyful then he looked for) lepte out of the grave and ran as faste as he could out of the churche at the place where he came in. At what time dayelight began to appeare, and he, with the ringe on his finger, wandred he wiste not whether till he came to the seaside and, at length, recovered his inne, where he founde his companye and his hoste al that night taking greate care for him. To whome recompting that whiche chaunced, his host gave him advise incontinently to get him out of Naples, whiche presently he did, and retourned to Perugia, having bestowed his 500 crownes upon a ringe, whiche he thought to have imployed upon horses, for whiche cause he made that journey.

Giletta, a physition's doughter of Narbon, healed the French king of a fistula, for reward whereof she demaunded Beltramo, counte of Rossiglione, to husband. The counte, being maried against his will, for despite fled to Florence and loved another. Giletta, his wife, by pollicye founde meanes to lie with her husbande in place of his lover and was begotten with childe of two sonnes. Which knowen to her husband, he received her againe, and afterwards he lived in great honour and felicitye.

In Fraunce there was a gentleman called Isnardo, the counte of Rossiglione, who, because he was sickely and diseased, kepte alwayes in his house a physition named maister Gerardo of Narbona.[1] This counte had one onely sonne, called Beltramo, a very yonge childe, amiable and faire, with whom there was nourished and brought uppe many other children of his age, amonges whom one of the doughters of the said physition, named Giletta, who fervently fill in love with Beltramo, more then was meete for a maiden of her age. This Beltramo, when his father was deade and left under the royall custody of the king, was sente to Paris; for whose departure the maiden was very pensife. A litle while after, her father being likewise deade, shee was desirous to go to Paris onelye to see the yonge counte, if for that purpose she could get any good occasion. But being diligently loked unto by her kinsfolke because she was riche and fatherlesse, she could see no convienient waye for her intended journey. And, being now mariageable, the love she bare to the counte was never out of her remembraunce, and refused manye husbandes with whom her kinsfolke woulde have matched her, without making them privye to the cause of her refusall.

Now it chaunced that she burned more in love with Beltramo than ever shee did before because she hearde tell that hee was growen to the state of a goodly yong gentleman. She heard by report that the French king had a swelling upon his breast which by reason of ill cure was growen to be a fistula, which did put him to marveilous paine and griefe, and that there was no physition to be found, although many were proved, that could heale it, but rather did impaire the griefe and made it worse and worse. Wherfore the king, like one in dispaire, would take no more counsell or helpe. Wherof the yong mayden was wonderfull glad, thinckinge to have by this meanes not onely a lawfull occasion to go to Paris but, if the disease were such as she supposed, easelye to bringe to passe that shee mighte have the Counte Beltramo to her husbande.

Whereuppon, with such knowledge as she had learned at her father's hands beforetime, shee made a pouder of certaine herbes which she thought meete for that disease, and rode to Paris. And the first thing she went about when she came thither was to see the Counte Beltramo. And then she repaired to the king, praying his grace to vouchsafe to shew her his griefe. The king, perceiving her to be a faire yonge maiden and a comelye, would not hide it but opened the same unto her.

So soone as shee saw it, shee put him in comforte that shee was able to heale him, saying: 'Sir, if it maye please your grace, I truste in God, without anye greate paine unto your highnesse, within eighte dayes to make you whole of this disease.'

The king, hearing her say so, began to mocke her, saying: 'How is it possible for thee, beinge a yong woman, to do that which the beste renowmed physitions in the world cannot?' Hee thancked her for her goodwill and made her a direct aunsweare that hee was determined no more to followe the counsaile of any physition.

Whereunto the maiden aunsweared: 'Sir, you dispise my knowledge because I am yonge and a woman, but I assure you that I do not minister physicke by profession but by the aide and helpe of God and with the cunninge of maister Gerardo of Narbona, who was my father and a physition of great fame so longe as he lived.'

The king, hearing those words, said to himselfe: 'This woman, peradventure, is sente unto me of God. And, therefore, why should I disdaine to prove her cunninge, for so muche as she

promiseth to heale me within a litle space without any offence
or griefe unto me?' And, being determined to prove her, he said:
'Damosel, if thou doest not heale me but make me to breake my
determination, what wilt thou shal folow therof?'

'Sir,' said the maiden, 'let me be kept in what guard and
keeping you list, and if I do not heale you within these eight
dayes, let me be burnt. But if I do heale your grace, what
recompence shall I have then?'

To whom the kinge aunswered: 'Because thou art a maiden
and unmaried, if thou heale me according to thy promise, I wil
bestow thee uppon some gentleman that shal be of right good
worship and estimation.'

To whom she aunsweared: 'Sir, I am very well content that
you bestow me in mariage, but I beseech your grace let me have
such a husband as myselfe shall demaund, without presumption
to any of your children or other of your bloud.' Which request
the king incontinently graunted.

The yong maiden began to minister her physicke, and in short
space (before her appointed time) she had throughly cured the
king. And when the king perceived himselfe whole, said unto
her: 'Thou hast well deserved a husbande, Giletta, even such a
one as thyselfe shalt chose.'

'I have then, my Lord', quoth she, 'deserved the Countye
Beltramo of Rossiglione, whom I have loved from my youth.'

The king was very loth to graunt him unto her, but, for
that he had made a promise which he was loth to breake, he
caused him to be called forth and said unto him: 'Sir countye,
knowing full well that you are a gentleman of great honour,
oure pleasure is that you returne home to your owne house
to order your estate according to your degree and that you
take with you a damosell which I have appointed to be your
wife.'

To whom the countye gave his humble thanks and demaunded
what she was. 'It is she', quoth the king, 'that with her medecines
hath healed me.'

The counte knew her wel and had already seen her. Although
she was faire, yet knowing her not to be of a stocke convenable
to his nobility, skornefully said unto the king: 'Will you then,
sir, give me a physition to wife? It is not the pleasure of God
that ever I should in that wise bestow myselfe.'

To whom the king said: 'Wilt thou then that wee should

breake our faith, which wee to recover health have given to the
damosell, who for a reward asked thee to husband?'

'Sir', quoth Beltramo, 'you may take from me all that I have
and give my person to whom you please because I am your subject. But I assure you I shal never be contented with that mariage.'

'Wel, you shall have her', said the king, 'for the maiden is
faire and wise and loveth you most intirely, thinking verely you
shal leade a more joyful life with her then with a lady of a
greater house.' The countye therewithal held his peace, and the
kinge made great preparation for the mariage.

And when the appointed day was come, the counte in the
presence of the king (although it were against his wil) maried
the maiden, who loved him better then her owne selfe. Which
done, the counte, determining before what he would do, prayed
licence to retourne to his countrye to consummat the mariage.
And when he was on horsebacke hee went not thither but toke
his journey into Tuscane, where, understanding that the Florentines and Senois were at warres, he determined to take the
Florentines' parte, and was willingly received and honourablye
intertaigned, and was made captaine of a certaine nomber of
men, continuing in their service a long time.[2]

The new-maried gentlewoman, scarce contented with his
unkindnes, hopinge by her well-doinge to cause him to retourne
into his countrye, went to Rossiglione, where she was received
of all his subjects for their lady. And perceiving that through the
counte's absence all thinges were spoiled and out of order, shee,
like a sage ladye, with greate diligence and care disposed his
thinges in order againe; whereof the subjects rejoised very much,
bearing to her their harty love and affection, greatly blaming the
counte because he coulde not content himselfe with her.

This notable gentlewoman, having restored all the countrye
againe to their auncient liberties, sent word to the counte her
husband by two knights to signifye unto him that, if it were for
her sake that hee had abandoned his countrye, uppon retourne
of aunsweare, she, to do him pleasure, would departe from
thence. To whom he chorlishly replied: 'Let her do what she
liste, for I do purpose to dwell with her when she shall have this
ring (meaning a ring which he wore) upon her finger and a
sonne in her armes begotten by mee.' He greatly loved that ring
and kepte it very carefully and never toke it from his finger for
a certaine vertue that he knew it had.[3]

The knights, hearinge the harde condition of two thinges impossible and seinge that by them he could not be removed from his determination, retourned againe to the lady, tellinge her his aunsweare; who, very sorowfull, after shee had a good while bethoughte her, purposed to finde meanes to attaine the two thinges, that thereby she might recover her husbande. And havinge advised herselfe what to doe, shee assembled the noblest and chiefeste of her countrye, declaring unto them in lamentable wise what shee had alreadye done to winne the love of the counte, shewinge them also what folowed thereof. And in the ende saide unto them that shee was lothe the counte for her sake should dwell in perpetuall exile; therefore, shee determined to spende the reste of her time in pilgrimages and devotion for preservation of her soule, prayinge theim to take the charge and governemente of the countrye and that they would let the counte understande that shee had forsaken his house and was removed farre from thence with purpose never to returne to Rossiglione againe. Many teares were shed by the people as she was speaking those wordes, and divers supplications were made unto him to alter his opinion, but all in vaine.

Wherefore, commending them all unto God, she toke her way, with her maide and one of her kinsemen, in the habite of a pilgrime, well furnished with silver and precious jewels, telling no man whither shee wente, and never rested till shee came to Florence; where, arrivinge by fortune at a poore widowe's house, shee contented herselfe with the state of a poore pilgrime, desirous to heare newes of her lord, whom by fortune she sawe the next day, passing by the house where she lay, on horsebacke with his company. And, althoughe shee knewe him well enoughe, yet shee demaunded of the good wife of the house what hee was; who aunsweared that hee was a straunge gentleman called the Counte Beltramo of Rossiglione, a curteous knight and wel beloved in the city, and that he was marvelously in love with a neighbour of hers that was a gentlewoman, verye poore and of small substance, neverthelesse of right honest life and good report, and by reason of her poverty was yet unmaried and dwelte with her mother, that was a wise and honest ladye.

The countesse, well noting these wordes and by litle and litle debating every particular point thereof, comprehending the effecte of those newes, concluded what to do. And when she had well understanded which was the house and the name of

the ladye and of her doughter that was beloved of the counte,
uppon a day repaired to the house secretely in the habite of a
pilgrime, where, finding the mother and doughter in poore estate
amonges their familye, after she had saluted them, told the
mother that shee had to saye unto her.

The gentlewoman, rising up, curteously intertained her; and,
being entred alone in a chamber, they sate downe, and the
countesse began to speake unto her in this wise: 'Madame,
methincke that ye be one upon whom Fortune doth frowne so
wel as upon me, but, if you please, you may both comfort me
and yourselfe.'

The lady answered that there was nothing in the world wherof
she was more desirous then of honest comfort.

The countesse, proceeding in her talke, said unto her: 'I have
neede now of your fidelitye and truste, whereuppon if I do staye,
and you deceive mee, you shall both undoe me and yourselfe.'

'Tell me then what it is, hardlye', said the gentlewoman, 'for
you shall never bee deceived of mee.'

Then the countesse beganne to recite her whole estate of love,
tellinge her what she was and what had chaunced to that present
daye, in such perfite order as the gentlewoman, beleevinge her
because shee had partly heard report before, began to have
compassion uppon her. And after that the countesse had
rehearsed the whole circumstance, she continued her purpose,
saying: 'Now you have heard (amonges other my troubles) what
two things they bee which behoveth mee to have if I doe recover
my husband, which I know none can helpe me to obtaine but
onelye you, if it be true that I heare, which is that the counte,
my husband, is farre in love with your doughter.'

To whom the gentlewoman said: 'Madame, if the counte love
my doughter, I knowe not, albeit the likelihoode is great. But
what am I able to doe in that which you desire?'

'Madame', aunsweared the countesse, 'I will tell you. But first
I will declare what I meane to doe for you if my purpose be
brought to effecte. I see your faire doughter of good age, readye
to marye, but (as I understande) the cause why shee is unmaried
is the lacke of substance to bestowe her.[4] Wherefore, I purpose,
for recompence of the pleasure which you shall doe for mee, to
give so much readye money to marye her honourablye as you
shall thincke sufficient.'

The countesse's offer was very well liked of the ladye because she was poore. Yet, having a noble hart, she said unto her: 'Madame, tell me wherein I may do you service, and, if it be a thinge honest, I will gladlye performe it and, the same being brought to passe, do as it shall please you.'

Then said the countesse: 'I thincke it requisite that, by someone whom you truste, you give knowledge to the counte, my husband, that your doughter is and shall be at his commaundement. And, to the intent she may be well assured that hee loveth her indeede above anye other, she must pray him to sende her a ring that hee weareth uppon his finger, which ring (as she knoweth) he loveth very dearely. And when he sendeth the ringe, you shal give it unto me and afterwards sende him woorde that your doughter is readye to accomplishe his pleasure. And then you shall cause him secretelye to come hither, and place me by him insteede of your doughter. Peradventure, God will give me the grace that I may be with child, and so, having this ring on my finger and the childe in mine armes begotten by him, I maye recover him and, by your meanes, continue with him as a wife ought to do with her husbande.'

This thinge seemed difficulte unto the gentlewoman, fearing that there woulde folowe reproche unto her doughter. Notwithstandinge, considering what an honest part it were to be a meane that the good ladye might recover her husbande and that shee mighte doe it for a good purpose, havinge affiaunce in her honest affection, not onely promised the countesse to bring this to passe, but, in fewe dayes, with greate subtiltye folowing the order wherein she was instructed, she had gotten the ringe, although it was with the counte's ill-will, and toke order that the countesse insteede of her doughter did lie with him. And at the first meeting, so effectuously desired by the counte, God so disposed the matter that the countesse was begotten with child, of two goodly sonnes, and her delivery chaunced at the due time. Whereuppon the gentlewoman not onelye contented the countesse at that time with the companye of her husbande, but at manye other times so secretly as it was never knowen; the counte not thinkinge that he had lien with his wife but with her whom he loved. To whom, at his uprising in the morning, he used many curteous and amiable woords and gave divers faire and precious jewels, which the countesse kept most carefully.

And when she perceived herselfe with child, she determined no more to trouble the gentlewoman but said unto her:

'Madame, thanckes be to God and you, I have the thing that I desire, and even so it is time to recompence your desert, that afterwards I may depart.' The gentlewoman said unto her that if she had done anye pleasure agreeable to her minde, she was right glad thereof; which she did not for hope of reward but because it appertained to her by well-doing so to doe. Whereunto the countesse said: 'Your sayinge pleaseth me well, and, for my part, I doe not purpose to give unto you the thing you shal demaunde in reward but for consideration of your well-doing, which dutye forceth me to do.' The gentlewoman, then constrained with necessity, demaunded of her with great bashfulnesse an hundred poundes to marie her daughter. The countesse, perceivinge the shamefastnesse of the gentlewoman and her curteous demaunde, gave her five hundred poundes and so many faire and costly jewels as almost amounted to like valour. For which the gentlewoman, more then contented, gave most harty thankes to the countesse, who departed from the gentlewoman and retourned to her lodging.

The gentlewoman, to take occasion from the counte of anye farther repaire or sendinge to her house, toke her doughter with her and went into the country to her frends. The Counte Beltramo, within fewe dayes after, being revoked home to his owne house by his subjectes (hearinge that the countesse was departed from thence), retourned. The countesse, knowinge that her husbande was goone from Florence and retourned home, was verye gladde, continuing in Florence till the time of her childbedde, being brought abedde of twoo sonnes, whiche were very like unto their father, and caused them carefully to be noursed and brought up.

And when she sawe time, she toke her journey (unknowen to anye) and arrived at Montpellier.[5] And resting her selfe there for certaine dayes, hearing newes of the counte and where he was and that upon the daye of Al Sainctes[6] he purposed to make a greate feaste and assembly of ladies and knightes, in her pilgrime's weede she repaired thither. And, knowing that they were all assembled at the palace of the counte readye to sitte downe at the table, shee passed through the people, without chaunge of apparell, with her twoo sonnes in her armes. And, when shee was come up into the hall, even to the place where the counte sat, falling downe prostrate at his feete, weeping, saying unto him: 'My lorde, I am thy poore infortunate wife, who, to th'intent thou mightest retourne and dwel in thine owne house, have bene a great while begging aboute the worlde. Therefore, I nowe beseche thee, for the honoure of God, that thou wilt observe the conditions which the twoo knightes that I sent unto thee did commaunde me to doe. For, beholde, here in mine armes, not only one sonne begotten by thee, but twaine, and likwise thy ring. It is nowe time then (if thou kepe promise) that I should be received as thy wife.'

The counte, hearing this, was greatly astonned, and knewe the ring, and the children also, they were so like him. 'But tell me', quod he, 'howe is this come to passe?'

The countesse, to the great admiration of the counte and of all those that were in presence, rehersed unto them in order all that whiche had bene done and the whole discourse thereof. For which cause the counte, knowing the thinges she had spoken to be true and perceiving her constant minde and good witte and the twoo faire young boyes, to kepe his promise made and to please his subjectes and the ladies that made sute unto him to accept her from that time foorth as his lawefull wife and to honour her, abjected his obstinate rigour, causing her to rise up, and imbraced and kissed her, acknowledging her againe for his lawefull wife. And after he had apparelled her according to her estate, to the great pleasure and contentation of those that were there and of al his other frendes, not onely that daye but many others he kept great chere. And from that time forth, hee loved and honoured her as his dere spouse and wife.[7]

*Philenio Sisterno, a scholler of Bologna, being
mocked of three faire gentlewomen, at a banket
made of set purpose he was revenged on them all.*

At Bologna, whiche is the noblest citye of Lombardye, the
mother of studies and accomplished with al things nedefull and
requisite for sutch a florishing state, there was a yong scholler, a
gentleman of the countrye of Crete named Philenio Sisterno, of
very good grace and behaviour.[1] It chanced that in his time there
was a great feast made in the citye, wherunto were bidden the
fairest dames and beste of reputation there. There was likewise
many gentlemen and schollers of Bologna, amonges whom was
this Philenio Sisterno. Who, following the manner of young
men, dallying sometime with one, sometime with another, and
perceiving them for his purpose, determined to daunce with one
of them. And comming to one whiche was called Emerentiana,
the wife of Sir Lamberto Bentivoglia,[2] hee prayed her to daunce.
Who, being verye gentle and of no less audacitye than beautiful,
refused not.

  Then Philenio leading forth the daunce very softly, sometimes
wringing her by the hand, spake somewhat secretly unto her
these wordes: 'Madame, your beautye is so great that without
doubt it surmounteth all that ever I sawe, and there is no woman
in the world to whome I beare so great affection as to your
persone. Whiche, if it were correspondent to me in Love, I
would thinke myself the beste contented man in the world;
otherwise I shall in shorte time bee deprived of life, and then
you shall be the cause of my death. And loving you (Madame)
as I doe, and as my dutye requireth, you ought to take me for
your servaunt, using me and those litle goodes whiche I have as
your owne. And I doe assure you, that it is impossible for me to
receive greater favour from Heaven, then to see myselfe subjecte
to sutch a gentlewoman as you be, whiche hath taken me in a

nette like a birde.'³ Nowe Emerentiana, whiche earnestly had marked those sweet and pleasaunt woordes, like a wise gentle-woman seemed to geve no eare thereunto, and made him no aunswere at all.

The daunce ended, and Emerentiana being set down in her place, this young scholler went to take another gentlewoman by the hand, and began to daunce with her. Whiche was not so sone begonne, but thus he said unto her: 'It nedeth not, madame, that by woordes I doe expresse the fervant love which I beare you, and will so doe so long as my poore spirite shall governe and rule my members. And if I could obtaine you for my maistress and singuler ladye, I would thinke myself the happiest man alive. Then, loving you as I do and being wholly yours, as you may easely understand, refuse me not, I besech you, for your humble servaunt, sithe that my life and all that I have dependenth upon you alone.' The yong gentlewoman, whose name was Panthemia, perceiving his meaning, did not aunswere him anything at that time, but honestly proceded in her daunce. And the daunce ended, smiling a litle, she sat downe with the other dames.

This done, amorous Philenio rested not until he had taken the thirde by the hand (who was the gentlest, fairest and trimmest dame in all Bologna) and began to daunce with her, roming abrode to shewe his cunning before them that came to behold him. And before the daunce was finished, he saide thus unto her: 'Madame, it may so be as I shall seme unto you very malapert to manifest the secret love that I have and doe beare you at this instant, for which you ought not to blame me, but your beautye, which rendreth you excellent above al the rest and maketh me your slave and prisoner. I speake not of your commendable behaviour, of your excellent and marvellous vertues, which be such and of so great effect as they would make the gods descend to contemplate the same. If then your excellent beautye and shape, so well favoured by nature and not by art, may seeme to content the immortall gods, you ought not to be offended, if the same do constraine me to love you and to inclose you in the privye cabane of my harte. I beseeche you then, gentle madame (the onely comfort of my life), to have pitye upon him that dieth a thousand times a daye for you. In so doing, my life shall be prolonged by you, commending me humbly unto your good grace.' This faire gentlewoman called

Simphorosia, understanding the sweete and pleasaunt woordes uttered from the very harte of Philenio, could not dissemble her sighes, but waying her honor, because she was maried, gave him no answere at all. And the daunce ended, she retourned to her place.

Nowe it chaunced, as these three ladies did sit together jocundly disposed to debate of sundrye mery talke, behold Emerentiana, the wife of seignior Lamberto, not for any evill, but in sporting wise, said unto her companions: 'Gentlewomen, I have to tell you a pleasaunt matter which happened to me this day.'

'What is that?' said her companions.

'I have gotten this night' (said she) 'in dauncing, a curteous lover, a very faire gentleman, and of so good behaviour as any in the worlde, who said that he was so inflamed with my beauty that he tooke no rest day nor night'; and from point to point rehearsed unto them all that he had said. Which Panthemia and Simphorosia understanding, answered that the like had chaunced unto them, and they departed not from the feaste before eche of theim knewe him that was their lover. Whereby they perceived that his woordes proceded not of faithfull love, but rather of follye and dissimulation, in suche wise as they gave so lighte credite thereunto, as of custome is geven to the woordes of those that bee sicke. And they departed not from thence untill all three with one accorde had conspired every one to give him mocke.

Philenio, continuing thus in love, sometime with one, sometime with another, and perceiving that every of them seemed to love him, hee determined with himselfe, if it were possible, to gather of them the last frute of his love. But he was greatly deceived in his desire, for that all his enterprise was broken.[4] And that done, Emerentiana, whiche could not any longer dissemble the love of the foolishe scholer, called one of her maides, which was of faire complexion and a joly wenche, charging her that she should devise meanes to speake with Philenio to geve him to understande the love which her maistress bare unto him and, when it were his pleasure, she willingly would one night have him at home at her house. Which newes when Philenio heard, he greatly rejoiced, and said to the maid: 'Returne to your maistresse, faire maide, and commend me unto her, telling her in my behalf that I doe praye her to loke for me this evening, if her husband be not at home.' During which time, Emerentiana caused a certaine number of fagots of sharpe thornes to be made and to be laid under her bedde still waiting for her minion.

When night was come, Philenio toke his sworde and went to the house of his enemy, and, calling at the dore with the watchworde, the same incontinently was opened. And after that they had talked a litle while together and banketted after the best maner, they withdrew themselves into the chamber to take their reste. Philenio had no soner put of his clothes to goe to bedde but seignior Lamberto her husband came home. Which the maistresse of the house perceiving, made as though she had bene at her wittes' ende, and could not tell whether to convey her minion, but prayed him to hide himself under the bedde. Philenio, seeing the daunger wherein both he and the wife were, not taking with him any other garmentes, but only his shirte, crept under the bed, where he was so cruelly prickt and scratched with the thornes as there was no parte of his body (from the toppe of his head to the sole of his foote) free from bloud. And the more he sought to defende himselfe in that darke place, the more sharpely and piteously he was tormented, and durst not crye for feare least seignior Lamberto would kill him. I will leave to your consideration in what plight this poore wretche was in, who, by reason of his miserable being, as he was brechelesse in that terrible purgatorye, even so was he speachlesse and durst not speake for his life. In the morning when segnior Lamberto was gone forth, the poore scholler put on his clothes so well as he could and, all bloudy as he was, returning to his lodging, was like to die. But being deligently cured by physicians, in short time he recovered his former health.

Shortly after, Philenio began to pursue again his love towardes the other two, that is to say, Panthemia and Simphorosia, and found convenient time one evening to speake to Panthemia, to whom he rehearsed his griefes and continuall tormentes, praying her to have pitye upon him. The subtile and wise wenche Panthemia, faining to have compassion uppon him, excused herselfe by lacke of meanes to content his desire, but in th'end, vanquished with faire supplications and marvellous sighes, shee made him to come home to her house. And, being unready, dispoiled of al his apparell to go to bed with his lady, she required him to go with her into a litle closet, wher all her swete smels and perfumes were, to the intent he might be well perfumed before he went to bedde. The young dolt, not doubting the subtiltye of this wicked woman, entred the closet and, setting his foote upon a borde unnnailed from the joist, fell so depe into a store house where marchauntes use to lay there cottons and wolles as he thought he had broken his necke and his legges;[5] notwithstanding, as fortune would, he had no hurt.

This poore scholler, being in that darke place, began to seke for some dore or ladder to go out, and, finding nothing for his purpose, he cursed the houre and time that ever he knew Pan-themia. When the dauning of the day began to appeare, the simple sot discried in one place of the storehouse certain ventes in the wall, which gave some light because they wer old and covered over with mosse; in such wise as he began with marvelous force to pluck out the stones in the moste decayed place of the wall and made so great a hole as he went out. And, being in a lane hard by the great streate, barefoote and bare-legged, and in his shirt, he went home to his lodging unknowen of any.

A litle while after, Simphorosia, understanding of the deceits whiche the other twoo had done to Philenio, attempted to geve him the thirde, whiche was not inferior to the other twaine. And for that purpose, she began afarre of to caste her amorous lokes upon him, letting him to knowe that shee was in great distresse for his love. This poore soule, having already forgotten his fortune paste, began to walke up and downe before her house, like a man altogether tormented and pained with love. Then Simphorosia, seing him to be farre in love with her, sent him a letter by an old woman, whereby she advertised him that his beautye and good behaviour so puissantly did governe her affections as she could take no rest night nor day, for the earnest love that she bare him; wherefore she prayed him, if it were his pleasure, to come and speake with her. Philenio receiving that letter and perusing the contentes, not considering the deceite prepared for him, ne yet any longer remembring the injuries past, was more joyfull and glad then ever he was before. Who, taking pen and paper, aunswered her againe that he for his parte suffered no lesse tormentes for her sake, yea and in respect of unfained love, that he loved her farre better than she did him, and at al times when shee pleased hee woulde be at her commaundement to do her service.

The aunswere read, and oportunitye found, Simphorosia
caused him to come home to her house, and after many false
sighes, she saide unto him: 'My deare frend Philenio, I knowe
none other in all the world that hath brought me into this state
and plighte wherein presently I am, but you, because your
beautye, good grace and pleasaunt talke have so sette my harte
on fire as I feele it to kindle and burne like drye woode.' Which
talke maister scholler hearing, thought assuredly that she consumed for love of him.

This poore nodgecock, contriving the time in sweete and
pleasaunt woordes with his dareling Simphorosia, the time
approched that he should go to bed with his faire lady, who said
unto him: 'My swete frend Philenio, abide awhile, and let us
make some banket and collation.' Who, taking him by the
hande, caried him into her closet adjoining, wher was a table
ready furnished with exquisit conficts and wines of the best.
This gentlewoman had made a composition in the wine to cause
this yong gallant to sleepe for a certain time. Philenio, thinking no hurte, toke the cup and filled it with the wine and dranke
it up at one draught. His spirits revived with this refreshing,
after he had bene very well perfumed and washed in swete
waters, he went to bedde. And, within a while after, this drinke
began to woorke, and hee slepte so soundly as canon shot or
the greatest gonnes of the worlde were not able to wake him.
Then Simphorosia, perceiving the drinke beginne to woorke,
called one of her sturdy maides that wel was instructed in the
game of this pageant. Both whiche carying this poor sleepy
scholler by the feete and armes, and opening the dore very
softlye, they faire and well bestowed him in the middeste of the
streete, a good stone's caste of from the house, where he lay all
the nighte.

But when the dawning of the daye did appeare, or an houre
before, the drinke lost his vertue, and the poore soule began to
awake, and thinking that he had bene abedde with the gentlewoman, he perceived himself brechelesse and in his shirt more
dead then alive, through the colde that he had endured by lying
starke naked uppon the earth. The poore wretche was not able
to help himselfe so much as with his armes and legges, ne yet to
stande uppon his feete without great paine. Notwithstanding,
through creping and sprawling, hee got home to his house,
unseene of anye, and provided so well as hee could for recovery

of his health. And had it not been for his youth, which did helpe him at that instant, his sinewes had been benommed for ever.

In the ende, having atteined his former state of health, he still remembred the injuries past, and, without shewing any signe of anger or displeasure, made as though he loved them all three better then ever he did before, and sometime seemed to be in love with the one, and sometime with another. They againe, for their part, nothing mistrusting the malice of Philenio, set a good face on the matter, usinge amorous cheere and countenance towards him, but when his backe was tourned, with mockes and floutes they toke their pleasure. He, bearing in his brest secrete despite, was still desirous with his hand to marke them in the face, but, like a wise man, waying the natures of women, he thought it woulde redounde to his greate shame and reproche if hee did them any hurt, and, therefore, restraining the heate of his choler, used pacience. And yet, by devising and practising how he might be even with them and revenged, hee was in great perplexitye.

Very shortly after, it chaunced that the scholler had invented a meane easely to satisfye his desire, and so sone as hee had fully resolved what to do, fortune therunto was favorable. Who hired in the citye of Bologna a very faire house which had a large hall and comodious chambers, and purposed to make a greate and sumptuous feast and to invite many ladies and gentlewomen to the same, amongs whom these three were the first that should be bidden. Which accordingly was done. And when the feast day was come, the three gentlewomen, that were not very wise at that instante, repaired thither, nothing suspecting the scholler's malice.

In the end, a litle to recreate the gentlewomen and to get them a stomacke, attendinge for supper time, the scholler toke these his three lovers by the hand and led them friendly into a chamber, somewhat to refresh them. When these three innocent women were come into the scholler's chamber, he shut fast the doore and, going towards them, he saide: 'Beholde, faire ladies, now the time is come for me to be revenged upon you and to make you suffer the penaunce of the torment wherwith ye punished me for my great love.' The gentlewomen, hearing those cruell woordes rather dead then alive, began to repent that ever they had offended him, and besides that, they cursed themselves for givinge credit unto him whom they ought to have abhorred.

The scholler with fierce and angry countenaunce commaunded them upon paine of their lives to strippe themselves naked. Which sentence when these three goddesses heard, they began to loke one uppon another, weeping and praying him that although he woulde not for their sakes, yet, in respect of his owne curtesye and naturrall humanitye, that he woulde save their honor above all thinges.[6] This gallant, rejoising at their humble and pitifull requestes, was thus curteous unto them that he would not once suffer them to stand with their garmentes on in his presence. The women, casting themselves downe at his feete, wept bitterly, beseeching him that he woulde have pitye upon them and not to be the occasion of a slaunder so great and infamous. But he, whose hart was hardened as the diamonde, said unto them that this facte was not worthy of blame but rather of revenge. The women dispoiled of their apparel (and standing before him, so free from covering as ever was Eve before Adam) appeared as beautifull in this their innocent state of nakednes as they did in their braverye. Insomuch that the yong scholler, viewing from toppe to toe those faire and tender creatures, whose whitenesse surpassed the snow, began to have pitye uppon them, but, calling to his remembraunce the injuries past and the daunger of death wherein he was, he rejected all pitye and continued his harde and obstinate determination. Then he toke all their apparell and other furnitures that they did weare and bestowed it in a little chamber, and with threatning words commaunded all three to lie in one bed. The women, altogether astonned, began to say to themselves: 'Alas, what fooles be we? What wil our husbands and our frendes say, when they shal understand that we be found naked and miserablye slaine in this bed? It had been better for us to have died in our cradels, than apprehended and found dead in this state and plight.'

The scholler seeing them bestowed one by another in the bed, like husband and wife, covered them with a very white and large sheete, that no part of their bodies might be seene and knowen, and, shutting the chamber doore after him, Philenio went to seeke their husbands, which were dauncing in the hall, and, the daunce ended, he intreated them to take the paines to goe with him. Who was their guide into the chamber where the three muses lay in their bedde, saying unto them: 'Sirs, I have broughte you into this place to shewe you some pastime and to let you see the fairest thinges that ever you saw in your lives.'

Then approching neere the bed, and holding a torch in his hand, he began faire and softly to lift up the shete at the bed's feete, discovering these faire ladies even to the knees. Ye should have seen, then, how the husbands did behold their white legges and their wel proporcioned feete; which don, he disclosed them even to the stomack, and shewed their legges and thighes farre whiter than alablaster, which seemed like two pillers of fine marble, with a rounde body so wel formed as nothing could be better. Consequently he tourned up the sheete a litle further, and their stomacks appeared, somewhat round and plumme, having two rounde breasts so firme and feate as they would have constrained the great god Jupiter to imbrace and kiss them. Whereat the husbandes toke so great pleasure and contentmente as coulde be devised. I omitte for you to thincke in what plighte these poore naked women weare, hearinge their husbandes to mocke them. All this while they laye verye quiet, and durst not so much as to hem or coughe, for feare to be knowen. The husbands were earnest with the scholler to discover their faces, but hee, wiser in other menne's hurtes than in his owne, would by no meanes consent unto it.

Not contented with this, the yong scholler shewed their apparel to their husbands, who, seing the same, were astonned. And, in viewing it with great admiration, they said one to another: 'Is not this the gowne that I once made for my wife? Is not this the coife that I bought her? Is not this the pendant that she weareth about her necke? Be not these the rings that set out and garnisht her fingers?' Being gone out of the chamber for feare to trouble the feast,[7] he would not suffer them to depart, but caused them to tarye supper.

The scholler, understandinge that supper was ready and that the maister of the house had disposed all thinges in order, he caused the geastes to sit downe. And whiles they were removing and placing the stooles and chaires, he returned into the chamber wher the three dames lay, and, uncovering them, he said unto them: 'Bongiorno, faire ladies. Did you heare your husbandes? They be here by, and do earnestly tarye for you at supper. What do ye meane to do? Up and rise, ye dormouses, rubbe your eyes and gape no more, dispatche and make you ready, it is time for you now to repaire into the hall, where the other gentlewomen do tarye for you.' Behold, now, how this scholer was revenged by interteigning them after this maner.

Then the poore desolate women, fearing least their case would sorte to som pitiful successe, dispairing of their health, troubled and discomforted, rose up expecting rather death than any other thing. And, tourning them toward the scholler, they said unto him: 'Maister Philenio, you have had sufficient reveng upon us. The best for you to do now is to take your sword and to bereve us of oure life, which is more lothsome unto us than pleasaunt. And if you will not do us that good tourne, suffer us to go home to our houses unknowen, that our honours may be saved.' Then Philenio, thinking that he had at pleasure used their persons, delivered them their apparel, and so sone as they were ready, he let them out at a litle dore, very secretlye, unknowen of anye, and so they went home to their houses.

So sone as they had put of their faire furnitures, they folded them up, and laid them in their chestes; which done, they went about their houshold busines till their husbands came home. Who being retourned, they founde their wives sowing by the fireside in their chambers. And because of their apparell, their ringes and jewels, which they had seene in the scholler's chamber, it made them to suspect their wives, every of them demaunding his severall wife, where she had bin that nighte and where their apparell was. They, well assured of themselves, aunswered boldly that they were not out of their house all the evening, and, taking the keyes of their cofers shewed them their aparell, their ringes and other things, which their husbandes had made them. Which when their husbandes saw, they could not tell what to say, and forthwith rejected all suspicion which they had conceived, telling them from point to point what they had seen that night. The women, understanding those woordes, made as though they knew nothing, and, after a little sport and laughter betweene them, they went to bed.

Many times, Philenio met his gentlewomen in the streates and saide unto them: 'Which of you was most afraide or worste intreated?' But they holding downe their heads, passed forth not speaking a word. In this maner the scholler was requited so well as he could of the deceites done against him by the three gentlewomen aforesaid.

The unhappy end and successe of the love of King Massinissa and Queene Sophonisba, his wife.

If men would have afore consideration of their owne doings before they do attempt the same, or els premeditate and study the scope and successe thereof, I do verely beleeve that a numbre would not cast themselves headlong into so many gulfs of miseries and calamities as they do, specially noblemen and princes, who oftentimes doe exceede in temerity and rashnesse, by lettinge the raines of their own lustes to farre to raunge at large, wherein they deepely plunge thimselves to their great prejudice and dishonour. As teacheth this goodly historye ensuinge, which declareth that there was a prince called Massinissa, the sonne of Gala, kinge of Massaezali (a people of Numidia), who warfaring with the Carthaginians in Spaine against the Romaines, havinge first fought honourably against Kinge Syphax in Numidia, it chaunced that Gala his father died. Uppon whose death his kingdome was invaded and occupied by other, wherefore, sustaininge stoutly the surges of adversity, combatinge with his enemies, sometimes getting part of his kingdome, and sometimes losinge, and many times molestinge both Syphax and the Carthaginians, was in divers conflicts like to be taken or slaine.[1]

With these his travels, impacient of no paine and trouble, he became very famous and renoumed, that amonges the people of Affrica he acquired the name and title of a valiant and puissant souldier and of a pollitique and provident captain. Afterwards he was generally wel beloved of the souldiers, bicause, not like the king's sonne or a prince, but as a private souldier and companion, his conversation and usuall trade of life was amongs them, calling every man by his propre name, cherishing and esteeming them according to their desert, observing neverthelesse a certaine comelinesse of a superiour.

This Massinissa, by meanes of one Syllanus being in Spaine, prively entred acquaintance and familiarity with that Scipio which afterwardes was surnamed Affricanus and who in those dayes, with the authority of proconsul in that province, victoriously subdued the Carthaginians. The same Massinissa entred league with the Romanes and inviolably so long as he lived observed amity with the Romane people and lefte the same to his children and posteritye as an inheritance.

When the Romanes began warres in Affrica, spedily with that power he was able to make, he repaired to his old friend Scipio. Within a while after, Syphax being overthrowen in battell and taken, Massinissa and Laelius were sent to surprise the chief city of that kingdom, which sometimes were King Syphax owne, called Cirta.[2]

In that city remained Sophonisba, the wife of Syphax and daughter to Hasdrubal of Giscon, who had alienated hir husband from the Romanes, being in league with them, and by hir persuasions went to aide and defend the Carthaginians.[3] Sophonisba, perceiving that the ennimies were entred the city of Cirta and that Massinissa was going towardes the palace, determined to meete him to prove his gentlenesse and curtesye. Whereupon in the middes of his souldiers' thronge, which were already entred the palace, she stoutly thrust and bouldly looked round aboute to prove if she could espye by some signes and tokens the personage of Massinissa.

She amongs that prease perceived one for whose apparel, armure, and reverence don unto him, semed unto hir that without doubt the same was the king, and therefore incontinently kneeled downe before him and pitiously began to speake in this manner: 'For so mutch (o puissante prince) as felicity and good fortune, but specially the favour of the gods immortall, have permitted that thou shouldest recover thine auncient kingdome descended unto the by righte and lawfull inheritaunce, and therewithall hast taken and vanquished thine ennimy, and now hast me at thy will and pleasure to save or spill, I poore wretched, miserable woman, brought into bondage from queenelike state, whilom leading a delicate life in princely courte accompanied with a royall traine of beautifull dames and nowe at thy mercifull disposition, doe humbly appeale to thy mercye and goodnesse. Whose princely majesty and comfortable aspect chereth up my woefull heart to loke for grace, and therefore am bold thus to presume with most humble voice to implore and crye out, beseeching thee to reach me hither thy victorious handes to kisse and salute.'

This lady was a passing faire gentlewoman of flourishing age and comely behaviour, none comparable unto her within the whole region of Affrica. And so much the more as hir pleasant grace by amiable gesture of complaint did increase, so much the heart of Massinissa was delited. Who, being lusty and of youthly age, according to the nature of the Numides was easily intrapped and tangled in the nettes of love. Whose glutting eyes were never ful, nor fiery hart was satisfied, in beholding and wondring at hir most excellent beauty, not foreseeing therefore or taking heede of the daungerous effect of beautye's snares, his heart being so fiercely kindled with the swinging flames of love. Who, causing hir to rise, exorted hir to prosecute hir supplication. Then she began to procede as foloweth: 'If it may be lawfull for me thy prisoner and bondwoman (o my soveraign lord) to make request, I humbly do, beseech thee by thy royal majesty, wherein no long time past my husband and I were magnificently placed in so kinglike guise as thou art now, and by that Numidicall name, common unto thee and my husbande Syphax, and by the savinge gods and patrons of this city, who with better fortune and more joyfull successe do receive thee into the same, that expelled Syphax out from thence: it may please thy sacred state to have pity on me.

'I require no hard and difficult thinge at thy handes. Use thine imperiall governement over me sutch as law of armes and reason of warre require. Cause me, if thou wilt, to pine in cruel prison, or do me to sutch death with torments as thou list to use. The sharp, fierce and cruel death that any wight can suffre or perillus bull shall not be dreadfull unto me, but more deare and acceptable than wonted life in pleasures led. For no death shal bee refused of mee, rather than to be rendred into the proud handes of the most cruell Romanes.[4] Rather had I tast the trust of a native Numidie, borne with me in Affrike soile, than the faith of straunger's kinde. I know full well that thou dost knowe what curtesy a Carthaginian and daughter of Hasdrubal shal surely looke for at the Romanes' hands; whose mind is fearfull of nothing more than of their pride and glory intollerable.

'If thou (my lord) haddest sisters of thine own or daughters of thy royal bloud brought forth, think that they may chaunce (if

Fortune frown) to slide into the pit of adverse lucke, so well as I am nowe. Of that forme Fortune's wheele is made which we daily see to be unstable, turninge and divers, that now peace and now warre it promiseth, now evill it threatneth, now mirth, now sorrow it bringeth, now advauncinge aloft, now tumbling downe the climbers-up. Let Syphax bee cleare and lively example to thee, which coulde never finde any stedfast stay under the moone's globe. He was the mightiest and the richest kinge that raigned in Affrica, and now is the most miserable and unlucky wight that liveth on land. The gods graunt that I bee no prophet or diviner of future evill, whose omnipotency I devoutly beseech to suffer thee and thy posterity in Numidie land and most happily to raigne.

'Vouchsafe then to deliver me from the Romanes' thraldome, which if thou bee not able safely to bring to passe, cause death (the ease of al woe) to be inflicted upon me.' In speaking those words, she tooke the kinge's right hande and many times sweetly kissed the same.

And then her teares turned to pleasant cheare, in sutch wise as not onely the minde of the armed and victorious prince was mooved to mercy but straungely wrapped in the amorous nets of the lady, whereby the victour was subdued by the vanquished, and the lord surprised of his captive. Whom with tremblinge voice thus he aunswered: 'Make an end, o Sophonisba, of thy large complaint. Abandon thy conceived feare, for I wil not onely ridde thee from the Romaine handes but also take thee to my lawfull wife (if thou therewith shalt be content). Whereby thou shalte not leade a prisoner's life but passe thy youthfull dayes and hoarye age (if gods doe graunt thy life so long) as quene unto a king, and wife unto a Romane frend.' When he had said so, with weeping teares he kissed and imbraced hir.

She, by the countenaunce, signes, gestes, and interrupted woordes, comprehending the minde of the Numide king to be kindled with fervent love, the more to inflame the same, beemoned herself with such heavinesse as the beastly heartes of the Hircane tigres would have bene made gentle and dispoiled of al fiercenesse if they had beheld her. And againe she fel downe at his feete, kissinge the armed sabbatons uppon the same and bedewinge them with hir warme teares.

After many sobbes and infinite sighes, comforted by him, she said: 'O the glorye and honor of all the kinges that ever were, bee or shall bee hereafter. O the safest aide of Carthage, mine unhappy countrey without desert, and now the present and most terrible astonishment. If my hard fortune and distresse after so great ruine might have bene relieved, what greater favour, what thing in all my life, coulde chaunce more fortunate unto me than to bee called wife of thee? O I, blessed above all other women to have a man so noble and famous to husband. O mine adventurous and most happy ruine. O my moste fortunate misery, that such a glorious and incomparable mariage was prepared for me. But bicause the gods be so contrary unto me, and the due ende of my life approcheth, ceasse from henceforth (my deare soveraigne lorde) to kindle againe in me my hope half dead, or rather consumed and spent, bicause I see myself wrapped in a state that in vaine against the pleasures of the gods, I go about to molest thee. A greate gift (and to say truthe) a right great good turne I make accompte to have received of thee, if mine owne death I should procure by thee. That dyinge by thy means or with thy handes (which were more acceptable) I shoulde escape the feare of the Romaines' thral and subjection, and this soule, delivered of the same, should streight passe into the Elysian fieldes.

'The final scope of this my humble plaint is to rid me from the hands of the Romanes, whose thraldom to suffer I had rather die. The other benefit which thou dost frankly offer to me pore wretch, I dare not desire, mutch lesse require the same, bicause the present state of my mishap dareth not presume so high. But for this thy pity and compassion joined with loving regard and mind toward me, mightye Love, with al the other gods, reward and blesse thy gotten kingdom in long raign, enlarging the same with more ample bounds to thine eternal renoum and praise. And I do not only render humble thanks for this thy kind and loving enterteinment, but also yeld myself thine own, so long as life governeth this caitif corps of mine.'

These words wer pronounced with such effect as Massinissa was not able for pity to hold his teares, which watred so his comely form as the dew therof soaked into his tender heart, and not able a long time to speake, at last thus hee said: 'Give over (o my quene) these cares and thoughts, dry up thy cries and plaints, make an end of al these dolorous sutes, and rejoice that frowarde Fortune hath changed hir mind. The gods no doubt with better successe wil perfourm the rest of thy living days.

Thou shalt henceforth remain my quene and wife; for pledg whereof the sacred godheads I cal to witnesse. But if perchaunce (which the thundring mighty God above forbid) that I shal be forced to render thee the Romanes' prisoner, be well assured that on live they shall not possesse the.'

For credit and accomplishment of this promise and in signe of his assured faith, he reached his right hand to Sophonisba and led hir into the inner lodging of the king's palace. Wher afterward Massinissa with himself considering how he might perform his promised faith, vexed and troubled with a thousand cogitations, seing in a maner his manifest overthrow and ruine at hand, provoked with mad and temerarious love, the very same day in open presence he toke hir to wife, solemnizing that mariage, which afterwardes bred unto him great vexation and trouble, meaninge by the same to have discharged Sophonisba from the Romanes' rule and order. But when Laelius was come and hearde tell thereof,[5] hee fretted and chafed, and with threatninge wordes commaunded Massinissa to send his new maried wife (as the booty and pray of the Romanes) together with Syphax to their captaine Scipio. Notwithstanding, vanquished with the supplications and teares of Massinissa, referring the matter wholy to the judgement of Scipio, he dispatched Syphax with the other prisoners and bootye to the Romane campe, and he himself remained with Massinissa for the recoverye of other places of the kingdome, minding not to returne before the whole province were brought under the Romane subjection.

In the meanetime Laelius gave intelligence unto Scipio of the successe of Massinissa his mariage. Who, knowing the same to be so hastilye celebrated, was marvellouslye offended and troubled in minde, mutche marvellinge that Massinissa woulde make sutch posthast before the comming of Laelius, yea, and, upon the very first day of his entrye into Cirta, that hee would consummate that unadvised wedding. And the greater was Scipio his displeasure towards Massinissa for that the love which he had conceived of that woman was unsemely and dishonest, wondering not a little that he could not find out some lady within the region of Spain of semblable beauty and comlinesse to please and content his honest and commendable intent. Wherfore, he judged Massinissa his fact to be done out of time to the prejudice and great decay of his honor and estimation.

Howbeit, like a wise and prudent personage, he dissembled his conceived griefe, expecting occasion for remedye of the same.

Now the time was come that Laelius and Massinissa were sent for to the campe. But to declare the tears and lamentable talke, the great mone and sighes uttered betwene this new-maried couple, time would want and tediousnesse would over-come the reader. He had scarce lien with his beloved two or three nights but Laelius (to their great grief and sorow) claimed hir to bee his prisoner. Wherfore, verye sorowfull and pensive, hee departed and retourned to the campe. Scipio in honourable wise accepted him and openly before his captaines and men of warre gave thanks to Laelius and him for their prowesse and notable exploites.

Afterwards, sending for him unto his tent, he said unto him: 'I do suppose (my dere frend Massinissa) that the vertue and benevolence which you saw in me did first of all provoke you to transfrete the straits to visite me in Spaine, wherein the goodwill of my valiaunt frend Syllanus did not a little availe to sollicite and procure amity betwene us. And the same afterwards, inducing your constant minde to retire into Affrica, committed both yourselfe and all your goods into my hands and keeping. But I, well pondering the quality of that vertue which moved you thereunto, you beinge of Affrica and I of Europa, you a Numidian borne and I a Latine and Romane, of divers customes and language different, thought that the temperance and absti-nence from venerial pleasures which you have sene to bee in me and experience therof wel tried and proved (for the which I render unto the immortal gods most humble thankes) would or ought to have moved you to follow mine example, being vertues which above all other I doe most esteme and cherish. For he that well marketh the rare giftes and excellent benefits wherwith Dame Nature hath arrayed you would thinke that ther should be no lacke of diligence and travell to subdue and overcome the carnall appetites of temporal beauty, which, had it bene applied to the rare giftes of nature planted in you, had made you a personage to the posterity very famous and renoumed.

'Consider wel my present time of youth, full of courage and youthly lust, which contrary to that naturall race I stay and prohibite. No delicate beauty, no voluptuous delectation, no feminine flattery can intice my youth and state to the perils and daungers whereunto that heedelesse age is most prone and subject. By which prohibition of amorous passions, temperatly raigned and governed, the tamer and subduer of those passions, closing his breast from lascivious imaginations and stopping his eares from the Sirenes and marmaides of that sexe and kinde, getteth greater glorye and fame than wee have gotten by our victory against Syphax.[6] Hanniball, the greatest ennimy that ever we Romanes felt, the stoutest gentleman and captain without peere, through the delites and imbracements of women effeminated, is no more the manlike and notable emperor that hee was wont to be.[7] The great exploits and enterprises which valiantly you have done in Numidia when I was farre from you, your care, readinesse, animosity, your strength and valor, your expedition and bold attemptes, with all the rest of your noble vertues worthy of immortal praise, I might and could perticulerly recite, but to commend and extol them my heart and minde shall never be satisfied, by renovacion wherof I should rather give occasion of blushing than myselfe could be contented to let them sleepe in silence.

'Syphax, as you know, is taken prisoner by the valiance of our men of warre; by reason whereof, himselfe, his wife, his kingdome, his campe, landes, cities and inhabitants, and, briefly, all that which was King Syphax, is the pray and spoile to the Romane people. And the king and his wife, albeit she was no citizen of Carthage, and hir father, although no captain of our ennimies, yet we muste send them to Rome, there to leave them at the pleasure and disposition of the Romane senate and people.

'Doe you not know that Sophonisba with her toyes and flatteries did alienat and withdraw King Syphax from our amitye and friendship and made him to enter force of armes against us? Be you ignoraunt that she, full of rancor and malice against the Romane people, endevoured to set al Affrica against us, and now, by her faire inticementes, hath gained and wonne you, not, I say, our ennemy, but an ennimy so farre as shee can, with her cruell inchauntments? What damage and hurt have lighted uppon divers monarches and princes through sugred lippes and venemous woordes I will not spend time to recite. With what provocations and conjured charmes shee hath already bewitched your good nature, I wil not now imagine, but referre the same to the deepe consideration of youre wisdome.

'Wherefore, Massinissa, as you have bene a conquerer over great nations and provinces, be now a conquerer of your own mind and appetites, the victorye whereof deserveth greater praise than the conquest of the whole world. Take heede, I say, that you blot not your good qualities and conditions with the spots of dishonor and pusillanimitye. Obscure not that fame which hitherto is advaunced above the region of the glitteringe starres. Let not this vice of feminine flatterye spoile the desertes of noble chivalrye and utterly deface those merites with greater ignominye than the cause of that offence is worthye of dispraise.'

Massinissa, hearinge these egree and sharpe rebukes, not onely blushed for shame but, bitterly weepinge, saide that his poor prisoner and wife was at the commaundement of Scipio. Notwithstanding, so instantly as teares coulde suffer him to speak, he besoughte him that, if it were possible, hee woulde give him leave to observe his faithe foolishlye assured, bicause hee had made an othe to Sophonisba that with life shee shoulde not bee delivered to the handes of the Romanes.

And after other talke betweene them, Massinissa retired to his pavilion, where, alone, with manifolde sighes and most bitter teares and plaintes, uttered with sutch houlinges and outcries as they were hearde by those which stoode nearehande, hee rested all the daye bewailinge his presente state. The most part of the nighte, also, hee spent with like heavinesse. And debating in his mind upon divers thoughts and devises, more confused and amazed than before, hee could by no meanes take rest. Somtimes he thought to flee and passe the straights commonly called the Pillers of Hercules, from thence to saile to the Fortunate Islandes with his wife.[8] Then againe, hee thoughte with hir to escape to Carthage and in aide of that city to serve against the Romanes. Somtimes hee proposed by sworde, poison, halter or som such meanes to end his life and finish his dolorous days. Many times hee was at pointe by prepared knife and sworde to pierce his heart, and yet stayed the same, not for feare of death but for preservation of his fame and honor.

Thus this wretched and miserable lover, burned and consumed in love, tossing and tumbling himselfe uppon his bedde, not able to find comfort to ease his paine, thus began to say: 'O Sophonisba, my deare beloved wife, o the life and comfort of my life, o the deinty repast of my joy and quiet, what shall become of us? Alas, and out alas, I crye that I shall see no more thine incomparable beauty, thy surpassing comely face, those golden lockes, those glistering eyes which a thousand times have

darkned and obscured the rayes and beames of the sunne itself.[9]
Alas, I say, that I can no longer be suffred to heare the pleasaunt
harmonye of thy voice, whose sweetenesse is able to force
Jupiter himselfe to mitigate his rage when with lightning thun-
derbolts and stormye claps in his greatest furye he meaneth to
plague the earth. Ah, that it is not lawfull any more for me to
throw these unhappy armes about thy tender neck, whose
whitenesse of face entermingled with semely rudds excelleth the
morning roses, which by sweete nightly dewes doe sproute and
budde.

'The gods graunt that I doe not long remaine on live without
thy sweete haunt and company, which can no longer draw forth
this breathing ghoste of mine than can a bodye live withoute
like breathe in it.[10] Graunt (o mighty Jupiter) that one grave
may close us twaine to live among the ghostes and shadowes
that be already past this world for like right loving fitts, if intent
of life be ment to mee without thy fellowship and delectable
presence. And who (o good god) shall be more blisful amongs
the Elysian Fields, wandring amids the spirites and ghostes of
departed soules, than I, if there we two may jette and stalke
amonge the shadowed friths and forest huge, besette with mirtle
trees, odoriferous and sweete? That there we may at large
recount and sing the sweete and sower pangs of those our passed
loves without anye stay or let at all. That there, I say, we may
remembre things already done, rejoicing for delights and sighing
for the paines. There shall no harde-hearted Scipio bee found;
there shal no marble-minded captain rest, which have not had
regard of love's toyes ne yet have pitied bitter pains, by having
no experience what is the force of love. He, then, with over-
cruell wordes shall not goe aboute to persuade me to forsake
thee or to deliver thee into the Romanes' handes to incurre
miserable and most cruell bondage. He shal there never checke
me for the fervent love I beare thee. We shal there abide without
suspition of him or any other. They can not seperate us; they be
not able to devide our sweetest companye.

'I would the gods above had graunted me the benefite that hee
had never arrived into Affrica but had still remained in Sicilia,
in Italy or Spaine. But what stand I upon these termes,[11] O, I,
fole and beast? what meanes my drousye head to dreame sutch
fansies? If he hadde not passed over into Affrica and made war
against King Syphax, how should I have ever seene my faire

Sophonisba, whose beauty farre surmounteth eche other wight, whose comelines is withoute peere, whose grace inspeakable, whose maners rare and incomparable, and whose other qualities, generally disparcled throughoute Dame Nature's mould, by speach of man cannot bee described? If Scipio had not transfraited the seas to arrive in Affrike soile, how should I (o onely hope and last refuge of my desires) have knowen thee? Neither should I have bene thy feere, ne yet my wife thou shouldest have ben, but great had ben thy gaine, and losse not much. Never shouldest thou have felt the present painfull state wherein thou art. Thy life (whereof most worthy no doubt thou art) shoulde not have lien in ballance poize or rested in doubtfull plight, which now in choise of enemies' thrall thou maist prolong, or else in Romanes' handes a praye or spoile by captive state. But I beseech the gods to prevent the choice to be a Romane prisoner.

'And who can thinke that Scipio ever ment to graunt me the life of one and goeth about to spoile me of the same? Did not he give me the pardon of one when he sent me to besiege the city of Cirta, where I found faire Sophonisba which is my life? A straunge kinde of pardon, by giving me a pardon to dispossesse me of the same! Who ever hard tel of such a pardon? So much as if he said to me thus: "Massinissa, go take the paine to cause the city yeld and ransack it by force, and I wil pardon thee thy life. And not with the onely benefit, but with Craesus goods I wil inrich thee,[12] and make thee owner of the happy soile of Arrabia." And when I have so done and rased the walles by mine indevor, wherein mine onely life and joy did rest at my retourne, for guerdone of that noble fact, insteede of life, hee choppeth of my head; and for faire promise of golden mountes, hee strips me naked and makes mee a Romane slave, according to which case and state he deales with me. For what availes my life if in griefe and sorrowe's gulffe I drown the pleasures of the same? Doth not he believe my life and bredes my death by dividing me from my faire Sophonisba?

'Ah caitife wretch, what lucke have I, that neither storme nor whirle winde could sende him home to Italian shore or set him packing to Sicile land? What ment cruell Scipio when, so sone as Syphax was taken, he did not streightway dispatch him to Rome to present the glorious sight of the Numidian king to the Romane people? If Scipio had not beene here, thou, Sophonisba, frankly hadst bene mine, for at Laelias' hands I could have found some grace. But surely if Scipio did once see Sophonisba and reclined his eyes to viewe hir perelesse beauty, I doubt not but he would be moved to have compassion upon hir and me, and would judge hir worthy not onelye to be queene of Numidia but of all the province besides.

'But what do I make this good accompt? The common proverbe saith that he which counteth before his hoste must recken twice,[13] and so perhaps may be my lot. For what know I, if Scipio did wel view hir, whether himselfe would be inamored of hir or not, and so utterly deprive me of that jewel? He is a man no doubt as others be, and it is impossible, methink, but that the hardnesse of his heart must bow to the view of such a noble beauty.

'But (beast as I am) what mean these wordes? What follies doe I vaunt by singing to the deafe and teaching of the blind? O wretch, wretch, nay more than miserable wretch. Marke the words of Scipio. He demaundeth Sophonisba as a thing belonging unto him, for which cause he saith that she is the pray, and part of the Romane spoile. But what shall I do? Shal I give hir unto him? He will have hir, hee constraines me, he exhortes mee, hee prayes mee, but I know full well whereunto those intreaties tend, and under the grasse what lurking serpent lieth. Shal I then put into his hands mine own Sophonisba? But before I so doe, the armipotent god above, with his flashing fires and flamming brands, shall thunder me downe into the depthe of Hell.[14] The gaping ground receive my corps, before I yeld to that request; the trampling steedes of savage kinde do teare my members in thousand gobbets, the desert beastes consume my flesh, the ravening gripes and carrain kites pick out my tongue and eyes, before I glutte his ravenous mind with that demaund to break the faith which by holy othe I have promised to performe.

'O curssed caitif, but what shall I doe then? It behoveth to obey and in despite of my teeth to do that which the Romane emperour commaundeth. Alas, by thinking upon that straight and needefull lot, I die a thousand deaths. Wherfore, of evils to chose the least of twaine and to preserve my plighted faith, o swete Sophonisba, thou must die and, by meanes of thy beloved feere, shalt void the yoke of Romanes' thral, for so it pleaseth unmindeful Jova to appoint. The wretched heavens by cruel fate have throwen their lot that I of mine owne mischiefe shal be the

minister. And so (o life most deere) I shall performe the effecte
to kepe the faith which last of all before thy face I did confirme.'

By this speach and maner of talke, the good prince bewailed
his case, excogitating by what meanes he might doe to death the
thing which above al the world he loved best. At length it came
unto his minde to sende hir a draught of poisoned drink, which
devise he had no sooner founde but he was driven into a new
kinde of fury and kindled with disdaine. His braines were on
fire with extreme madnesse, and, as though Sophonisba had
bene before him, hee talked and raved in Bedlemwise. Somtimes
with taunts he checked hir to hir teeth; sometimes lamented hir
unfortunate state. Sometimes, with pawes displayed, he seemed
to rampe into hir face, and then, againe, into amorous toyes his
passions drove him forth.

When I doe thinke what kinde of man Massinissa was, who
indeede was a crowned and most noble king, and who with
sutch prudence governed his new conquered and recovered
kingdoms and so constantly persevered in amity of the Romane
people, I pray to God to graunt my frendes and myselfe also not
to enter into so intricat and lovesome labyrinth[15] wherein this
noble Prince was tangled, and with more temperaunce to
governe our beloved things.

But retourning againe to this afflicted gentleman Massinissa,
he sent unto his beloved wife and queene a pot of poison to rid
hir of hir life, but, yet staying his messenger, he cried out these
words: 'God forbid that I should commit this infamous murder
upon hir whom I most deerley love. I would rather convey hir
into the extreme partes of the unknowen sandy coaste of Lybia,
where the countrey is full of venemous beasts and crawling
poisoned serpents, in which we shal be safe and sure from the
danger of cruell and inexorable Scipio. By which meanes, he
shall never see the rare and divine beauty which the serpents,
once beholding, will mitigate and asswage their bitter poison,
and for whose sake they will not annoy ne yet hurt me, hir
loving husband and companion. Wherefore let us make hast to
flee thither to avoide the bondage and death prepared for us.
And if so be we be not able to cary with us gold and silver, yet
shal we not want there some reliefe to maintain our lives. For
better it is to feede on bread and water then to live in perpetual
thraldome. And living with thee (sweete wife) what poverty and
beggery am not I able to sustaine? The stormes of exile and

penury I have already suffred. For, beinge driven out of my kingdome many times, I have repaired to obscure dens and caves where I have hidden myselfe and lived in the wildernesse among the savage beasts.

'But what meane I thus to say of myselfe, whom no misadventure can affray or mislike?[16] But thou deare wife, which hast ben trained up and nourished amongs the delicacies and bankets of the court, accompanied with traines of many faire and noble ladies, living like a queene in al kinde of pleasures and delights, what shall I doe with thee? I knowe thy heart will not suffer thee to follow me, and yet if the same would serve thee, from whence shall I procure present shippinge? Upon the sea the Roman fleete beares swinge; upon the land Scipio with his army occupieth every coast and is generall lord of the field. What, then, shall I, most miserable and infortunate caitife, do? For whilest I am thus makinge my bitter plaints the night is past away, daylight approcheth and the bright shining morning beginneth to cleare the earth. And behold, yonder commeth the general's messanger for Sophonisba, whom I must either deliver into his handes or else commit her to present slaughter, beinge assured that she had rather make choise to dy than fall into the laps of the cruell Romans.'

Whereupon he determined to send hir the poison, and for very sorrow fell down upon the ground like a man halfe deade. Afterwards, being come againe to himselfe, he cursed the earth, the aire, the fire, Heaven, Hell, and all the gods of the same, and exclaming in lamentable wise he called unto him one of his most faithfull servants, who, according to the custome of those dayes, always kept poison in store, and saide unto him: 'Receive this cuppe of golde, and deliver the same with the poison to Queene Sophonisba, now abiding within the city of Cirta, and tel hir that I with greatest goodwill would faine have kept the mariage knot and the firste faith which I plighted unto hir, but the lorde of the fielde, in whose power I am, hath utterly forbidden the same. I have assayed all possible meanes to preserve hir my wife and queene at liberty, but he which commaundeth me hath pronounced such hard and cruell sentence as I am forced to offend myself and to be the minister of mine own mischief. This poison I send hir with so dolefull message as my poore hearte (God knoweth) doth only fele the smart, being the most sorowfull present that ever was offred to any faire lady. This is the way alone to save hir from the Romanes' handes. Pray hir to consider the worthines of hir father, the dignity of hir countrey and the royal majesty of the 2 kings hir husbands, and to do as hir mind and wil shall fansye best. Get the hence with all possible spede, and lose no time to do this message, for thou shalt cary the bane and present death of the fairest ladye that ever Nature framed within hir fairest mould.' The servaunt with this commaundment did departe, and Massinissa, like a childe beaten with the rodde, wept and cried.

The messenger, being come to the queene and giving hir the cup with the poison, declared his cruell ambassage. The queene took the poisoned cuppe and said unto the messenger: 'Geeve the king thy maister mine humble thankes, and say unto him that I receive and drinke this poison with a will so good as if hee had commaunded me to enter in triumph with laurel garlande over mine ennymies. For a better gifte a husbande cannot give to wife than accomplishment of assured faith, the funeralles whereof shall bee done with present obsequye.'[17]

And sayinge nothinge else unto the messenger, shee tooke the cuppe, and, minglinge well together the poison within, she unfearfully quafft it up. And when she had dronke it, shee delivered the messenger his cuppe againe and laied hirselfe upon hir bed, commaunding hir gentlewomen in comely wise to cover hir with clothes; and withoute lamentation or signe of feminine minde, shee stoutly waighted for approching death. The gentle-women which waited upon hir bewailed the rufull state of their maistresse; whose plaints and schriches were heard throughout the palace, wherof the brute and rumor was great. But the good queene, vanquished with the strong force of the poison, con-tinued not long before she died. The messanger returned these heavye newes unto Massinissa, who so sorowfully complained the losse of his beloved wife in such wise as many times hee was like to kill himselfe that his soule might have accompanied the ghost of hir which was beloved of him above al the dearest things of the worlde.

The valiant and wise capitaine Scipio, understanding the newes hereof, to the intente Massinissa shoulde not commit any cruelty against himselfe or perpetrate other uncomely deede, called him beefore him and comforted him with the sweetest wordes he could devise, and frendly reproved him. The next day, in the presence of al the army, hee highly commended him and rewarded him with the kingdome of Numidia, geving him many rich jewels and treasures, and brought him in great estimation amonges the Romaines; which the senate and people of Rome very well approved and confirmed with most ample privileges, attributinge unto him the title of kinge of Numidia and Freende of the Romaines. Sutch was the ende of the unhappy love of Kinge Massinissa and of the faire and lucklesse Queene Sophonisba.

*The infortunate mariage of a gentleman called
Antonio Bologna with the duchesse of Malfi, and the
pitifull death of them both.*

The greater honor and authority men have in this world and the
greater their estimation is, the more sensible and notorious are
the faultes by theim committed, and the greater is their slaunder.
In like manner more difficult it is for that man to tolerate and
sustaine fortune, which al the dayes of his life hath lived at his
ease, if by chaunce he fall into any great necessity, than for him
which never felt but woe, mishap and adversity. Dionysius, the
tiraunt of Scicilia, felt greater paine when hee was expelled his
kingdome than Milo did beinge banished from Rome; for so
mutch as the one was a soveraigne lorde, the sonne of a kinge, a
justiciary on earth, and the other but a simple citizen of a citty,
wherein the people had lawes, and the lawes of magistrates were
had in reverence.¹ So, likewise, the fall of a high and lofty tree
maketh greater noise than that which is low and little. High
towers and stately palaces of princes bee seene further of than
the poore cabans and homely sheepeheardes' sheepecotes; the
walles of lofty citties more aloofe doe salute the viewers of the
same than the simple caves which the poore doe digge belowe
the mountaine rockes. Wherefore, it behooveth the noble and
sutch as have charge of common-wealth to live an honest life,
and beare their port upright, that none have cause to discourse
uppon their wicked deedes and naughty life. And, above all,
modesty ought to be kept by women, whom, as their race, noble
birth, aucthority and name maketh them more famous, even so
their vertue, honesty, chastity and continencye more praise-
worthy. And behoveful it is that like as they wishe to be
honoured above all other, so their life do make them worthy of
that honour, without disgracing their name by deed or worde or
blemishing that brightnesse which may commend the same. I

greatly feare that all the princely factes, the exploites and conquests done by the Babylonian Queene Semiramis never was recommended with sutch praise as hir vice had shame in records by those which left remembrance of auncient acts.[2]

Thus I say, because a woman being as it were the image of sweetenesse, curtesye and shamefastnesse, so soone as she stoppeth out of the right tract, and abandoneth the sweete smel of hir duety and modesty, besides the denigration of hir honour, thrusteth her selfe into infinite troubles, causeth ruine of sutch which should bee honoured and praised, if womens' allurementes solicited theim not to folly. I will not heere indevour myselfe to seeke for examples of Samson, Salomon or other which suffred themselves fondly to be abused by women and who by meane of them be tumbled into great faults and have incurred greater perils,[3] contentinge myselfe to recite a right pitifull history done almost in our time, when the French, under leadinge of that notable capitaine Gaston de Foix, vanquished the force of Spaine and Naples at the journey of Ravenna in the time of the French kinge called Lewes the Twelfth,[4] who married the lady Mary, daughter to Kinge Henry the Seventh, and sister to the victorious prince of worthy memory Kinge Henry the Eight, wife (after the death of the said Lewes) to the puissaunt gentleman Charles, late duke of Suffolke.[5]

In the very time then lived a gentleman of Naples called Antonio Bologna, who having bin master of household to Frederieke of Aragon, somtime king of Naples, after the French had expelled those of Aragon out of that citty, the saide Bologna retired into Fraunce, and thereby recovered the goods, which hee possessed in his countrey.[6] The gentleman, besides that he was valiant of his persone, a good man of warre, and wel esteemed amongs the best, had a passing numbre of good graces, which made him to be loved and cherished of every wight; and for riding and managing of greate horse he had not his fellow in Italy. He could also play exceedinge well and trim upon the lute, whose faining voice so wel agreed thereunto that the moste melancholike persons would forget their heavinesse upon hearing of his heavenly noise; and besides these qualities, he was of personage comely and of good proportion. To be short: nature having travailed and dispoiled hir treasure house for inriching of him, he had by arte gotten that which made him most happy and worthy of praise, which was the knowledge of good letters, wherein he was so well trained, as by talke and dispute thereof, he made those to blush that were of that state and profession.

Antonio Bologna, having left Fredericke of Aragon in Fraunce, who expulsed out of Naples was retired to King Lewes, went home to his house to live at rest and to avoid trouble, forgetting the delicates of courtes and houses of great men, to bee the only husband of his owne reveneue. But what? It is impossible to eschue that which the heavens have determined upon us or to shunne the unhappe which seemeth to follow us, as it were naturally proceeding from our mother's wombe; in sutch wise as, many times, he which seemeth the wisest man, guided by misfortune, hasteth himself with stouping head to fall headlonge into his death and ruine. Even so it chaunced to this Neapolitane gentleman; for in the very same place where he attained his advauncement he received also his diminution and decay, and by that house which preferred him to what he had, he was deprived both of his estate and life; the discourse whereof you shall understande.

I have tolde you already that this gentleman was maister of the kinge of Naples household, and being a gentle person, a good courtier, wel trained up, and wise for government of himself in the courte and in the service of princes, the duchesse of Malfi thought to intreate him that he would serve hir in that office which he served the king. This duchesse was of the house of Aragon and sister to the cardinall of Aragon, which then was a rich and puissant personage. Being resolved and persuaded that Bologna was devoutly affected to the house of Aragon, as one brought up there from a childe, shee sent for him home to his house, and upon his repaire used unto him these or like woordes: 'Maister Bologna, sith your ill fortune, nay rather the unhap of our whole house, is sutch as your good lord and maister hath forgon his state and dignity and that you therwith-all have lost a good maister, without other recompence but the praise which every man giveth you for your good service, I have thought good to intreat you to doe me the honor as to take charge of the government of my house and to use the same as you did that of the king your maister. I know well that the office is to unworthy for your calling; notwithstanding, you be not ignorant what I am and how neare to him in bloud to whom you have bene a servaunte so faithfull and loving. And albeit that I am no queene, endued with greatest revenue, yet with that little portion I have I beare a princely heart; and sutch as you by experience do knowe what I have done, and daily do, to those which depart my service, recompensing them according to their paine and travaile: magnificence is observed as well in the courts of poore princes as in the stately palaces of great kings and monarches. I do remembre that I have read of a certain noble gentleman, a Persian borne, called Ariobarzanes, who used great examples of curtesye and stoutness towards King Artaxerxes, wherewith the king wondred at his magnificence and confessed himself to be vanquished.[7] You shal take advise of this request, and in the meanetime do think you will not refuse the same, as well for that my demaund is just as also being assured that our house and race is so well imprinted in your heart as it is impossible that the memory thereof can be defaced.'

The gentleman, hearinge that curteous demaund of the duchesse, knowing himselfe how deeply bound he was to the name of Aragon, and led by some unknowen provocation to his great il luck, answered hir in this wise: 'I would to God, madame, that with so good reason and equity I were able to make deniall of your commaundment, as justly you maye require the same. Wherfore, for the bounden duety which I owe to the name and memorye of the house of Aragon, I make promise that I shall not only sustaine the travell but also the daunger of my life, daily to be offred for your service, but I feele in minde I know not what which commaundeth me to withdraw myselfe to live alone at home within my little house and to be content with that I have, forgoing the sumptuous charge of princes' houses, which life would be wel liked of myself, were it not for the feare that you, madame, should be discontented with my refusall and that you should conceive that I disdained your offred charge or contempne your court for respect of the great office I bare in the courte of the king, my lord and maister; for I cannot receive more honour than to serve hir which is the paragon of that stock and royal race. Therfore, at all adventures, I am resolved to obey your will and humbly to satisfy the duety of the charge wherein it pleaseth you to imploy me, more to pleasure you for avoiding of displeasure then for desire I have to live an honorable life in the greatest prince's house of the world, sith I am discharged from him in whose name resteth my comfort and only stay, thinking to have lived a solitarye life and to passe my yeres in rest, except it were in the pore abilitye of my service to that house wherunto I am bound continually to be a faithfull servaunt. Thus, madame, you see me to be the readiest man of the world to fulfil the request and accomplishe sutch other service wherein it shall please you to imploy me.'

The duchesse thanked him very heartily and gave him charge of all hir housholde traine, commaunding ech person to do him sutch reverence as to hirself and to obey him as the chief of al hir family.

This lady was a widow, but a passing faire gentlewoman, fine and very yong, having a yong sonne under hir guard and keping, left by the deceased duke hir husband, togither with the duchy, the inheritaunce of hir child. Now consider hir personage being sutch, her easy life and delicate bringing up, and hir daily view of the youthly trade and manner of courtiers' life, whether she felt hirself prickt with any desire, which burned hir heart the more incessantly as the flames were hidden and covert; from the outward shew whereof shee stayed hirself so well as shee coulde. But shee, followinge beste advice, rather esteemed the proofe of mariage, than to burne with so little fire or to incurre the exchange of lovers, as many unshamefaste strumpets do, which be rather given over, than satisfied with pleasure of love.[8]

And to say the truthe, they be not guided by wisedom's lore which suffer a maiden ripe for mariage to be long unwedded or yong wife long to live in widowe's state, what assurance soever they make of their chaste and stayed life. For bookes be to full of sutch enterprises and houses stored with examples of sutch stolne and secrete practises, as there neede no further proofe for assurance of our cause; the daily experience maketh plaine and manifest. And a great folly it is to build the fantasies of chastitye amid the follies of worldly pleasures. I will not goe about to make those matters impossible, ne yet will judge at large, but that there be som maidens and wives which wiselye can conteine themselves amongs the troupe of amorous suters. But what? The experience is very hard, and the proofe no lesse daungerous, and perchaunce in a moment the mind of some perverted, which all their livinge dayes have closed their eares from the sute of those that have made offer of loving service. And hereof we neede not run to forraine histories, ne yet to seeke records that be auncient, sith wee may see the daily effects of the like, practised in noble houses, and courtes of kings and princes. That this is true, example of this faire duchesse, who was moved with that desire which pricketh others that be of flesh and bone.

This lady waxed very weary of lying alone and grieved hir hearte to be withoute a match, specially in the night, when the secrete silence and darkenesse of the same presented beefore the eyes of hir mind the image of the pleasure which she felt in the lifetime of hir deceased lord and husband, where of now feeling hirselfe despoiled, she felt a continuall combat and durst not attempte that which she desired most, but eschued the thing wherof hir mind liked best. 'Alas' (said shee) 'is it possible, after the taste of the value of honest obedience which the wife oweth unto hir husband, that I should desire to suffer the heat which burneth and altereth the martyred minds of those that subdue themselves to love? Can sutch attempt pierce the heart of me to become amorous by forgetting and straying from the limmetts of honest life? But what desire is this? I have a certaine unacquainted lust, and yet very well know not what it is that moveth me and to whom I shall vow the spoile thereof. I am truely more fond and foolishe than ever Narcissus was, for there is neither shadow nor voice upon which I can well stay my sight, nor yet simple imagination of any worldly man, whereuppon I can arrest the conceipt of my unstayed heart and the desires which provoke my minde. Pygmalion loved once a marble piller, and I have but one desire, the colour whereof is more pale than death.[9] There is nothing which can geve the same so mutch as one spot of vermilion rud. If I doe discover these appetites to any wight, perhaps they will mock me for my labor, and for all the beauty and noble birth that is in me, they will make no conscience to deeme me for their jesting stock and to solace themselves with rehersall of my fond conceits. But sith there is no enemy in the field and that but simple suspicion doth assaile me, why breake I not the same and deface the entier remem-braunce of the lightnesse of my braine? It appertaineth unto mee to shewe myselfe as issued from the noble house of Aragon; to me it doeth belonge to take heede how I erre or degenerate from the royall bloud whereof I came.'

In this sort that faire widow and young princesse fantasied in the night uppon the discourse of hir appetites. But when the day was come, seeing the great multitude of the Neapolitan lords and gentlemen that marched up and downe the citty, eyinge and beholdinge their best beloved or using talke of love with them whose servaunts they were, all that which she thought upon in the night vanished so sone as the flame of burned straw or the pouder of cannon shot, and purposed for any respect to live no longer in that sort, but promised the conquest of some frend that was lusty and discreete. But the difficulty rested in that she knew not upon whom to fixe hir love, fearing to bee slaundered and, also, that the light disposition and maner of most part of youth were to be suspected; in sutch wise as, giving over al them which vauted upon their gennets, Turkey palfreys, and other coursers alonge the citty of Naples, shee purposed to take repast of other venison than of that fond and wanton troupe.[10] So hir mishap began already to spin the threede which choked the aire and breath of hir unhappy life.

Yee have heard before that maister Bologna was one of the wisest and most perfect gentlemen that the land of Naples that time brought forth, and for his beauty, proportion, galantnesse, valiaunce and good grace without comparison. His favour was so sweete and pleasant, as they which kept him company had somwhat to do to abstaine their affection. Who then could blame this faire princesse if (pressed with desire of match to remove the ticklish instigations of her wanton flesh and having in hir presence a man so wise) shee did set hir minde on him or fantasy to mary him? Would not that party for calming of his thirst and hunger, being set at a table before sundry sorts of delicate viands, ease his hunger? Methinke the person doth greatly forget himselfe, which, having handfast upon occasion, suffreth the same to vanish and fly away, sith it is wel known that she, being bald behinde, hath no place to sease upon when desire moveth us to lay hold upon hir.[11] Which was the cause that the duchesse became extremely in love with the maister of hir house. In sutch wise as, before al men, she spared not to praise the great perfections of him whom she desired to be altogether hirs. And so she was inamored that it was as possible to see the night to be voide of darknesse as the duchesse without the presence of hir Bologna, or els by talke of words to set forth his praise, the continuall remembrance of who (for that shee loved him as hirselfe) was hir onely minde's repast.

The gentleman, that was full wise and had at other times felt the great force of the passion which proceedeth from extreeme love, immediatly did mark the countenaunce of the duchesse and perceived the same so neere as unfainedly hee knew that very ardently the lady was in love with him; and, albeit he sawe the inequality and difference betweene them both, she being sorted out of the royall bloud and himself of meaner calling, yet, knowing love to have no respect to state or dignity, determined to folow his fortune and to serve hir which so lovingly shewed hirselfe to him.

Then, sodainely reproving his fonde conceit, he said unto himself: 'What folly is that I enterprise to the prejudice and peril of mine honor and life? Ought the wisedome of a gentleman to stray and wandre through the assaults of an appetite rising of sensuality, and that reason gieve place to that which doeth participate with brute beasts deprived of all reason by subduinge the minde to the affections of the body? No, no, a vertuous man ought to let shine in himselfe the force of the generosity of his minde. This is not to live according to the spirite, when pleasure shall make us forget our duty and savegard of our conscience. The reputation of a wise gentleman resteth not only to be valiant and skilfull in feates of armes or in service of the noble, but needefull it is for him by discreation to make himselfe praise-worthy and by vanquishinge of himselfe to open the gate to fame, whereby he may everlastingly make himselfe glorious to all posterity. Love pricketh and provoketh the spirite to do well, I do confesse, but that affection ought to be addressed to some vertuous end, tending to mariage, for otherwise that unspotted image shall be soiled with the villany of beastly pleasure.'

'Alas', said he, 'how easye it is to dispute when the thing is absent which can both force and violently assaile the bulwarks of most constant hearts. I full well doe see the troth, and doe feele the thing that is good, and knowe what behoveth mee to follow, but, when I view the pereles beauty of my lady, hir graces, wisedome, behaviour and curtesye, when I see hir to cast so lovinge an eye upon me, that she useth so great familiarity that she forgetteth the greatnesse of hir house to abase hirselfe for my respect, how is it possible that I should be so foolish to dispise a duety so rare and precious and to set light by that which the noblest would pursue with all reverence and devoire? Shall I be so voide of wisdome to suffer the yonge princesse to see hirselfe contempned of mee, thereby to convert hir love to teares, by setting hir minde upon another that shall seek mine overthrow? Who knoweth not the fury of a woman, specially the noble dame, by seeing hirselfe despised?'

'No, no, she loveth me, and I will be hir servaunt and use the fortune proffred. Shal I be the first simple gentleman that hath married or loved a princesse? Is it not more honourable for mee to settle my mind upon a place so high than uppon some simple wench by whom I shall neither attaine profit or advancement? Baldouine of Flaunders, did not he a noble enterprise when he carried away Judith the daughter of the French kinge, as she was passing upon the seas into England, to be married to the kinge of that countrey?[12] I am neither pirat nor adventurer, for the lady loveth me. What wrong doe I then to any person by rendringe love againe? Is not she at liberty? To whom ought shee to make accoumpt of hir deedes and doinges, but to God alone and to hir owne conscience? I will love hir and cary like affection for the love which I know and see that she beareth unto me, beinge assured that the same is directed to good ende and that a woman so wise as she is will not hazard the bleamish of hir honor.'

Thus Bologna framed the plot for intertainment of the duchesse (albeit hir love already was fully bent upon him) and fortified himselfe against all perillous mishap and chaunce that might succeede, as ordinarily you see that lovers conceive all things for their advauntage and fantasye dreames agreeable to their most desire, resemblinge the mad and Bedlem persons which have before their eyes the figured fansies which cause the conceipt of their fury and stay themselves upon the vision of that which most troubleth their offended braine.

On the other side, the duchesse was in no lesse care of hir lover, the will of whom was hid and secret, which more did vexe and torment hir than the fire of love that burned hir fervently. She could not tell what way to hold to do him understand hir heart and affection. She feared to discover the same unto him, doubtinge either some fond and rigorous aunswere or the reveilinge of hir minde to him whose presence pleased hir more than all of the men of the world.

'Alas', said shee, 'am I happed into so straunge misery that with mine owne mouth I must make request to him which with all humility ought to offer mee his service? Shall a lady of sutch bloud as I am be constrained to sue, where all other be required by importunate instance of their suters?

'Ah Love, Love, whatsoever he was that clothed thee with sutch puissance, I dare say he was the cruell ennimy of man's freedom. It is impossible that thou hadst thy being in heaven, sith the clemency and curteous influence of the same investeth man with better benefits than to suffer hir nourse children to be intreated with sutch rigor. He lieth which saith that Venus is thy mother, for the swetenes and good grace that resteth in that pitifull goddesse, who taketh no pleasure to see lovers perced with so egre travailes as that which afflicteth my heart. It was some fierce cogitation of Saturne that brought thee forth[13] and sent thee into the worlde to breake the ease of them which live at rest without any passion or griefe.

'Pardon me, Love, if I blaspheme thy majesty, for the stresse and endlesse grief wherein I am plunged maketh me thus to rove at large, and the doubts which I conceive do take away the health and soundnesse of my minde. The little experience in thy schole causeth this amaze in me, to be solicited with desire that countersayeth the duty, honor and reputation of my state. The party whom I love is a gentleman, vertuous, valiant, sage and of good grace. In this there is no cause to blame Love of blindnesse, for all the inequality of our houses, apparant upon the first sight and shew of the same. But from whence issue monarchs, princes and great lords but from the naturall and common masse of earth whereof other men do come? What maketh these differences betwene those that love ech other, if not the sottish opinion which we conceive of greatnesse and preheminence, as though naturall affections bee like to that ordained by the fantasye of men in their lawes extreme. And what greater right have princes to joine with a simple gentlewoman than the princesse to mary a gentleman, and sutch as Anthonio Bologna is, in whom Heaven and nature have forgotten nothinge to make him equall with them which march amongs the greatest? I thinke we be the daily slaves of the fond and cruell fantasye of those tyraunts which say they have puissance over us, and that, straininge our will to their tyranny, we be still bound to the chaine like the galley slave.

'No, no, Bologna shall be my husband, for of a freend I purpose to make my loyall and lawful husband, meaning therby not to offend God and men together and pretend to live without offence of conscience, wherby my soule shal not be hindred for anything I do, by marying him whom I so straungely love. I am sure not to be deceived in love. He loveth me so mutch or more as I do him, but he dareth not disclose the same, fearing to be refused and cast of with shame. Thus 2 united wils and 2 hearts tied togethers with equal knot cannot chose but bring forth fruites worthy of sutch society. Let men say what they list, I will doe none otherwise than my heade and mind have already framed. Semblably I neede not make accompt to any persone for my fact, my body and reputation beinge in full liberty and freedome. The bond of mariage made shall cover the faulte which men woulde finde, and leaving mine estate I shall do no wrong but to the greatnesse of my house, which maketh me amongs men right honorable. But these honors be nothing worth where the mind is void of contentation and wher the hearte prickte forwarde by desire, leaveth the bodye and minde restlesse without quiet.'

Thus the duchesse founded hir enterprise, determining to mary hir houshold maister, seeking for occasion and time meete for disclosing of the same, and albeit that a certaine naturall shamefastnesse, which of custome accompanieth ladies, did close hir mouth and made hir to deferre (for a certain time) the effect of hir resolved minde. Yet, in the ende, vanquished with love and impacience, she was forced to breake of silence and to assure hirself in him, rejecting feare conceived of shame to make hir waye to pleasure, which she lusted more than mariage, the same serving hir but for a maske and coverture to hide hir follies and shamelesse lusts, for which she did the penaunce that hir folly deserved. For no colorable dede or deceitful trompery can serve the excuse of any notable wickednesse.

She, then, throughly persuaded in her intent, dreaming and thinking of nought else but upon the imbracement of hir Bologna, ended and determined hir conceits and pretended follies and upon a time, sent for him up into hir chamber, as commonly she did for the affaires and matters of hir house, and taking him aside unto a window having prospect into a garden, she knew not how to begin hir talk. For the heart being seased, the mind troubled and the witts out of course, the tongue failed to do his office; in sutch wise as of long time she was unable to speake one onely woord. He, surprised with like affection, was more astonied by seeing the alteration of his ladye.

So the two lovers stoode still like images, beholding one another without any moving at all, untill the lady, the hardiest of them bothe, as feelinge the most vehement and greatest grief, tooke Bologna by the hand, and dissembling what she thought, used this or sutch language: 'If any other besides yourselfe, gentleman, should understand the secret which now I purpose to disclose, I doubt what speeach were necessary to colour what I shall speake, but, being assured of your discretion and wisdom and with what perfection nature hath indued you – and arte having accomplished that in you which nature did begin to worke, as one bred and brought up in the royal court of the seconde Alphonse, of Ferdinando and Frederick of Aragon my cousins – I wil make no doubt at all to manifest to you the hidden secretes of my heart, being well persuaded that when you shall both heare and savor my reasons and tast the light which I bring forth for me, easily you may judge that mine advice cannot be other than just and reasonable.

'But if your conceits shall straye from that which I determine, I shal be forced to thinke and saye that they which esteeme you wise and sage and to be a man of good and ready witte be marvelously deceived. Notwithstanding my heart foretelleth that it is impossible for maister Bologna to wandre so farre from equitye but that by and by he wil enter the listes and discerne the white from blacke and the wronge fro that which is just and righte, for so mutch as hitherto I never saw thinge done by you which preposterated or perverted the good judgement that all the world esteemeth to shine in you, the same well manifested and declared by your tongue, the right judge of the minde.

'You knowe and see how I am a widow through the death of that noble gentleman of good remembrance, the duke my Lord and husbande; you be not ignoraunt also that I have lived and governed myself in sutch wise in my widow state as there is no man so hard and severe of judgement that can blason reproch of mee in that which appertaineth to the honestye and reputation of sutch a lady as I am, bearing my port so righte as my conscience yeldeth no remorse, supposinge that no man hathe wherewith to bite and accuse me.

'Touching the order of the goods of the duke my sonne, I have used them with diligence and discretion, as, besides the dettes, which I have discharged sithens the death of my lord, I have purchased a goodly manor in Calabria, and have annexed the same to the dukedome of his heire,[14] and at this day doe not owe one peny to any creditor that lent money to the duke, which he toke up to furnish the charges in the warres which he sustained in the service of the kinges, our soveraine lords, in the

late warres for the kingdome of Naples. I have, as I suppose, by
this meanes stopped the slaunderous mouth and given cause
unto my sonne, during his life, to accompt himself bound unto
his mother.

'Now, having till this time lived for other and made myselfe
subject more than nature could beare, I am entended to chaunge
both my life and condition. I have till this time run, travailed
and removed to the castels and lordeships of the dukedome, to
Naples and other places, being in mind to tary as I am a widow.
But what new affaires and new councel hath possest my mind? I
have travailed and pained myself inoughe. I have to long abidden
a widowe's life. I am determined therefore to provide a husbande, who, by loving me, shall honor and cherish me according
to the love which I shall beare him and my desert.

'For to love a man without mariage God defend my hearte
should ever think, and shal rather die a hundred thousand
deathes than a desire so wicked should soile my conscience,
knowing well that a woman which setteth hir honor to sale is
lesse than nothing and deserveth not the common aire should
breathe upon hir, for all the reverence that men do beare unto
them. I accuse no person, albeit that many noble women have
their forheds marked with the blame of dishonest life and, being
honored of some, bee neverthelesse the common fable of the
worlde.[15] To the intente then that sutch mishappe happen not
to me, and perceiving myselfe unable still thus to live, being
younge as I am, and (God bee thanked) neither deformed nor
yet painted, I had rather bee the loving wife of a simple feere
than the concubine of a kinge or great prince. And what? Is the
mighty monarche able to washe away the faulte of his wife
which hath abandoned him contrary to the duety and honesty
which the undefiled bed requireth? No lesse then princesses that
whilom trespassed with those which were of baser stuffe than
themselves. Messalina with hir imperiall robe could not so wel
cover hir faults, but that the historians do defame hir with the
name and title of a common woman. Faustina, the wife of the
sage monarch Marcus Aurelius, gained like reporte by rendringe
hirselfe to others' pleasure, bisides hir lawfull spouse.[16]

'To mary myselfe to one that is mine equall it is impossible,
for so mutch as there is no lorde in all this countrey meete for
my degree but is to olde of age, the rest being dead in these later
warres. To mary a husband that yet is but a childe is folly

extreeme for the inconveniences which daily chaunce thereby
and the evil intreaty that ladies do receive when they come
to age when their nature waxeth cold; by reason whereof,
imbracements be not so favourable and their husbandes, glutted
with ordinary meate, use to run in exchange.[17] Wherefore I
am resolved, without respite or delay, to choose some well
qualified and renoumed gentleman that hath more vertue than
richesse, that is of better fame and brute then of wealth and
revenue, to the entent I may make him my lord, espouse and
husbande. For I cannot imploy my love upon treasure, which
may bee taken away from him in whom richesse of the minde
doth faile, and shall bee better content to see an honest
gentleman with little living to be praised and commended of ech
degree for his good deedes than a rich carle curssed and detested
of all the world.

'Thus mutch I say, and it is the summe of all my secretes,
wherein I pray your councel and advice. I know that some wil
be offended with my choise, and the lords my brothers, specially
the cardinall, will thincke it straunge and receive the same with
ill digesture, that mutch ado shall I have to bee agreed with
them and to remove the griefe they shall conceive against mee
for this mine attempt. Wherefore I would the same should
secretly be kept, until without peril and daunger either of myself
or him whome I pretende to marry, I may publish and manifest
not my love but the mariage, which I hope in God shall soone
bee consummate and accomplished with one whome I doe love
better than myself, and who, as I ful well do know, doeth love
me better than his owne propre life.'

Maister Bologna, which till then hearkned to the oration of
the duchesse without moving, feeling himselfe touched so neare,
and hearinge that his lady had made hir approche for mariage,
stode still astonnied, his tongue not able to frame one word,
onely fantasied a thousand chimeraes in the aire and formed like
number of imaginations in his minde, not able to conjecture
what hee was, to whom the duchesse had vowed hir love and
the possession of hir beauty. He could not thinke that this joy
was prepared for himselfe, for that his lady spake no word of
him, and he lesse durst open his mouth, and yet was wel assured
that she loved him beyond measure. Notwithstanding, knowing
the ficklenesse and unstable heart of women, he said unto
himselfe that she would change hir minde, for seeing him to be

so great a coward, as not to offer his service to a lady by whom hee saw himselfe so many times both wantonly looked uppon and intertained with some secresye more than familiar.

The duchesse, which was a fine and subtile dame, seeinge hir friend rapt with the passion and standing still unmooveable through feare, pale and amazed, as if hee had bene accused and condempned to dy, knew, by that countenaunce and astonishment of Bologna, that she was perfectly beloved of him. And so, meaning not to suffer him any longer to continue in that amaze, ne yet to further feare him with dissembled and fained mariage of any other but with him, she tooke him by the hand, and, beholdinge him with a wanton and luring eye (in sutch sort as the curious philosophers themselves would awake, if sutch a lampe and torche did burne within their studies),[18] she saide thus unto him: 'Seignor Anthonio, I pray you be of good cheere, and torment not yourselfe for anything that I have said. I know well, and of long time have perceived, what good and faithful love you beare mee and with what affection you have served me sithens you first came into my company. Thinke me not to bee so ignorant but that I know ful wel by outward signes what secret thoughts be hid in the inner heart, and that conjectures many times do geve me true and certaine knowledge of concealed things, and am not so foolish to thinke you to be so undiscrete but that you have marked my countenaunce and maner, and thereby have knowen that I have bene more affectioned to you than to any other.

'For that cause', saide shee, straininge him by the hand very lovingly and with cheerefull colour in hir face, 'I sware unto you and doe promise that, if you thinke meete, it shal be none other but yourself whom I wil have and desire to take to husband and lawful spouse, beinge assured so much of you as the love, which so longe time hath ben hidden and covered in our hartes, shall appeare by so evident proofe as onely death shal end and undo the same.'

The gentleman, hearing sutch sodain talke, and the assurance of that which he most wished for, albeit he saw the daunger extreme wherunto he launched himself by espousing this great ladye and the ennimies he should get by entring sutch aliaunce, notwithstandinge, building upon vaine hope, and thinking at length that the choler of the Aragon brother would passe away if they understoode the mariage, determined to pursue the purpose and not to refuse that greate preferment, being so prodigally offred.

For which cause hee answered his lady in this manner: 'If it were in my power, madame, to bring to passe that which I desire for your service by acknowledging the benefits and favors which you depart unto me, as my mind presenteth thanks for the same, I would think myself the happiest gentleman that liveth, and you the beste-served princesse of the world. For one beter beloved (I dare presume to say, and so long as I live wil affirme) is not to be found.

'If till this time I delayed to open that which now I discover unto you, I beseeche you, madame, to impute it to the greatnesse of your estate and to the duty of my calling and office in your house, being not seemelye for a servaunte to talk of sutch secrets with his lady and mistresse. And truely the paine which I have indured to hold my peace and to hide my grief hath been more noisom to me than one hundred thousand like sorrowes together, although it had bene lawfull to have revealed them to some trusty friend. I doe not denye, madame, but of long time you did perceive my follye and presumption, by addressing my minde so high as to the Aragon bloud and to sutch a prinesse as you be. And who can beguile the eye of a lover, specially of hir whose paragon for good minde, wisedome and gentlenesse is not?

'And I confesse to you, besides, that I have most evidentlye perceived how a certain love hath lodged in your gracious hearte, wherwith you bare me greater affection than you did to anye other within the compasse of your family. But what? Great ladies' heartes be fraught with secretes and conceites of other effects than the minds of simple women, which caused me to hope for none other guerdon of my loyal and faithful affection than deathe, and the same very short, and, sith that, little hope accompanied with great, nay, rather, extreme, passion is not able to give sufficient force both to suffer and to stablish my heart with constancye. Nowe for so mutch as of your motion, grace, curtesye and liberality the same is offred, and that it pleaseth you to accept me for yours, I humblye beseche you to dispose of me not as husband but of one which is, and shal be, your servaunt for ever, and sutch as is more ready to obey, than you to commaund. It resteth now, madame, to consider how and in what wise our affaires are to be directed that, things being in assurance, you may so live without perill and bruite of slaunderous tongues, as your good fame and honest report may continue without spot or blemish.'

Beholde the first acte of this tragedy[19] and the provision of the fare which afterwardes sent them bothe to their grave, who immediatly gave their mutual faith. And the houre was assigned the next day that the faire princesse should be in hir chamber alone, attended upon with one onely gentlewoman which had ben brought up with her from the cradle and was made privy to the heavy mariage of those two lovers which was consummate in hir presence.[20] And for the present time they passed the same in words, for ratification whereof they went to bed togither. But the pain in the end was greater than the pleasure, and had ben better for them bothe, yea and also for the third,[21] that they had shewed themselves so wise in the deede as discrete in keeping silence of that which was don. For albeit their mariage was secrete, and therby politikely governed themselves in their stelthes and robberies of love, and that Bologna more ofte helde the state of the stewarde of the house by daye than of lorde of the same, and by nighte supplied that place, yet, in the ende, the thinge was perceived which they desired to bee closely kepte.

And as it is impossible to till and culture a fertile grounde but that the same muste yelde some fruicte, even so the duchesse after many pleasures (being ripe and plentifull) became with childe, which at the firste astonned the maried couple. Neverthelesse, the same so well was provided for as the first childbed was kept secret, and none did know thereof. The childe was nourced in the towne, and the father desired to have him named Frederick, for remembraunce of the parents of his wife.

Nowe Fortune, which lieth in daily waite and ambushment and liketh not that men should longe loiter in pleasure and passetime, being envious of sutch prosperity, cramped so the legges of our two lovers, as they must needes chaunge their game and learne some other practise. For so mutch as the duchesse, beinge great with childe againe and delivered of a girle, the businesse of the same was not so secretly done but that it was discovered. And it sufficed not that the brute was noised through Naples, but that the sound flew further of. As eche man doth know that Rumor hath many mouthes, who with the multitude of his tongues, and trumps, proclaimeth in divers and sundry places the things which chaunce in al the regions of the earth,[22] even so that bablinge foole caried the newes of that second childbed to the eares of the cardinall of Aragon, the duchesse brother, being then at Rome.

Think what joy and pleasure the Aragon brothers had by hearinge the report of their sister's fact. I dare presume to say that, albeit they were extremely wroth with this happened slaunder and with that dishonest fame which the duchesse had gotten throughout Italy, yet farre greater was their sorrow and griefe for that they did not know what hee was that so curteously was allied to their house and in their love had increased their ligneage. And therefore, swelling with despite and rapt with fury to see themselves so defamed by one of their bloude, they purposed, by all meanes whatsoever it cost them to know the lucky lover that had so wel tilled the duchesse, their sister's field. Thus desirous to remove that shame from before their eyes, and to bee revenged of a wrong so notable, they sent espials round about, and scouts to Naples, to view and spy the behaviour and talke of the duchesse, to settle some certaine judgement of him, which stealingly was become their brother-in-lawe.

The duchesse courte beinge in this trouble, she did continually perceive in hir house hir brothers' men to marke hir countenance and to note those that came thither to visite hir and to whom she used greatest familiaritye, bicause it is impossible but that the fire, although it be raked under the ashes, must give some heat. And albeit the two lovers used eche other's company without shewing any signe of their affection, yet they purposed to chaung their estate for a time by yelding truce to their pleasures. Yea, and although Bologna was a wise and provident personage, fearing to be surprised upon the facte, or that the gentlewoman of the chamber, corrupted with money or forced by feare, should pronounce any matter to his hinderance or disadvantage, determined to absent himself from Naples, yet not so sodainly but that he made the duchesse, his faithfull lady and companion, privy of his intent.

And as they were secretly in their chamber together, he used these or sutchlike words: 'Madame, albeit the right good intent and unstained conscience is free from faulte, yet the judgement of men hath further relation to the exterior apparance than to vertue's force and innocency itself, as ignoraunt of the secrets of the thought. And so, in things that be well done, wee must of necessity fall into the sentence of those whom beastly affection ravisheth more than ruled reason.

'You see the solempne watch and guarde which the servaunts of the lordes your brothers do within your house, and the suspition which they have conceived by reason of your second childbed, and by what meanes they labor truely to know how your affaires procede and things do passe. I feare not death where your service may be advaunced, but if herein the maiden of your chamber be not secrete, if she bee corrupted and if she keepe not close that which shee ought to doe, it is not ignoraunt to you that it is the losse of my life, and shall die suspected to bee a whoremonger and varlot, even I (I say) shal incurre that perill, which am your true and lawfull husband. This separation chaunceth not by justice or desert, sith the cause is to righteous for us, but rather your brethren will procure my death, when I shall thinke the same in greatest assurance. If I had to do but with one or two, I would not chaunge the place, ne march one step from Naples, but bee assured that a great band, and the same well armed, will set uppon me.

'I pray you, madame, suffer me to retire for a time, for I am assured that, when I am absent, they will never soile their hands or imbrue their sweardes in your bloud. If I doubted any thing at all of perill touching your owne person, I had rather a hundred hundred times die in your company than live to see you no more, but out of doubt I am, that, if our affaires were discovered and they knew you to be begotten with child by me, your safety would be provided for, wher I should sustain the penaunce of the fact, committed without fault or sinne. And therfore I am determined to goe from Naples, to order mine affaires, and to cause my revenue to be brought to the place of mine abode, and from thence to Ancona, until it pleaseth God to mitigate the rage of your brethren and recover their good wills for consent to our mariage. But I meane not to do or conclude anything without your advise, and if this intente doe not like you, give me councell, madame, what I were best to doe, that both in life and death you may knowe your faithfull servaunt and loving husband is ready to obey and please you.'

This good lady, hearing hir husband's discourse, uncertaine what to do, wept bitterly, as well for grief to lose his presence as for that she felt herself with child the third time. The sighes and teares, the sobbes and heavy lookes, which she threwe forth

uppon hir sorrowful husband gave sufficient witnesse of hir
paine and grief, and if none had hard hir, I thinke her plaintes
would have well expressed hir inwarde smarte of minde. But
like a wise ladye, seing the alleaged reasons of hir husbande,
licensed him, although againste hir minde, not without utterance
of these fewe words before hee went out of hir chamber: 'Deare
husbande, if I were so well assured of the affection of my
brethren as I am of my maide's fidelity, I would entreat you not
to leave me alone – specially in the case I am, beinge with childe.
But knowing that to be just and true which you have saide, I am
content to force my will for a certaine time, that hereafter we
may live at rest together, joining our selves in the companye of
our children and familye, voide of those troubles which greate
courts ordinarily beare within the compasse of their palaces. Of
one thing I must intreat you, that, so often as you can by trusty
messenger, you send me word and intelligence of your health
and state, bicause the same shall bring unto me greater pleasure
and contentation than the welfare of mine owne, and bicause,
also, upon sutch occurentes as shall chaunce, I may provide for
mine owne affaires, the surety of my self, and of our children.'

In saying so, she embraced him very amorously, and he kissed
hir with so great sorrow and grief of heart as the soule was
ready out of his body to take hir flight, sorowful beyond measure
so to leave hir whome he loved, for the great curtesies and honor
which hee had received at hir hands. In the end, fearing that the
Aragon espials woulde come and discrie them in those privities,
Bologna tooke his leave and bad his lady and spouse farewell.

And this was the second acte of this tragicall historie, to see a
fugitife husband secretly to mary, especially hir upon whome
hee ought not so mutch as to loke but with feare and reverence.
Behold here (o ye folish lovers) a glasse of your lightnesse, and
yee women, the course of your fond behavior. It behoveth not
the wise sodainly to execute their first motions and desires of
their heart, for so mutch as they may be assured that pleasure is
pursued so neare with a repentaunce so sharp to be suffred, and
hard to be digested, as their voluptuousnesse shall utterly
discontent them. True it is that mariages be don in Heaven and
performed in Earth, but that saying may not be applied to fooles
which governe themselves by carnall desires, whose scope is but
pleasure, and the reward many times equall to their follye. Shall
I be of opinion that a houshold servaunt oughte to sollicite, nay

rather suborne, the daughter of his lorde without punishment, or that a vile and abject person dare to mount upon a prince's bed? No, no, pollicye requireth order in all, and eche wight ought to bee matched according to their qualitye, without makinge a pastime of it to cover their follies, and knowe not of what force love and desteny be, except the same be resisted. A goodly thinge it is to love, but where reason looseth place, love is withoute his effecte, and the sequele – rage and madnesse. Leave we to discourse of those which beleve that they be constrained to folowe the force of their minde, and may easilye subdue themselves to the lawes of vertue and honesty, like one that thrusteth his heade into a sack and thinkes he cannot get out. Sutch people do please themselves in their losse and thinke all well that is noisome to their health, daily folowing their owne delightes.

Come wee againe, then, to sir Bologna, who, after he had left his wife in hir castell, went to Naples. And, having sessed a rent upon hir lands and levied a good summe of money, he repaired to Ancona, a city of the patrimonye of the Romane church,[23] whither hee caried the two children which he had of the duchesse, causing them to be brought up with suche diligence and care as it is to be thought a father well affectioned to his wife would doe, and who delighted to see a braunch of the tree that to him was the best-beloved fruict of the world. There he hired a house for his traine and for those that waited uppon his wife. Who in the meane time was in great care and could not tell of what woode to make hir arrowes,[24] perceiving that hir belly began to swell and grow to the time of hir delivery, seeing that from day to day hir brothers' servaunts were at hir back, voide of counsel and advise, if one evening she had not spoken to the gentlewoman of her chamber, touching the doubts and peril wherein she was, not knowing how she might be delivered from the same.

That maiden was gentle and of a good mind and stomake, and loved hir mistresse very derely, and seeing hir so amazed and tormenting hirself to death, minding to fray hir no further, ne to reprove hir of hir fault which could not be amended, but rather to provide for the daunger wherunto she had hedlong cast hirselfe, gave hir this advise: 'How now, Madame?' (said shee). 'Is that wisdom, which from your childhode hath ben so familiar in you, dislodged from your brest in time when it ought chiefly to rest for incountring of those mishaps that are comming upon us? Think you to avoid the dangers by thus tormenting yourself, except you set your hands to the work therby to give the repulse to adverse fortune? I have heard you many times speake of the constancye and force of minde which ought to shine in the deedes of princesses more clerely than amongs those dames of baser house, and which ought to make them appeare like the sunne and the little starres, and yet I see you nowe astonned, as though you had never forseene that adversity chaunceth so wel to catch the great within his clouches as the base and simple sort.

'It is but now that you have called to remembraunce that which might insue your mariage with sir Bologna? Did his onely presence assure you against the waits of fortune, and was it the thought of paines, feares and frights which now turmoileth your dolorous mind? Ought you thus to vexe yourselfe, when nede it is to thinke how to save both your honor and the fruicte within your intrailes? If your sorrow be so great over sir Bologna, and if you feare your childbed wil be descried, why seeke you not meanes to attempt some voyage for covering of the fact, to beguile the eyes of them which so diligently do watch you? Why sweat and freat you before you make me answer?'

'Ah, sweetehearte,' (answered the duchesse) 'if thou feltest the paine which I do suffer, thy tongue would not be so mutch at will as thou shewest it now to bee for reproofe of my small constancye. I do sorrow specially for the causes which thou alleagest and, above all, for that I know well, that if my brethren had never so litle intelligence of my beinge with child, I were undone and my life at an end, and, peradventure, poore wench, thou shouldest beare the penaunce for my sinne. But what way can I take, that stil these candels may not give light, and I voided of the traine which ought to waighte upon my brethren? I thinke if I should descend into Hell they would know whither any shadowe there were in love with me. Now gesse if I should travaile the realme or retire to any other place, whither they would let me live in peace? Nothing lesse, for suspect they would that the cause of my departure proceeded of desire to live at liberty, to dallye with him whom they judge to be other than my lawfull husband. And it may so be that, as they bee wicked and suspicious, so will they doubte of my beinge with childe, and thereby shall I bee farre more infortunate by travailing than

here in miserye amidde mine anguishe. And you, the reste that
be keepers of my councell, fall into greater daunger; uppon
whome no doubte they will bee revenged and fleshe themselves
for your unhappy waiting and attendance upon us.'

'Madame', said the bolde maiden, 'be not afraide, and followe
mine advise, for I hope that it shall be the meanes both to see
your spouse and to rid those troublesome verlets out of your
house, and in like maner safely to deliver you into good
assuraunce.'

'Say your mind', quod the ladye, 'for it may bee that. I will
governe myself according to the same.'

'Mine advise is, then', said the gentlewoman, 'to let your
houshold understand that you made a vowe to visite the holy
temple of Our Lady of Loretto (a famous pilgrimage in Italy)
and that you commaund your train to make themselves ready to
wait upon you for accomplishment of your devotion, and from
thence you shall take your journey to sojourne at Ancona,
whither, before you goe hence, you shall send your moveables
and plate, with sutch moneye as you thinke necessarye for
furnishing of your charges. And afterwards God will performe
the rest and through his holy mercy will guide and direct al your
affaires.'[25]

The duchesse, hearing the maiden speake her good advise and
amazed of her sodaine invention, could not forbear to imbrace
and kisse hir, blessing the houre wherein she was borne and that
ever she chaunced into hir company. To whome afterwards shee
said: 'My wenche, I had well determined to give over mine estate
and noble porte, joyfully to live a simple gentlewoman with my
deare and wel-beloved husband, but I could not devise how I
should conveniently departe this countrey without suspition of
some folly. And sith that thou hast so well instructed mee for
bringing that same to passe, I promise thee that so diligentlye
thy counsel shal be performed as I see the same to be right good
and necessary, for rather had I see my husband, beinge alone
without title of duchesse or great lady, than to live without him
beautified with the graces and names of honor and
preheminence.'

This devised plot was no soner grounded but she gave order
for execution of the same and brought it to passe with sutch
dexterity as the ladye in lesse than 8 dayes had conveyed and
sente the most part of hir moveables, and specially the chiefest

and beste, to Ancona, taking in the meanetime hir way towards
Loretto after she had bruted hir solempne vow made for that
pilgrimage. It was not sufficient for this folish woman to take a
husband more to glut hir libidinous appetite than for other
occasion, except shee added to hir sinne another excreable
impietye, making holy places and dueties of devotion to be as it
were the shadowes of hir folly.

But let us consider the force of lovers' rage, which, so soone
as it hath seased upon the minds of men, we see how marvellous
be the effects thereof and with what straint and puissaunce that
madnesse subdueth the wise and strongest worldlings. Who
woulde thinke that a great lady, besides the abandoning hir
estate, hir goodes and child, would have misprised hir honor
and reputation to follow, like a vagabond, a pore and simple
gentleman, and him besides that was the household servaunt of
hir courte? And yet you see this great and mighty duchesse trot
and run after the male, like a female wolfe or lionesse (when
they goe to sault) and forget the noble bloud of Aragon whereof
she was descended to couple hirself almost with the simplest
person of all the trimmest gentlemen of Naples.

But turne we not the example of follies to be a matter of
consequence; for if one or two become bankrupt of their honor,
it followeth not, good ladies, that their fact should serve for a
matche to your deserts, and mutch lesse a patron for you to
folow. These histories be not writen to traine and trap you to
pursue the thousand thousand slippery sleightes of love's gallantise, but rather carefully to warne you to behold the semblable
faultes, and to serve for a drugge to discharge the poison which
gnaweth and fretteth the integritye and soundnesse of the soule.
The wise and skilfull apothecary or compositor of drugges
dresseth viper's flesh to purge the patient from hote corrupted
bloud which conceiveth and engendreth leprosye within his
body.[26] In like manner, the fonde love and wicked ribauldry of
Semiramis, Pasiphae, Messalina, Faustina and Romilda is
shewed in writ, that every of you maye feare to be numbred and
recorded amongst sutch common and dishonourable women.[27]
You princes and great lords, read the follies of Paris, the
adulteries of Hercules, the dainty and effeminate life of Sardanapalus, the tyranny of Phalaris, Busiris or Dionysius of Sicile,
and see the history of Tiberius, Nero, Caligula, Domitian, and
Heliogabalus, and spare not to recompte them amongst our

wanton youthes which soile themselves villaines more filthily
than the swine do in the durt. Al this intendeth it an instruction
for your youth to follow the infection and whoredome of those
monsters? Better it were all those bokes were drenched in
bottomlesse depth of seas than Christian life by their meanes
should be corrupted. But the example of the wicked is induced
for to eschue and avoid them, as the life of the good and honest
is remembred to frame and addresse our behavior in this world
to be praiseworthy and commended. Otherwise the holinesse of
sacred writ should serve for an argument to the unthrifty and
luxurious to confirm and approve their beastly and licencious
wickednesse.

Come we againe then to our purpose. The good pilgrime of
Loretto went forth hir voyage to atchieve hir devotions by
visiting the saint for whose reliques she was departed the country
of the duke, hir sonne. When she had done hir suffrages at
Loretto, hir people thought hir voyage to be at an end and that
she would have returned again into hir countrey. But she said
unto them that, forsomutch as she was so neare Ancona, being
but xv miles of, she would not retire but she had seen that
auncient and goodlye city, which divers histories do greatly
recommend, as wel for the antiquitye as for the pleasant seat
therof. Al were of hir advise and went forward to see the
antiquities of Ancona, and she to renue the pleasures which she
had before begon with hir Bologna, who was advertised of all
hir determination, resting now like a god, possessed with the
jewels and richesse of the duchesse, and had taken a faire palace
in the great streat of the city, by the gate wherof the traine of
his lady must passe. The harbinger of the duchesse posted before
to take up lodging for the train, but Bologna offred unto him
his palace for the ladye. So Bologna, which was already wel-
beloved in Ancona, and newely entred amitye and great aquain-
taunce with the gentlemen of the citye, with a goodlye troupe of
them wente forthe to meete his wife, to whom he presented his
house, and besought hir that shee and hir traine would vouchsafe to lodge there. She received the same very thankfully, and
withdrew hirselfe unto his house; who conducted hir thither not
as a husband, but like him that was hir humble and affectionate
servaunte.

But what needeth great discourse of woordes? The duchesse,
knowing that it was impossible but eche man must be privy to

hir facte and know what secretes hath passed betweene hir and hir husband, to the ende that no other opinion of hir childebed should be conceived but that which was good and honest, and done since the accomplishment of the mariage, the morrow after hir arrivall to Ancona, assembled all her traine in the hall, of purpose no longer to keepe cloase that sir Bologna was hir husbande, and that alreadye shee had had two children by him and againe was great with childe with a third.

And when they were come togither after dinner, in that presence of hir husbande, shee used unto them these woordes: 'Gentlemen, and al ye my trusty and loving servaunts, highe time it is to manifest to every of you the thing which hath been done before the face and in the presence of him who knoweth the most obscure and hidden secrets of our thoughts.[28] And needefull it is not to keepe silente that which is neither evill done ne hurtfull to any person. If things might be kept secrete and stil remaine unknowen, except they were declared by the doers of them, yet would not I commit the wrong in concealing that which to discover unto you doth greatly delite me and delivereth my mind from exceeding grief, in sutch wise as if the flames of my desire could break out with sutch violence as the fire hath taken heate within my mind, ye should see the smoke mount up with greater smoulder than that which the mount Gibel doeth vomit forth at certaine seasons of the yeare.

'And to the intent I may not keepe you long in this suspect, this secret fire within my heart, and that which I shal cause to flame in open aire, is a certain opinion which I conceive for a mariage by me made certain yeares past, at what time I chose and wedded a husband to my fantasye and liking, desirous no longer to live in widow state, being unwilling to do the thing that should prejudice and hurt my conscience. The same is done, and yet in one thing I have offended, which is by long keeping secrete the performed mariage; for the wicked brute dispearsed through the realme by reason of my childbed, one yeare paste, hath displeased some. Howbeit, my conscience receiveth comforte for that the same is free from fault or blot.

'Now shall ye know, therefore, what he is whom I acknowledg for my lord and spouse, and who it is that lawfully hath me espoused in the presence of this gentlewoman here present, which is the witnesse of our nuptials and accorde of mariage. This gentleman, also, Antonio Bologna, is he to whom I have sworn and given my faith, and hee againe to mee hath ingaged his. He it is whom I accompt for my spouse and husband and with whome henceforth I meane to rest and continue. In consideration whereof, if there be any heere amongs you all that shal mislike of my choise and is willing to wait uppon my sonne the duke, I meane not to let them of their intent, prayinge them faithfully to serve him and to be careful of his person, and to be unto him so honest and loyall as they have bene to me so longe as I was their mistresse. But if any of you desire stil to make your abode with me, to be partakers of my wealth and woe, I will so entertaine them as they shall have good cause to be contented; if not, let them departe hence to Malfi, and the steward shal provide for them according to their degre. For, touching myself, I do mind no more to be termed an infamous duchesse. Rather would I be honored with the title of a simple gentlewoman, or with that estate which shee can have that hath an honest husband and with whom she holdeth faithfull and loyall company, than reverenced with the glory of a princesse, subject to the despite of slaunderous tongues.'

'Ye know' (said she to Bologna) 'what hath passed betwene us, and God is the witnesse of the integrity of my conscience, wherfore I pray you bring forth our children, that eche man may beholde the fruictes raised of our alliance.'[29]

Havinge spoken those woordes, and the children broughte forthe into the hall, all the companye stoode still, so astonned with that newe successe and tale as though hornes sodainly had started forth their heads, and rested unmoveable and amazed, like the great marble piller of Rome called Pasquile,[30] for so mutch as they never thought ne conjectured that Bologna was the successor of the duke of Malfi in his mariage bed.

This was the preparative of the catastrophe and bloudy end of this tragedie. For, of all the duchesse' servaunts, there was not one that was willing to continue with their aunciant mistresse. Who, with the faithfull maiden of hir chamber, remained at Ancona, enjoying the joyful embracements of hir husbande in all sutch pleasure and delights as they doe, which, having lived in fear, be set at liberty and out of al suspition; plunged in a sea of joy and fleting in the quiet calme of al passetime, where Bologna had none other care but how to please his best beloved, and she studied nothing else but how to love and obey him as the wife ought to doe hir husband. But this faire weather lasted

not long, for as the joyes of men do not long endure but wast in
little time, so bee the delights of lovers lesse firme and stedefast
and passe away almost in one moment of an houre.

Now the servaunts of the duchesse which wer retired and
durst tary no longer with hir, fearing the fury of the cardinal of
Aragon, brother to the lady, the verye day they departed from
Ancona devised amongs themselves that one of them should ride
in post to Rome to advertise the cardinal of the ladye's mariage,
to the intente that the Aragon brethren might conceive no cause
to seke revenge of their disloyalty. That determination spedily
was accomplished, one posting towardes Rome, and the rest
galloping to the countrey castles of the duke.

These newes reported to the cardinal and his brother, it may
be conjectured how grievously they toke the same, and that they
were not able to digest them with modestye. The yongest of the
brethren yalped forth a thousand cursses and despites, againste
the simple sexe of womankind.[31] 'Ha', said the prince (trans-
ported with choler, and driven into deadly furye) 'what law is
able to punish or restraine the folish indiscretion of a woman
that yeldeth hirself to hir own desires? What shame is able to
bridle and withdrawe a woman from hir mind and madnesse?
Or with what fear is it possible to snaffle them from execution
of their filthinesse? Ther is no beast, be he never so wilde, but
man sometime may tame and bring to his lure and order.[32] The
force and diligence of man is able to make milde the stronge and
proude, and to overtake the swiftest beaste and foule, or
otherwise to attaine the highest and deepest things of the world.
But this incarnate divelish beaste, the woman, no force can
subdue hir, no swiftnesse can approch hir mobility, no good
mind is able to prevent hir sleightes and deceites; they seem to
be procreated and borne againste all order of nature and to live
withoute lawe, which governeth al other things indued with
some reason and understanding.

'But howe great abhomination is this, that a gentlewoman, of
sutch a house as ours is, hath forgotten hir estate and the
greatnesse of hir deceased husband, with the hope of the toward
youthe of the duke, hir sonne and our nephew. Ah, false and
vile bitch, I sweare, by the Almighty God and by his blessed
wounds,[33] that if I can catch thee and that wicked knave thy
chosen mate, I wil pipe ye both sutch a wofull galiard, as in
your imbracements ye never felt like joy and mirthe. I wil make

ye daunce sutch a bloudy bargenet, as your whorish heate for ever shall be cooled.

'What abuse have they committed under title of mariage, which was so secretly don as their children do witnesse their lecherous love, but their promise of faith was made in open aire and serveth for a cloke and visarde of their moste filthy whoredom. And what if mariage was concluded, be we of so little respect as the carion beast could not vouchsafe to advertise us of hir entent? Or is Bologna a man worthy to be allied or mingled with the royal bloud of Aragon and Castille? No, no, be he never so good a gentleman, his race agreeth not with kingly state. But I make to God a vow that never will I take one sound and restful slepe untill I have dispatched that infamous fact from our bloud, and that the caitif whoremonger be used according to his desert.'

The cardinal also was out of quiet, grinding his teeth togither, chattering forth of his Spanish mosel jackanapes Pater-noster, promising no better usage to their Bologna than his yonger brother did. And the better to intrap them both (without further sturre for that time) they sent to the lord Gismondo Gonsago, the cardinal of Mantua, than legate for Pope Julius the Second at Ancona, at whose hands they enjoyed sutch friendship as Bologna and all his family were commaunded spedily to avoid the city.

But for al that the legat was able to do, of long time he could not prevail; Bologna had so greate intelligence within Ancona. Neverthelesse, whiles hee differred his departure, he caused the most part of his traine, his children and goods to be conveyed to Siena, an auncient city of Thoscane, which, for the state and liberties, had long time bin at warres with the Florentines; in sutch wise as, the very same day that newes came to Bologna that hee should depart the citty within 15 dayes, hee was ready and mounted on horseback to take his flight to Siena; which brake for sorrow the hearts of the Aragon brethren, seeinge that they were deceived and frustrate of their intent, bicause they purposed by the way to apprehend Bologna and to cut him in peeces.

But what? The time of his hard lucke was not yet expired, and so the marche from Ancona served not for the theatre of those two infortunate lovers' overthrow, who certaine moneths lived in peace in Thoscane. The cardinall night nor day did sleepe, and his brother still did wait to performe his othe of revenge. And seeinge their ennimy out of feare, they dispatched a post to Alfonso Castruccio, the cardinall of Siena, to entreat the lord Borgliese, cheife of the seigniory there, that their sister and Bologna should be banished the countrey, and limits of that city; which with small suite was brought to passe.[34]

These two infortunate, husband and wife, were chasid from all places, and so unlucky as whilom Achastus was when he was accursed or Oedipus, after his father's death and incestious mariage with his mother, uncertaine to what sainct to vow themselves and to what place to take their flight.[35] In the ende they determined to goe to Venice, but first to Ramagna, there to imbarke themselves for to retire in saulfty to the city environned with the sea Adriaticum, the richest in Europa.[36] But the poore soules made their reconinge there without their hoaste, failinge halfe the price of their banket. For, being uppon the territory of Forli, one of the traine afarre of did see a troupe of horsemen galloping towardes their company, which by their countenaunce shewed no signe of peace or amity at all; which made them consider that it was some ambush of their enimies.

The Neapolitan gentleman, seeing the onset bendinge uppon them, began to feare death, not for that hee cared at al for his mishap and ruine, but his heart began to cleave for heavinesse to see his wife and little children ready to be murdered and serve for the passetime of the Aragon brethren's eyes. For whose sakes he knew himselfe already predestinate to dy, and that for despite of him and to accelerate his death by the overthrow of his wife and children, he was assured that they would dispatch them all before his face and presence. But what is there to be done where counsell and meanes to escape do faile? Full of teares, therefore, astonishment and feare, he expected death so cruell as man could devise and was already determined to suffer the same with good courage, for anything that the duchesse could say unto him. He might well have saved himself and his eldest sonne by flight, being both wel mounted upon two good Turkey horsses, whiche ran so fast as the quarrel out of a crosbow. But he loved to mutch his wife and children and woulde kepe them company both in life and death.

In th'ende the good lady said unto him: 'Sir, for all the joyes and pleasures which you can do me, for God's sake save yourselfe and the litle infant next you, who can well indure the galloping of the horse. For sure I am that, you being out of our company, we shall not neede to feare any hurt, but if you do tary, you wil be the cause of the ruine and overthrow of us all, and we shal receive thereby no profit or advauntage. Take this purse, therefore, and save yourself, attending better fortune in time to come.'

The poore gentleman Bologna, knowing that his wife had pronounced reason, and fearing that it was impossible from that time forth that she or hir traine could escape their hands, taking leave of hir, and kissing his children, not forgetting the money which she offred unto him, willed his servants to save themselves by sutch meanes as they thought best. So gieving spurs unto his horse, he began to fly amaine, and his eldest sonne, seeing his father gone, began to followe in like sorte. And so, for that time, they two were saved by breaking of the intended ill luck like to light upon them. And where he thought to rescue himselfe at Venice, he turned another way, and by great journeys arrived at Millan.

In the meanetime, the horsemen were approched neere the duchesse; who seeing that Bologna had saved himselfe, very courteously began to speake unto the lady, were it that the Aragon brethren had geven theim that charge, or feared that the lady would trouble them with hir importunate cries and lamentations. One, therefore, amongs the troupe saide thus unto hir: 'Madam, we be commaunded by the lordes your brethren to conduct you home unto your house, that you may receive againe the government of the duchy and the order of the duke your sonne, and do marvell very mutch at your folly for giving yourselfe thus to wander the countrey after a man of so smal reputation as Bologna is, who, when he had glutted his lusting lecherrous minde with the comelines of your noble personage, wil despoile you of your goods and honour and then take his legs into som straung countrey.'

The simple lady, albeit greevous it was unto hir to heare sutch speech of hir husband, yet helde hir peace and dissembled what she thought, glad and wel contented with the curtesy done unto hir, fearinge before that they came to kill hir and thought hirselfe already discharged, hopinge uppon their courteous dealinges that shee and hir children from that time forth should live in good assuraunce. But she was greatly deceived, and knew, within shorte space after, the goodwill that hir brethren bare

hir. For so soone as these gallants had conducted hir into the
kingdome of Naples to one of the castels of hir sonne, she was
committed to prison with hir children, and she also that was the
secretary of hir infortunate mariage. Til this time fortune was
contented to proceede with indifferent quiet against those lovers,
but henceforth yee shall heare the issue of their little-prosperous
love, and how, pleasure having blinded them, never forsooke
them until it had given them the overthrow.

It booteth not heere to recite any fables or histories, contenting myself that ladies do reade, without to many weping teares,
the pitifull end of that miserable princesse; who, seeing hirselfe
a prisoner in the company of hir litle children and wel-beloved
maiden, paciently lived in hope to see hir brethren appaised,
comforting hirselfe for the escape of hir husband out of the
hands of his mortal foes.

But hir assurance was changed into an horrible feare, and hir
hope to no expectation of surety, when, certaine dayes after hir
imprisonment, hir gaoler came in and saide unto hir: 'Madame,
I do advise you henceforth to consider and examine your
conscience, for so mutch as I suppose that even this very day
your life shall be taken from you.'[37]

I leave for you to thinke what horrour and traunce assailed
the feeble heart of this poore lady and with what eares she
received that cruell message, but hir cries and moanes together
with hir sighes and lamentations declared with what chere she
received the advertisement. 'Alas' (said she) 'is it possible that
my brethren should so far forget themselves as, for a fact
nothing prejudicial unto them, cruelly to put to death their
innocent sister and to imbrue the memory of their fact in the
bloud of one which never did offend them? Must I against al
right and equity be put to death before the judge or majestrate
have made triall of my life and knowne the righteousnesse of
my cause?

'Ah God, most rightfull and bountifull father, beholde the
mallice of my brethren and the tyrannous cruelty of those which
wrongfully doe seeke my bloud. Is it a sinne to marry? Is it a
fault to fly and avoide the sinne of whoredome? What lawes be
these, where marriage bed and joined matrimony is pursued
with like severity that murder, theft and advoutry are? And
what Christianity in a cardinall to shed the bloud which hee
ought to defend? What profession is this, to assaile the innocent

by the highway side and to reve them of life in place to punish theeves and murderers?

'O Lord God thou art just and dost al things in equity. I see wel that I have trespassed against thy majesty in some more notorious crime than in marriage. I most humbly therefore beseech thee to have compassion on mee and to pardon mine offences, accepting the confession and repentaunce of mee, thine humble servaunt, for satisfaction of my sinnes, which it pleased thee to washe away in the precious bloud of thy sonne our Saviour, that being so purified, I may appeare at the holy banket in thy glorious kingdome.'[38]

When shee had thus finished hir prayer, two or three of the ministers, which had taken hir besides Forli, came in and said unto hir: 'Now, Madame, make ready yourselfe to goe to God, for beholde your houre is come.'

'Praised be that God' (said she) 'for the wealth and woe that it pleaseth him to send us. But I beseech you, my friendes, to have pitty uppon these little babes and innocent creatures. Let them not feele the smarte which I am assured my brethren beare againste their poore unhappy father.'

'Well, well, madame', said they, 'we wil convey them to sutch place as they shal not want.'

'I also recommend unto you' (quod she) 'this pore imprisoned maiden, and entreate hir well, in consideration of hir good service done to the infortunate duchesse of Malfi.' As she had ended those words, the two ruffians did put a coarde about her neck, and strangled hir.

The maiden, seeing the pitious tragedy commensed upon hir maistresse, cried out amaine, cursing the cruell malice of those tormenters, and besought God to be witnesse of the same; and crying out upon his divine majesty, she humbly prayed unto him to bend his judgement against them which causelesse (being no magistrates) had killed so innocent creatures.

'Reason it is' (said one of the tyrants) 'that thou be partaker of thy maistresse' innocency, sith thou hast bene so faithfull a minister and messenger of hir fleshly follies.' And sodainly caught hir by the haire of the head and insteade of a carcanet placed a roape about her necke.

'How now' (quoth shee) 'is this the promised faith you made unto my lady?' But those words flew into the aire with hir soule, in company of the miserable duchesse.

And now hearken the most sorowfull scene of all the tragedy.
The little children, which had seene all this furious game
executed upon their mother and hir maide, as nature provoked
them, or as some presage of their mishap might leade them
thereunto, kneeled upon their knees before those tyrants and,
embracinge their legges, wailed in sutch wise as I thinke that
any other, except a pitilesse heart spoiled of all humanity, would
have had compassion. And impossible it was for them to unfolde
the embracementes of those innocent creatures, which seemed
to forejudge their death by savage lookes and countenaunce of
those roisters. Whereby I think that needes it must be confessed
that Nature hath in hirselfe and in us imprinted some signe of
divination, and specially at the houre and time of death, so as
the very beastes doe feele some forewarninges, although they see
neither sworde nor staffe, and indevoure to avoide the cruell
passage of a thinge so fearefull as the separation of two thinges
so neerely united, even the body and soule; which, for the
motion that chaunceth at the very instant, sheweth how nature
is constrained in that monstrous division and more than horrible
overthrow.

But who can appease a heart determined to worke mischief
and hath sworne the death of another, forced thereunto by some
special commaundment? The Aragon brethren ment hereby
nothing else but to roote out the whole name and race of
Bologna. And therfore the two ministers of iniquity did like
murder and slaughter upon those two tender babes, as they had
done before upon their mother, not without some motion of
horror, for an act so detestable.

Behold here how far the cruelty of man extendeth, when it
coveteth nothing else but vengeance, and marke what excessive
choler the mind of them produceth which suffer themselves to
be forced and overwhelmed with fury. Leave we apart the
cruelty of Euchrates, the sonne of the kinge of Bactria, and of
Phraates, the sonne of the Persian prince, of Timon of Athenes,
and of an infinit number of those which were rulers and
governors of the empire of Rome, and let us match with these
Aragon brethren one Vitoldus, duke of Lituania, the cruelty of
whom constrained his own subjects to hang themselves for feare
leaste they should fall into his furious and bloudy hands.[39] We
may confesse also these brutall brethren to be more butcherly
than ever Otho, erle of Monferrato and prince of Urbin, was,

who caused a yeoman of his chamber to be wrapped in a sheete poudred with sulpher and brimstone and afterwards, kindled with a candle, was scalded and consumed to death, bicause he waked not at an hour by him appointed. Let us not excuse them also from some affinity with Manfredus, the sonne of Henry, the second emperor, who smoldered his own father, being an old man, between two coverlets. These former furies might have some excuse to cover their cruelty, but these had no other color but a certain beastly madnesse which moved them to kil those litle children, their nephews, who by no means could prejudice or anoy the duke of Malfi or his title in the succession of his duchye, the mother having withdrawen hir goods and had her dowrye assigned hir.[40] But a wicked hart wrapt in malice must nedes bring forth semblable workes.

In the time of these murders, the infortunate lover kept himself at Millan with his sonne Frederick and vowed himself to the lord Silvio Savello, who that time besieged the castell of Millan in the behalf of Maximilian Sforcia; which in the end he conquered and recovered by composition with the French within.[41] But that charge being atchieved, the general Savello marched from thence to Cremona with his campe, whither Bologna durst not folow, but repaired to the marquize of Britone. In which time the Aragon brethren so wroughte as his goods were confiscate at Naples and he driven to his shiftes to use the golden duckates which the Duchesse gave him to relieve himselfe at Millan; whose death, althoughe it were advertised by many, yet hee could not be persuaded to beleve the same, for that divers, which went about to betray him and feared he shoulde flye from Millan, kept his beake under the water (as the proverb is) and assured him both of the life and welfare of his spouse and that shortly his brethren-in-law would be reconciled because many noble men favored him well and desired his returne home to his countrey.

Fed and filled with that vaine hope, he remained more than a yeare at Millan, frequenting good company, who was well entertained of the richest marchaunts and best gentlemen of the citye. And above all other, he had familiar accesse to the house of the ladye Hippolita Bentivoglia,[42] where, uppon a daye after dinner, taking his lute in hand, whereon he could exceedingly well play, he began to sing a sonnet which he had composed uppon the discourse of his misfortune, the tenor whereof insueth:

The song of Antonio Bologna, the husband of the duchesse of Malfi
If love, the death, or tract of time, have measured my distresse,
Or if my beatinge sorrowes may my languor well expresse:
Then love come soone to visit me, which most my heart desires,
And so my dolor findes some ease, through flames of fancye's
    fires.
The time runnes out his rollinge course, for to prolong mine ease,
To th' end I shall enjoy my love, and heart himselfe appease,
A cruell darte brings happy death, my soule then rest shall find:
And sleepinge body under toumbe, shall dreame time out of
    minde,
And yet the love, the time, nor death, lookes not how I decreace:
Nor geveth eare to anythinge, of this my wofull peace.
Full farre I am from my good hap, or halfe the joye I crave,
Whereby I chaung my state with teares, and draw full neere my
    grave.
The courteous gods that gives me life, now mooves the planets
    all:
For to arrest my groning ghost, and hence my sprite to call.
Yet from them still I am separd, by thinges unequall heere,
Not ment the gods may be unjust, that breedes my chaunging
    cheere,
For they provide by their foresight, that none shall doe me harme:
But she whose blasing beauty bright, hath brought me in a
    charme.
My mistresse hath the powre alone, to rid me from this woe:
Whose thrall I am, for whom I die, to whom my sprite shall goe.
Away, my soule, goe from the griefs, that thee oppresseth still,
And let thy dolor witnesse beare, how mutch I want my will.
For since that love and Death himselfe, delights in guiltlesse
    bloud,
Let time transport my troubled sprite, where destiny seemeth
    good.[43]

This song ended, the poor gentleman could not forbeare from
pouring forth his lukewarme tears, which abundantly ran downe
his heavy face, and his pantinge sighes truly discovered the
alteration of his minde, which mooved ech wight of that
assembly to pitty his mournful state; and one, specially, of no
acquaintance, and yet knew the devises that the Aragon brethren
had trained and contrived again him. That unacquainted gentle-

man, his name was Delio, one very well learned and of trim invention, who very excellently hath endited in the Italian vulgar tongue.[44]

This Delio, knowing the gentleman to be husband to the deceased duchesse of Malfi, came unto him, and taking him aside, said: 'Sir, albeit I have no great acquaintance with you, this being the first time that ever I saw you to my remembrance, so it is that vertue hath sutch force and maketh gentle mindes so amorous of their like as, when they doe beholde ech other, they feele themselves coupled as it were in a bande of mindes, that impossible it is to divide the same. Now, knowinge what you be and the good and commendable qualities in you, I coumpt it my duty to reveale that which may chaunce to breede you damage. Know you, then, that I of late was in company with a nobleman of Naples, which is in this citty, banded with a certaine company of horsemen, who tolde mee that he had a speciall charge to kill you, and therefore prayed me (as it seemed) to require you not to come in his sight, to the intent he might not be constrained to doe that which should offend his conscience and grieve the same all the dayes of his life. Moreover, I have worse tidinges to tell you. The duchesse, your wife, deade by violent hand in prison, and the most part of them that were in hir company. Besides this, assure yourselfe that, if you doe not take heede to that which this Neapolitane capitaine hath differred, other will doe and execute the same. This mutch I have thought good to tell you, bicause it would very mutch grieve me that a gentleman so excellent as you be should be murdered in that miserable wise, and I should deeme myselfe unworthy of life if, knowing these practises, I should dissemble the same.'

Whereunto Bologna aunswered: 'Sir Delio, I am greatly bound unto you and geve you hearty thankes for the goodwill you beare me. But in the conspiracy of the brethren of Aragon and of the death of my lady, you be deceived, and some have given you wrong intelligence. For within these two dayes, I received letters from Naples wherein I am advertised that the right honorable and reverend cardinal and his brother be almost appeased and that my goods shall bee rendred againe and my dear wife restored.'

'Ah, sir,' saide Delio, 'how you be beguiled, and fedde with follies, and nourished with sleights of court. Assure yourselfe that they which write these trifles make sutch shamefull sale of your life as the butcher doth of his flesh in the shambles, and so wickedly betray you as impossible it is to invent a treason more detestable. But bethinke you well thereof.' When he had said so, he tooke his leave and joined himselfe in company of fine and pregnaunt wittes, there assembled together.

In the meanetime, the cruell spirite of the Aragon brethren were not yet appeased with the former murders, but needes must finish the last act of Bologna his tragedy by losse of his life, to keepe his wife and children company so well in another worlde as he was united with them in love in this fraile and transitory passage. The Neapolitan gentleman before spoken of by Delio, which had taken this enterprise to satisfye the barbarous cardinall to berieve his countreyman of life, havinge chaunged his minde, and differring from day to day to sorte the same to effect, it chaunced that a Lombarde of larger conscience than the other,[45] inveigled with covetousnesse and hired for ready money, practised the death of the duchesse' poore husband. This bloudy beaste was called Daniel de Bozola, that had charge of a certaine bande of footemen in Millan. This newe Judas and pestilent manqueller, who within certaine dayes, after knowinge that Bologna oftentimes repaired to heare service at the church and convent of S. Fraunces, secretly conveyed himself in ambush, hard besides the church of S. James (being accompanied with a certaine troupe of souldiers) to assaile infortunate Bologna, who was sooner slaine than hee was able to thinke upon defence, and whose mishap was sutch as hee which killed him had good leisure to save himselfe by reason of the little pursuite made after him.

Beholde heere the noble fact of a cardinall and what saver it hath of Christian purity to commit a slaughter for a fact done many yeres past, upon a poore gentleman which never thought him hurt! Is this the sweete observation of the Apostles, of whom they vaunt themselves to be the successours and followers?[46] And yet we cannot finde nor reade that the Apostles, or those that stept in their trade of life, hired ruffians and murderers to cut the throates of them which did them hurt. But what? It was in the time of Julius the Second, who was more martiall than Christian and loved better to shed bloud than give blessing to the people.

Sutch ende had the infortunate mariage of him which ought to have contented himselfe with that degree and honor that he had acquired by the deedes and glory of his vertues, so mutch by ech wight recommended. We ought never to climb higher than our force permitteth, ne yet surmount the bounds of duty, and lesse suffer ourselves to be haled fondly forth with desire of brutal sensuality. Which sinne is of sutch nature that he never giveth over the party whom he maistereth until he hath brought him to the shame of some notable folly. You see the miserable discourse of a princesse' love that was not very wise, and of a gentleman that had forgotten his estate. Which ought to serve for a lookinge-glasse to them which bee over-hardy in makinge enterprises and doe not measure their ability with the greatnesse of their attemptes, where they ought to maintaine themselves in reputation and beare the title of well-advised; foreseeing their ruine to be example for all posterity, as may bee seene by the death of Bologna and by all them which sprang of him and of his infortunate spouse his lady and maistresse. But we have discoursed inough hereof, sith diversity of other histories do call us to bring the same in place, which were not mutch more happy than the bloudy end of those whose history ye have already heard.

Two gentlemen of Venice were honourably deceived of their wives, whose notable practises and secret conference for atchievinge their desire occasioned divers accidentes and ingendred double benefit; wherein also is recited an eloquent oration made by one of them, pronounced before the duke and state of that cittye, with other chaunces and actes concerninge the same.

Heere have I thought good to summon 2 gentlewomen of Venice to appeare in place and to mount on stage amongs other Italian dames to shew cause of their bolde incountrey against the folly of their two husbands, that uncharitably, without respect of neighbourhoode, went about to assaile the honesty of either's wife; and, weening they had enjoyed other's felicity, by the women's prudence, foresight and ware government were both deceived and yet attained the chiefest benefit that mariage state doth looke for. So that, if search bee made amonges antiquities, it is to be doubted wheather greater chastity and better pollicy could be founde for accomplishment of an intended purpose.

Many deedes have ben done by women for savegard of their husbandes' lives, as that of the Minyae, a sort of women whose husbandes were imprisoned at Lacedaemon and for treason condemned, who, to save their lives, entred into prison the night before they should dy and, by exchange of apparell, delivered them and remained there to suffer for them; of Hipsicratea, also, the queene and wife of Mithridates, king of Pontus, who spared not hir noble beauty and golden lockes to manure hirselfe in the use of armes to keepe hir husband company in perils and daungers, and, being overcome by Pompeius and flying away, never left him unaccompanied ne forsooke sutch travaile as he himselfe sustained; the like also of Aemilia, Turia, Sulpitia, Portia and other Romane dames.[1] But that sutch have prevented their husband's folly, seldome we reade, saving of Queene Marie, the wife of Don Pietro, king of Arragon, who, marking the insolency of hir husband and sory for his disordred life, honest jealousye opening hir continent eyes forced hir to seeke meanes to remove his wanton acts or at least wise by pollicy and wise foresight to make him husbande and culture his own soile that for want of seasonable tillage was barren and voide of fruicte. Wherefore, consulting with the lord chamberlaine, who of custome brought whom the king liked best, was in place of his woman bestowed in his bed, and of her that night begat the yong Prince Giacomo, that afterwardes proved a valiaunte and wise king.[2] These passing good pollicies of women many times abolish the frantik lecherous fits of husbands gieven to superflu-ous lusts, when first by their chast behaviour and womanly patience they containe that which they be loth to see or heare of and then, demaunding counsell of sobriety and wisedome, excogitate sleights to shun folly and expell discurtesye by husbandes' carelesse use. Sutch practises and devises these two gentlewomen whom I now bringe forth disclose in this discourse ensuing.

In the city of Venice (which for riches and faire women excelleth all other within the region of Italy) in the time that Francesco Foscari, a very wise prince, did governe the state, there were two young gentlemen, the one called Girolamo Bembo and the other Anselmo Barbadico, betwene whom, as many times chaunceth amongs other, grew sutch great hatred and cruel hostility, as ech of them by secret and all possible meanes divised to doe other shame and displeasure, which kindled to sutch outrage, as it was thought impossible to be pacified.[3] It chaunced that at one time both of them did mary two noble young gentlewomen, excellent and faire, both brought up under one nurse and loved ech other like two sisters and as though they had been both borne of one body. The wife of Anselmo, called Isotta, was the daughter of messer Marco Gradenigo, a man of great estimation in that citty, one of the procuratours of San Marco, whereof there were not so great number in those dayes as there bee now, because the wisest men and best approved of life were chosen to that great and noble dignity, none allotted thereunto by bribes or ambition. The wife of Girolamo Bembo was called Lucia, the daughter of messer Gian Francesco Valerio, Cavaliere,[4] a gentleman very well learned, and many times sent by the state ambassador into divers countreys, and, after he had bene orator with the pope, for his wisedome in the execution of the same, was in great estimation with the whole citty.

The two gentlewomen, after they were maried and heard of the hatred betwene their husbandes, were very sorrowfull and pensive, because they thought the freendship and love betwene them twaine, continued from their tender yeares, could not bee but with greate difficulty kept or else altogither dissolved and broken; notwithstanding, being discrete and wise, for avoiding occasion of eche husbande's offence, determined to cease their accustomed conversation and lovinge familiarity and not to frequent other's company but at places and times convenient. To whom fortune was so favourable as not onely their houses were neere together but also adjoininge; in the backsides whereof their gardeins also confined, seperated onely with a little hedge, that every day they might see one another and many times talke together. Moreover the servauntes and people of either houses were freendly and familiar, which didde greately content the two lovinge gentlewomen, bicause they also, in the absence of their husbandes, mighte at pleasure in their gardens disport themselves.

And continuing this order the space of three yeares, neither of them within that terme were with childe. In which space Anselmo, many times viewing and casting his eyes upon madonna Lucia, fell earnestly in love with hir and was not that day well at ease wherein he had not beholden hir excellent beauty. She, that was of spirite and wit subtle, marked the lookes and maner of Anselmo; who, neither for love ne other cause, did render like lookes on him, but to see to what ende his loving cheere and countenaunce would tend. Notwithstanding, she seemed rather desirous to behold him than elswhere to imploye hir lookes. On the other side, the good behaviour, the wise order and pleasaunt beauty of madonna Isotta was so excellent and plausible in the sight of maister Girolamo as no lover in the world was better pleased with his beloved than he with hir; who, not able to live without the sweete sight of Isotta (that was a crafty and wily wench), was by hir quickly perceived. She, being right honest and wise, and loving hir husband very dearely, did beare that countenaunce to Girolamo that she generally did to any of the citty or to other straunger that she never saw before. But hir husband more and more inflamed, having lost the liberty of himselfe, wounded and pierced with the amorous arowes of love, coulde not convert his minde to any other but to mistresse Lucia.

These two women wonted to heare service every day ordinarily at the church of Sanfantino, bicause they lay long abed in the mornings, and, commonly, service in that church was said somewhat late, their pewes also somwhat distant one from an other. Whether their 2 amorous husbands continually used to follow them aloofe of and to place themselves where either of them might best view his beloved; by which custome they seemed to the common people to be jealous over their wives. But they prosecuted the matter in sutch wise as either of them, without shipping, sought to send other into Cornovale.[5]

It came to passe, then, that these 2 beloved gentlewomen, one knowing nothing of another's intent, determined to consider better of this love, because the great goodwill long time borne should not be interrupted. Uppon a certaine day when their husbands were abrode, resorting together to talk at their garden hedge according to their wonted manner, they began to be pleasaunte and merry, and, after lovinge salutations, mistresse Lucia spake these woordes unto hir companion: 'Isotta, my deare beloved sister, I have a tale to tell you of your husband that perchaunce will seeme straunger than anye newes that ever you heard.'

'And I' (answered mistresse Isotta). 'I have a story to tel you that wil make you no lesse to wonder than I at that which you have to say, and it may be will put you into some choler and chafe.'

'What is that?' quod the one and other.

In the ende, either of them told what practizes and love their husbands went about. Whereat, although they were in great rage for their husbandes' follye, yet, for the time, they laughed out the matter and thought that they were sufficient (as in very deede they were, a thing not to be doubted) and able to satisfye their husbands' hunger, and therewithall began to blame them and to say that they deserved to learn to play of the cornets, if they had no greater feare of God and care of honesty than their husbands had; then, after mutch talke of this matter, concluded that they should do wel to expect what their husbands would demaund. Having taken order as they thought meete, they agreed dailye to espye what shoulde chaunce and purposed first with sweete and pleasaunte lookes to baite and lure eche other feere to put them in hope therby that they should satisfye their desires; which done, for that time, they departed.

And when at the church at Sanfantino or other place in Venice they chanced to meete their lovers, they shewed unto them cheareful and mery countenaunce; which the lovers well noting were the gladdest men of the worlde. And, seeing that it was impossible in speache to utter their mindes, they purposed by letters to signify the same. And, having found purcivants to goe betwene parties (whereof this city was wont to be ful), either of them wrote an amorous letter to his beloved, the content whereof was that they were verye desirous secretly to talke with them, thereby to expresse the burninge affections that inwardly they bare them, which, without declaration and utterance by mouthe in their owne presence, woulde breede them torments more bitter than deathe. And within fewe dayes after (no great difference of time betweene) they wrote their letters.

But Girolamo Bembo, having a pregnant wit, who coulde well endite both in prose and rime, wrote an excellent sonnet in the praise of his darling in Italian meeter and with his letter sent the same unto hir; the effect whereof doth follow:[6]

> A lively face and pearcing beauty bright
> Hath linkt in love my sely sences all:
> A comely porte, a goodly shaped wight
> Hath made me slide that never thought to fall:
> Hir eyes, hir grace, hir deedes and maners milde,
> So straines my heart that love hath wit begilde.
>
> But not one dart of Cupide did me wounde,
> A hundred shaftes lights all on me at ones:
> As though Dame Kind some new devise had founde,[7]
> To teare my flesh, and crash atwo my bones:
> And yet I feele sutch joy in these my woes
> That as I die my sprite to pleasure goes.
>
> These newfound fits sutch change in me doe breede,
> I hate the day and draw to darknesse, lo!
> Yet by the lampe of beauty doe I feede

In dimmest dayes and darkest nights also,
Thus altring state and changing diet still,
I feele and know the force of Venus' will.

The best I finde, is that I doe confesse,
I love you, dame, whose beauty doth excell:
But yet a toy doth breede me some distresse,
For that I dread you will not love me well;
Than love yee wot shall rest in me alone,
And fleshly brest, shall beare a heart of stone.

O goddesse mine, yet heare my voice of ruthe,
And pitye him that heart presents to thee:
And if thou want a witnesse for my truth
Let sighes and teares my judge and record be,
Unto the ende a day may come in hast,
To make me thinke I spend no time in waste.

For nought prevailes in love to serve and sue
If full effect joine not with words at neede,
What is desire or any fansies newe
More than the winde? That spreades abroade in deede,
My words and works, shall both in one agree,
To pleasure hir, whose servaunt would I bee.

The subtill dames receiving those amorous letters and song,
disdanfully at the first seemed to take them at the bringers'
hands, as they had determined, yet afterwardes they shewed
better countenaunce. These letters were tossed from one to
another, whereat they made great pastime and thought that the
same would come to very good successe, either of theim
keepinge still their husbande's letter, and agreed without injury
done one to another trimly to deceive their husbands: the maner
how you shall perceive anone.

They devised to send word to their lovers that they were ready
at al times to satisfye their sutes, if the same might be secretly
done, and safely might make repaire unto their houses when
their husbands were absent, which in any wise, they saide, must
be done in the night, for feare least in the daytime they were
discried. Againe these provident and subtill women had taken
order with their maides, whom they made privy to their practise,
that through their gardens they should enter into other's house
and bee shut in their chambers without light, there to tary for

their husbands and by any meanes not to bee seene or knowne. This order prescribed and given, mistresse Lucia first did hir lover to understand that the night insuing at foure of the clock at the posterne dore, which should be left open, he should come into hir house, where hir maide should be ready to bring him up to hir chaumbre, because hir husband maister Girolamo woulde that night imbarke himselfe to goe to Padua. The like mistresse Isotta did to maister Girolamo, appointing him at five of the clock, which she said was a very convenient time, bicause maister Anselmo that night would sup and lie with certaine of his friends at Murano, a place besides Venice. Upon these newes, the 2 lovers thought themselves the most valiaunt and fortunate of the world; no enterprise now there was but seemed easye for them to bring to passe, yea if it were to expell the Saracens out of Hierusalem or to deprive the great Turke of his kingdome of Constantinople.[8] Their joy was sutch as they coulde not tell where they were, thinking every houre a whole day till night.

At length, the time was come so long desired, and the husbandes accordingly gave diligent attendaunce and let their wives to understande (or at leastwise beleeved they had) that they could not come home that night for matters of great importaunce. The women, that were very wise, seeing their ship saile with so prosperous winde, fained themselves to credite all that they offered. These young men tooke either of them his gondola (or as we tearm it their barge) to disport themselves, and, having supped abroade, rowed in the canali, which is the water that passeth through divers streates of the citty, expecting their appoincted houre. The women, ready at three of the clocke, repaired into their gardens, and, after they had talked and laughed together a prety while, went one into another's house and were by the maides brought up to the chaumbers. There either of them, the candle being light, began diligently to view the order and situation of the place, and by little and little marked the chiefest things they looked for, committing the same to memory.

Afterwards they put out the candle, and both in trembling maner expected the comming of their husbandes. And just at foure of the clocke the maiden of madonna Lucia stoode at the dore to waite for the comminge of maister Anselmo, who within a while after came and gladly was let in by the maide and by hir conducted up to hir bedside. The place there was

so dark as Hel and impossible for him to know his wife. The
two wives were so like of bignesse and speach as by darke
without great difficulty they could be known. When Anselmo
had put of his clothes, he was of his wife amorously intertained, thinking the wife of Girolamo had received him betwene hir armes, who above a thousande times kissed hir very
sweetely, and she for hir parte sweetely rendred againe to him
so many. What followed it were folly to describe.[9] Girolamo
likewise at 5 of the clocke appeared and was by the maide
conveyed up to the chamber, where he lay with his own wife, to
their great contentations.[10] Now, these 2 husbands, thinking
they had been imbraced by their beloved ladies, to seeme brave
and valiaunt men of warre, made greater proofe of their
manhoode than they were wont to do. At what time their wives
(as it pleased God to manifest by their delivery) were begotten
with child of 2 faire sons, and they the best contented women of
the world.

This practise continued betwene them many times, fewe
weekes passing but in this sort they lay together. Neither of
them for all this perceived themselves to be deluded or conceived
any suspition of collusion for that the chamber was still without
light, and in the day the women commonly failed not to be
together. The time was not longe but their bellies began to swell,
whereat their husbandes were exceeding joyfull, beleeving verily
that either of them had fixed hornes upon the other's head.
Howbeit the poore men, for all their false beliefe, had bestowed
their laboure uppon their owne soile, watred onely with the
course of their proper fountaine.

These two jolly wenches seeing themselves by this amorous
practize to be with childe, beganne to devise howe they might
break of the same, douting least some slaunder and ill talke
should rise and, thereby, the hatred and malice betwene their
husbandes increase to greater fury. And as they were aboute this
devise an occasion chaunced utterly to dissolve their accustomed
meetinges, but not in that sorte as they woulde have had it. For
the women determined, as merily they had begon, so jocundlye
to ende. But Fortune, the guide of humane life, disposeth all
enterprises after hir owne pleasure, who like a puissant lady
caryeth with hir the successe of eche attempte. The beginning
she offereth freely to him that list; the ende she calleth for as a
ransome or tribute payable unto hir.[11]

In the same streate, or as they call it rio, and canale, not farre from their houses, there dwelled a young woman very faire and comely, not fuly twenty yeares of age, which then was a widow and, a little before the wife of M. Niccolo Delphino and the daughter of M. Giovanni Moro, called Gismonda.[12] She, besides hir father's dowrye (which was more than a thousand pound), had left hir by hir husband, a great porcion of money, jewels, plate and houshold furnitures. With hir fell in love Aloisio Foscari, the nephewe of the duke, who, making greate sute to have hir to wife, consumed the time in beholding his ladye and at length had brought the matter to so good passe, as one nighte she was contented, at one of the windowes of hir house directly over againste a little lane, to heare him speake.

Aloisio, marvellous glad of those desired newes, at the appointed night, about five or sixe of the clocke, with a ladder made of roapes (bicause the window was very high) went thither alone. Being at the place and making a signe concluded uppon betweene them, attended when the gentlewoman should throw down hir cord to draw up the ladder accordingly as was appointed, which not longe after was done. Gismonda, when shee had received the ende of the ladder, tied it fast to the jawme of the window and gave a token to hir lover to mount. He, by force of love being very venturous, lively and lustely scaled the window. And when he was uppon the top of the same, desirous to caste himselfe in, to embrace his lady, and shee not readye to receive him or else uppon other occasion, he fel downe backe-warde, thinking as he fell to have saved himselfe twice or thrice by catching holde uppon the ladder, but it would not be. Notwithstanding, as God would have it, the poise of his body fell not uppon the pavement of the streate fully, but was stayed by some lets in the fall, which had it not bene so, no doubt he had bene slayne out of hande, but yet his bones were sore bruised and his heade deepely wounded.

The infortunate lover, seeing himselfe sore hurt with that pitifull fall, albeit hee thought that hee had received his death's wounde and impossible to live any longer, yet the love that he bare to the widow did so far surmount his paine and the griefe of his body sore crushed and broken, that, so well as he could, hee rose up and with his hands stayed the bloud that ranne from his heade, to the intente it mighte not raise some slaunder uppon the widow whom hee loved so wel, and went alonges the streate towarde the houses of Girolamo and Anselmo aforesaid. Being come thither with greate difficulty, not able to goe anye further for verye paine and griefe, hee fainted and fell downe as deade, where the bloude issued in sutch aboundaunce as the grounde therewith was greatly imbrued, and everyone that saw him thought him to be voide of life. Mistresse Gismonda, exceeding sorrowful for this mischaunce, doubted that he had broken his necke, but, when she saw him depart, she comforted him so well as she could and drewe up the ladder into hir chamber.

Sutch chaunces happen to earnest lovers, who, when they think they have scaled the top of their felicity, sodainly tomble downe into the pit of extreme despaire, that better it had been for them leisurely to expect the grace of their ladies at convenient place and houre than hardily without providence to adventure like desperat souldiers to clim the top of the vamure, without measuring the height of the wals or viewinge the substaunce of their ladders, do receive in the ende cruell repulse and fal down headlonge either by present death or mortall wounde, to receive everlasting reproche and shame.[13] But turne we againe now to this disgraced lover, who lay gasping betwene life and death. And as he was in this sorrowful state, one of the captaines, a nobleman appointed to see orders observed in the nighte, with his bande (which they call *zaffi*) came thither, and, finding him lying upon the ground, knew that it was Aloisio Foscari, and, causing him to be taken up from the place wher he lay (thinking he had ben dead), commanded that he should be conveyed into the church adjoining, which immediately was done. And when he had wel considered the place where hee was founde, hee doubted that either Girolamo Bembo or Anselmo Barbadico, before whose dores hee thought the murder committed, had killed him; which afterwards he beleved to be true, bicause he heard a certaine noise of menne's feete at one of their doores. Wherefore he devided his company, placing some on the one side of their houses and some on the other, besieging the same so well as he coulde. And as Fortune woulde, he founde by negligence of the maids the dores of the 2 houses open. It chaunced also that night that the two lovers one in other's house were gone to lie with their ladies, who hearinge the hurly-burly and sturre made in the house by the sergeants, sodainely the women lept out of their beds and, bearing their apparell uppon their shoulders, went home to their houses throughe their gardeins unseene of any and in fearefull wise did attende what should be the end of the same.

Girolamo and Anselmo, not knowing what rumor and noise that was, although they made hast in the darke to cloth themselves, were by the officers, without any field fought, apprehended in ech other's chamber, and remained prisoners at their mercy, whereat the captaine and his band did greatly marvell, knowing the hatred betweene them. But when torches and lights were brought and the two gentlemen caried out of doores, the wonder was the greater for that they perceived them almoste naked, and prisoners taken in eche other's house. And besides this admiration, sutch murmur and slaunder was bruted as the quality of everye vulgar heade coulde secretlye devise or imagine, but specially of the innocente women, who howe faultlesse they were, every man by what is saide before maye conceive, and yet the cancred stomackes of that troupe bare sutch malice againste them, as they jarred and brawled against them like currishe curres at straunge dogges whom they never sawe before.[14]

The gentlemen immediately were caried to prison, ignorant uppon what occasion. Afterwards, understandinge that they were committed for the murder of Aloisio Foscari and imprisoned like theeves, albeit they knew themselves guiltlesse of murder or theft, yet their grief and sorrowe was very greate, beinge certaine that all Venice should understande howe they, betweene whome had ben mortall hatred, were nowe become copartners of that which none but the true possessours ought to enjoy; and, althoughe they coulde not abide to speake together, like those that deadely did hate one another, yet both their mindes were fixed uppon one thought.

In the ende, conceiving fury and despite againste their wives, the place being so darke that no light or sunne coulde pierce into the same, whereby without shame or disdaine one of them began to speake to another, and with terrible othes they gave their faith to disclose the troth in what sort either of them was taken in other's chamber and frankely told the way and meane howe eche of them enjoyed his pleasure of other's wife. Whereupon the whole matter (according to their knowledge) was altogether by little and little manifest and knowne. Then they accompted their wives to be the most arrant strumpets within the whole city, by dispraising of whom their olde rancor was forgotten and they agreed together like two friends, who thought that for shame they should never be able to looke men in the face, ne yet to shew themselves openlye within the citye; for sorrow whereof, they deemed death the greatest good turne and best benefit that could chance unto them. To be short, seeing no meanes or occasion to comfort and relieve their pensive and heavy states, they fell into extreeme despaire; who, ashamed to live any longer, devised way to rid themselves of life, concluding to make themselves guilty of the murder of Aloisio Foscari. And after mutch talke betweene them of that cruell determination, still approving the same to be their best refuge, they expected nothing else, but when they should be examined before the magistrates.

Foscari, as is before declared, was carried into the churche for deade and the priest straightly charged with the keepinge of him; who caused him to be conveyed into the middes of the church, setting 2 torches alight, the one at his heade and the other at his feete. And when the company was gone, he determined to goe to bed the remnant of the night to take his rest, but before he went, seeing the torches were but short and could not last paste two or three houres, he lighted two other and set them in the others' place, for that it should seeme to his frends, if any chaunced to come, what care and worship he bestowed upon him.

The priest, ready to depart, perceived the body somewhat to move; with that, looking uppon his face, espied his eyes a little to begin to open. Wherewithall, somewhat afraide, he, crying out, ran awaye. Notwithstanding, his courage began to come to him again, and laying his hand upon his breast, perceived his heart to beate, and then 'twas out of doubt that he was not dead, although, by reason of losse of his bloud, he thought little life to remaine in him. Wherefore he with one of his fellow priests which was abed and the clerck of the parish caried maister Foscari so tenderly as they could into the priest's chamber, which adjoined next the church. Then he sente for a surgeon that dwelt hard by and required him diligently to search the wounde; who so well as he could purged the same from the corrupt bloud, and, perceiving it not to be mortall, so dressed it with oiles and other precious ointments, as Aloisio came again to himself. And when he had anointed that recovered body with certaine precious and comfortable oiles, he suffred him to take his rest. The priest also went to bed and slepte till it was daye; who, so soone as he was up, went to seeke the captaine to tel him that maister Aloisio was recovered.

The captaine at that time was gone to the pallace at San Marco to give the duke advertisement of this chaunce; after whom the priest went and was let into the duke's chamber, to whom he declared what he had done to Aloisio.[15] The duke, very glad to heare tell of his nephewe's life, although then very pensive for the newes broughte unto him by the captaine, intreated one of the *signor de notte* to take with him two of the best surgions and to call him that had already dressed his nephew to goe to visite the wounded gentleman, that hee might be certified of the truth of that chaunce.

All which together repaired to the prieste's chaumber, where, findinge him not asleepe and the wounde faire inoughe to heale, did thereunto what their cunning thoughte meete. And then they began to inquire of him, that was not yet full recovered to perfecte speache, howe that chaunce happened, telling him that he might frankelye confesse unto them the trouthe. The more diligent they were in this demaunde, bicause the surgeon that dressed him first alleaged that the wounde was not made with sworde but received by some greate fall, or blowe with mace or clubbe, or rather seemed to come of some high fall from a windowe, by reason his head was so grievously brused. Aloisio, hearinge the surgeon's sodaine demaunde, presentlye aunswered that he fell downe from a windowe and named also the house. And he had no sooner spoken those woordes but he was very angry with himselfe and sorrye. And wherewithall his dismayde spirites began to revive in sutch wise as sodainlye he choise rather to die than to speake anythinge to the dishonoure of mistresse Gismonda. Then the *signior di notte* asked him what he did thereaboute that time of the night, and wherfore hee did climb up to the windowe, beinge so highe. Which hee coulde not keepe secrete, considering the authoritye of the magistrate that demaunded the question, albeit hee thoughte that if his tongue hadde runne at large and committed a faulte by rashe speakinge, his bodye should therefore suffer the smart.

Wherefore before hee woulde in any wise give occasion to slaunder hir whome hee loved better than his owne life, deter-mined to hazarde his life and honoure to the mercye of justice and saide: 'I declared even nowe, which I cannot denye, that I fell downe from the windowe of mistresse Gismonda Mora. The cause thereof (beeinge now at state wherein I knowe not whether I shall live or die) I will truelye disclose. Mistresse Gismonda, beinge a widowe and a younge woman withoute anye man in hir house, bicause by reporte shee is very rich of jewels and money, I purposed to robbe and dispoile. Wherefore I devised a ladder to climbe up to hir windowe, with minde full bent to kill all those that should resiste me. But my mishappe was sutch as the ladder, being not well fastened, fell downe, and I myselfe therwithall; and, thinking to recover home to my lodging with my corded ladder, my spirites beganne to faile, and tombled downe I wotte not where.'

The *signor de notte*, whose name was Domenico Mariperto,[16] hearing him say so, marvelled greatly and was very sorye, that all they in the chamber, which were a great number (as at sutch chaunces commonly be), did heare those woordes. And, bicause they were spoken so openly, he was forced to saye unto him: 'Aloisio, it doth not a little grieve me that thou hast committed sutch follye, but for so mutch as sorrowe now will not serve to remedye the trespasse, I muste needes shew myselfe both faithfull to my countrey and also carefull of mine honor, withoute respect of persons. Wherefore thou shalte remaine here in sutch safe custody as I shal appoint, and when thou art better amended, thou must, according to desert, be referred to the gaole.'

Leaving him there under sure keeping, he went to the Counsell of the *Dieci*[17] (which magistrates in that city be of greatest authority) and, finding the lords in counsell, he opened the whole matter unto them. The presidentes of the counsell, which had hearde a great numbre of complaints of many theftes don in the night within the citye, tooke order that one of the captaines that were appointed to the diligente watche and keeping of Aloisio, remaining in the prieste's house, should cause him to be examined and with tormentes forced to tell the truth, for that they did verely beleeve that hee had committed many robberies besides, or at the least was privy and accessarye to the same and knew where the theves were become.

Afterwardes, the said counsell did sitte uppon the matter of Girolamo Bembo and Anselmo Barbadico, found at midnight naked in eche other's chambre and committed to prison as is before remembred. And bicause they had many matters besides of greater importaunce to consult uppon, amongs which the warres betwene them and Philippo Maria Visconte, duke of Milane,[18] the aforesaide causes were deferred till another time, notwithstanding in the meanewhile they were examined.

The duke himselfe, that time being in counsell, spake most severely against his nephew. Neverthelesse, he did hardly beleeve that his nephew, being very rich and indued with great honesty, would abase himselfe to a vice so vile and abhominable as theft is; whereuppon he began to consider of many thinges, and in the ende talked with his nephew secretly alone and by that meanes learned the trouth of the whole matter.

In like maner Anselmo and Girolamo were examined by commissioners appoincted by the state, what one of them did in another's chamber at that houre of the night, who confessed that many times they had seene Aloisio Foscari to passe up and down before their houses at times inconvenient, and that night by chaunce, one of them not knowing of another, espied Aloisio, thinking that he lingered about their houses to abuse one of their wives; for which cause they went out and with their weapons sodenly killed him. Which confession they openly declared accordingly, as whereupon before they were agreed. Afterwardes, with further circumstaunce being examined upon the article of being one in another's chaumber, it appeared that their first tale was utterly untrue. Of all which contradictions the duke was advertised and was driven into extreeme admiration, for that the truth of those disorders coulde not be to the full understanded and knowne.

Whereuppon the *Dieci* and the assistauntes were againe assembled in councell, according to the maner. At what time, after all things throughly were debated and ended, the duke, being a very grave man of excellent witte, advaunced to the dukedome by the consent of the whole state, as every of theim were about to rise up, hee saide unto them: 'My lordes, there resteth one thinge yet to be moved, which peradventure hitherto hath not bene thought upon. There are before us two complaints, the effect whereof in my judgement is not throughly conceived in the opinions of divers. Anselmo Barbadico and Girolamo Bembo, betwene whom there hath bene ever continuall hatred, left unto them, as a man may say, even by fathers' inheritance, both of them in either of their chaumbers were apprehended in a manner naked by our sergeaunts, and, without torments or for feare to bee racked, upon the onely interrogatories of oure ministers, they have voluntarily confessed that before their houses they killed Aloisio our nephew. And albeit that our saide nephew yet liveth and was not striken by them or any other as should appeare, yet they confesse themselves guilty of murder. What shall be said then to the matter? Doth it not seeme doubtfull?

'Our nephew again hath declared that in going about to rob the house of mistresse Gismonda Mora, whom he ment to have slaine, he fel downe to the ground from the top of a window; wherefore, by reason so many robberies have bene discovered within the citty, it may be presumed that hee was the theefe and malefactor who ought to be put to the torments, that the truth may be knowne, and, being found guilty, to feele the severe punishment that he hath deserved. Moreover, when he was found lying upon the ground, he had neither ladder nor weapon, whereupon may bee thought that the fact was otherwise done than hitherto is confessed.

'And because amongs morall vertues temperance is the chiefest and worthy of greatest commendation, and that justice not righteously executed is injustice and wronge, it is meete and convenient for us in these straunge accidents rather to use temperaunce than the rigor of justice. And that it may appeare that I do not speake these words without good grounde, marke what I shall saye unto you. These two most mortall enimies doe confesse that which is impossible to be true, for that our nephew (as is before declared) is alive and his wounde was not made by sworde, as hee himselfe hath confessed. Now, who can tell or say the contrary, but that shame for being taken in their severall chambers, and the dishonesty of both their wives, hath caused them to despise life and to desire death? We shall finde, if the matter be diligently inquired and searched, that it will fall out otherwise than is already supposed by common opinion. For the contrariety of examinations, unlikelihoode of circumstances and the impossibility of the cause rendreth the matter doubtfull. Wherefore it is very needeful diligently to examine these attempts and thereof to use more advised consideration.

'On the other side, our nephew accuseth himselfe to be a theefe and, which is more, that hee ment to kill mistresse Mora when hee brake into hir house. Under this grasse, my lords, as I suppose, some other serpent lieth hiden that is not yet thought of. The gentleman, yee know, before this time was never defamed of sutch outrage, ne suspected of the least offence that may be objected. Besides that, all yee doe know (thanks therefore be geven to almighty God) that he is a man of great richesse and possessions and hath no neede to rob. For what necessity should drive him to rob a widowe, that hath of his owne liberally to bestow upon the succour of widowes? Were there none els of substance in the citty for him to geve attempt but to a widdowe, a comfortlesse creature, contented with quiet life to live amonges hir family within the boundes of hir owne house? What if hir richesse, jewels and plate be great? Hath not Aloisio of his owne to redouble the same? But truly this robbery was done after some other manner than hee hath confessed. To us then, my lords, it appertaineth, if it so stande with your pleasures, to make further inquiry of the same, promisinge unto you uppon our faith that wee shall imploy our whole diligence in the true examination of this matter and hope to bring the same to sutch good ende as none shall have cause to blame us, the finall sentence whereof shall bee reserved to youre judgement.' This grave request and wise talke of the duke pleased greatly the lordes of the counsaile, who referred not onely the examination, but also the finall sentence, unto him.

Whereuppon the wise prince, beinge fully enformed of the chaunce happened to his nephewe, attended onely to make search if he could understand the occasion why Bembo and Barbadico so foolishly had accused themselves of that which they never did. And so, after mutch counsaile and great time contrived in their several examinations, his nephew then was well recovered and able to goe abroade, being set at liberty.

The duke then, havinge bestowed his travaile with the other two prisoners, communicated to the lords of the aforesaid councel called *Dieci* the whole trouth of the matter. Then he caused, with great discretion, proclamation to be made throughout Venice that Anselmo and Girolamo shold be beheded betwene the two pillers and Aloisio hanged, whereby he thought to know what sute the women would make, either with or against their husbandes, and what evidence mistresse Gismonda woulde geve against Aloisio. The brute hereof dispersed, divers talke thereuppon was raised and no communication of anything els in open streats and private houses but of the putting to death of those men. And bicause all three were of honorable houses, their kinsmen and friendes made sute by all possible meanes for their pardon. But their confessions published, the rumor was made worse (as it daily chaunceth in like cases) than the matter was indeede, and the fame was noised how Foscari had confessed so many theftes done by him at divers times as none of his freends or kin durst speake for him.

Mistresse Gismonda, which bitterly lamented the mischaunce of hir lover, after she understoode the confession hee had made and evidently knew that, because hee woulde not bleamish hir honour, he had rather willingly forgo his owne, and therewithall his life, felt hirselfe so oppressed with fervent love as shee was ready presently to surrender hir ghost. Wherefore shee sent him woorde that he should comfort himselfe, because shee was determined to manifest the very trouth of the matter and hoped, uppon hir declaration of true evidence, sentence shoulde bee revoked, for testimony whereof shee had his lovinge letters yet to shewe, written to hir with his owne handes, and would bring forth in the judgement place the corded ladder, which she had kept stil in her chamber. Aloisio, hearinge these loving newes and of the evidence which his lady woulde give for his defence, was the gladdest man of the worlde and caused infinite thankes to be rendred unto hir, with promise that, if hee might bee rid and discharged out of prison, he woulde take hir for his loving spouse and wife. Whereof the gentlewoman conceived singuler solace, loving hir deere freende with more entier affection than hir owne soule.

Mistresse Lucia and mistresse Isotta, hearing the dispercled voice of the death of their husbands, and understanding the case of mistresse Gismonda by another woman, laid their heads together likwise to divise meanes for saving their husbandes' lives and, entring into their barge, or gondola, wente to seeke mistresse Gismonda; and, when they had debated uppon the trouthe of these events, concluded with one assent to provide for the safegarde and deliverye of their husbandes, wherein they shewed themselves both wise and honest.

For what state is more honorable and of greater comforte than the married life, if indeede they that have yoaked themselves therein be conformable to those delightes and contentation which the same conduceth?[19] Wealth and riches maketh the true united couple to rejoice in the benefits of Fortune, graunted by the sender of the same, either of them providing for disposing thereof against the decripite time of olde age, and for the bestowing of the same uppon the fruicte accrued of their bodies. Poverty in any wise dothe not offend them, both of them glad to laboure and travaile like one body to sustaine their poore and neady life, either of them comfortably doth minister comforte in the cruell time of adversity, rendring humble thankes to God for his sharp rodde and punishment enflicted uppon them for their manifolde sinnes committed againste his majestye, travailinge by night and daye by sweatinge browes to get browne breade and drinke ful thin to cease the cries and pitifull cravinges of their tender babes, wrapt in cradle and instant on their mother to fill their hungry mouthes. Adverse fortune maketh not one to forsake the other. The loving wife ceaseth not by painfull sute to trot and go by night and day in heate and colde to relieve the miserye of hir husband. He likewise spareth not his paine to get and gaine the living of them both. He abrode and at home according to his called state, she at home to save the lucre of that labor and to doe sutch necessary travaile incident to the married kinde. He carefull for to get, she heedeful for to save, he by trafique and arte, shee by diligence and housholde toile. O the happy state of married folke! O surpassing delights of mariage bed! Which maketh these 2 poore gentlewomen, that by honorable pollicy saved the honor of themselves and honesty of their husbandes, to make humble sute for their preservation, who were like to be berieved of their greatest comforts.

But come we again to declare the last act of this comical discourse. These maried women, after this chaunce befell, upon their husbandes' imprisonment began to be abhorred of their friendes and parentes for that they were suspected to be dishoneste, by reason whereof dolefully lamenting their misfortune, notwithstandinge their owne conscience voide of faulte, did bid them to be of good cheere and comfort. And when the daye of execution came, they did their friends and parents to understand that their conceived opinion was untrue and prayed them to forbeare their disdain and malice till the truth should be throughly manifested, assuring them that in the end their owne innocencye and the guiltlesse crime of their husbands should openly be revealed to the worlde. In the meanetime they made request unto their friendes that one of the lordes called *Avogadori*[20] might be admitted to understande their case, the rest to be referred to themselves, wherein they had no neede either of proctor or advocate. This request seemed verye straunge to their friends, deeming their case to be shameful and abhominable; nevertheles, diligently they accomplished their request and, understanding that the counsell of the *Dieci* had committed the matter wholy to the duke, they made a supplication unto him in the name of the three gentlewomen, wherein they craved nothing else but their matter might be hearde. The duke, perceivying his advise like to take effect, assigned them a day, commaundinge them at that time before him and the lords of the councell and all the college of the estate to appeare.

The day being come, all the lordes assembled, desirous to see to what issue this matter would grow.

On the morning the three gentlewomen, honestly accompanied with other dames, went to the palace, and, goinge along the streate of San Marco, the people began to utter many railing words against them. Some cried out (as we see by unstable order the vulgare people in like cases use to do) and doinge a certain curtisy by way of disdain and mockery: 'Behold the honest women, that, without sending their husbands out of Venice, have placed them in the Castell of Cornetto,[21] and yet the arrante whoores bee not ashamed to shewe themselves abrode, as thoughe they hadde done a thinge that were honeste and praiseworthye.' Other shot forth their boltes, and with their proverbes proceeding from their malicious mouthes thwited the pore women at their pleasure. Other also seeing mistresse Gismonda in their company, thought that she went to declame against maister Aloisio Foscari, and none of them all hapned on the trouth. Arrived at the pallace, ascending the marble staires or steps of the same, they were brought into the great hal wher the duke appointed the matter to be heard. Thither repaired the friends and those of nearest kin to the three gentlewomen, and before the matter did begin, the duke caused also the thre prisoners to be brought thither. Thither also came many other gentlemen, with great desire to see the end of those events.

Silence being made, the duke, turning his face to the women, said unto them: 'Ye gentlewomen have made requeste by supplication to graunt you publike audience according to justice, for that you do alleage that law and order doth so require, and that every wel-ordred commonwealth condemneth no subjecte withoute due answere by order of lawe. Beholde, therefore, that we, desirous to do justice, bee ready in place to heare what ye can say.'

The two husbands were very angrye and wrathfull against their wives, and the more their stomackes did fret with choler and disdaine by how mutch they saw their impudente and shamelesse wives with sutch audacity to appeare before the majesty of a counsel so honourable and dreadfull, as though they had ben the most honeste and chast women of the world. The two honeste wives perceived the anger and displeasure of their husbands and for all that were not afraide ne yet dismayde, but smiling to themselves and somewhat moving their heads in decente wise seemed unto them as though they had mocked them. Anselmo, more angry and impacient then Girolamo, brake out into sutch furye as, had it not been for the majesty of the place and the companye of people to have stayed him, woulde have killed them. And seing he was not able to hurt them, he began to utter the vilest woords that he possibly could devise against them.

Mistresse Isotta, hearing hir husband so spitefully to spit forth his poison in the presence of that honourable assemblye, conceived courage and, cravinge licence of the duke to speake, with merrye countenance and good uttrance began thus to say her mind: 'Most excellent prince, and yee right honourable lordes, I doe perceive how my deare husbande uncomely and very dishonestly doth use himselfe against me in this noble company, thincking also that maister Girolamo Bembo is affected with like rage and minde against this gentlewoman mistresse Lucia his wife, although, more temperate in words, he do not expresse the same. Against whom if no reply be made, it may seeme that he doth well and hath spoken a truth, and that we by silence do condemne ourselves to be those most wicked women whom hee alleageth us to be. Wherefore by your gratious pardon and licence (most honourable) in the behalfe of mistresse Lucia and myselfe, for our defence I purpose to declare the effect of my minde, although my purpose be cleane altered from that I had thought to say, being now justly provoked by the unkinde behaviour of him whom I love better than myselfe, and whose disloyalty, had hee beene silent and not so rashly runne to the overthrow of me and my good name, coulde I have concealed, and onely touched that which had concerned the purgation and savegard of them both, which was the onely intent and meaning of us, by making our humble supplication to your majesties. Neverthelesse, so farre as my feeble force shall stretch, I will assay to do both the one and the other, although it be not appropriate to our kinde in publike place to declaime, nor yet to open sutch bold attempts, but that necessity of matter and oportunity of time and place dothe bolden us to enter into these termes, whereof we crave a thousand pardons for our unkindely dealings, and render double thanks to your honours for admitting us to speake.

'Be it knowne, therefore, unto you that our husbands against duety of love, lawes of mariage, and against all reason do make their heavy complaints, which by and by I will make plaine and evident. I am right well assured that their extreme rage and bitter hearts' sorrow do proceede of 2 occasions: the one, of the murder whereof they have falsely accused themselves; the other, of jealousye, which grievously doth gnawe their hearts, thinking us to be vile and abhominable women, because they were surprised in ech other's chaumber.

'Concerning the murder, if they have soiled their handes therein, it appertaineth unto you my lords to render their desert. But how can the same be laid to our charge, for so mutch as they (if it were done by them) committed the same without our knowledge, our help and counsel? And truly I see no cause why any of us ought to be burdened with the outrage, and mutch lesse cause have they to laye the same to our charge. For meete it is that he that doth any unlawful act, or is accessary to the same, should suffer the due penalty and severe chastisement accordingly as the sacred lawes do prescribe, to be an example for other to abstaine from wicked facts. But hereof what neede I to dispute, wherein the blind may see to bee none offence, because (thankes bee to God) maister Aloisio liveth, which declareth the fonde confession of our ungentil husbandes to bee contrary to trouth? And if so be our husbands indeede had done sutch an abhominable enterprise, reason and duety had moved us to sorrowe and lament them, because they be borne of noble bloud and be gentlemen of this noble citty, which like a pure virgin inviolably doth conserve hir lawes and customes. Great cause, I say, had we to lament them if like homicides, and murderers, they had spotted their bloud with sutch fowle bleamish thereby deserving death, to leave us yong women widowes in wofull plight.

'Nowe it behoveth me to speake of the jealousye they have conceived of us, for that they were in ech other's chamber, which truly is the doubtfull knot and scruple that forceth all their disdaine and griefe. This I knowe well is the naile that pierceth their heart. Other cause of offence they have not; who, like men not well advised, without examination of us and our demeanour, bee fallen into despaire and, like men desperate, have wrongfully accused themselves. But because I may not consume words in vaine, to stay you by my long discourse from matters of greater importaunce, I humbly beseech you (right excellent prince) to commaunde them to tell what thing it is which so bitterly doth torment them.'

Then the duke caused one of the noblemen assistaunt there to demaund of them the question. Who aunswered that the chiefest occasion was bicause they knew their wives to be harlots, whom they supposed to be very honest. And, forsomutch as they knew them to be sutch, they conceived sorrow and griefe, which with sutch extremity did gripe them at the heart as, not able to sustaine that great infamy, ashamed to be sene of men, were induced through desire of death to confesse that they never did.

Mistresse Isotta, hearing them say so, began to speak againe, turning hirselfe unto them: 'Were you offended then at a thinge which yee thought inconvenient and not meete to be done? Wee then have greatest cause to complaine. Why then, sweete husband, went you to the chaumber of mistresse Lucia at that time of the night? What had you to do there? What thing thought you to finde there more than was in your own house? And you maister Girolamo, what constrained you to forsake your wive's bed to come to my husband's, where no man ever had, or at this present hath, to do but himselfe? Were not the sheetes of the one so white, so fine, neate and sweete as the other?

'I am (most noble prince) sory to declare my husbande's folly and ashamed that hee should forsake my bed to go to another, that did accompt myselfe so well worthy to entertaine him in mine owne as the best wife in Venice; and now, through his abuse, I abstaine to shewe myselfe amonges the beautifull and noble dames of this citty. The like misliking of hirselfe is in mistresse Lucia, who (as you see) may be numbred amonges the fairest.

'Either of you ought to have bene contented with your wives, and not (as wickedly you have done) to forsake them to seeke for better breade than is made of wheate or for purer golde than whereof the angell is made.[22] O worthy deede of yours, that have the face to leave your owne wives that be comely, faire and honest, to seeke after straunge carrion! O beastly order of men that cannot conteine their lust within the boundes of their owne house, but must goe hunt after other women as beastes do after the nexte of their kinde that they chaunce uppon! What vile affection possessed your hearts to lust after other's wife? You make complainte of us, but wee with you have right good cause to be offended; you ought to bee grieved with your owne disorder and not with other's offence, and this your affliction patiently to beare, bicause you went about to beguile one another's love, like them that be weary and glutted with their owne fare, seekinge after other dainties more delicate if they were to be founde. But, praised be God and our provident discretion, if any hurt or shame hath chaunced, the same doth light on you.

'Moreover, I know no cause why men should have more liberty to doe evill than we women have; albeit, through the weaknes and cowardise of our sexe, yee men will doe what ye list. But ye be now no lords, not we servaunts, and husbands we do you call bicause the holy lawes of matrimony (which was the first Sacrament given by God to men after the creation of the worlde) doe require equall faith, and so well is the husband bound to the wife as she unto him. Go to, then, and make your complaint; the next asse or beast ye meete take hir to be your wife. Why do yee not know that the balance of justice is equall and wayeth downe no more of one side than of other? But let us nowe leave of to reason of this matter and come to that for which we be come hither.

'Two things (most righteous prince) have moved us to come before your majesty and all this honourable assembly, which had they not bene we would have bene ashamed to shewe our faces, and lesse presumed to speake or once to open our lippes in this noble audience, which is a place only meete for them that be most expert and eloquent orators, and not for us, to whom the needle and distaffe be more requisite. The first cause that forced us to come forth of our owne house was to let you understand that our husbands be no murderers, as is supposed, neither of this gentleman present maister Aloisio, ne yet of any man els; and thereof we have sufficient and worthy testimony.

But herein we neede not to travaile mutch, or to use many wordes. For neither maister Aloisio is slaine, ne any other murdred that is known or manifest hitherto. One thing resteth, which is that madonna Lucia and I do humbly beseech youre excellente majestye that youre grace, and the authoritye of the right honourable lords here present, will vouchsafe to reconcile us to our husbands, that we may obtaine pardon and favor at their handes, bicause we have so manifestly made their acts to appeare, and for that we be the offence, and they the offendours, and yet by their owne occasions we have committed the error (if it may be so termed.)

'And now to come to the conclusion, I doe remember, sithens I was a childe, that I have heard the gentlewoman my mother saye (whose soule God pardon) many times unto me and other my sisters and to mistresse Lucia, that was brought up with us, being by hir instructed in divers good and vertuous lessons, that all the honor a woman can doe unto hir husband, whereby she beautifieth him and his whole race and family, consisteth in hir honest, chast and vertuous life, without which, she oughte rather to die than live. And that a gentleman's wife, when she hath given hir body to the use of another man, is the common marke for every man to point at in the streate where she goeth, hir husband therby incurring reproche and shame, which no doubt is the greatest injury and scorne that an honest gentleman can receive and the moste shamefull reproche that can deface his house. Which lesson we so well remembring, desirous not to suffer the carelesse and unbrideled appetites of our husbandes to be unrained and runne at large to some dishonest ende, by a faithfull and commendable pollicy did provide for the mischiefe that mighte ensue.

'I neede not heere rehearse the enimitye and debate that manye yeares did raigne betweene our husbandes' fathers, bicause it is knowne to the whole city. Wee too, therefore, here presente, the wives of those noble gentlemen, brought up together from oure cradle, perceiving the malice betwene our husbandes, made a vertue of necessity, deeminge it better for us to lose our sweete and auncient conversation, than to minister cause of disquietnesse. But the nearenesse of our houses would not that naturall hatred shoulde defraude and take away olde ingrafted amity. Wherefore many times when our husbands were gone forth we met together and talked in our gardens, betwene which there is but a slender hedge beset with primme and roses,[23] which commoditye in their absence we did discretly use. And as sometimes for pleasure we walked with oure husbandes there, ye' (shee turninge unto them) 'did cast your eyes upon ech other's wife, and were straighteway in love, or else perchance you fained yourselves to bee. Which espied by us, many times betwene ourselves did devise uppon the same, and red your amorous letters and sonnet sent unto us. For which disloyalty and treason toward us your wives we sought no dishonour to youre persons; wee were content to suffer you to bee abused with your fond love. We blabbed it not abroade to our gossips, as many leude and fantasticall women bee wont to doe, thereby to raise slaunder to our husbands and to sturre up ill reporte upon them, whose infirmities it becommeth us to conceale and hide. We devised meanes by some other way to let you understand your fault, and did cast upon you many times right lovinge lookes. Which, although it were againste our owne desire, yet the cause and full conclusion of the same was to practise, if it were possible, to make you frendes.

'But consideringe that this love and allurementes of either parts could not tend to other end, as wee conjectured, but to increase displeasure and to put the swords into your handes, we therefore consulted, and uniformely in one minde agreed for the appeasinge and satisfaction of all partes. At sutch nightes as ye fained to go into divers places about earnest affaires, as yee alleaged, mistresse Lucia with the help of Cassandra my maide, through the gardeine came into my chamber, and I, by meanes of Jane hir maide, by like way repaired unto hirs. And yee, poore men, guided by our maides were brought unto your chambers where ye lay with your owne wives, and so by tilth of other's land in straunge soile (as yee beleeved) yee lost no labour. And bicause your embracements then were like to those atchieved by amorous gentlemen, usinge us with more earnest desire than you were wont to do, both wee were begotten with childe. Which ought to be very gladsome and gratefull unto you, if yee were so faine to have children as yee shewed yourselves to bee.

'If, then, none other offence doth grieve you, if remorse of conscience for other cause doeth not offend you, if none other sorrowe doeth displease you, gieve over your griefe. Remit your displeasure. Be glad and joyfull. Thanke us for our pollicy and pleasaunt disport that wee made you. If hitherto yee have been enimies, henceforth be frends; put of that auncient mallice so long continued, mitigate your hatefull moode, and live yee from henceforth like friendly gentlemen; yelde up your rancor into the lap of your countrey, that shee may put him in exile for ever, who like a pitifull and loving mother woulde gladly see all hir children of one accorde and minde.[24] Which if yee doe (ye shall do singulare pleasure to your friendes), ye shall doe great discomfort to your foes, yee shall do singular good to the commonwealth, yee shall doe greatest benefit to yourselves, ye shall make us humble wives, yee shall encrease your posterity, yee shall be praised of all men, and finally shall depart the best contented that ever the world brought forth.

'And now, because yee shall not thinke that wee have picked out this tale at our fingers' ends, thereby to seeke your savegard and our owne fame and praise, beholde the letters which you sent us; beholde your owne handes subscribed to the same; beholde your seales assigned thereunto, which shall render true testimony of that which unfainedly we have affirmed.' Then both delivered their letters, which viewed and seene were well knowne to be their owne husbands' hands, and the same so well approved her tale as their husbands were the gladdest men of the world and the duke and seignory marvailously satisfied and contented. Insomutch as the whole assembly with one voice cried out for their husbands' deliveraunce. And so, with the consent of the duke and the whole seignory, they were clearly discharged.

The parents, cosins and friends of the husbands and wives were wonderfully amazed to heere this long history and greatly praised the maner of their delivery, accoumpting the women to be very wise, and mistresse Isotta to be an eloquent gentle-woman for that shee had so well defended the cause of their husbands and of themselves. Anselmo and Girolamo openly in the presence of all the people embraced and kissed their wives with great rejoising. And then the husbands shaked one another by the hands, betwene whom began a brotherly accorde, and from that time forth lived in perfect amity and friendship, exchaunging the wanton love that either of them bare to other's wife into brotherly friendship, to the great delight of the whole citty.

When the multitude assembled to heare this matter throughly

was satisfied, the duke with cheerefull countenaunce lookinge toward Gismonda, saide thus unto hir: 'And you, faire gentlewoman, what have you to say? Bee bolde to utter your minde, and wee wil gladly heare you.'

Mistresse Gilsmonda, bashfull to speake, began wonderfully to blush, into whose cheekes entred an orient rud, intermixed with an alabaster white, which made her countenaunce more amiable than it was wont to be. After she had stode still awhile with hir eyes declined towards the ground, in comly wise lifting them up againe with shamefast audacity, she began thus to speake: 'If I, most noble prince, in open audience should attempt to discourse of love, whereof I never had experience or knew what thing it was, I should be doubtfull what to say thereof, and peradventure durst not open my mouth at al. But hearing my father (of worthy memory) many times to tel that your majesty in the time of your youth disdained not to open your heart to receive the amorous flames of love, and being assured that there is none but that doth love little or mutch, I do not doubt but for the words which I shal speake to obtaine both pity and pardon.

'To come then to the matter: God, I thanke him of his goodnesse, hath not permitted me to bee one of those women that like hypocrites do mumble their Paternoster to saincts, appearing outwardly to be devout and holy, and in fruict doe bring forth devils and al kinds of vices, specially ingratitude, which is a vice that doth suck and dry up the fountaine of godly piety. Life is deare to mee (as naturally it is to all) next which I esteeme mine honor, which is to be preferred before life, bicause without honor life is of no regard. And where man and woman do live in shame notorious to the world, the same may be termed a living death rather than a life.

'But the love that I beare to mine onely beloved Aloisio here present I do esteeme above al the jewels and treasures of the world, whose personage I do regard more than mine owne life. The reason that moveth me thereto is very great, for before that I loved him or ever ment to fixe my mind that way, he dearely regarded me, continually devising which way he might win and obtain my love, sparing no travel by night and day to seeke the same. For which tender affection should I shew myself unkind and forward? God forbid. And to be plain with your honors, he is more deare and acceptable unto me than the balles of mine own eyes, being the chiefest things that appertain to the furniture of the body of man, without which no earthly thing can be gladsome and joyful to the sense and feelings. Last of all, his amorous and affectionate demonstration of his love towards me, by declaringe himselfe to be carefull of mine honor, rather more willinge to bestow his owne than to suffer the same to be touched with the least suspicion of dishonesty, I cannot choose but so faithfully imbrace as I am ready to guage my life for his sake rather than his finger shoulde ake for offence.

'And where hath there bene ever found sutch liberality in any lover? What is he that hath bene ever so prodigall to employ his life (the most speciall pledge in this worlde) rather than hee would suffer his beloved to incurre dishonoure? Many histories have I red and chronicles of our time, and yet I have found few or none comparable unto this gentleman, the like of whom be so rare and seldome as white crowes, or swannes of colour blacke. O singuler liberality, never hearde of before! O fact that can never be sufficiently praised! O true love most unfained! Maister Aloisio, rather than he would have my fame any one iote to be impaired, or to suffer any shadow of suspition to bleamish the same, frankly hath confessed himselfe to be a theefe and murdrer, regardinge mee and mine honor more than himselfe and life. And albeit that he might a thousand wayes have saved himselfe without the imprisonment and adversity which he hath sustained, neverthelesse, after he had said, beinge then past remembrance through the fall, that he fell downe from my window, and perceived how mutch that confession would prejudice and hurt my good name and hurt the known honesty of the same, of his goodwill did chose to die rather than to speake any words that might breede ill opinion of mee, or the least thinge of the worlde that might ingender infamy and slaunder. And therefore, not able to revoke the words hee had spoken of the fall, nor by any meanes coulde coloure the same, hee thought to save the good name of another by his owne hurt.

'If he then thus redily and liberally hath protruded his life into manifest daunger for my benefit and saveguard, preferring mine honour above the care of himselfe, shall not I abandon all that I have, yea and therewithall hazard mine honor for his salvation? But what? Shall I disdaine bountifully to imploy myselfe and all the endevor of my frendes for his delivery? No, no (my lords) if I had a thousand lives and so many honors at my commaundement, I woulde give them al for his releife and comfort, yea if it were possible for me to recover afresh 1,000,000 lives, I woulde so frankly bestow them all, as ever I desired to live, that I might enjoy mine owne Aloisio. But I am sorry, and ever shal be sorry, for that it is not lawful for me to do more for him, than that which my power and possibility is able. For if he should die, truely my life could not endure; if he were deprived of life, what pleasure should I have to live in this world after him? Whereby (most honorable and righteous judge) I beleeve, before the honest not to loose any one iote of mine honor, bicause I being (as you may see) a younge woman and a widow desirous to marry againe, it is lawful for me to love and to bee beloved, for none other intent (whereof God is the onely judge) but to attaine a husbande according to my degre. But if I should lose my reputation and honor, why should not I adventure the same for him that hath not spared his own for me?

'Now to come to the effect of the matter: I do say with al dutifull reverence that it is an accusation altogither false and untrue that ever maister Aloisio came to my house as a theefe against my wil. For what neede he to be a thefe, or what nede had he of my goodes, that is a lorde and owner of twenty times so mutch as I have? Alas, good gentleman, I dare depose and guage my life that he never thoughte, mutch lesse did, any robbery or thing unlawful wherewith justly he may be charged, but he repaired to my house with my consent as a loving and affectionate lover, the circumstance whereof, if it be duly marked, must advouch the same to be of trouth infallible. For if I had not given him licence to come, how was it possible for him to convey his ladder so high, that was made but of ropes, and to fasten the same to the jaume of the window if none within did helpe him? Againe, howe could the window of the chaumber be open at that time of the night, which is still kept shut, if it had not bene by my consent? But I with the helpe of my maide threwe downe to him a little rope, whereunto he tied his ladder, and drewe the same up, and making it so fast, as it could not undo, gave a signe for him to mounte. But as both our ill-fortune would have it, before I could catch any hold of him, to mine inestimable griefe and hart's sorrow he fell downe to the ground.

'Wherefore (my lords) I beseech your honours to revoke the confession wherein he hath made himselfe to be a theefe. And you, maister Aloisio, declare the trouth as it was, sith I am not ashamed in this honourable assemble to tel the same. Beholde the letters (my lordes) which so many times he wrote unto me, wherein hee made suite to come to my speache, and continually in the same doth call me wife. Beholde the ladder, which till nowe did still remaine in my chaumber. Beholde my maide which in all mine affaires is, as it were, mine owne hande and helper.'

Aloisio being hereupon demaunded by the lordes of the articles which she in hir tale had recited, confessed them al to be true; who also at the same instant was discharged. The duke greatly commended them both: hir for hir stoute audacity in defence of an innocent gentleman, and him for his honour and modesty by seeking to preserve the fame and good reporte of a vertuouse gentlewoman. Which done, the Counsell disassembled and brake up. And the friendes of both the parties accompanied them home to the house of mistresse Gismonda, where, to the great rejoice and pleasure of all men, they were solemnely maried in sumptuous and honourable wise, and Aloisio with his wife lived in great prosperity long time after. Mistresse Lucia and mistresse Isotta, at the expired time, were delivered of two goodly sonnes, in whom the fathers tooke great joy and delight. Who with their wives after that time lived very quietly and well, one loving another like naturall brethren, many times sporting among themselves discretely at the deceipts of their wives. The wisedome of the duke also was wonderfully extolled and commended of all men, the fame whereof was increased and bruted throughout the region of Italy. And not without cause. For by his prudence and advise the dominion of the state and commonwealth was amplified and dilated. And yet in th'ende beeing old and impotent, they unkindly deposed him from his dukedom.

THE LADY OF BOEME

*Two barons of Hungarye, assuring themselves to
obtain their sute to a faire lady of Boeme, received
of hir a straung and marvelous repulse, to their great
shame and infamy, cursinge the time that ever they
adventured an enterprise so foolish.*

Penelope, the woful wife of absent Ulysses, in hir tedious longing
for the home retourne of that hir adventurous knight, assailed
with carefull heart amid the troupe of amorous suters and
within the bowels of hir royall pallace, deserved no greater fame
for hir valiaunt encountries and stoute defence of the invincible
and adamant fort of hir chastity than this Boeme lady doth by
resisting two mighty barrons that canoned the walles and well-
mured rampart of hir pudicity.[1] For, being threatned in his
prince's court (whether al the well-trained crew of eche science
and profession did make repaire), being menaced by Venus'
band – which not onely summoned hir fort and gave hir a
camisado by thick *al' armes*, but also forced the place by fierce
assault – she, like a couragious and politike captaine, gave those
brave and lusty souldiers a fowle repulse and, in end taking
them captives, urged them for their victuals to fall to woman's
toile, more shamefull than shamelesse Sardanapalus amid his
amorous troupe.[2]

I neede not amplifye by length of preamble the fame of this
Boeme lady, nor yet briefly recompt the triumph of hir victory.
Vaine it were also by glorious hymnes to chaunte the wisedome
of hir beleving maake, who – not carelesse of hir life – employed
his care to serve his prince and by service atchieved the cause
that drave him to a souldier's state. But yet, for trustlesse faith
in the prime conference of his future porte,[3] hee consulted with
a Pollaco for a compounded drugge to ease his suspect mind;
which medicine so eased his maladye as it not onely preserved

him from the infected humour,[4] but also made hir happy for
ever. Sutch fall the events of valiaunt mindes, though many
times mother Jealosye (that cancred witch) steppeth in hir foote
to anoy the well-disposed heart. For had he joined to his
valiaunce credite of his lovinge wife without the blinde advise of
sutch as professe that blacke and lying science, double glorye
hee had gained: once for endevoring by service to seeke honour,
the seconde for absolute truste in hir that never ment to beguile
him, as by hir firste aunswere to his first motion appeareth.

But what is to be objected against the barons? Let them
answere for their fault in this discourse ensuing, which so
lessoneth all noble mindes as warely they ought to beware how
they adventure upon the honour of ladies, who bee not altogither of one selfe and yelding trampe, but wel forged and
steeled in the shamefast shoppe of loyaltye – which armure
defendeth them against the fond skirmishes and unconsidred
conflicts of Venus' wanton band. The majesties also of the king
and queene are to be advaunced above the starres for their wise
dissuasion of those noblemen from their hot and hedlesse
enterprise and then their justice for due execution of their
forfait. The particularity of which discourse in this wise doth
beginne.

Mathie Corvine, sometime king of Hungarye, aboute the
yeare of Oure Lorde 1458, was a valiaunt man of warre and of
goodly personage. Hee was the first that was famous or feared
of the Turks of any prince that governed that kingdome. And,
amongs other his vertues, so well in armes and letters as in
liberallity and curtesye he excelled al the princes that raigned in
his time. He had to wife Queene Beatrice of Arragon, the
daughter of olde Ferdinando, king of Naples, and sister to the
mother of Alphonsus, duke of Ferrara, who in learning, good
conditions and all other vertues generally dispersed in hir was a
surpassing princesse and shewed hirself not onely a curteous
and liberall gentlewoman to King Mathie hir husband but to all
other that for vertue seemed worthy of honour and reward.[5] In
sutch wise as to the court of these two noble princes repaired
the most notable men of al nations that were given to any kind
of good exercise, and every of them (according to their desert
and degree) welcomed and entertained.

It chaunced in this time that a knight of Boeme, the vassal of
Kinge Mathie (for that he was likewise king of that countrey),

born of a noble house, very valiant and wel exercised in armes, fell in love with a passing faire gentlewoman of like nobility and reputed to be the fairest of al the country, and had a brother that was but a pore gentleman, not lucky to the goods of fortune. This Boemian knight was also not very rich, having onely a castle, with certain revenues therunto, which was scarce able to yeld unto him any great maintenance of living. Falling in love, then, with this faire gentlewoman, he demaunded hir in mariage of hir brother and with hir had but a very little dowrye. And this knight, not wel forseeing his poore estate, brought his wife home to his house, and there, at more leisure considering the same, began to fele his lacke and penury and how hardly and scant his revenues were able to maintein his port. He was a very honest and gentle person and one that delighted not by any meanes to burden and fine his tenants, contenting himself with that revenue which his ancesters left him, the same amounting to no great yerely rent.

When this gentleman perceived that he stode in neede of extraordinary reliefe, after many and divers considerations with himself, he purposed to folow the court and to serve King Mathie, his soverain lord and master, there by his diligence and experience to seke meanes for ability to sustaine his wife and himself. But so great and fervent was the love that he bare unto his lady as he thought it impossible for him to live one houre without hir, and yet judged it not best to have hir with him to the court, for avoidinge of further charges incidente to courting ladies, whose delight and pleasure resteth in the toyes and tricks of the same that cannot be wel avoided in poore gentlemen without their names in the mercer's or draper's jornals, a heavy thing for them to consider, if for their disport they like to walke the stretes.[6] The daily thinking thereupon brought the poore gentleman to great sorrow and heavinesse.

The lady, that was young, wise and discrete, marking the maner of hir husband, feared that he had some misliking of hir. Wherefore, upon a day, she thus said unto him: 'Dere husband, willingly would I desire a good turne at your hand, if I wist I should not displease you.'

'Demaund what you will', said the knighte, 'if I can, I shall gladly performe it, bicause I do esteeme your satisfaction as I do mine owne life.'

Then the lady very sobrely prayed him that he would open

unto hir the cause of that discontentment which hee shewed outwardly to have, for that his mind and behaviour seemed to bee contrary to ordinary custome and contrived daye and nighte in sighes, avoidinge the company of them that were wont specially to delight him.

The knight, hearing his ladye's request, paused a while and then said unto hir: 'My wel-beloved wife, forsomutch as you desire to understand my thoughte and minde and whereof it commeth that I am sad and pensife, I will tell you. All the heavinesse wherewith you see me to be affected doth tend to this end: faine would I devise that you and I may in honour live together according to our calling. For, in respect of our parentage, our livelode is very slender; the occasion whereof were our parents, who morgaged their lands and consumed a great part of their goods that our auncestors lefte them. I, daily thinking hereupon and conceiving in my head divers imaginations, can devise no meanes but one that in my fansye seemeth best, which is that I go to the court of our soveraine lord Mathie, who at this present is inferring warres upon the Turk, at whose hands I do not mistrust to receive good intertainment, beinge a most liberal prince and one that esteemeth al sutch as be valiant and active. And I for my parte will so governe myselfe (by God's grace) that by deserte I will procure sutch living and favour as hereafter we may live in oure old wayes a quiet life to oure great stay and comforte. For althoughe Fortune hitherto hath not favoured that state of parentage whereof we be, I doubt not with noble courage to win that, in despite of Fortune's teeth, which obstinately hitherto she hath denied. And the more assured am I of this determination because at other times I have served under the vaivoda in Transylvania against the Turke, where many times I have bene required to serve also in the courte by that honourable gentleman the counte of Cilia.[7] But when I did consider the beloved company of you (deare wife), the swetest companion that ever wight possessed, I thought it unpossible for me to forbeare your presence, which if I should doe I were worthy to sustaine that dishonour which a great number of carelesse gentlemen doe who, following their private gaine and will, abandon their young and faire wives, neglectinge the fire which nature hath instilled to the delicate bodies of sutch tender creatures. Fearing therewithall that, so soone as I shoulde depart, the lusty yong barons and gentlemen of the countrey would pursue the gaine of that love (the price whereof I do esteeme above the crowne of the greatest emperour in all the world and woulde not forgoe for all the riches and precious jewels in the fertile soile of Arabie) who no doubte would swarme togethir in greater heapes than ever did the wowers of Penelope within the famous graunge of Ithaca, the house of wandering Ulysses. Which pursute if they did attaine, I shoulde for ever hereafter be ashamed to shewe my face before those that be of valour and regard. And this is the whole effect of the scruple (sweete wife) that hindreth me to seeke for our better estate and fortune.' When he had spoken these words, he held his peace.

The gentlewoman, which was wise and stout, perceiving the great love that her husband bare hir, when hee had stayed himselfe from talke, with good and merry countenance answered him in this wise: 'Sir Ulrico' (which was the name of the gentleman) 'I, in like manner as you have done, have devised and thoughte upon the nobilitye and birth of our auncestors, from whose state and port (and that without oure fault and crime) we be far wide and devided. Notwithstanding, I determined to set a good face upon the matter and to make so mutch of our painted sheath as I could. Indeede, I confesse myselfe to be a woman and you men doe say that women's heartes be faint and feeble.[8] But to bee plaine with you, the contrary is in me; my hearte is so stoute and ambitious as peradventure not meete and consonant to power and ability, although we women will finde no lacke if our hartes have pith and strength inough to beare it out. And faine woulde I support the state wherein my mother maintained me. Howebeit, for mine owne part (to God I yeld the thanks) I can so moderate and stay my little great heart that contented and satisfied I can be with that which your abilitye can beare and pleasure commaund.

'But to come to the point, I say that debating with myselfe of our state as you full wisely do, I do verily think that (you being a yong gentleman, lusty and valiaunt) no better remedy or devise can be found than for you to aspire and seeke the king's favor and service. And it must needes rise and redounde to your gaine and preferment, for that I heare you say the king's majestye doth already knowe you. Wherefore I do suppose that his grace (a skilfull gentleman to way and esteeme the vertue and valor of ech man) cannot chose but reward and recompence the well-doer, to his singular contentation and comfort. Of this mine opinion I durst not before this time utter word or signe for feare of your displeasure. But nowe, sith yourselfe hath opened the way and meanes, I have presumed to discover the same; do what shal seeme best unto your good pleasure.

'And I, for my parte, although that I am a woman (accordingly as I saied even now) that by nature am desirous of honor and to shew myselfe abrode more rich and sumptuous than other, yet in respect of our fortune, I shall be contented so long as I live to continue with you in this our castell, where, by the grace of God, I will not faile to serve, love and obey you and to keepe your house in that moderate sorte as the revenues shall be able to maintaine the same. And no doubt but that poore living we have orderly used shal be sufficient to finde us two and five or sixe servaunts with a couple of horse, and so to live a quiet and merry life. If God doe send us any children, til they come to lawfull age we will, with our poore living, bring them us so well as wee can and then to prefer them to some noblemen's services, with whome by God's grace they may acquire honoure and living to keepe them in their aged dayes. And I doe trust that wee two shall use sutch mutuall love and rejoice that so long as our life doth last in wealth and woe our contented mindes shall rest satisfied.

'But I, waying the stoutnesse of your minde, doe know that you esteeme more an ounce of honor than all the golde that is in the world. For as your birth is noble, so is your heart and stomacke. And, therefore, many times seeing your great heavinesse and manifolde muses and studies, I have wondred with myselfe whereof they should proceede, and, amongs other my conceipts, I thought that either my behavior and order of dealing or my personage did not like you, or else that your wonted gentle minde and disposition had ben altered and transformed into some other nature. Many times, also, I was contente to thinke that the cause of your disquiet minde did rise uppon the disuse of armes, wherein you were wonte dailye to accustome youreselfe amonges the troupes of the honourable, a company indede most worthy of your presence.

'Revolving many times these and sutchlike cogitations, I have sought meanes by sutch alurementes as I could devise to ease and mitigate your troubled minde and to withdraw the great unquiet and care wherewith I sawe you to be affected. Bicause I do esteeme you above all the worlde, deeming your onely griefe to be my double paine, your aking finger a fervent fever fit, and the least woe you can sustaine moste bitter death to me that loveth you more dearelye than myselfe. And, for that I doe perceive you are determined to serve our noble king, the sorrowe which without doubte will assaile mee by reason of your absence I will sweeten and lenifye with contentation to see your commendable desire appeased and quiet. And the pleasaunt memory of your valiaunt facts beguile my pensife thoughts, hoping our nexte meeting shall bee more joyfull than this our disjunction and departure heavy.

'And where you doubt of the confluence and repaire of the dishoneste which shall attempt the winning and subduing of mine heart and unspotted bodye, hitherto inviolably kepte from the touch of any person, cast from you that feare, expel from your minde that fonde conceipt; for death shall sooner close these mortall eyes than my chastitye shall bee defiled. For pledge whereof I have none other thing to give but my true and simple faith, which, if you dare trust it, shal hereafter appeare so firme and inviolable as no sparke of suspition shal enter your careful minde, which I may wel terme to be carefull bicause some care beforehand doth rise of my behavior in your absence. The triall wherefore shall yelde sure evidence and testimony by passing my careful life (which I may with better cause so terme in your absence) that, God knoweth, wil be right pensife and carefull unto mee, who joyeth in nothinge else but in your welfare. Neverthelesse, all meanes and wayes shall bee agreeable unto my minde for your assurance and shall breede in me a wonderful contentation, which lusteth after nothing but your satisfaction. And if you list to close me up in one of the castell towers til your return, right glad I am there to continue an ankresse life,[9] so that the same may ease your desired mind.'

The knight, with great delight, gave ear to the aunswere of his wife, and when she had ended hir talke he began to reply unto hir: 'My wel-beloved, I doe like wel and greatly commended the stoutnesse of your heart. It pleaseth me greatly to see the same agreeable unto mine. You have lightned the same from inestimable woe by understanding your conceived purpose and determination to gard and preserve your honor (praying you therein to persevere), still remembering that when a woman hath lost hir honor, shee hath forgone the chiefest jewel she hath in this life and deserveth no longer to be called woman.

'And touching my talke proposed unto you, although it be of great importaunce, yet I meane not to depart so soone. But if it do come to effect, I assure thee, wife, I will leave thee lady and mistresse of all that I have. In the meanetime I will consider better of my businesse and consult with my friendes and kinsmen, and then determine what is best to be done. Til when, let us live and spend our time so merely as we can.'

To bee shorte, there was nothing that so mutch molested the knight as the doubt he had of his wife, for that she was a very fine and faire yong gentlewoman. And, therefore, he stil devised and imagined what assurance he might finde of hir behavior in his absence.

And, resting in this imagination, not long after it cam to passe that, the knight being in company of divers gentlemen and talking of sundry matters, a tale was tolde what chaunced to a gentleman of the countrey which had obtained the favoure and goodwill of a woman by meanes of an olde man called Pollacco, which had the name to be a famous enchaunter and physitian, dwelling at Cutiano, a citye of Boeme where plenty of silver mines and other metals is. The knight, whose castle was not far from Cutiano, had occasion to repaire unto that citye and, according to his desire, found out this Pollacco, which was a very old man, and talking with him of divers things, perceived him to be of great skil. In end, he entreated him that forsomutch as he had don pleasure to many for apprehension of their love, he wold also instruct him how he might be assured that his wife did keepe hirself honest all the time of his absence and that by certaine signes hee might have sure knowledge whether she brake hir faith by sending his honesty into Cornwall.[10] Sutch vaine trust this knight reposed in the lying science of sorcery, which although to many other is found deceitful, yet to him served for sure evidence of his wife's fidelity.

This Pollacco (which was a very cunning enchaunter as you have heard) said unto him: 'Sir, you demaund a very straunge matter, sutch as wherwith never hitherto I have bene acquainted, ne yet searched the depthe of those hidden secrets, a thing not commonly sued for ne yet practized by me. For who is able to make assurance of a woman's chastity or tel by signes (except he were at the deede doing) that she had done amisse? Or who can gaine, by proctor's writ to summon or sue at spiritual courte, peremptorily to affirme, by never so good evidence or testimony, that a woman hath hazarded hir honesty (except he sweare *rem* to be in *re*), which the greatest civilian that ever Padua bred never sawe by processe duely tried?[11] Shall I then warrante you the honesty of such slippery catell, prone and ready to lust, easy to be vanquished by the suites of earnest pursuers? But blameworthy surely I am thus generally to speake; for some I know, although not many, for whose poore honesties I dare adventure mine owne. And yet that number (how small soever it be) is worthy all due reverence and honoure.

'Notwithstanding (bicause you seeme to bee an honeste gentleman) of that knowledge which I have, I will not bee greatelye squeimishe. A certaine secrete experiment indeede I have, wherewith perchaunce I may satisfy your demaund. And this is it: I can by mine arte, in smal time, by certaine composi-tions, frame a woman's image, which you continually in a little boxe may carry about you and (so ofte as you list) behold the same. If the wife doe not breake hir mariage faith, you shall still see the same so faire and wel coloured as it was at the first making and seeme as though it newly came from the painter's shop, but if perchaunce she meane to abuse hir honesty, the same wil waxe pale. And, indeede committing that filthy fact, sodainly the colour will bee blacke, as arayed with cole or other filth, and the smel thereof wil not be very pleasaunt. But at al times when she is attempted or pursued, the colour will be so yealow as gold.'

This marvellous secrete devise greatly pleased the knight (verely beleving the same to be true) specially mutch moved and assured by the fame bruted abrode of his science, whereof the citizens of Cutiano tolde very straunge and incredible things. When the price was paied for this precious jewel, hee received the image and joyfully returned home to his castell, where, tarryinge certain dayes, he determined to repaire to the court of the glorious King Mathie, making his wife privy of his intent.

Afterwards, when he had disposed his household matters in order, he committed the government therof to his wife, and havinge prepared all necessaries for his voyage, to the great sorrow and grief of his beloved, he departed and arrived at Alba Regale,[12] where that time the king lay with Beatrix his wife, of whom hee was joyfully received and entertained. He had not long continued in the court but he had obtained and won the favor and goodwill of all men. The king (which knew him full well) very honorably placed him in his courte and by him accomplished divers and many waighty affairs, which very wisely and trustely he brought to passe according to the king's mind and pleasure.

Afterwards he was made colonell of a certain number of footmen sent by the king against the Turks to defende a holde which the enimies of God began to assaile under the conduct of Mustapha Basca.[13] Which conduct he so wel directed and therin stoutly behaved himself as he chased al the infidels oute of those coasts, winning therby the name of a most valiaunt soldier and prudent captaine; whereby he merveilously gained the favor and grace of the king, who (over and besides his daily intertainment) gave unto him a castle and the revenue in fee farme for ever.[14] Sutch rewards deserve all valiaunt men which for the honour of their prince and countrey do willingly imploy their service; worthy no doubt of great regard and chearishinge upon their home returne because they hate idlenes to win glory, desiringe rather to spende whole dayes in fielde than houres in courte. Which this worthy knight deserved, who (not able to sustaine his poore estate) by politick wisdome and prowesse of armes endevored to serve his lord and countrey, wherein surely hee made a very good choise. Then he devoutly praised God for that he put into his minde sutch a noble enterprise, trusting daily to atchieve greater fame and glory. But the greater was his joy and contentation bicause the image of his wife inclosed within a boxe (which still hee caried about him in his purse) continued freshe of coloure without alteration.'

It was noised in the court how this valiaunt knight Ulrico had in Boeme the fairest and goodliest lady to his wife that lived either in Boeme or Hungary. It chaunced as a certain company of young gentlemen in the courte were together (amongs whom was this knight) that a Hungarian baron said unto him: 'How is it possible, sir Ulrico, being a yeare and a halfe since you departed out of Boeme, that you have no minde to returne to see your wife, who, as the common fame reporteth, is one of the goodliest women of all the countrey? Truely it seemeth to me that you care not for hir, which were great pitty if hir beauty be correspondent to hir fame.'

'Sir' (quod Ulrico) 'what hir beauty is I referre unto the world. But howsoever you esteeme me to care of hir, you shall understand that I doe love hir and wil do so duringe my life.

And the cause why I have not visited hir of long time is no little proofe of the great assurance I have of her vertue and honest life. The argument of hir vertue I prove, for that she is contented that I should serve my lord and king, and sufficient it is for me to give hir intelligence of my state and welfare, which many times by letters at opportunity I faile not to do. The proofe of my faith is evident by reason of my bounden duety to our soveraigne lord (of whom I have received so great and ample benefites) and the warrefare which I use in his grace's service upon the frontiers of his realme against the enimies of Christe, whereunto I bear more goodwill than I doe to wedlocke love, preferring duety to prince before mariage. Albeit my wife's faith and constancy is sutch as freely I may spend my life without care of hir devoir, being assured that, besides hir beauty, shee is wise, vertuous and honest, and loveth me above al worldly things, tendring me so dearely as she doth the balles of hir owne eyes.'

'You have stoutly said', answered the baron, 'in defence of your wive's chastity, whereof she can make unto hirselfe no great warrantice, because a woman sometimes will bee in minde not to be mooved at the requests and gifts offred by the greatest prince of the world who afterwards, within a day, upon the onely sight and view of some lusty youth, at one simple worde uttered with a few teares and shorter suite, yeldeth to his request. And what is she, then, that can conceive sutch assuraunce in hirselfe? What is hee that knoweth the secretes of heartes which be impenetrable? Surely none, as I suppose, except God himselfe.

'A woman of hir owne nature is mooveable and pliant and is the moste ambitious creature of the worlde. And (by God) no woman doe I know but that she lusteth and desireth to be beloved, required, sued unto, honored and cherished. And oftentimes it commeth to passe that the most crafty dames, which thincke with fained lookes to feede their divers lovers, be the first that thrust their heads into the amorous nets, and, like little birdes in hard distresse of weather, be caught in lovers' lime-twigges. Whereby, sir Ulrico, I do not see that your wife (above all other women compact of flesh and bone) hath sutch priviledge from God, but that she may be soone entised and corrupted.'[15]

'Well, sir', said the Boeme knight, 'I am persuaded of that

which I have spoken and verely doe beleve the effect of my
beliefe most true. Every man knoweth his owne affaires, and the
foole knoweth better what hee hath than his neighbors do, be
they never so wise. Beleve you what you thincke for goode. I
meane not to disgresse from that which I conceive. And suffer
me (I pray you) to beleve what I list, sith beliefe cannot hurt me,
nor yet your discredite can hinder my beliefe, being free for ech
man in semblable chaunces to thinke and believe what his minde
lusteth and liketh.'

There were many other lordes and gentlemen of the court
present at there talke, and (as we commonly see at sutch like
meetinges) every man uttereth his minde. Whereupon sundry
opinions were produced touching that question. And because
divers men be of divers natures and many presuminge upon the
pregnancy of their wise heads, there rose some stur about that
talke, each man obstinate in his alledged reason, more froward
peradventure than reason more rightly required.

The communication grew so hot and talke brake forth so
loude as the same was reported to the queene. The good lady,
sory to heare tell of sutch strife within hir court (abhorring
naturally all controversy and contention) sent for the parties
and required theim from poinct to poinct to make recitall of the
beginning and circumstaunce of their reasons and arguments.
And when she understoode the effect of al their talke she said
that every man at his owne pleasure might beleeve what he list,
affirming it to be presumptuous and extreme folly to judge all
women to be of one disposition, in like sort as it were a great
errour to say that all men bee of one quality and condicion, the
contrary by daily experience manifestly appearing. For, both in
men and women, there is so great difference and variety of
natures as there bee heades and wits. And how it is commonly
seene that two brothers (and sisters) borne at one birth bee yet
of contrary natures and complexions, of manners and conditions
so divers, as the thinge which shall please the one is altogather
displeasaunt to the other. Where uppon the queene concluded
that the Boeme knight had good reason to continue that good
and honest credit of his wife, as having proved hir fidelity of
long time, wherein she shewed hirself to be very wise and
discret.

Now because (as many times we see) the natures and appetites
of divers men be insaciable and one man sometimes more foolish

hardy than another, even so (to say the troth) were those two Hungarian barons, who seeming wise in their owne conceiptes, one of them said to the queene in this manner: 'Madame, your grace doth wel maintaine the sexe of womankinde, because you be a woman. For by nature it is gieven to that kinde stoutly to stand in defence of themselves, because their imbecillity and weakenes otherwise would bewray them. And although good reasons might be alledged to open the causes of their debility and why they be not able to attaine the hault excellency of man, yet for this time I doe not meane to be tedious unto your grace, least the little heart of woman should rise and display that conceit which is wrapt within that little moulde. But to retourne to this chaste lady, through whom our talke began, if we might crave licence of your majesty and saulfe-conduct of this gentleman to knowe hir dwelling place and have leave to speake to hir, we doubt not but to breake with our batteringe talke the adamant walles of hir chastity that is so famous and cary away that spoile which victoriously we shall atchieve.'

'I know not,' aunswered the Boeme knight, 'what yee can or will doe, but sure I am that hitherto I am not deceived.'

Many things were spoken there, and sundry opinions of either partes alledged. In ende, the two Hungarian barons persuaded themselves and made their vaunts that they were able to climbe the skies, and both would attempt and also bring to passe any enterprise were it never so great, affirming their former offer by othe, and offering to guage all the landes and goods they had that within the space of 5 moneths they would either of them obtaine the gentlewoman's goodwill to do what they list, so that the knight were bound neither to returne home ne yet to advertise hir of their determination. The queene and all the standers-by laughed heartely at this their offer, mocking and jesting at their foolish and youthly conceites.

Which the barons perceiving, saide: 'You thinke, madame, that we speake triflingly and be not able to accomplish this our proposed enterprise, but, madame, may it please you to gieve us leave, wee meane by earnest attempt to gieve proofe thereof.'

And as they were thus in reasoninge and debating the matter, the kinge (hearinge tell of this large offer made by the barons) came into the place where the queene was, at such time as she was about to dissuade them from the frantik devise. Before whom, he being entred the chamber, the two barons fell downe upon their knees and humbly besought his grace that the compact made betwene Sir Ulrico and them might proceede, disclosing unto him in few wordes the effect of all their talke, which franckly was graunted by the king. But the barons added a provisio that, when they had won their wager, the knight by no meanes shoulde hurt his wife and from that time forth should grieve over his false opinion that women were not naturally gieven to the sutes and requests of amorous persons.

The Boeme knight, who was assured of his wive's great honesty and loyall faith, beleeved so true as the gospell the proportion and quality of the image, who in all the time that hee was farre of never perceived the same to bee either pale or black. But at that time lookinge upon the image, hee perceived a certaine yealow colour to rise, as hee thought his wife was by some love pursued, but yet sodeinly it returned againe to his naturall hewe, which boldned him to say these words to the Hungarian barons: 'Yee be a couple of pleasaunt and unbeleeving gentlemen and have conceived so fantasticall opinion as ever men of your calling did. But sith you proceede in your obstinate folly, and wil needes guage all the lands and goods you have that you bee able to vanquishe my wive's honest and chaste heart, I am contented (for the singuler credite which I repose in hir) to joine with you, and will pledge the poore livinge I have for proofe of mine opinion, and shall accomplishe al other your requestes made here before the majesties of the kinge and queene. And, therefore, may it please your highnesse, sith this fond device cannot be beaten out of their heads, to gieve licence unto those noblemen the lords Vladislao and Alberto' (so were they called) 'to put in proofe the mery conceipt of their disposed mindes (whereof they do so greatly bragge), and I, by your good grace and favoure, am content to agree to their demaundes.'

'And wee,' answered the Hungarians, 'do once againe affirme the same which wee have spoken.'

The king, willing to have them give over that strife, was intreated to the contrary by the barons. Whereupon the kinge, perceivinge their follies, caused a decree of the bargaine to be put in writing, either parties interchaungeably subscribing the same. Which done, they tooke their leaves.

Afterwards, the two Hungarians began to put their enterprise in order and agreed betweene themselves Alberto to bee the firste that should adventure uppon the lady. And that within sixe weekes after, upon his returne, the lord Vladislao should proceede.

These things concluded and all furnitures for their severall jorneys disposed, the lord Alberto departed in good order with two servaunts, directly travailing to the castle of the Boeme knight, where, being arrived, hee lighted at an inne of the towne adjoining to the castle. And demaunding of the hoste the conditions of the lady, hee understoode that shee was a very faire woman and that hir honesty and love towards hir husbande farre excelled hir beauty. Which wordes nothing dismayede the amorous baron, but when hee had pulled of his bootes and richely arayed himselfe he repaired to the castle and, knockinge at the gates, gave the lady to understand that he was come to see hir. She (which was a curteous gentlewoman) caused him to be brought in and gently gave him honourable intertainment.

The baron greatly mused uppon the beauty and goodlinesse of the lady, singularly commending hir honest order and behaviour. And, beinge set down, the young gentleman said unto hir: 'Madame, mooved with the fame of your surpassing beauty, which now I see to bee more excellent than fame with hir swiftest wings is able to cary, I am come from the court to view and see if that were true or whether lyinge brutes had scattered their vulgar talke in vaine. But, finding the same farre more fine and pure than erst I did expect, I crave licence of your ladyship to conceive none offence of this my boulde and rude attempt.'

And herewithall hee began to joine many trifling and vaine words, which dalyinge suters by heate of lusty bloude bee wont to shoote forth to declare theimselves not to be speachlesse or tongue-tied. Which the lady, well espying, speedily imagined into what porte his rotten barke would arrive. Wherefore, in the ende, when shee sawe his shippe at roade, began to enter in prety lovinge talke by little and little to incourage his fond attempt. The baron, thinkinge hee had caught the ele by the taile, not well practised in Cicero his schoole,[16] ceased not fondly to contrive the time, by making hir beleeve that he was farre in love. The lady, weary (God wrote) of his fonde behaviour and amorous reasons, and yet not to seeme scornfull, made him good countenaunce, in sutch wise as the Hungarian two or three dayes did nothing else but proceede in vaine pursute.

Shee, perceiving him to bee but a hauke of the first coate,[17] devised to recompence his follies with sutch entertainement, as during his life, he shoulde keepe the same in good remembraunce. Wherefore, not long after, faining as though his great wisedome, uttered by eloquent talke, had subdued hir, shee said thus unto him: 'My lord, the reasons you produce and your pleasaunt gesture in my house have so inchaunted mee that impossible it is but I must needes agree unto your will. For, where I never thought during life to staine the purity of mariage bed and determined continually to preserve myselfe inviolably for my husbande, your noble grace and curteous behaviour have (I say) so bewitched mee that ready I am to bee at your commaundement, humbly beseeching your honour to beware that knowledge hereof may not come unto mine husband's eares, who is so fierce and cruell and loveth me so dearely as no doubt he will without further triall either himselfe kill me or otherwise procure my death. And to the intent none of my house may suspect our doings, I shall desire you tomorrow in the morninge about nine of the clock, which is the accustomed time of your repaire hither, to come unto my castle; wherein, when you be entred, speedily to mount up to the chaumber of the highest tower, over the doore whereof yee shall finde the armes of my husband entailed in marble, and, when you be entred in, to shut the doore fast after you. And in the meanetime I will waite and provide that none shall molest and trouble us, and then we shall bestowe ourselves for accomplishement of that which your love desireth.' Nowe (in very deede) this chaumber was a very strong prison ordained in auncient time by the progenitours of that territory to imprison and punishe the vassals and tenants of the same for offences and crimes committed.

The baron, hearinge this liberall offer of the ladye, thinking that he had obteined the summe of al his joy, so glad as if he had conquered a whole kingdome, the best-contented man alive, thanking the lady for hir curteous answere, departed and retourned to his inne. God knoweth uppon howe merry a pinne the hearte of this young baron was sette.[18] And, after he had liberally banketted his hoste and hostesse, pleasantly disposing himself to mirth and recreation, he wente to bed, where joy so lightned his merry head, as no slepe at all could close his eyes. Sutch be the savage pangs of those that aspire to like delights, as the best reclaimer of the wildest hauk could never take more

paine or desire mo shiftes to man the same for the better
atchieving of hir pray than did this brave baron for bringing his
enterprise to effect.

The nexte day early in the morning, hee rose, dressing himselfe
with the sweete perfumes and puttinge on his finest suite of
apparell. At the appoincted houre, hee went to the castell and,
so secretly as he could, accordinge to the ladye's instruction, hee
conveyed himselfe up into the chaumber, which hee founde
open, and when he was entred hee shut the same. The maner of
the doore was sutch as none within coulde open it without a
key, and, besides the strong locke, it hadde both barre and bolt
on the outside, with sutch fasteninge as the devill himselfe, being
locked within, could not breake forth. The lady (which waited
hard by for his comming) so soone as she perceived that the
doore was shut, stept unto the same and both double-locked the
doore and also without she barred and fast bolted the same,
carying the key away with hir. This chamber was in the highest
tower of the house (as is before said) wherein was placed a
bedde with good furniture, the window whereof was so high
that none coulde looke out without a ladder. The other partes
thereof were in good and convenient order, apt and meete for
an honest prison. When the lorde Alberto was within, hee sat
downe, waiting (as the Jewes do for Messias)[19] when the lady,
according to hir appoinctment, shoulde come.

And as he was in this expectation, building castles in the aire
and devising a thousand chimeras in his braine, behold he heard
one to open a little wicket that was in the doore of that chamber,
which was as straight as scarcely able to receive a loafe of bread
or cruse of wine used to be sent to the prisoners. He, thinking
that it had ben the lady, rose up and hearde the noise of a little
girle who, looking in at the hole, thus said unto him. 'My lord
Alberto, the lady Barbara, my mistresse' (for that was hir name)
'hath sent me thus to say unto you: that forasmuch as you be
come into this place by countenaunce of love to dispoile hir of
hir honour, shee hath imprisoned you like a theefe, accordinge
to your deserte, and purposeth to make you suffer penance
equall to the measure of your offence. Wherefore, so long as
you shal remain in this place, she mindeth to force you to gaine
your bread and drinke with the arte of spinning, as poore
women doe for gaine of their livinge, meaninge thereby to coole
the heate of your lusty youth and to make you tast the sorrow

of sauce meete for them to assay that go about to robbe ladies
of their honour.[20] She bad me likewise to tell you that the more
yarne you spin, the greater shall be the abundance and delicacye
of your fare; the greater paine you take to earne your foode, the
more liberall she will be in distributing of the same. Otherwise
(she sayeth) that you shall faste with breade and water. Which
determinate sentence she hath decreed not to be infringed and
broken for any kinde of sute or intreaty that you be able to
make.' When the maiden had spoken these wordes, she shut the
little dore and returned to hir lady.

The baron (which thought that he had ben commen to a
mariage) did eate nothing al the morning before, bicause he
thought to be enterteined with better and daintier store of
viandes, who nowe at those newes fared like one out of his
wittes and stoode still so amazed as though his leggs would have
failed him. And in one moment his spirites began to vanish and
his force and breath forsoke him, and fel downe upon the
chamber flore in sutch wise as hee that had beheld him would
have thought him rather dead than living. In this state he was a
great time. And afterwardes somewhat comminge to himselfe,
he could not tel whether hee dreamed or else that the words
were true which the maiden had saide unto him.

In the end, seeing and beinge verely assured that he was in a
prison so sure as bird in cage, through disdaine and rage was
like to die or else to lose his wits, faring with himselfe of long
time like a maddeman, and not knowing what to do, passed the
rest of the day in walking uppe and downe the chaumber,
raving, stamping, staring, cursinge and using words of greatest
villanye, lamenting and bewailinge the time and day that (so like
a beast and brutish man) he gave the attempt to dispoile the
honesty of another man's wife. Then came to his mind the losse
of all his lands and goods, which by the king's authority were
put in comprimise; then the shame, the scorne and rebuke which
hee should receive at other men's handes beyonde measure
vexed him. And reporte bruted in the courte (for that it was
impossible but the whole worlde should knowe it) so grieved
him as his heart seemed to be strained with two sharp and biting
nailes, the paines whereof forced him to loose his wittes and
understandinge.

In the middes of which pangs, furiously vaunting up and
downe the chaumber, hee espied by chaunce in a corner a

distaffe furnished with good store of flaxe and a spindle hanging thereuppon. And overcome with choler and rage, hee was about to spoile and breake the same in pieces. But, remembring what a harde weapon necessitye is, hee stayed his wisedome, and albeit he hadde rather to have contrived his leisure in noble and gentlemanlike pastime, yet, rather than he would be idle, he thought to reserve that instrument to avoide the tedious lacke of honest and familiar company.

When supper time was come, the maiden retourned againe, who opening the portall dore, saluted the baron, and saide: 'My lord, my mistresse hath sent mee to visite your good lordship and to receive at youre good handes the effecte of your laboure, who hopeth that you have sponne some substanciall store of threede for earning of your supper which being done shall be readily brought unto you.'

The baron (full of rage, furye and felonious moode) if before he were fallen into choler, now, by protestation of these words, seemed to transgresse the bounds of reason and began to raile at the poore wench, scolding and chiding hir like a strumpet of the stews, faring as though he would have beaten hir or don hir some other mischiefe. But his moode was stayed from doing any hurt.

The poore wench, lessoned by her mistresse, in laughing wise, said unto him: 'Why (my lord) do you chafe and rage againste mee? Methinks you do me wrong to use sutch reprochful words, which am but a servaunt and bounde to the commaundement of my mistresse. Why, sir, do you not know that a pursivaunt or messanger suffreth no paine or blame? The greatest king or emperour of the worlde, receiving defiaunce from a meaner prince, never useth his ambassador with scolding wordes, ne yet by villany or rebuke abuseth his person. Is it wisdome, then, for you, being a present prisoner at the mercy of your kepers, in this dishonorable sorte to revile me with disordred talke?

'But, sir, leave of your rages and quiet yourselfe for this present time, for my mistresse marvelleth much why you durst come (for al your noble state) to give attemptes to violate hir good name, which message shee required me to tell you, over and besides a desire shee hath to know whether by the science of spinning you have gained your meat, for you seeme to kicke against the wind and beat water in a morter, if you think from hence to goe before you have earned a recompense for the meat

which shal be given you. Wherefore it is your lot paciently to
suffer the penance of your fond attempt, which I pray you gently
to sustaine and think no scorn thereof hardely, for desperate
men and hard adventures must needes suffer the daungers
thereunto belonging. This is the determinate sentence of my
mistrese mind, who fourdeth you no better fare than bread and
water if you cannot shewe some prety spindle full of yarne for
signe of your goodwill at this present pinch of your distresse.'

The maiden, seeing that hee was not disposed to shewe some
part of willing mind to gaine his living by that prefixed science,
shut the portall doore and went her way. The unhappy baron
(arrived thether in very ill time) that night had neither breade
nor broth, and therefore he fared accordinge to the proverbe:
'He that goeth to bed supperlesse, lieth in his bed restlesse', for,
during the whole night no sleepe could fasten his eyes.

Now, as this baron was closed in prison faste, so the ladye
tooke order that secretly with great cheare his servauntes should
be interteined, and his horse with sweete haye and good
provender well mainteined, all his furnitures, sumpture, horse
and cariages conveyed within the castle, where wanted nothing
for the state of sutch a personage but onely liberty; making the
host of the inne beleve (wher the lord harbored before) that he
was returned into Hungarye.

But now turne we to the Boeme knight, who (knowinge that
one of the two Hungarian competitors were departed the court
and ridden into Boeme) did still behold the quality of the
inchaunted image, wherein by the space of thre or foure dayes
(in which time, the baron made his greatest sute to his ladye) he
marked a certaine alteration of coloure in the same, but afterwards returned to his native forme. And seeing no greater
transformation, he was wel assured that the Hungarian baron
was repulsed and imployed his labor in vaine. Whereof the
Boeme knight was excedingly pleased and contented, bicause he
was well assured that his wife had kept hirselfe righte pure and
honest. Notwithstanding, his minde was not wel settled, ne yet
his heart at rest, doubting that the lord Vladislao (which as yet
was not departed the courte) would obtaine the thing and
acquite the faulte which his companion had committed.

The imprisoned baron (which all this time had neither eaten
nor dronken, nor in the night could sleepe) in the morning, after
he had considred his misadventure and well perceived no remedy

for him to goe forth, except hee obeyed the ladye's hest, made of necessity a vertue and applied himselfe to learne to spinne by force, which freedome and honour could never have made him to do. Whereuppon, he toke the distaffe and beganne to spinne. And albeit that hee never sponne in al his life before, yet, instructed by necessity, so well as he could he drewe out his threede, now small and then great, and manye times of the meanest sort, but verye often broade, il-favored, ill-closed, and worse twisted, all oute of fourme and fashion that sundry times very heartely he laughed to himselfe to see his cunning, but would have made a cunning woman spinner burst into ten thousand laughters, if she had ben there.

Thus all the morning he spent in spinning, and when dinner came his accustomed messenger, the maiden, repaired unto him againe and, opening the window, demaunded of the baron how his worke went foreward and whether he were disposed to manifest the cause of his comming into Boeme. Hee (well beaten in the schoole of shame) uttered unto the maide the whole compact and bargaine made betweene him and his companion and the Boeme knighte hir maister, and afterwards shewed unto hir his spindle ful of threde.

The young wenche, smiling at his woorke, said, 'By Sainct Marie, this is well done! You are worthy of victual for your hire, for now I well perceive that hunger forceth the woulf oute of hir denne. I conne you thanck that like a lord you can so puissantly gaine your living. Wherefore, proceeding in that which you have begonne, I doubt not but shortely you will prove sutche a workeman as my mistresse shall not neede to put oute hir flax to spinne (to hir great charge and coste) for making of hir smockes, but that the same may wel be don within hir own house, yea althoughe the same doe serve but for kitchen cloathes for dresser bordes or cleaninge of hir vessell before they bee served forth. And as your good deserts doe merite thankes for this your arte, now well begonne, even so your new-told tale of comming hither requireth no lesse, for that you have disclosed the trouth.' When she had spoken these woords, she reached him some store of meates for his dinner and bade him farewell.

When shee was returned unto hir lady, shee shewed unto hir the spindle full of threde and told hir therewithall the whole story of the compact betwene the knight Ulrico and the two Hungarian barons. Whereof the lady (sore astonned for the snares laid to entrappe hir) was not withstanding wel contented, for that shee had so well forseene the same, but most of all rejoised that hir husband had so good opinion of hir honest life. And before she would advertise him of those events, she purposed to attend the comming of the lord Vladislao, to whome she ment to do like penance for his carelesse bargaine and dishonest opinion accordingly as he deserved, marvelling very mutch that both the barons were so rash and presumptuous daungerously (not knowing what kind of woman she was) to put their landes and goodes in hazard. But considering the nature of divers brainsick men which passe not how carelesly they adventure their gained goods and inherited lands, so they may atchieve the pray after which they vainely hunt for the prejudice and hurt of other, she made no accompt of these attemptes, sith honest matrones force not uppon the sutes or vaine consumed time of light-brained cockscombs that care not what fond cost or ill-imployed houres they waste to anoy the good renoume and honest brutes of women.

But not to discourse from point to point the particulers of this intended jorney, this poore deceived baron in short time proved a very good spinner, by exercise whereof he felt sutch solace as not onely the same was a comfortable sporte for his captive time, but also for want of better recreation it seemed so joyfull as if he had bene pluming and feding his hawke or doing other sports belonging to the honourable state of a lord. Which (his well accrived labour) the maiden recompensed with abundance of good and delicate meates. And although the lady was many times required to visite the baron, yet she would never to that request consent.

In which time the knight Ulrico ceased not continually to viewe and revewe the state of his image, which appeared still to bee of one well-coloured sorte, and although this use of his was divers times marked and seene of many, yet being earnestly demaunded the cause thereof hee would never disclose the same. Many conjectures thereof were made, but none could attaine the trouthe. And who would have thought that a knight so wise and prudente had worne within his pursse any inchaunted thing? And albeit the king and queene had intelligence of this frequent practise of the knight, yet they thought not mete for the private and secrete mystery to demaund the cause.

One moneth and a halfe was passed now that the lorde

Alberto was departed the court and become a castle knighte and cunning spinster. Which made the lord Vladislao to muse, for that the promise made betweene them was broken, and hearde neither by letter or messenger what successe he had received. After divers thoughts imagined in his minde, he conceived that his companion had happily enjoyed the ende of his desired joy and had gathered the wished fruicts of the lady and, drowned in the maine sea of his owne pleasures, was overwhelmed in the bottome of oblivion. Wherefore he determined to set forward on his journey to give onset of his desired fortune. Who, without long delay for execution of his purpose, prepared all necessaries for that voyage and, mounted on horsebacke with two of his men, he journeyed towards Boeme and (within a few dayes after) arrived at the castle of the faire and most honest lady.

And when hee was entred the inne where the lord Alberto was first lodged, he diligently enquired of him and heard tell that he was returned into Hungarye many dayes before, whereof, mutch marvelling, could not tel what to say or think. In the end, purposing to put in profe the cause wherefore he was departed out of Hungarye, after diligent searche of the maners of the lady, he understoode by general voice that she was without comparison the honestest, wisest, gentlest and comeliest lady within the whole countrey of Boeme. Incontinently the lady was advertised of the arrival of this baron and, knowing his message, she determined to paye him also with that money which she had already coined for the other.

The next day the baron went unto the castle and, knocking at the gate, went in woord how that he was come from the court of King Mathie to visite and salute the lady of that castle. And as she did entertaine the first baron in curteous guise and with loving countenaunce, even so she did the second, who thought thereby that he had attained by that pleasaunt entertainment the game which he hunted. And discoursing uppon divers matters, the lady shewed hirselfe a pleasaunt and familiar gentlewoman, which made the baron to think that in short time he should win the price for which he came. Notwithstanding, at the firste brunt he would not by any meanes descend to any particularity of his purpose, but his words ran general, which were: that hearinge tell of the fame of hir beauty, good grace and comelinesse, by having occasion to repaire into Boeme to doe certaine his affaires, he thought it labor wel spent to ride some portion of his journey, though it were besides the way, to digresse to do reverence unto hir whom fame advaunced above the skies. And thus passing his first visitation, he returned againe to his lodging.

The lady, when the baron was gone from hir castle, was rapt into a rage, greatlye offended that those two Hungarian lordes so presumptuously had bended themselves like common theeves to wander and rove the countreys not onely to robbe and spoile hir of hir honour but also to bring hir in displeasure of hir husband and thereby into the daunger and perill of death. By reason of which rage (not without cause conceived), she caused another chamber to be made ready, next wall to the other baron that was become sutch a notable spinster. And upon the nexte returne of the lord Vladislao she received him with no lesse good entertainement than before, and when night came caused him to be lodged in hir owne house in the chamber prepared as before, where he slept not very soundly all that night through the continuall remembraunce of his ladye's beauty.

Next morning, he perceived himself to be locked fast in a prison. And when he had made him readye, thinking to descend to bid the lady good morrow, seeking meanes to unlock the doore and perceiving that he could not, he stoode still in a dumpe. And as hee was thus standing, marvelling the cause of his shutting in so fast, the maiden repaired to the hole of the dore, giving his honor an unaccustomed salutation, which was that hir mistresse commaunded hir to give him to understand that if hee had any lust or appetite to his breakfast or if he minded from thenceforth to ease his hunger or conteine life, that he should give himselfe to learne to reele yarne. And for that purpose she willed him to looke in sutch a corner of the chamber, and he should find certaine spindles of thred and an instrument to winde his yarn upon. 'Wherefore' (quod she) 'apply your self thereunto and loose no time.'

He that had that time beholden the baron in the face would have thought that hee had seene rather a marble stone than the figure of a man. But, converting his could conceived moode into mad anger, he fell into ten times more displeasure with himselfe than is before described by the other baron. But seeinge that his mad behaviour and beastly rage was bestowed in vaine, the next day he began to reele.

The lady, afterwardes, when shee had intelligence of the good and gainefull spinning of the lord Alberto and the wel-disposed and towardly reeling of the lord Vladislao, greatly rejoiced for makinge of sutch two notable workemen, whose workemanship exceeded the labours of them that had been apprentizes to the occupation seven yeares togeather.[23] Sutch bee the apt and ready wits of the souldiers of love, wherein I would wishe all Cupide's dearlings to be nousled and applied in their youthly time. Then, no doubt, their passions woulde appease and rages assuage, and would give over bolde attempts, for which they have no thancke of the chaste and honest.

And to this goodly sight the lady brought the servaunts of these noblemen, willing them to marke and beholde the diligence of their maisters and to imitate the industry of their gallant exercise, who never attained meate before by labour they had gained the same. Which done, shee made them take their horse and furnitures of their lords and to depart; otherwise, if by violence they resisted, she would cause their choller to be caulmed with sutchlike service as they saw their lordes doe before their eyes. The servaunts, seeing no remedy but must needes depart, tooke their leave. Afterwards, she sent one of hir servaunts in poast to the court to advertise hir husband of all that which chaunced.

The Boeme knight, receiving these good newes, declared the same unto the king and queene, and recited the whole story of the two Hungarian barons accordingly as the tenor of his wive's letters did purport. The princes stoode still in great admiration and highly commended the wisedome of the lady, esteeming hir for a very sage and polliticke woman. Afterwards, the knight Ulrico humbly besought the king for execution of his decree and performaunce of the bargaine. Whereupon the king assembled his counsell and required every of them to saye their minde.

Upon the deliberation whereof, the lord chauncellor of the kingdome with two counsellers were sent to the castle of the Boeme knight to enquire and learne the processe and doinges of the two lordes. Who diligently accomplished the kinge's commaundement and, havinge examined the lady and hir maiden with other of the house, and the barons also, whom a little before the arrivall of these commissioners the lady had caused to be put together that by spinning and reeling they might comfort one another. When the lord chauncellor had framed and digested in order the whole discourse of this history, returned to the court, where the king and queene with the pieres and noblemen of his kingdome caused the acts of the same to be divulged and bruted abroade.

And after mutch talk and discourse of the performaunce of this compact, pro and contra, the queene taking the ladye's part and favoring the knight, the kinge gave sentence that sir Ulrico should wholly possesse the landes and goods of the two barons to him and to his heires for ever, and that the barons should be banished the kingdomes of Hungary and Boeme, never to returne upon paine of death. This sentence was put in execution, and the unfortunat barons exiled, which, specially to those that were of their consanguinity and bloud, seemed to severe and rigorous. Nevertheless, the covenaunt being most plaine and evident, to most men the same seemed to bee pronounced with greate justice and equity, for example in time to come to lesson rash wits how they judge and deeme so indifferently of women's behaviours, amongs whom no doubt there bee both good and bad as there bee of men.

Afterwards, the 2 princes sent for the lady to the court. Who there was courteously intertained and, for this hir wise and polliticke fact, had in great admiration. The queene then appointed hir to be one of hir women of honor and esteemed hir very deerely. The knight also daily grew to great promotion, well beloved and favored of the king. Who with his lady long time lived in greate joy and felicity, not forgetting the cunning Pollacco (that made him the image and likenes of his wife), whose frendship and labor he rewarded with money and other benefits very liberally.

A TALE FROM

THE SACK-FULL OF NEWES

THE OLD MAN AND HIS YOUNG WIFE

There was an old man that could not well see, who had a fair young wife, and with them dwelt a young man which had long wooed his mistress to have his pleasure of her, who at the last consented to him. But they knew not how to bring it to pass, for she did never go abroad but in her husband's company and led him always. At last she devised a very fine shift and bad her servant that he should that night about midnight come into her chamber where her husband and she lay, and she would find some device for him.

Night came, and the old man and wife went to bed, but she slept not a wink, but thought still upon her pretended purpose. But a little before the time prefixed, she awakned her husband and said thus unto him: 'Sir, I will tell you a thing in secret which your servant was purposed to do. When I am alone, I can never be at quiet for him, but he is always enticeing me to have me at his will, and so at the last, to be quiet with him, I consented to meet him in the garden, but for mine honesty's sake I will not. Wherefore, I pray you, put on my cloathes and go meet him, so when he comes to you, beat him well and chide him, for I know well he will not strike you because you are his master, and then he may amend himself and prove a good servant.'

And the man was well pleased therewith. So the good man put on his wive's cloaths and took a good cudgel in his hand and went into the garden. At length there came the servant to his mistress where she lay in bed and did what he would with her, and she was content. And then she told him how she had sent her husband into the garden in her apparel, and wherefore, and to what purpose.

So the servant arose and (as she bad him) took a good staff with him and went into the garden, as though he knew not it was his master, and said unto him: 'Nay, you whore, I did this but only to prove thee, whether thou wouldest be false to my good master, and not that I would do such a vile thing with thee.' Whereupon he fell upon his master, giving him many sore stripes and beating him most cruelly, still calling him nothing but: 'Out, you whore, will you offer this abuse to my good master?'

'Alas', quoth his master, 'good John, I am thy master, strike me no more, I pray thee.'

'Nay, whore', quoth he, 'I know who thou art well enough.' And so he struck him again, beating him most grievously.

'Good John', said his master, 'feel, I have a beard.' Then the servant felt, knowing well who it was. Who presently kneeled down and cried his master mercy. 'Now thanks be to God', quoth his master, 'I have as good a servant of thee as a man can have, and I have as good a wife as the world affords.'

Afterwards the master went to bed and his servant also. When the old man came to bed to his wife, she demanded of him how he sped. He answered and said: 'By my troth, wife, I have the trustiest servant in the world, and as faithful a wife, for my servant came thither with a great staff and did beat me right sore, thinking it had been you. Wherefore I was well pleased therewith.'

But ever after the servant was well-beloved of his master but better of his mistress, for his master had no mistrust of him, though he had made him a cuckold. So the poore man was cruelly beaten and made a summer's bird nevertheless.[1]

A TALE FROM

THE FORREST OF FANCY

Seigneor Fransisco Vergelis, for a fair ambling gelding, suffered one Seigneor Richardo Magniffico to talk with his wife, who gave him no aunswere at all; but he aunswering for her in such sort as if she herself had spoken it, according to the effect of his wordes, it came afterwards to passe.

Many there are that conceive so well of themselves as, in respect of their owne wisedome and knowledge, they thinke all other men to be but fooles and void of understanding, and yet we oftentimes see that these fine-headed fellowes, whilst they indevour by their subtle devises to deceive others, are in the end most deceived themselves.

And therefore in my opinion he is worthy much blame that goeth about by suche indirect meanes to make more narrow triall of other men's wits then is needefull. And for more perfect proofe of their folly, you shall heare what happened to a knight of Pistoy upon the like occasion.

In the city of Pistoy hard by Florence, there was sometime amongst the famely of the Vergelesies,[1] a knight called Fransisco, a man very rich, wise and well experimented in many matters, but therewithall beyonde all measure covetous. Hee, having occasion to goe to Milan to be potentate there,[2] was provided of all thinges fitte for his purpose and agreeable to the honorable estate he was called unto, save onely of an ambling gelding for himself to ride upon, and could get none to his contentmente, but that he alwayes thoughte the price to great that he should pay for it. There was the same time in Pistoy a yong man named Richardo, decended of a base parentage, but yet very riche, who for the neatnesse and bravery that he used in his apparrell was of every man commonly called Magniffico,[3] and had of long time loved and diverse times courted (without any comforte of that he craved) the wife of Seigneor Fransisco, that was exceeding faire and withall very honest.

Now it so happened that this Magniffico had the fairest ambling gelding in all Tuscan, which, for the bewtye and goodnesse of it, he highly esteemed. And being manifestlye knowne, throughout the cittye, that he was enamoured of the saide lady, there was some that told Seigneor Fransisco that if he woulde request it in gift, he might easily obtain it for the love he bare unto his wife. Seigneor Fransisco, burning with avirice, sent to seeke Magniffico and requested to buy his horse, to the end hee shoulde offer to give it him. Magniffico, hearing this, was very well pleased and aunswered: 'Sir, if you would give mee all that ever you have in the world I would not sell him. But yet you may have him in gifte if you please, upon the condition that, before you have him, I may with your leave and in your presence utter certaine words to your wife so farre from you that none may heare me but only she.' Seigneor Fransisco, being led by covetousnes and hoping to delude Magniffico, answered that he was very wel content wheresoever he wold, and, having left him in the hall, hee wente to his wife's chamber and told her howe easilye hee might obtaine the ambling gelding, commaunding her to come and heare what Magniffico would say but not to answere him to anything that hee shoulde alledge unto her. The ladye misliked much of this practise, but yet, being bound to obay her husbande's mind, she promised to do it and followed him into the hall to heare what Magniffico woulde say.

Who, having againe confirmed the covenaunte made with her husband, set himselfe downe by her in one of the corners of the hall, farre ynough from anybody, and began to say in this manner: 'Madame, I know your wisedome to be such as I am wel assured you have long since plainely perceived how great the love is that your bewty (which passeth without comparison all other that ever I saw) hath constrained mee to beare unto you. I leave to speake of the commendable quallities and rare vertues that remain in you, whiche have power to vanquish the most dainty hart in the whole world, wherefore it is not needefull by wordes to declare unto you that the love I beare you is farre greater and more fervent then ever man bare to any other woman living, whereby I am almost brought to that passe that my miserable life is scarcely able to sustaine my poore weakened members, and yet dare I be bolde to saye more unto you that if it be lawfull for men to love when they are dead as they may doe being alive I will love you for ever.[4]

'And therefore you may well assure youreselfe, that you have nothing, whatsoever it be, either deare or good cheape, that you may so well esteeme your owne or make so sure accoumpt of as of me, and of that I may be and semblably of all that ever I injoy.[5] And to the end you may be the more certain of that I say, I assure you I should accoumpt it for a singuler favour that you would vouchsafe to commaund me anything that I am able any way to performe and may be agreeable to your good liking, for, whatsoever it were, though all the world should saye and swere the contrarye, I would surely put it in practise.

'Now, madame, being so muche youre owne as you heare I am, I take boldnesse (not without great reason) to addresse my prayers to your highnesse, on whome onelye and on none other my rest, welth and safety wholy dependeth. And as your most humble servaunt, I humbly besech you, my dearest good and the only hope of my love, which nourisheth itselfe in the amourous fire, hoping in you that your goodwill shall be great and your rigour (whiche you have of long time extended towardes mee that am youre own) so mollified that, feeling myselfe recomforted by your compassion, I may say that as by your bewtye I became amourous, so doe I thereby also injoy the life which (if your hauty hart incline not to my prayers) would without doubt be in such sort consumed as I shoulde shortelye die. And so might you be called and accoumpted the murtherer of me, and yet should my death be no honor at al unto you, notwithstanding, I beleeve, that when at any time the same should come to youre hearing, you woulde saye to yourselfe: "Alas, what evill have I done in not having compassion of my Magniffico." And beeing then to late to repente you of anything that is past, it will be unto you an occasion of very great greefe. Wherfore, to the end that it come not so to passe, have now some compassion upon mee, and before I be past remedy render me that which may releve me. For in you onelye doth it rest to make mee the moste contented or most discontented creature living, hoping alwayes that your curtesy shall be so great as you wil not suffer me to receive death for recompence of suche and so great goodwill as I beare unto you, but will with a joyfull and gracious aunswere recomforte my pore sprightes which, altogither overcome with feare, doe tremble at your presence.'

Then Magniffico, making an ende and having shedde some teares, after many greevous sighes he began to harken what the lady wold answere. Now she, whom neither the long sutes made unto her, the justes and turneyes,[6] nor lost time, or anye suchlike thing which Magniffico had done for the love of herre had never before mooved anyething at all to love him, was nowe mooved thereunto by the effectuall words uttered by her moste fervente lover and began to feele that which she had never felt before, and judged this to proceede only of love. And though, to fulfill the charge that her husbande had given her, shee held her peace, notwithstanding, by the secret sighes which she sent forth it mighte easilye bee conjectured what aunswere she would willingly have made to her beloved Magniffico if she might.

He, having awhile attended her aunswere and perceiving that shee aunswered nothing at all, greatlye mervailed and beganne to perceive the deceipte and subtiltye of her husband, but yet in regarding her countinance and perceiving some glaunces of her eyes cast upon him and, besides that, remembring the sighes which shee sent foorth from the bottome of her hart, he received some good hope. And, building hereuppon, bethought himselfe and then began to aunswere her, as though she herselfe had saide, in this manner:

'Friend Magniffico, I did long since surmise that thy love towardes me was very great and perfecte and nowe am more certaine of it by thy words, whiche are of farre greater force, wherewith I am as well contented as may be; notwithstanding, if it seeme unto thee that I have hitherto bene hard and cruell unto thee, yet woulde I not have thee to thinke that my harte hath bene suche as my conntinance hath shewed me to be, but rather that I have loved and held thee more deare then any other, but it was meete I shoulde for that time conceale it, as well for feare of others as to keepe my good name unspotted; but now the time commeth that I may make thee more plainely to understand whether I love thee or no and give thee a meete guerdon for the love which thou hast so long borne unto me. Wherefore comfort thyselfe and have good hope, for seigneor Fransisco must go within these fewe dayes as potentate to Millan (as thou thyselfe knowest), when thou for my sake hast given him thy good ambling gelding, and so soone as he is gone thou shalt be most welcome unto me, and we wil then give ful accomplishment to our love. And therefore have regarde from henceforth when thou findest two kerchefes hanging out of my chamber window over the garden, and then in the evening when it is somewhat darke repaire thou unto me by the garden dore, having good regard that nobody see thee, and there thou shalt finde me ready to receive thee. Then will we take our pleasure togither all the whole night and make as greate cheare as we may.'

When Magnifico had in the person of the lady spoken all this, he began to aunswere for himselfe and saide: 'Deare lady, my spirites are so much occupied by the aboundaunt joy that I conceive by your wordes that I can hardlye frame an aunswere or utter anyething to give you condigne thankes for the same, and if I could, yet should I not finde sufficient time to gratifye youre goodwil as I desire, and as it is mete I should, and therfore I beseeche you that whatsoever I desire to do (and cannot by wordes declare it) you will vouchsafe to conceive the same in your minde. Only I assure you that without faulte I will performe your charge and order all my actions according to your good direction, and, when meete opportunity shall serve me to receive the favour whiche you have so freely promised, I wil inforce myself in all I may to yeeld you the greatest thankes that I am able. And now, having no more to saye unto you at this presente, wishing you such joy and welfare as your hart desireth, I commit you to God.'

For all this the lady aunswered not a word, wherefore Magnifico rise and began to retourne towards her husband, who, seeing him up, went to meete him and said: 'O sir, what thinke you now? Have I kept promise with you?'

'No, sir', aunswered Magnifico, 'for you promised me that I should talk with your wife, and you have made me to speake with an image of stone.'

This answere greatly pleased seigneor Fransisco, who, although he had a good opinion of his wife before, yet now he thought better of her then ever he did, and said: 'But yet the ambling gelding that was yours is now mine.'

Whereunto Magnifico aunswered: 'Yea, sir, but if I had thought to reape no better fruite then this by the favour I found at your handes, without demaunding the same I would freely have given you my gelding.'

Seigneor Fransisco laughed hartely at this aunswere, and, seing himself so wel provided of an ambler, shortly after set forward on his jorney towards Millan.

The lady then remaining in her house all alone, thinking upon the wordes that Magniffico had beforetime used unto her, remembring his love and how he had for her sake given her husband his good ambling gelding, seing also the said Magniffico diverse times to passe to and fro before her dore, she said unto herselfe: 'What shall I doe? Wherefore should I lose my youth? My husband is gone to Millan and will not retourne again these sixe monthes, and when will hee ever bee able to paye his aretrages?[7] What, when I am old and care not for it? Besides that, when shall I ever finde such a friende as Magniffico? I am now alone and in care of nobody, and if it were knowne, yet is it better to doe it and afterwards so repent me, then not to doe it and to be sorrye that I did it not.'

And having thus debated with herself, in the end determining to take the time whilst it served, she hanged one day two kerchefes out at the garden windows. Which Magniffico perceiving (being very glad of it), he went all secretely, so soone as the night was come, to the garden dore and found it open and from thence went to another dore which was at the entraunce of the house, where he mette with the lady, that attended his comming. Who, seing him come, rise up and went to meete him and received him with great joy. He, having kissed and imbrased her a hundred times, followed her up the staires into her chamber, where, being arived, they went by and by to bedde togither, and then they knew the finall end of their love. And although this were the firste time, yet was it not the last, for whilst seigneor Fransisco was at Millan, and also after his retourne, Magniffico frequented the house to the great comfort and contentment of them both.

HIS FAREWELL TO MILITARIE PROFESSION

OF APOLONIUS AND SILLA

The Argument

Apolonius, duke, having spent a yere's service in the warres against the Turke, returning homward with his companye by sea, was driven by force of weather to the ile of Cypres, where he was well received by Pontus, gouvernour of the same ile, with whom Silla, daughter to Pontus, fell so straungely in love that after Apolonius was departed to Constantinople Silla with one man followed, and, comming to Constantinople, she served Apolonius in the habite of a manne, and, after many prety accidentes falling out, she was knowne to Apolonius, who, in requitall of her love, maried her.[1]

There is no child that is borne into this wretched worlde but, before it doeth sucke the mother's milke, it taketh first a soope of the cupp of errour, which maketh us, when we come to riper yeres, not onely to enter into actions of injurye, but many times to straye from that is right and reason. But in all other thinges wherein wee shewe ourselves to bee moste dronken with this poisoned cuppe, it is in our actions of love. For the lover is so estranged from that is right and wandereth so wide from the boundes of reason that he is not able to deeme white from blacke, good from badde, vertue from vice, but onely led by the apetite of his owne affections, and grounding them on the foolishnesse of his owne fancies, will so settle his liking on such a one as either by desert or unworthinesse will merite rather to be loathed then loved.

If a question might be asked: What is the ground indeede of reasonable love whereby the knot is knit of true and perfect freendship? I thinke those that be wise would aunswere: deserte, that is, whether the partye beloved dooeth requite us with the like. For otherwise, if the bare shewe of beautye or the comelinesse of personage might bee sufficient to confirme us in our love, those that bee accustomed to goe to faires and markettes might sometimes fall into love with twentye in a daye! Desert must then bee (of force) the grounde of reasonable love. For to love them that hate us, to followe them that flye from us, to faune on them that froune on us, to currye favour with theim that disdaine us, to bee glad to please theim that care not how they offende us, who will not confesse this to be an erronious love, neither grounded upon witte nor reason? Wherfore, right curteous gentilwomen, if it please you with pacience to peruse this historye, following, you shall see Dame Errour so playe her parte with a leishe of lovers, a male and twoo femalles, as shall woorke a wonder to your wise judgement in noting the effecte of their amorous devises and conclusions of their actions. The firste, neclecting the love of a noble dame, yong, beautifull and faire, who onely for his goodwill played the parte of a serving-manne, contented to abide any maner of paine onely to behold him, he again setting his love of a dame that despising him (being a noble duke) gave herself to a serving-manne (as she had thought), but it otherwise fell out, as the substance of this tale shall better discribe. And because I have been something tedious in my first discourse, offending your pacient eares with the hearing of a circumstaunce overlong, from henceforthe that whiche I minde to write shall bee done with suche celeritye as the matter that I pretende to penne maye in any wise permit me, and thus followeth the historye.[2]

During the time that the famous citye of Constantinople remained in the handes of the Christians, emongst many other noble menne that kepte their abiding in that florishing citye there was one whose name was Apolonius, a worthye duke, who, being but a verye yong man and even then newe come to his possessions, whiche were verye greate, levied a mightye bande of menne at his owne proper charges, with whom he served againste the Turke during the space of one whole yere.[3] In whiche time, although it were very shorte, this yong Duke so behaved himself, as well by prowesse and valiaunce shewed with his owne handes as otherwise by his wisedome and liberalitye used towardes his souldiours, that all the worlde was filled with the fame of this noble duke. When he had thus spent one yeare's service, he caused his trompet to sounde a retraite, and, gathering his companye together and imbarking theimselves, he sette saile, holding his course towardes Constantinople. But, beeing uppon the sea, by the extreamitye of a tempest whiche sodainly fell, his fleete was desevered, some one waye and some another, but he himself recovered the ile of Cypres, where he was worthily received by Pontus, duke and gouvernour of the same ile, with whom he lodged while his shippes were newe repairing.[4]

This Pontus, that was lorde and governour of this famous ile, was an auncient duke and had twoo children, a soone and a daughter. His sonne was named Silvio, of whom hereafter we shall have further occasion to speake, but at this instant he was in the partes of Africa serving in the warres.

The daughter her name was Silla, whose beautye was so perelesse that she had the soveraintye emongest all other dames, as well for her beautye as for the noblenesse of her birthe. This Silla, having heard of the worthinesse of Apolonius, this yong duke, who besides his beautye and good graces had a certaine naturall allurement, that being now in his company in her father's courte, she was so strangely attached with the love of Apolonius that there was nothing might content her but his presence and sweete sight. And although she saw no maner of hope to attaine to that she moste desired, knowing Apolonius to be but a geaste and readye to take the benefite of the next winde and to departe into a straunge countrey, whereby she was bereved of all possibilitye ever to see him againe and therefore strived with her self to leave her fondenesse, but all in vaine. It would not bee, but, like the foule whiche is once limed, the more she striveth, the faster she tieth herself.[5]

So Silla was now constrained, perforce her will, to yeeld to love, wherefore from time to time she used so great familiaritye with him as her honour might well permitte and fedde him with suche amourous baites as the modestye of a maide could reasonably afforde. Whiche when she perceived did take but small effecte, feeling her self so muche outraged with the extreamitye of her passion, by the onely countenaunce that she bestowed uppon Apolonius it might have been well perceived that the verye eyes pleaded unto him for pitye and remorse. But Apolonius, comming but lately from out the feelde from the chasing of his enemies, and his furye not yet throughly desolved nor purged from his stomacke, gave no regarde to those amourous enticementes whiche, by reason of his youth, he had not been acquainted withall. But his minde ranne more to heare his pilotes bring newes of a merye winde to serve his turne to Constantinople, whiche in the ende came very prosperously.

And giving Duke Pontus hartye thankes for his greate entertainment, taking his leave of himself and the ladye Silla his daughter,
departed with his companye and, with a happye gaale arived at
his desired porte.

Gentlewomen, according to my promise, I will heare for
brevitye's sake omit to make repetition of the long and dolorous
discourse recorded by Silla for this sodaine departure of her
Apolonius, knowing you to bee as tenderly harted as Silla
herself, whereby you maye the better conjecture the furye of her
fever.[6]

But Silla, the further that she sawe herself bereved of all hope
ever any more to see her beloved Apolonius, so muche the
more contagious were her passions, and made the greater speede
to execute that she had premeditated in her minde, whiche was
this: emongest many servaunts that did attend uppon her, there
was one whose name was Pedro, who had a long time waited
uppon her in her chamber, wherby she was well assured of his
fidelitye and trust. To that Pedro, therefore, she bewrayed first
the fervencye of her love borne to Apolonius, conjuring him in
the name of the goddes of love herself, and binding him by the
duetye that a servaunte ought to have that tendereth his mistresse' safetye and good liking, and desiring him with teares
trickling doune her cheekes that he would give his consent to
aide and assiste her in that she had determined, whiche was, for
that she was fully resolved to goe to Constantinople, where she
might againe take the vewe of her beloved Apolonius, that he,
according to the trust she had reposed in him, would not refuse
to give his consent secretly to convaye her from out her father's
courte, according as she would give him direction, and also to
make himself pertaker of her journey and to waite upon her till
she had seen the ende of her determination.

Pedro, perceiving with what vehemencye his ladye and mistresse had made request unto him, albeeit he sawe many perilles
and doubtes depending in her pretence, notwithstanding gave
his consent to be at her disposition, promising her to further her
with his beste advice and to be readye to obeye whatsoever she
would please to commaunde him. The match being thus agreed
upon and all thinges prepared in a readinesse for their departure,
it happened there was a gallye of Constantinople ready to
departe. Whiche Pedro understanding came to the captaine
desiring him to have passage for himself and for a poore maide

that was his sister, whiche were bounde to Constantinople uppon certaine urgent affaires. To whiche request the captaine graunted, willing him to prepare aborde with all speede because the winde served him presently to departe.

Pedro now comming to his mistres and telling her how he had handeled the matter with the captaine, she liking verye well of the devise, disguising herself into verye simple atire, stole awaye from out her father's court and came with Pedro, whom now she calleth brother, aboarde the galleye, where all thinges being in readinesse and the winde serving verye well, they launched forthe with their oores and set saile.

When they were at the sea, the captaine of the galleye, taking the vewe of Silla, perceiving her singular beautye, he was better pleased in beholding of her face then in taking the height either of the sunne or starre.[7] And thinking her by the homelinesse of her apparell to be but some simple maiden, calling her into his cabin, he beganne to breake with her after the sea fashion, desiring her to use his owne cabin for better ease, and during the time that she remained at the sea she should not want a bedde. And then, whispering softly in her eare, he saied that, for want of a bedfellow, he himself would supplye that rome. Silla, not being acquainted with any suche talke, blusshed for shame but made him no aunswere at all. My captaine, feeling suche a bickering within himself the like whereof he had never indured upon the sea, was like to bee taken prisoner aboard his owne shippe and forced to yeeld himself a captive without any cannon shot. Wherefore, to salve all sores and thinking it the readiest waye to speed, he began to breake with Silla in the waye of mariage, telling her how happye a voyage she had made to fall into the liking of such a one as himself was, who was able to keepe and maintaine her like a gentilwoman, and for her sake would like-wise take her brother into his fellowship, whom he would by some meanes prefarre, in suche sorte that bothe of theim should have good cause to thinke theimselves thrise happye: she to light of suche a housbande, and he to light of suche a brother. But Silla, nothing pleased with these prefermentes, desired him to cease his talke for that she did thinke herself, indeede to bee too unworthye suche a one as he was, neither was she minded yet to marrye, and therefore desired him to fixe his fancye uppon some that were better worthye then herself was and that could better like of his courtesye then she could dooe.

The captaine, seeing himself thus refused, being in a greate chafe, he saied as followeth: 'Then, seeing you make so little accompte of my courtesye, proffered to one that is so farre unworthye of it, from henceforth I will use the office of my aucthoritye. You shall knowe that I am the captaine of this shippe and have power to commannde and dispose of thinges at my pleasure, and, seing you have so scornfully rejected me to be your loyall housbande, I will now take you by force and use you at my will, and so long as it shall please me will kepe you for mine owne store. There shall be no man able to defende you, nor yet to perswade me from that I have determined.'

Silla, with these wordes being stroke into a great feare, did thinke it now too late to rewe her rashe attempte, determined rather to die with her owne handes then to suffer herself to be abused in suche sorte. Therefore she moste humbly desired the captaine so muche as he could to save her credite, and, seing that she must needes be at his will and disposition, that for that present he would depart and suffer her till night, when in the darke he might take his pleasure without any maner of suspition to the residue of his companye. The captaine, thinking now the goole to be more then half wonne, was contented so farre to satisfye her request and departed out, leaving her alone in his cabin.

Silla, being alone by herself, drue out her knife readye to strike her self to the harrt, and, falling upon her knees, desired God to receive her soule as an acceptable sacrifice for her follies whiche she had so wilfully committed, craving pardon for her sinnes and so forthe continuing a long and pitifull reconciliation to God, in the middest whereof there sodainly fell a wonderfull storme, the terrour whereof was suche that there was no man but did thinke the seas would presently have swallowed them. The billowes so sodainly arose with the rage of the winde that they were all glad to fall to heaving out of water, for otherwise their feeble gallye had never bin able to have brooked the seas.

This storme continued all that daye and the next night, and they, being driven to put romer before the winde to keepe the gallye ahed the billowe,[8] were driven uppon the maine shore, where the gallye brake all to peeces. There was every man providing to save his own life. Some gat upon hatches, boordes, and casks, and were driven with the waves to and fro, but the greatest nomber were drouned, amongst the whiche Pedro was

one. But Silla herself being in the caben, as you have heard, tooke
holde of a cheste that was the captaine's, the whiche by the onely
providence of God brought her safe to the shore the whiche when
she had recovered, not knowing what was become of Pedro her
manne, she deemed that bothe he and all the rest had been
drouned, for that she sawe nobodye uppon the shore but herself.

Wherefore, when she had awhile made greate lamentations,
complaining her mishappes, she beganne in the ende to comforte
herself with the hope that she had to see her Apolonius and
found suche meanes that she brake open the chest that brought
her to lande, wherin she found good store of coine and sondrye
sutes of apparell that were the captaine's. And now, to prevent
a nomber of injuries that might be proffered to a woman that
was lefte in her case, she determined to leave her owne apparell
and to sort herself into some of those sutes, that, being taken
for a man, she might passe through the countrye in the better
safetye. And as she changed her apparel, she thought it likewise
convenient to change her name, wherefore, not readily happening of any other, she called herself Silvio, by the name of her
owne brother, whom you have heard spoken of before.

In this maner she travailed to Constantinople, where she
inquired out the palace of the Duke Apolonius, and thinking
herself now to be bothe fitte and able to playe the serving-man,
she presented herself to the duke, craving his service. The duke,
verye willing to give succour unto strangers, perceiving him to
bee a proper smogue yong man, gave him entertainment. Silla
thought herself now more then satisfied for all the casualties
that had happened unto her in her journey, that she might at her
pleasure take but the vew of the Duke Apolonius, and above the
reste of his servauntes was verye diligent and attendaunt uppon
him. The whiche the duke perceiving beganne likewise to growe
into good liking with the diligence of his man and, therefore,
made him one of his chamber. Who but Silvio then was moste
neate aboute him in helping of him to make him readye in a
morning, in the setting of his ruffes, in the keeping of his
chamber? Silvio pleased his maister so well that above all the
reste of his servaunts aboute him he had the greatest credite,
and the duke put him moste in trust.

At this verye instaunt there was remaining in the citye a noble
dame, a widowe, whose housbande was but lately deceased, one
of the noblest men that were in the partes of Grecia, who left

his lady and wife large possessions and great livinges. This ladye's name was called Julina, who, besides the aboundance of her wealth and the greatness of her revenues, had likewise the soveraigntye of all the dames of Constantinople for her beautye. To this ladye Julina, Apolonius became an earnest suter, and, according to the maner of woers, besides faire woordes, sorrowfull sighes, and piteous countenaunces, there must bee sending of loving letters, chaines, bracelettes, brouches, ringes, tablets, gemmes, juels, and presentes. I knowe not what. So my duke, who in the time that he remained in the ile of Cyprus had no skill at all in the arte of love, although it were more than half proffered unto him, was now become a schollear in love's schoole and had alreadye learned his first lesson, that is, to speake pitifully, to looke ruthfully, to promise largely, to serve diligently and to please carefully. Now he was learning his seconde lesson, that is, to reward liberally, to give bountifully, to present willingly and to write lovingly. Thus Apolonius was so busied in his newe studye that I warrant you there was no man that could chalenge him for plaiying the truant, he followed his profession with so good a will. And who must bee the messenger to carrye the tokens and love letters to the lady Julina but Silvio, his manne. In him the duke reposed his onely confidence to go betweene him and his ladye.

Now, gentilwomen, doe you thinke there could have been a greater torment devised wherewith to afflicte the harte of Silla then herself to bee made the instrumente to woorke her owne mishapp and to playe the atturney in a cause that made so muche againste herself? But Silla, altogether desirous to please her maister, cared nothing at all to offende herself, followed his businesse with so good a will as if it had been in her owne preferment.

Julina, now having many times taken the gaze of this yong youth Silvio, perceiving him to bee of suche excellente perfecte grace, was so intangeled with the often sight of this sweete temptation that she fell into as great a liking with the man as the maister was with herself. And on a time Silvio, being sent from his maister with a message to the ladye Julina, as he beganne very earnestly to solicet in his maister's behalfe, Julina interrupting him in his tale, saied: 'Silvio, it is enough that you have saied for your maister. From henceforthe either speake for yourself or saye nothing at all.'

Silla, abashed to heare these wordes, began in her minde to accuse the blindnesse of love, that Julina, neglecting the goodwill of so noble a duke, would preferre her love unto suche a one as nature itself had denaied to recompense her liking.

And now for a time leaving matters depending, as you have heard, it fell out that the right Silvio indeede (whom you have heard spoken of before, the brother of Silla) was come to his father's courte into the ile of Cypres, where, understanding that his sister was departed in maner as you have heard, conjectured that the very occasion did proceade of some liking had between Pedro her man (that was missing with her) and herself. But Silvio, who loved his sister as dearly as his owne life and the rather for that as she was his naturall sister, bothe by father and mother, so the one of theim was so like the other in countenaunce and favour that there was no man able to descerne the one from the other by their faces, saving by their apparell, the one being a man, the other a woman. Silvio, therefore, vowed to his father not onely to seek out his sister Silla but also to revenge the villainye whiche he conceived in Pedro for the carrying awaye of his sister.

And thus departing, having travailed through many cities and tounes without hearing any maner of news of those he wente to seeke for, at the laste he arrived at Constantinople, where, as he was walking in an evening for his owne recreation on a pleasaunte greene yarde without the walles of the citye,[9] he fortuned to meete with the ladye Julina, who likewise had been abroad to take the aire. And as she sodainly caste her eyes uppon Silvio, thinking him to bee her olde acquaintaunce by reason they were so like one another as you have heard before, saied unto him: 'Sir Silvio, if your haste be not the greater, I praye you let me have a little talke with you, seeing I have so luckely mette you in this place.'

Silvio, wondering to heare himself so rightlye named, beeing but a straunger not of above twoo daye's continuaunce in the citye, verye courteouslye came towardes her, desirous to heare what she would saye.

Julina, commaunding her traine somthing to stande backe, saied as followeth: 'Seing my goodwill and frendly love hath been the onely cause to make me so prodigall to offer that I see is so lightly rejected, it maketh me to thinke that men bee of this condition, rather to desire those thinges whiche they cannot come by then to esteeme or value of that whiche both largely and liberallye is offered unto theim. But if the liberalitye of my proffer hath made to seme lesse the value of the thing that I ment to present, it is but in your owne conceipt, considering how many noblemen there hath been here before, and be yet at this present, whiche hath bothe served, sued and moste humbly intreated to attaine that whiche to you of myself I have freely offred, and I perceive is dispised or at the least verye lightly regarded.'

Silvio, wondering at these woordes, but more amazed that she could so rightlye call him by his name, could not tell what to make of her speeches, assuring himself that she was deceived and did mistake him, did thinke, notwithstanding, it had been a poincte of greate simplicitye if he should forsake that whiche Fortune had so favorably proffered unto him, perceiving by her traine that she was some ladye of great honour, and, vewing the perfection of her beautye and the excellencye of her grace and countenaunce, did thinke it unpossible that she should be despised, and therefore aunswered thus: 'Madame, if before this time I have seemed to forgett myself in neglecting your courtesye whiche so liberally you have ment unto me, please it you to pardon what is paste, and from this daye forewardes, Silvio remaineth readye preste to make suche reasonable amendes as his abilitye maye anywayes permit, or as it shall please you to commaunde.'

Julina, the gladdest woman that might bee to heare these joyfull newes, saied: 'Then, my Silvio, see you faile not tomorrowe at night to suppe with me at my owne house, where I will discourse farther with you what amendes you shall make me.'

To whiche request Silvio gave his glad consente, and thus they departed verye well pleased. And as Julina did thinke the time verye long till she had reapte the fruite of her desire, so Silvio, he wishte for harvest before corne would growe, thinking the time as long till he sawe how matters would fall out. But not knowing what ladye she might bee, he presently (before Julina was out of sight) demaunded of one that was walking by what she was and how she was called. Who satisfied Silvio in every poincte, and also in what parte of the toune her house did stande whereby he might enquire it out.

Silvio, thus departing to his lodging, passed the night with verye unquiet sleapes, and the nexte morning his minde ran so muche of his supper that he never cared neither for his breakfast nor dinner; and the daye, to his seeming, passed awaye so slowlye that he had thought the statelye steedes had been tired that drawe the chariot of the sunne, or els some other Josua had commanded them againe to stande, and wished that Phaeton had been there with a whippe.[10]

Julina, on the other side, she had thought the clocke-setter had played the knave, the daye came no faster forewardes. But sixe a clocke beeing once stroken recovered comforte to bothe parties, and Silvio hastening himself to the pallace of Julina, where by her he was frendly welcomed, and, a sumpteous supper beeing made readye, furnished with sondrye sortes of delicate dishes, they satte theim doune, passing the supper time with amarous lokes, loving countenaunces and secret glaunces conveighed from the one to the other, whiche did better satisfye them then the feeding of their daintye dishes.

Supper time beeing thus spent, Julina did thinke it verye unfitly if she should tourne Silvio to goe seeke his lodging in an evening, desired him therefore that he would take a bedde in her house for that night. And bringing him up into a faire chamber that was verye richely furnished, she founde suche meanes that when all the reste of her housholde servauntes were abedde and quiet, she came herself to beare Silvio companye, where, con-cluding uppon conditions that were in question betweene them,[11] theye passed the night with suche joye and contentation as might in that convenient time be wished for, but onely that Julina, feeding too muche of some one dishe above the reste received a surfet whereof she could not bee cured in fourtye wekes after, a naturall inclination in all women whiche are subjecte to longing and want the reason to use a moderation in their diet. But the morning approching, Julina tooke her leave and conveighed herself into her owne chamber, and when it was faire dayelight, Silvano, making himself readye, departed like-wise about his affaires in the toune, debating with himself how thinges had happened, being well assured that Julina had mistaken him, and therefore, for feare of further evilles, deter-mined to come no more there, but tooke his journey towardes other places in the partes of Grecia to see if he could learne any tidinges of his sister Silla.

The Duke Apolonius, having made a long sute and never a

whit the nerer of his purpose, came to Julina to crave her direct aunswere, either to accept of him and of suche conditions as he proffered unto her, or els to give him his laste farewell.

Julina, as you have heard, had taken an earnest penye of another, who she had thought had been Silvio, the duke's man, was at a controversye in herself what she might doe. One while she thought, seing her occasion served so fitt, to crave the duke's goodwill for the marrying of his manne. Then againe she could not tell what displeasure the duke would conceive in that she should seeme to preferre his man before himself, did thinke it therefore beste to conceale the matter till she might speake with Silvio to use his opinion how these matters should be handled, and hereupon resolving herself, desiring the duke to pardon her speeches, saied as followeth: 'Sir duke, for that from this time forwardes I am no longer of myself, having given my full power and authorytye over to another whose wife I now remaine by faithfull vowe and promise, and albeeit I knowe the worlde will wonder when they shall understande the fondnesse of my choice, yet I trust you yourself will nothing deslike with me, sithe, I have ment no other thing then the satisfying of mine owne contentation and liking.'

The duke, hearing these woordes, aunswered: 'Madam, I must then content myself, although against my wil, having the lawe in your owne handes to like of whom you liste and to make choise where it pleaseth you.'[12]

Julina, giving the duke greate thankes that would content himself with suche patience, desired him likewise to give his free consent and goodwill to the partye whom she had chosen to be her housebande.

'Naye surely, madam' (quoth the duke) 'I will never give my consent that any other man shall enjoye you than myself. I have made too greate accompt of you then so lightly to passe you awaye with my goodwill. But seeing it lieth not in me to let you, having, as you saye, made your own choise, so from hencefor-wardes I leave you to your owne liking, alwaeys willing you well, and thus will take my leave.'

The duke departed towardes his owne house, verye sorrowfull that Julina had thus served him. But in the meane space that the duke had remained in the house of Julina, some of his servauntes fell into talke and conference with the servaunts of Julina. Where, debating betwene them of the likelihood of the mariage betweene the duke and the ladye, one of the servauntes of Julina saied that he never sawe his ladye and mistres use so good countenaunce to the duke himself as she had doen to Silvio, his manne, and began to report with what familiaritye and courte-sye she had received him, feasted him and lodged him, and that, in his opinion, Silvio was like to speede before the duke, or any other that were suters.

This tale was quickly brought to the duke himself, who, making better enquirye in the matter, founde it to be true that was reported, and, better considering of the woordes whiche Julina had used towardes himself, was verye well assured that it could bee no other then his owne manne that had thrust his nose so farre out of jointe; wherefore, without any further respect, caused him to be thrust into a dongeon, where he was kept prisoner in a verye pitifull plight.

Poore Silvio, having gotte intelligence by some of his fellowes what was the cause that the duke his maister did beare such displeasure unto him, devised all the meanes he could, as well by mediation by his fellowes as otherwise by petitions and supplication to the duke, that he would suspende his judgemente till perfect proofe were had in the matter, and then if any maner of thing did fall out againste him wherby the duke had cause to take any greef, he would confesse himself worthye not onely of imprisonmente but also of moste vile and shamefull death. With these pititions he daiely plied the duke, but all in vaine, for the duke thought he had made so good proofe that he was throughly confirmed in his opinion against his man.

But the ladye Julina, wondering what made Silvio that he was so slacke in his visitation and why he absented himself so long from her presence, beganne to thinke that all was not well. But in the ende, perceiving no decoction of her former surfette, received as you have heard, and finding in herself an unwonted swelling in her beallye, assuring herself to bee with child, fearing to become quite banckroute of her honour, did thinke it more than time to seeke out a father, and made suche secret searche and diligent enquirye that she learned the truthe how Silvio was kepte in prison by the duke, his maister. And minding to finde a present remedye, as well for the love she bare to Silvio as for the maintainaunce of her credite and estimation, she speedily hasted to the pallace of the duke, to whom she saied as followeth: 'Sir duke, it maye bee that you will thinke my comming to your house in this sorte doeth something passe the limites of modestye, the whiche I protest before God proceadeth of this desire that the worlde should knowe how justly I seke meanes to maintaine my honour. But to the ende I seeme not tedious with prolixitye of woordes, nor to use other then direct circumstaunces, knowe, sir, that the love I beare to my onely beloved Silvio, whom I doe esteeme more then all the jewells in the worlde, whose personage I regard more then my owne life, is the onely cause of my attempted journey, beseching you that all the whole displeasure whiche I understand you have conceived against him maye be imputed unto my charge and that it would please you lovingly to deale with him whom of myself I have chosen rather for the satisfaction of mine honest liking then for the vaine preheminences or honourable dignities looked after by ambicious minds.'

The duke, having heard this discourse, caused Silvio presently to be sent for and to be brought before him, to whom he saied: 'Had it not been sufficient for thee, when I had reposed myself in thy fidelitye and the trustinesse of thy service, that thou shouldest so traiterously deale with me? But since that time haste not spared still to abuse me with so many forgeries and perjured protestations, not onely hatefull unto me, whose simplicitye thou thinkest to bee such that by the plotte of thy pleasaunt tongue thou wouldest make me beleeve a manifest untrothe, but moste ahbominable bee thy doinges in the presence and sight of God, that hast not spared to blaspheme his holy name by calling him to bee a witnesse to maintaine thy leasinges, and so detestably wouldest forsweare thyself in a matter that is so openly knowne.'

Poore Silvio, whose innocencye was suche that he might lawfully sweare, seing Julina to be there in place, aunswered thus: 'Moste noble duke, well understanding your conceived greefe, moste humbly I besecche you paciently to heare my excuse, not minding thereby to aggravate or heape up youre wrathe and displeasure, protesting before God that there is nothing in the worlde whiche I regarde so muche or doo esteeme so deare as your good grace and favour. But, desirious that your grace should know my innocencye and to cleare myself of such impositions wherewith I knowe I am wrongfully accused, whiche, as I understande, should be in the practising of the ladye Julina, who standeth here in place, whose acquitaunce for my better discharge now I moste humbly crave, protesting before the almightye God that neither in thought, worde nor deede I have not otherwise used myself than according to the bonde and duetye of a servaunte that is bothe willing and desirous to further his maister's sutes. Which, if I have otherwise saied then that is true, you, madame Julina, who can verye well deside the depthes of all this doubte; I moste humbly beseche you to certifye a trothe, if I have in anything missayed or have otherwise spoken then is right and just.'

Julina, having heard this discourse whiche Silvio had made, perceiving that he stoode in greate awe of the duke's displeasure, aunswered thus: 'Thinke not, my Silvio, that my comming hither is to accuse you of any misdemeanor towardes your maister. So I dooe not denaye but in all suche imbassages wherein towardes me you have been imployed, you have used the office of a faithfull and trustye messenger. Neither am I ashamed to confesse that the first daye that mine eyes did beholde the singuler behaviour, the notable curtesye, and other innumerable giftes wherwith my Silvio is endued, but that beyonde all measure my harte was so inflamed that impossible it was for me to quenche the fervente love or extinguishe the least parte of my conceived torment before I had bewrayed the same unto him and of my owne motion craved his promised faithe and loyaltye of marriage. And now is the time to manifest the same unto the worlde which hath been doen before God and betwene our-selves, knowing that it is not needefull to keepe secret that whiche is neither evill done nor hurtfull to any persone. There-fore (as I sayed before) Silvio is my housbande by plited faithe, whom I hope to obtaine without offence or displeasure of anyone, trusting that there is no manne that will so farre forget himself as to restraine that whiche God hath left at libertye for every wight, or that will seeke by crueltye to force ladies to marrye otherwise then according to their owne liking. Feare not then, my Silvio, to keepe your faith and promise whiche you have made unto me, and as for the reste, I doubte not thinges will so fall out as you shall have no maner of cause to complaine.'

Silvio, amased to heare these woordes, for that Julina by her speeche semed to confirme that whiche he moste of all desired to bee quite of, sayed: 'Who would have thought that a ladye of so great honour and reputation would herself bee the embassadour of a thing so prejudicial and uncomely for her estate. What plighted promises be these whiche bee spoken of? Altogether ignoraunt unto me, whiche if it bee otherwise then I have saied, you sacred goddes consume me straight with flashing flames of fire. But what woordes might I use to give credite to the truthe and innocencye of my cause? Ah, madame Julina, I desire no other testimonye then your owne honestye and vertue, thinking that you will not so muche blemishe the brightnesse of your honour, knowing that a woman is or should be the image of curtesye, continencye and shamfastness, from the whiche so sone as she stoopeth and leaveth the office of her duetye and modestye, besides the degraduation of her honour, she thrusteth herself into the pitte of perpetuall infamye. And as I cannot thinke you would so farre forgette yourself, by the refusall of a noble duke, to dimme the light of your renowne and glorye, whiche hetherto you have maintained emongest the beste and noblest ladies, by suche a one as I knowe myself to bee too farre unworthy your degree and calling, so moste humbly I beseche you to confesse a trothe, whereto tendeth those vowes and promises you speake of, whiche speeches bee so obscure unto me as I knowe not for my life how I might understande them.'

Julina, something nipped with these speeches, sayed: 'And what is the matter that now you make so little accoumpt of your Julina, that beeing my housbande in deede you have the face to denaye me to whom thou art contracted by so many solemne othes? What, arte thou ashamed to have me to thy wife? How muche oughtest thou rather to be ashamed to breake thy promised faithe and to have despised the holye and dreadfull name of God. But that time constraineth me to laye open that whiche shame rather willeth I should dissemble and keepe secret, behold me then here, Silvio, whom thou haste gotten with childe, who, if thou bee of suche honestye as I trust, for all this, I shall finde, then the thing is doen without prejudice or any hurte to my conscience, considering that by the professed faithe thou diddste accoumpt me for thy wife and I received thee for my spouse and loyall housbande, swearing by the almightye God that no other than you have made the conquest and triumphe of my chastitye whereof I crave no other witnesse then yourself and mine owne conscience.'

I pray you, gentlewomen, was not this a foule oversight of Julina, that would so precisely sweare so great an othe that she was gotten with childe by one that was altogether unfurnisht with implementes for suche a tourne? For God's love, take heede, and let this bee an example to you, when you be with childe, how you sweare who is the father before you have had good proofe and knowledge of the partye, for men be so subtill and full of sleight that, God knoweth, a woman may quickly be deceived.

But now to returne to our Silvio, who, hearing an othe sworne so divinely that he had gotten a woman with childe, was like to beleeve that it had bin true in very deede, but remembring his owne impediment, thought it impossible that he should committe suche an acte, and therefore half in a chafe, he sayed: 'What lawe is able to restraine the foolishe indiscretion of a woman that yeeldeth herself to her owne desires? What shame is able to bridle or withdrawe her from her mind and madnesse, or with what snaffell is it possible to holde her backe from the execution of her filthinesse? But what abhomination is this that a ladye of suche a house should so forget the greatnesse of her estate, the aliaunce whereof she is descended, the nobilitye of her deceased housbande, and maketh no conscience to shame and slaunder herself with suche a one as I am, being so farre unfit and unsemely for her degree? But how horrible is it to heare the name of God so defased that wee make no more acompt but for the maintenaunce of our mischifes, we feare no whit at all to forsweare his holy name, as though he were not in all his dealinges most righteous, true and juste, and will not onely laye open our leasinges to the worlde but will likewise punishe the same with moste sharpe and bitter scourges.'

Julina, not able to indure him to proceede any farther in his sermon, was alreadye surprised with a vehement greefe, began bitterly to crye out, uttering these speeches following: 'Alas, is it possible that the soveraigne justice of God can abide a mischiefe so great and cursed? Why maye I not now suffer death rather than the infamye which I see to wander before mine eyes? Oh happye, and more than right happye, had I bin if inconstant fortune had not devised this treason wherein I am surprised and caught. Am I thus become to be intangled with snares, and in the handes of him who, injoying the spoils of my honour, will openly deprive me of my fame by making me a common fable to al posteritye in time to come? Ah, traitour and discourtious wretche, is this the recompense of the honest and firme amitye

which I have borne thee? Wherin have I deserved this discourte-
sye? By loving thee more then thou art able to deserve? Is it I,
arrant theefe, is it I uppon whom thou thinkest to worke thy
mischives? Doest thou think me no better worthe but that thou
mayest prodigally waste my honour at thy pleasure? Didest thou
dare to adventure uppon me, having thy conscience wounded
with so deadly a treason? Ah, unhappye, and above all other
most unhappye, that have so charely preserved mine honour,
and now am made a praye to satisfye a yong man's lust that
hath coveted nothing but the spoyle of my chastitye and good
name.' Herewithal the teares so gushed doune her cheekes that
she was not able to open her mouth to use any farther speeche.

The duke, who stoode all this while and heard this whole
discourse, was wonderfully moved with compassion towardes
Julina, knowing that from her infancye she had ever so honourably used herself that there was no man able to detect her of any
misdemeanour otherwise than beseemed a ladye of her estate.
Wherefore, being fully resolved that Silvio his man had committed this villainye against her, in a greate furye drawing his rapier,
he sayed unto Silvio: 'How canst thou (arrant theefe) showe
thyself so cruell and carelesse to suche as doe thee honour? Hast
thou so little regard of suche a noble ladye as humbleth herself
to suche a villaine as thou art, who, without any respecte either
of her renowme or noble estate, canst be content to seeke the
wracke and utter ruine of her honour? But frame thyself to
make such satisfaction as she requireth (although I knowe,
unworthye wretche, that thou art not able to make her the least
parte of amendes), or I sweare by God that thou shalt not escape
the death which I will minister to thee with my owne handes,
and therefore advise thee well what thou doest.'

Silvio, having heard this sharpe sentence, fell doune on his
knees before the duke, craving for mercye, desiring that he might
be suffered to speake with the ladye Julina aparte, promising to
satisfye her according to her owne contentation.

'Well' (quoth the duke) 'I take thy worde, and therewithall I
advise thee that thou performe thy promis, or otherwise I protest
before God I will make thee suche an example to this worlde
that all traitours shall tremble for feare how they doe seek the
dishonouring of ladies.'

But now Julina had conceived so greate greefe againste Silvio
that there was muche adooe to perswade her to talke with him.

But, remembering her owne case, desirous to heare what excuse he could make, in the ende she agreed, and being brought into a place severally by themselves, Silvio beganne with a piteous voice to saye as followeth: 'I knowe not, madame, of whom I might make complaint, whether of you or of myself, or rather of fortune, whiche hath conducted and brought us both into so great adversitye. I see that you receive greate wrong, and I am condemned againste all right, you in perill to abide the brut of spightfull tongues, and I in daunger to loose the thing that I moste desire. And although I could alledge many reasons to prove my sayings true, yet I referre myself to the experience and bountye of your minde.'

And herewithall loosing his garmentes down to his stomacke and shewed Julina his breastes and pretye teates, surmounting farre the whitenesse of snowe itself, saying: 'Loe, madame, behold here the partye whom you have chalenged to bee the father of your childe. See, I am a woman, the daughter of a noble duke, who, onely for the love of him whom you so lightly have shaken of, have forsaken my father, abandoned my countrye, and in maner as you see, am become a serving-man, satisfying myself but with the onely sight of my Apolonius. And now, madame, if my passion were not vehement and my tormentes without comparison, I would wish that my fained greefs might be laughed to scorne and my desembled paines to be rewarded with floutes. But my love being pure, my travail continuall and my greefs endlesse, I trust, madame, you will not onely excuse me of crime but also pitye my destresse, the which I protest I would still have kept secrete if my fortune would so have permitted.'

Julina did now thinke herself to be in a worse case then ever she was before, for now she knewe not whom to chalenge to be the father of her child. Wherfore, when she had told the duke the very certantye of the discourse which Silvio had made unto her, she departed to her owne house with suche greefe and sorrowe that she purposed never to come out of her owne doores againe alive to be a wonder and mocking stocke to the worlde.

But the duke, more amased to heare this strange discourse of Silvio, came unto him whom, when he had vewed with better consideration, perceived indeede that it was Silla, the daughter of Duke Pontus, and imbrasing her in his armes, he sayed: 'Oh, the braunch of all vertue and the flowre of curtesye itself, pardon me, I beseche you, of all suche discourtesies as I have ignorantlye committed towardes you, desiring you that, without farther memorye of auncient greefs, you will accept of me, who is more joyful and better contented with your presence then if the whole worlde were at my commaundement. Where hath there ever been founde suche liberalitye in a lover, whiche having been trained up and nourished emongest the delicacies and banquettes of the courte, accompanied with traines of many faire and noble ladies, living in pleasure and in the middest of delightes, would so prodigallye adventure yourself, neither fearing mishapps nor misliking to take suche paines as I knowe you have not been accustomed unto? O liberalitye never heard of before! O facte that can never bee sufficiently rewarded! O true love moste pure and unfained!'

Herewithall, sending for the moste artificiall woorkmen, he provided for her sondrye sutes of sumpteous apparell, and the marriage daye appoincted. Whiche was celebrated with great triumphe through the whole citye of Constantinople, everyone praising the noblenesse of the duke. But so many as did behold the excellent beautye of Silla gave her the praise above all the rest of the ladies in the troupe.

The matter seemed so wonderfull and straunge that the brute was spreade throughout all the partes of Gretia insomuche that it came to the hearing of Silvio, who, as you have heard, remained in those partes to enquire of his sister. He, being the gladdest manne in the worlde, hasted to Constantinople, where, comming to his sister, he was joyfullye received and moste lovinglye welcomed and entertained of the duke his brother-in-lawe. After he had remained there twoo or three dayes, the duke revealed unto Silvio the whole discourse how it happened betweene his sister and the ladye Julina, and how his sister was chalenged for getting a woman with childe. Silvio, blushing with these woordes, was stricken with great remorse to make Julina amendes, understanding her to bee a noble ladye, and was lefte defamed to the worlde through his default. He therefore bewrayed the whole circumstaunce to the duke, whereof the duke being verye joyfull, immediatlye repaired with Silvio to the house of Julina, whom they found in her chamber in great lamentation and mourning. To whom the duke said: 'Take courage, madam, for beholde here a gentilman that will not sticke both to father your child and to take you for his wife: no inferior persone but the sonne and heire of a noble duke, worthye of your estate and dignitye.'

Julina, seing Silvio in place, did know very well that he was the father of her childe, and was so ravished with joye that she knewe not whether she were awake or in some dreame. Silvio, imbracing her in his armes, craving forgivenesse of all that past, concluded with her the mariage daye, which was presently accomplished with greate joye and contentation to all parties. And thus Silvio, having attained a noble wife, and Silla, his sister, her desired houssband, they passed the residue of their dayes with suche delight as those that have accomplished the perfection of their felicities.

OF TWO BRETHREN AND THEIR WIVES

The Argument

Two brothers making choise of their wives, the one chouse for beautye, the other for riches. It happened unto them after they were married, the one of their wives proved to bee of light disposition,[1] the other a common scolde. In what maner they lived with their housbandes, and how in the ende the first became to live orderly and well, but the other could be brought by no devise to any reason or good maner.

Gentlewomen, before I will proceede any farther in this historye, I muste desire you to arme yourselves with pacience in reading hereof, that if you finde anything that might breede offence to your modeste mindes, take it in this sorte: that I have written it onely to make you merrye and not to sette you a-snarring or grudging against me. For although I meane to present you with a chapter of knaverye, yet it shall be passable and suche as you maye very well permit, and the mattere that I minde to wright is upon this question: whether a man were better to bee married to a wise harlot or to a foolishe, overthwart and brauling woman?

This question, I know, will seeme very doubtful unto some, and yet in my opinion very easye to bee aunswered. And to speake my minde without dissimulation of bothe those evilles, I thinke the first is leaste and therefore is to be chosen. And herein I could alledge for my better proofe an example of the aunisent Romaines, who in all their governmentes were moste wise and politique, amongst whom the infirmite of the firste was borne withall, because it proceeded of the frailtye of the fleshe, but the outrage of the second was ever condemned, for that it did abounde from a wicked and mischevous minde. And in common reason is it not lesse noisome for a man to live accompanied with a wife who, although she will sometime flye out, can so wisely dissemble with her housbande that he shall never so

muche as suspecte her, whereby he shall receive no discontentment in his minde, then to be bed-fellowe with Xantippa,[2] a
common scold, who dayely and hourely will be checking,
taunting and railing at him in such sorte that he shall thinke
himself moste blest and happye when he is farthest from her
companye?

But for your better confirmation I have set forthe this historye
of twoo brethren, the one of them married to a wenche that
could so cunninglye behave herself towardes him that he had
thought she had beleved there had been no other God but
himself, and yet, by your leave, she would take reason when it
was proffered her, but what of that? The harte never greeves
what the eyes see not. The other was married to a dame that
from her navill douneward was more chast and continent, but
otherwise of her tong suche a devill of helle that the poore man
her housbande could never enjoye merrye daye nor houre,
although he devised many a pretye remedye, as by the reading
of the processe of this tale you shall better perceive, whiche
followeth in this sorte.

There was somtime remaining in a famous citye twoo brethren. The eldest (according to the custome of the place) enjoyed
his father's goodes and possessions after his death, wherby he
was well able to live. The yongest had neither landes nor
livinges, saving that his father had trained him up in learning,
whereby he was able to governe himself in all maner of
companies wheresoever he became. These twoo brethren, being
wearye of their single lives, disposed themselves to mariage. The
eldest, beeing of himself well able to live, sought a wife onely
for her beauty, without any other respect either to her conditions
or riches, and, as the proverbe is (he that sekes shall finde),[3] so
in the ende he lighted on a gentlewoman, called by the name of
mistres Dorithe, whose beautye indeede was verye excellent, and
therewithall had a passing readye witte, marye her training-up
had not been after the beste nor worst maner but, as a man
might saye, after the common sorte. This gentlewoman he
married, who could so well handle him with kissinges, cullinges
and other amarous exercises that her housebande thought
himself the most fortunate manne that lived to light on suche a
wife, although she cunningly armed his hedde with hornes,[4] as
after you shall heare.

The second brother, left (as you have heard) without mainten-

aunce or living, sought for a wife onely to releve his want, and
fortuned to hit of a widowe, indeede with greate wealthe, but in
conditions so overthwart and so spitfull of her tongue that the
poore man had not been married fullye out a moneth but he
more then a thousande times cursed the priest that maried him,
the sexten that opened the churche doore when he went to bee
married, yea, and his owne unhappye legges that had carried his
bodye to bee yoked to so greate a mischeef.

But because I doe minde more orderly to tell you the maners
of these twoo gentlewomen, I will firste beginne with mistres
Doritye. Whose housebande, after they had been a while maried,
fortuned to fall sicke, and then, according to that countrey
maner, a doctor of physicke was presently sent for. Who,
comming many times to visite his pacient, began to beholde and
contemplate the lively beautye of this gentlewoman and lent her
many rowling looke and secrete countenaunces, in suche sorte
that mistres Doritye, being well practised in the arte of love and
seing maister doctor to be a man as sufficient to content a
gentlewoman in her chamber that was whole as to minister
medicines to those that were sicke, did not onely requite him
againe with looke for looke, but she yeelded him a large usurye
and payed him more then fourtye in the hundred.

Maister doctor, who was likewise skilfull enough, could well
perceive whereto those lookes did tende. Upon a time, being
alone in her companye, he sayed unto her as followeth: 'Mistres
Doritye, if the experience whiche I have learned in physicke's
arte might crave credite and make my tale to bee the better
beleeved, assure yourself then that I minde to saye nothing but
that that shall bee to your owne behoofe. And the reason that
makes me to enter into this discourse is the pitye that I take to
see so proper a gentlewoman as yourself should bee so deceived
in a housebande, who, although you shall finde him bothe
honeste, gentle and loving – yea, and peradventure maye content
you with suche rightes as appertaine to the marriage bedde – yet
assure yourself he shall never be able to get you with child,
considering your natures and complexitions be so farre different
the one from the other, whereby you are like for ever to remaine
without issue. And one of the greateste comfortes that maye
happen unto us in this worlde is to see ourselves as it were
regenerate and borne anewe in our children. And barreness in
the auncient time hath been accompted not onely infamous but

also moste hatefull emongst women, insomuche that Sara gave her owne handmaide to her houseband, because she could not herself conceive a child.[5] But I would wishe women more witee then to followe Sara's example. God defende they should be so foolishe to give their maidens to their housebandes; I woud wishe them rather themselves to take their menne. It hath been ever holden for the greater wisedome rather to take then to give, and sure they shal finde it more for their owne profites that, if their housbande's want be suche that he is not able to get a child, to take helpe of some other that maye supplye his imperfections. But I truste I shall not neede to use many perswasions, considering that every wise woman will thinke that I have reason on my side. Thus, mistres Doritye, you have heard the somme of my tale, protesting that if my service maye any wayes stand you in steade, I am as readye to obeye as he over whom you have power to commaunde.'

Mistres Doritye, who all this while had well pondered his woordes, knewe verye well how to whet maister doctor on, and the more to set his teeth on edge,[6] aunswered him thus: 'I perceive, maister doctor, you are something pleasantly disposed, and hereafter when I shall finde my housbande's infirmitye to be suche as you have sayed, I meane to sende for you, desiring you that you would not be out of the waye, to helpe me when I have need.'

The doctour knewe not well how to understande these woordes, whether they were merily spoken or otherwise in disdaine of his former talke, aunswered thus: 'Alas, mistres Doritye, pardon me if my woordes seeme anything offensive unto you, assuring you that in this meane space that I have made my recourse to your housebande (whose healthe, by the sufferance of God, I have now well restored) am myself falne into a fever so extreame as neither Galen, Hypocrates, Avicen, Pliniy,[7] nor any other that ever gave rules of physicke could yet prescribe a medicine for the malladye or diet to suppresse the humour that feedes it. I shall not neede to use longe circumstaunce in the matter, knowing your wisedome to bee suche that you can well conceive the somme of all my greef. It is your beautye that is like to breede my bane and hath alreadye driven me into the greatest depth of daunger, unlesse some plaintes of pitye maye prevaile to yeelde remorse to him that vowes himself to doe you service during life.'

Mistres Doritye, seing the matter forced out as she looked for, could tell well enough how to handle maister doctor. And to make him the more eger she delayed him of with doubtfull speeches, but yet fedde him still with suche entising and pleasant countenaunces that ministered greate hope of comfort to his desease. She aunswered thus: 'And could you then finde in your harte (maister doctor) to deceive your very freend of his deare and loving wife? How can you offer him so manifest an injurye, to whom you are so lately linckt in so great a league of freendship as is betweene my houseband and yourself? I cannot thinke, maister doctor, that it is goodwill that hath caused you to move this sute unto me but rather to see how I were disposed or, peradventure, you use these wordes for exercise' sake, knowing the fashion of you men to bee suche as, by praising of our beautye, you thinke to bring us into a foole's paradize, that we well give credite straightwaye that you love us so soone as you shall but tell us the tale. But for my part (maister doctor), although I want wit to encounter you with wordes, so likewise I want wil to beleve anything that you have said, to be otherwise then wordes of course.'[8]

These speeches did ingender suche a nomber of swete and sowre alterations in maister doctor that for his life he wiste not how to understande them. One while they were like to drive him to dispaire. Another while they something quieted him with hope, but in the ende determining to followe what he had begonne, he sayed: 'Swete mistres, moste humbly I desire you to accompt of me not according to my desertes, which as yet are none at all, but according to the dutifull service which hereafter I vowe faithfully to doe unto you. And for the better testimonye of my wordes which (as you saye) seme to be of suche ordinary course, I desire no other credite maye bee given theim then shall bee agreable to my deedes, when it shall please you to commaunde. But, alas for the injurye which you speake of, that I should offer to your housebande, who indeede I make accompt to bee my verye freende. What is he, I praye you, that is able to prescribe lawes to love? And as love is without lawe, so it is without respect either of freende or foe, father or brother, riche or poore, mightye or weake, vertuous or vicious. The examples are so many and generall that I should but waste the time to repeate them. But (mistres Doritye) I proteste the verye cause that maketh me to move this matter unto you is for no ill-will that I bear to your housbande, but for the goodwil I beare to your swete self. You maye use your housbande as your housbande and me as your freende, glad to stande at reversion when your houseband maye take his fill of the banket and be glutted with more then enough. Farther, if you make so greate accompte of your housbande's good liking as you saye, what wives be ever better beloved or more made of by their housbandes then those that have discretion to helpe their frendes when they neede? But what sottishe opinion is this, which so many doeth holde, that they thinke it so greate an injurye for a man to seke the wife of his freende when he is attached by love, whose arrest neither goddes nor men have ben ever able to resist? But I praye you (mistres Doritye), if I might aske you this question, would you not thinke your goodwill better bestowed upon your housbande's freende then his foe? If you love your housebande, I am sure you wil saye I have reason. What should I longer trouble you, then, with circumstances? I knowe you are wise, and now I desire you for the goodwill that you beare to your housebande to pitye me, his freende, whom I trust you will restore with one drop of mercy, and the rather for your housband's sake.'

How thinke you, gentlewomen? Bee not these gentle perswasions to bee used by a doctor? Marye, he was no doctor of devinitye, and therefore you neede not followe his doctrine, unlesse you liste, yourselves, but this pitifull gentlewoman, seing maister doctor at suche desperate poinctes, for feare of daming of her owne soule that so deare a freende to her housbande as maister doctor was should perishe and bee so wilfully caste awaye through her default, she received him for her freend, and so I praye God give them joye.

But it fortuned afterwardes this gentlewoman to light into the companye of a lawyer, who, perceiving this dame to be of suche excellent beautye, joining himself something nere her, he sayed: 'Gentlewoman, although I have no skill in the arte of painting, yet assure yourself, your forme and passing beautye is so surely engraven and fixed in my minde that, although yourself were absent, I could drawe your perfect counterfecte, saving that I thinke all the apothecaries in this citye were not able to furnishe me with colours to make the perfecte distaine of the beautye in your face.'

Mistres Doritye, knowing whereto these speeches pretended, aunswered: 'Indeede, sir, it should seeme you would prove a passing painter, that can so cunningly painte forthe with wordes that which I knowe is too farre unworthye of so excellent a florishe as you would give it.'

'Mistres' (quoth the lawyer) 'if I have committed any offence in these woordes whiche I have spoken, it is in that I have taken upon me to praise your beautye and not able to give it suche due commendations as I see it doeth deserve, the sight whereof doeth so captivate my affections and hath so creepled all my sences that it hath caused me in maner to forgette myself. No marvaile, then, though my tongue doeth faile and is not able to expresse the perfection of you unto whom, with vowe of continuall service, I subjecte my life, living and libertye, if it please you to accept of it.'

This gentlewoman, that had yet but one freend to truste uppon, besides her housebande, beganne to thinke that store was no sore,[9] and therefore determined not to forsake his frendlye offer. But firste she demaunded of him of his facultye, and what trade of life he used, to whiche he aunswered that he was a gentleman appertaining to the lawe.

'It may well be so' (quoth she) 'for I perceive by your experience that this is not the firste plea that you have framed.'

'And yet, beleeve me' (quoth the lawyer) 'I was never brought before to pleade at beautye's barre, but, sithe my happe is suche, I humblye holde up my bandes, desiring to be tried by your courtesye and mine owne loyaltye, contenting myself to abide suche dome and judgement as it shall please you to appoincte, beeing the cheef and soveraigne judge yourself.'

She, replying, sayed: 'Seeing you have constituted me to give sentence at my pleasure, it is not the office of a good justicer to bee parciall in his owne cause, and therefore this is the hope you shal looke for at my bandes: that if hereafter in your deedes I shall see as plaine proofe of perfecte goodwill as your woordes by pretence importe likelihood of earnest love, you shall finde me ready to render suche recompence as shall fall out to your owne contentation and liking.' This comfortable answere verye well pleased him, and within a verye little space after he so handeled the matter that he had entered his action in her common place.[10]

Thus, what betweene maister doctor on the one side, who was still ministering of physicke unto her so long as there were any drugges remaining in his storehouse, and the lawyer on the other side, who sufficiently enstructed her with his lawe, they used suche haunt unto this gentlewoman's companye that the one beganne to growe suspicious on the other and, eche of theim desirous to have her severall to himself, beganne in the ende to envaigh the one against the other, the doctor against the lawyer, and the lawyer against the doctor, and to tel her to her face what they suspected, the one against the other. But mistres Doritye, beeing very angrye with theim bothe, that would so narrowlye looke into her doinges, did thinke it had been sufficient for reasonable men that she had received them into her favor and, as often as it had pleased them to come, she welcomed them as themselves did desire, and what can a man desire any more then to drinke so often as he shal be athirst? But with faire speeches she contented them bothe for a time. But she thought in th'ende to finde a remedy for that mischeef.

And thus it fell out that a souldiour who was lately retoured from the warres, I gesse about the same time that King Henry the Fift was retourned from the winning of Agincourt feelde,[11] this souldier, I saye, braving it out aboute the streates of the citye (as commonly the custome of souldiours is, to spend more in a moneth then they get in a yere), as he roomed to and fro and fortuned to espye this blasing starre looking out at a windowe, was sodainly stroken into a greater maze to see this lampe of light then ever he had been in the feelde to see the ensignes of his enemies, and was so farre overcharged with her love that, but for feare to have been marked by the passers-by, he would have stoode still gazing and looking uppon her. But, learning in the ende that she was the mistres of the house, he began to devise how he might make her understande the fervencye of his love, on whiche he determined to write unto her. But then he knewe not how to beginne his letter, because souldiours are verye seldome accustomed to endite, especially any of these loving lines. And to speake unto her, he was likewise to learne how to use his tearmes, neither wiste he how to come into her presence, but you shall see fortune favoured him.

For in an evening as he passed through the streate she was sitting alone in her doore to take the aire and, comming unto her, not knowing for his life how to begin his tale, in the ende, 'Mistres,' (quoth he) 'I praye you, is your housebande within?'

'No, surely, sir' (quoth she) 'he is abroade in the toune, but I knowe not where.'

'And I would gladlye have spoken with him' (quoth the souldiour) 'if he had ben within.'

'Beleeve me, sir, he is not within' (quoth she) 'but if it please you to leave your arrande with me, at his comming home I will shew him your minde.'

'In faith, mistress' (quoth the souldiour) 'my arrande is not greate. I would but have craved his helpe in chusing me a wife, because I perceive he hath some experience in the facultye or els I think he could never have chosen so well for himself.'

'If your arrande be no other then this' (quoth mistres Doritye) 'you maye at your owne leisure come and doe it yourself. And, as for my housebande's experience that you speake of, although peradventure it bee not fitting to your fancye, yet I am well assured that he hath made his choise of suche a one as he himself very wel liketh.'

'I beleeve it well' (quoth the souldiour) 'and if without offence I might speake it, I sweare, so God help me, I like his choise so well that I would thinke myself more then a thousand times happye if I might be his halfe, or if my unworthinesse deserved not so great a portion, I would crave no more then yourself would willingly bestow on me, accordingly as you should see me able to deserve it.'

'Why, sir' (quoth mistres Doritye) 'I doe not understande whereunto your speeches doeth tende, neither what part you would have me to give you, when I have alreadye bestowed of my housebande bothe my hande, my harte, my minde and goodwill.'

'Alas, gentlewoman' (quoth the souldiour) 'these bee none of them that I would crave. There is yet an overplus whiche you have not yet spoken of, whiche if you please to bestow of a souldiour, I should think myself the happiest man alive, whose love and good liking towardes you is suche that I trust in time to come yourself will judge me worthye for my well-deserving zeale to have deserved hire.'

'Souldiours are seldome seene' (quoth mistres Doritye) 'to marche under the banner of Venus, but whatsoever you bee, doe you thinke to overthrowe my vertues with the assault of your wanton perswasions, or would you make me beleeve that you love me as you saye when you have no more respect to the hurt of my soule?'

'Gentlewoman' (quoth the souldiour) 'I am not able to

encounter you with wordes, because it hath not been my profession, nor training-up, but if you doubte of my love and good liking, please it you to make triall, commaund any thing that yourself shall thinke requisite, whiche if I doe not performe to the uttermoste, then esteme my love indeede to be but feined, and where you thinke that I goe aboute to seeke the prejudice or hurte of your soule beleeve me I never ment it.'

Mistres Doritye, who had beene well acquainted before with many suiters, had never been apposed with such a rough-hewen fellowe that was so blunt and plaine, as well in his gesture as in his tearmes. Beganne to thinke with herself that he might well bee a souldiour, for she knewe that they had little skill in the courting of gentlewomen, yet she perceived by his countenaunce the vehemencye of the love he bare unto her and, perceiving his plainesse, she beganne to thinke him more fitter for her diet then either maister doctor or maister lawyer, that could not bee contented the one with the other when she gave them bothe so muche as they could crave. And, therefore, thinking with herself that to loose any longer time were but a poinct of follye, taking the souldiour by the hande, she ledde him up into a chamber, where other speeches were passed betweene them in secrete, which I could never yet understande.[12] And what they did farther when they were by themselves, gentlewomen, I praye gesse you, but this I must advertise you of: that before they came forth of the chamber againe, the souldiour had pleased mistres Doritye so wel that both maister doctor and maister lawyer were put quite out of conceipt, so that from that time forwards when they came of their visitation the gentlewoman was not well at ease, or she had companye with her, or she was not at home, that they could no more speake with her. Which tourned them both into a wonderful agonye. The doctor had thought she had forsaken him for the love of the lawyer. The lawyer he thought as muche by the doctor, that in the ende, not knowing otherwise how to spitte out their venime against her, they devised eache of them a letter, whiche they sent her.

The first of these letters delivered unto her came from the doctor. Which letter he left unpointed of purpose, because that in the reading of it, it might bee poincted two wayes and made to seeme either to her praise or dispraise, but mistres Doritye herself in the reading of it poincted it as I have set it doune, and followeth in this sorte.[13]

'And who would have thought, mistres Doritye, that for the loving advertisementes given you by your frende, you could so lightly have shaken him of, if I burdened you with anything that might seeme greevous unto you, thinke it was love that ledde me unto it, for that I protest inwardly in my minde, I never did esteeme you otherwise then for as honest a gentlewoman as lives this daye in Bridewell,[14] I have heard saye some have been scourged more upon evill will, then for any desertes whereof they might justly be accused, so if it be my happe to suffer undeserved penaunce, I must impute it to my owne misfortune, but yet contrarye to my expectation, considering how I have ever taken you to be given in your conditions to practise unseemly, filthye, and detestable thinges. I knowe you have ever abhored to live chastly, decently, and orderly. You have ever been trained up to be wanton, proude, and incontinent. You never tooke delight in that was good, honest, or commendable. You wholye gave yourself to leudenesse, luste and lecherye. You were an open enemye to vertue: a friend to vice. What should I saye, I doe but waste the time in the setting of you forth, and therefore will leave you like as I founde you.'

This letter brought mistres Doritye into suche a furye when she had perused it that she sware by no beggers[15] she would be so revenged upon the doctor that she would make him a spectacle to all the physitions in the worlde how they should abuse an honest gentlewoman while they lived. And in the middest of her melancholye her dearest freende, the souldiour, happened to come in, whom she made partaker of all her secretes, shewing him the letter whiche maister doctor had sent her. And as they were devising how to use revengemente a messenger was knocking at the doore to deliver a letter from the lawyer, the tenure whereof followeth in this maner:

'Maye this bee the rewarde of my true and faithfull love, whiche so firmely I have borne thee? Or is this the delight of thy dalliaunce, whiche so many times thou haste used with me? So careleslye to shake me of, as though I had committed some notable abuse, when indeede I have loved thee a greate deale more then I perceive thou art worthye of.

'Oh feminine flatterye, o fained fauning, o counterfect courtesye, oh depe dissimulation. But what hope is otherwise to be looked for in these rites of Cresside's kinde?[16] Or what constancye maye any man thinke to finde in a woman? No, no, if a man

maye generally speake of their sexe, you shall never finde them
but counterfect in their courtesye, fained in their frendship,
dissembling in their deedes, and in all their actions moste
daungerous for men to deale withall. For is she have a faire face,
it is ever matched with a cruell harte, their heavenly lookes with
hellishe thoughtes, their modest countenaunces with mercilesse
mindes. They have witte, but it is in wiles. If they love, it is too
vehement. When they hate it is to the death. But, good God,
with how many fopperies are they accustomed to feede fooles? I
meane suche as bee lovemakers and suiters unto theim whom
they delaye with as many devises as they be in number that
seekes to serve them. Some they lure with lookes. Some they
practise with promises. Some they feede with flattery. Some they
delaye with daliance. Some they winde in with wiles. Some they
keepe with kisses. Some they diet with dissimulation. One must
weare her glove. Another must weare her garter. Another must
weare her coulers. Another shall weare the spoile of as muche
as she can gette from all the reste by cousonage. And yet, to see
how daintye these darlinges wil seeme to those that be not
acquainted with their customes were able to dash a young man
out of countenaunce. I warrant you, they can make it more nice
then wise, more coye then comely, more fine then honest.[17] And
to whom doe they make the matter most daungerous but to
them that deserveth best to be rewarded? For where they see a
man that is drouned in affection towards them, over him they
will triumph and can tell how to ride the foole without a snaffle.
One while they will crosse him with froward language, then
againe comfort him with some fained looke. Now she drives
him into desperation with frouning face, by and by she baites
him againe with banquettes of uncertaine hope. Suche is their
evill nature (as I saye) that they will shewe themselves moste
squemishe and daintye to him that loves them moste entirely,
and him that seekes them least dishonestly, him they rewarde
with their coldest courtesye. For better proofe, lette a man seeke
to winne one of these tender peeces that goes for a maide
honestly and in the waye of mariage, and, I warrant you, she
will make the matter more coye and nice to him that meanes
good earnest then to another that comes but to trye and prove
them.[18] And what signes of shamefastnesse will they seeme to
make when a man doeth but touch them. Faining themselves to
be too young, when (indeede) if they once past the age of fifteen

yeres (if they were not afeard of breeding of bugges in their beallye), by their good willes they would never be without the companye of a man.[19] Thus to conclude, their nature is openly to scorne all men, bee their loves never so honest, and secretly to refuse no manne, be his lust never so leude. Full aptly did Salomon in his Proverbes compare you to wine that can make us so dronken with your devises that, notwithstanding we see the snares with our eyes whiche you have sette to entangle us, wee cannot shunne the baite, whiche wee knowe will breede our bane.[20]

'Thus muche, mistres Doritye, I have thought good to signifye unto you, whose discourtisye at this time hath caused me so generally to envaye against your whole sexe, not otherwise minding to accuse yourself perticularly, knowing that if you should otherwise have used me then you have, you should have degressed and swarved quite from your kinde, and so I leave you.'

Gentlewomen, I beseche you, forgive me my fault in the publishing this infamous letter. I promise you I doe but signifye it according to the copye which this unhappye lawyer sent to mistres Doritye, and when I had well considered the blasphemye that he had used against your sexe, I cutte my penne all to peeces, wherewith I did copye it out, and if it had not been for the hurting of myself, I promise you I would have cutte and mangled my owne fingers, wherewith I held the penne while I was writing of it. And, trust me, according to my skill, I could well have founde in my harte to encountre him with an aunswere in your defence, but then I was interrupted by another, as you shall well perceive.[21] For the souldiour, whiche you have heard spoken of, that was remaining with mistres Doritye, when he had perused this letter was put into a wonderfull chafe, and in the middest of his furye he uttered these wordes.

'Ah, moste vile and blasphemous beast, what art thou that with suche exclamations goest about to defame those whom by all honest humanitye and manhood we be willed specially to love, honour and reverence? What art thou? A man, a devill or a subtill lawyer, yea surelye, and so thou mayest well bee, and herein haste thou shewed thyself no whit at al to desgresse from thy profession. For, as at the firste the lawes were constituted to minister justice and to give everyone his right, so now are they made, by the practise of a nomber of pettiefoggers, the instruments of all iniquitye and wrong. Even so, that worthye sexe whiche at the first were given unto man by the almightye God himself to be his cheefest comfort and consolation, see here the practise of a wicked caitife who with his eloquence would perswade us that they were our greatest ruine and desolatione. Ah, wicked wretche that thou art, how thinkest thou to escape thus to blowe forthe thy blasphemye against those blessed ones, whom God hath perfited above all other creatures? For at their firste creation, they were made of the moste beste and purified mettall of mane, where man himself was framed but of slime and drosse.[22] What reason, then, that, being at the first framed moste pure and perfecte creatures, but that they should continue their firste perfection to the ende of the worlde. And like as at the first they were made more excellent then man, where should wee now seeke for grace, vertue and goodnese but onely in the feminine sexe, according to their singuler creation.

'I trust this is so evident that there is no man able to denaye it, and enough to prove that as women at the first were created moste perfecte, so they have still remained the storehouse of all grace, vertue and goodness, and that if there be anything founde in us men that is worthye of commendation, we are onely to give thankes to women from whom wee receive it, as being descended from out their entrailes. But with how great and manifolde miseries should wee men bee daily afflicted were it not for the comforte wee finde at women's handes, for besides that by their industrye we be netified, made mor clendly, and kept swete, who otherwise of ourselves we should become to bee moste filthye and lothsome creatures, so at all times and seasons they bee so necessarye and convenient aboute us that it were impossible for us to bee without their blessed companies. First, in our health they content us with their familiaritye, in our sicknesse they cherish us; in our mirth they make it more abounde, in sorrowe their companye doeth beguile our pensive thoughtes; in pleasure they bee our cheefe delightes, in paine their presence bredeth comfort to our grief; in wealth what greater treasure then to enjoye our beloved, in want what greater wealth then a loving a faithfull wife; in peace we labour still to get their liking, in warres they make us shew ourselves more valiaunt. But how is it possible that women should behave themselves but that there are some wil finde faught with them. First, if she be familiare, wee judge her to be light; if she seeme anything straunge in her conversation, "Ah," we saye, "she is a dangerous dame"; if merrye wee thinke her to be naught; if sad, we saye she is more grave then honest; if she bee talkative, we saye she is a doudye or a slut; if they denaye us their curtesye when we sue unto them, wee saye they be cruell tigers, beares and bugges; if they have compassion of us, we discredit them amongst our companions.

'But see the cunning of a caitife, that would wreste the wordes of Salomon to the dispraise of women, because in his Proverbes he compareth them to wine. But, to interprete the words of Salomon by Salomon himself, in another place of the same proverbes, he willeth wine should bee given to comforte those that bee feeble and weake.[23] Now, compare these places together and see what harme he hath doen to women, and, in my opinion, he could not more aptly have made a comparison, for as wine is a comforte to those that are feeble and weake, so are women our greatest solace, both in sicknesse and in health. But if any wil saye that wine maketh us dronken and from reasonable men to become more brute then beastes, I aunswere that the faught is not to be imputed to the wine, but to the beastlinesse of him that taketh more then enough, for there is nothing so precious for our behoofes, but by our own abuse we make it seeme most vile and lothsome. And thus, graunting maister lawyer his comparison to be true, he hath doen little hurt, saving he hath shewed himself a diligent scholler to his maister the devill, who is father of all lies, in maintaining so manifest a lie against suche harmelesse creatures.'

There were many other speeches pronounced by this souldiour in the behaulf of women, whiche I have forgot to recite. But I pray, gentlewomen, how like you by this souldiour? Doe you not thinke him worthye a sargante's fee for his aunswere? In my opinion, you ought to love souldiours the better for his sake.

But to retourne to mistres Doritye, those two letters had so vexed her that there was nothing in her minde but how she might be revenged. Her freende the souldiour promised for her sake that he would so cudgill bothe maister doctor and the lawyer, that they should not in one moneth after be able to lift their armes to their heds, saving he wist not how to get them into a place convenient, for that it was dangerous to deale with them in the open streates. Mistres Doritye, giving him twentye kisses for his courtesye, tolde him she would devise to bring them into some place where he might worke his will.

Presently after, mistres Doritye sent for maister doctor, whom she knewe very well how to handle, and in a milde maner she began greatly to blame him that being wise, as she knewe him to be, would so rashly judge of her, for that he might well know that there was some great cause that moved her to use him as she had doen otherwise then he had conjectured. And thus, with many other like speeches, she so smothed the matter with maister doctor that she made him beleeve her housbande had some suspition in their familiaritye and that by his commaunde-ment she had abstained his companye for a time. 'The which, maister doctor' (quoth she) 'I did for no evill will that I beare you, but for a time to bleare my housbande's eyes, thinking in the ende so to have handled the matter that we might have continued our accustomed freendship without any maner of suspition.' And then, drawing forthe the letter whiche the doctor had sent her, she sayed: 'But see, maister doctor, your good opinion conceived in me. Loe, here the reward that I have for my courtesye bestowed of you thus to raile and rage against me as though I were the moste notable strumpet in a countrey.'

The doctour, knowing in what forme he had wright the letter and desirous againe to renue his late acquaintaunce, aunswered that he never writte letter unto her whereby he had given any occasion for her to take any greef.

'No have?' (quoth mistres Doritye) 'read you then heare your owne lines', taking him the letter, whiche the doctor, as I told you before, had lefte unpointed, and therefore in the reading he poincted it after this maner:

'And who would have thought (mistres Doritye) that for the loving advertisementes given you by your freende, you could so lightly have shaken him of, if I burdeined you with anything, that might seme greevous unto you, thinke it was love that ledde me unto it, for that I protest inwardlye in my minde, I did never esteeme you otherwise, then for as honest a gentlewoman as lives this daye. In Bridwell I have heard saye, some have been scourged more upon evill will, then for any desertes whereof they might justly be accused. So if it be my hap to suffer undeserved penaunce, I must impute it to mine owne misfortune, but yet contrarye to my expectation, considering how I have ever taken you to be given in your conditions. To practise unseemly, filthye, and detestable thinges, I knowe you have ever abhorred. To live chastlye, decentlye, and orderly, you have ever bin trained up. To be wanton, proude, and incontinent, you never tooke delight. In that was good, honest or commendable, you wholye gave yourself. To lewdnesse, luste, and lecherye, you were an open enemye, to vertue a freende, to vice, what should I saye, I dooe but waste the time in the setting of you foorthe, and therefore will leave you like as I founde you.[24]

'I praye you, mistres Doritye' (quoth the doctor) 'where is this railing and raging you speake of? I trust I have written nothing that might discontent you.' Mistres Doritye, perceiving the knaverye of the doctour, and seeing the matter fell out so fitte for her purpose, first giving him a freendly busse, she said, 'Alas, my deare freend, I confesse I have trespassed in misconstering of your lines. But forgive me, I praye you, and now have compassion of her whose love towarde you is suche that it is impossible for me to live without your good liking. And seing that my housebande's jelousye is so muche that you can have no longer accesse to my house but it must needes come to his eare by suche spye and watche as he hath layed, neither myself can goe abroade to any place, but I am dogged and followed by suche as he hath appointed. But now, if your love bee but halfe so muche towardes me as I trust I have deserved and hereafter doe meane to requite, I have alreadye devised a meane how for ever I might enjoye my desired freend without either lette or molestation of anyone, seeme he never so muche to be offended at the matter.'

The doctor, the gladdest man in the worlde to heare these newes, aunswered: 'And what is it then that should make you stagger or doubt of the frendship of your loving doctor? No, not if thereby I should hazard the losse both of life and goodes.'

'Alas' (quoth mistres Doritye) 'God defende I should woorke you so greate a prejudice, and I beseche you use no more suche speeches unto me that I should goe about to put you into any suche perill, the remembraunce whereof is more greevous unto me then if I had felte the force of a thousande deathes. And now behold my determination and what I have devised. You have a house not farre hence standing in the feeldes, whiche you keepe for your solace and recreation in the time of sommer. To this house I have devised how you maye so secretly conveigh me that you maye there keepe me at your pleasure to your owne use and to my greate contentation, where I maye at pleasure enjoye him more dearely beloved unto me then the balles of mine owne eyes.' And herewithall she gave him other Judas kisse,[25] that the doctor desired her of all freendship not to bee long in her determination, for that he was readye to followe her direction whensoever it would please her to commaunde. Yea, if it were presently, he was readye.

Mistres Doritye, who had driven the matter to that passe she looked for, sayed: 'Naye, maister doctour, there resteth yet another thing. My housebande's jelousye (as I tolde you) is suche that there muste bee great circumspection used in the conveighing me awaye, and therefore give eare to that I have devised: I have in my house a certaine male with stuffe that is left with me to bee sent by the carriers into the countrye, whereof my housbande doeth knowe verye well. This stuffe I will cause to bee secretly taken forthe and to bee sent to the carrier's, trust up in some other thing, without any knowledge to any, saving to my maide, that shall woorke this feate herself, whose trustinesse I knowe to bee suche as there is no suspition to be had in the matter. The whiche when she hath done, she shall trusse up me in the same male. Then see that you faile not tomorowe in the evening about eight of the clocke, disguised in a porter's weede, to come to my house to enquire for the same male, whiche you shall saye you will beare to the carrier's. My maide, who shall of purpose bee readye to waite for your comming at the houre, shall make no bones to deliver you this male, and thus, without either doubte or jealousye of any one, you maye carrye me into the feeldes, where for your better ease you maye take me forthe, and disguising ourselves wee maye walke together to your house aforesayed, where I maye remaine, without any maner of suspition or knowledge to any, so long as it shall please yourself.'

'O most excellent devise' (quoth the doctor). 'I have this matter alreadye at my fingers' endes, and I warrant you, you shal see me playe the porter so cunninglye that how many soever I meete, there shall none of them be able to suspect me.' Thus with a feigned kisse that she againe bestowed of him, for that time they departed.

Mistres Doritye in like maner sent for the lawyer, whom she handeled in like sorte as she had done the doctor, making him beleeve that her housebande's jealousye was suche, as she durst no more come in his companye. But of herself she loved him so entirely that she would hazard anything for his sake, and because he should the better beleeve it: 'Tomorrowe (quoth she) 'in the afternoone, my housebande will be forthe of the dores, wherefore I praye you faile not aboute three of the clocke to come and visite me, when we shall have leisure to disporte ourselves to our better contentation.'

Many like enticing wordes she used, whiche so perswaded the lawyer. Then, dreading no badde measure at all, he promised her not to faile but he would keepe his hower, and thus departed verye joyfull that he had againe recovered his mistres. And the nexte daye, even as it had stroke three of the clocke, he was knocking at the doore of this gentlewoman, who, looking for his comming, was readye to receive him. And up they goe together to a chamber whiche she had appointed for the purpose, where for a time she dalied him of with devices, and sodainly her maide (according as her mistres had given her instructions) came hastely to the chamber doore, calling her mistres, saying that her maister was come in and had asked for her.

Mistres Doritye, who was not to learne to playe her parte, seemed to be striken into a wonderful feare.[26] 'Alas' (quoth she to the lawyer) 'for the love of God, keepe yourself secret for a time that I maye goe doune and ridde him awaye, if it be possible.' And, thus going her waye doune, she shuttes the doore after her.

The lawyer, who was readye to beraye himself for feare, crepte under the bedde, where she lette him alone the space of an hower, and then, comming up into the chamber and could not see him, she beganne to muse what was become of him. He, hearing one was come in at the chamber doore, beganne to prye out under the bedde's feete, and perceiving by the skirt of her goune who it was, with a faint voice he sayed: 'Alas, my deare, what newes? Is your housebande gone?'

'Ah, my loving freende' (quoth she) 'I was never so hardlye beset sith I was borne. My housebande is come home with three or fower of his frendes, whiche he mette withall in the citye and bee come out of the countrey of purpose to make merrye with him, and here they bee appoincted this night to suppe, and hether bee come to their beddes so long as they remaine in the citye, and this chamber is appoincted for twoo of them to lie in that, for my life, I knowe not what shifte to make nor how to conveigh you hence.'

'Alas' (quoth the lawyer) 'then am I utterly undone. For the love of God, devise some meanes to conveigh me out of the house, for I would not remaine all night in this perplexitye, no, not for all the golde in the worlde.'

Mistres Doritye, making a little pause, sodainlye, as though she had an invention but even then come into her hedde, she sayed: 'I have this onely remedye left. Here is in the house a male full of stuffe, whiche should this night be sent to the carriers. My devise is therefore to take forthe the stuffe and laye it aside till somtime the next weeke, when I will make shift to sende the stuffe awaye verye well, and you shall bee presently packed up in this male, whiche my maide shall doe while I am below with my housebande and his freendes. And so causing a porter to be sent for, he shall carrye you to your chamber, or to any other place where it shall please yourself, so that my housebande, seeing this male got forthe of doores, will thinke it is the stuffe whiche he knoweth this night should be sent.'

'No better devise in the worlde' (quoth the lawyer) 'and let the porter conveigh this male to my chamber, you knowe where, and deliver it to my manne, as sent from his maister, and will him to give him fourtye pence for his labour.'

The matter thus determined, mistres Doritye sent up her maide with this emptye male, wherein she trussed up the lawyer, and there she left him lying from five of the clocke untill it was past eight. And in the sommer season, the weather being verye hotte, the lawyer had like to have been smothered where he laye. At the length, according to poinctmente comes maister doctour, disguised like a right porter, with a longe gaberdine doune to the calfe of his legges, and he enquires for a male that should goe to the carriers. 'Yea, Marye' (quoth the maide) 'if you please to come in, it is ready for you.' The doctor, beeing a good sturdye lubber, tooke up the male verye easily, for feare of brusing the gentlewoman's tender ribbes, whom he had thought he had upon his backe, and thus forthe of dores he goes, taking the next waye towardes his lodging.

Mistres Doritye, with her beloved soldiour (whom she had made privye to her devise), stoode where she might see maister doctor in his porter's weede going with his carriage. Whereat, when they had a while sported themselves, the souldiour folowed maister doctor an easye pase, but onely to kepe the sight of him. And the doctour he tooke his waye through the stretes with a maine pase till he had recovered the feeldes, where, looking aboute him to see what companye was stirring, sawe nobodye neare him but the souldiour, whom he did not know. And then, crossing the waye from the common pathes, he came to the side of a bancke, and being wearye (as he was not to be blamed, considering the knavishe burthen that he had borne uppon his backe), he, laying downe the male tenderlye uppon the side of the bancke, seeing nobodye but the souldiour, who was but a little distance from him, sayed: 'Ah, my sweete wenche, I can see no creature stirring in al the feeldes but one manne, which is comming this waye, who so soone as he is paste, I will undoe the male.'

The lawyer in the male, when he felt the porter lay him doune, was in a good hope that he had been in his owne chamber, but, hearing by these speeches that he was in the feeldes, began to conjecture assuredly that the porter had spoken those wordes to some woman that was in his companye with whom he was confederate for the stealing of suche thinges as they should finde in the male and that, when they should open the male and finde him there, they would not sticke to cut his throte for feare least he should bewraye them and for the onely spoile of suche thinges as he had about him, that the lawyer was in suche a perplexitye that he wiste not for his life what he might doe. One while he had thought to have cried out for helpe, then he thought it would the soner bring him to his ende.

And as he continued thus in the middest of his muse, the souldiour was come to the place, and, speaking to the doctor, he sayed: 'Porter, it seemeth thou haste been knavishly loden, for I perceive thou art very hot. But what hast thou in thy male, I praye thee, that thou art carrying this waye so late in the evening?'

'Marrye', quoth the doctor, 'I have ware there, suche as it is.'

'Hast thou ware, knave?' (quoth the souldiour). 'Is that a sufficiente aunswere? What ware is it? Menne's ware, or women's ware?'

'Sir, I knowe not', quoth the porter, 'I have but the carrying of it to a gentleman's house that is here hard by.'

'Well,' quoth the souldiour, 'undoe your trusse, for I will see what wares you have there before you and I depart.'

'Why, sir' (quoth the porter) 'should I be so bolde to undoe a gentleman's male that is delivered me in trust to be caried? No, sir, you shall pardon me, if you were my father.' And herewithall he tooke the male upon his backe and beganne to goe his wayes. But the souldiour, knowing better what was in the male then the porter himself that carried it, and beeing provided for the purpose with a good cudgell, let drive halfe a dosen blowes at the male, as it laye upon his backe, so surely, that the lawyer cries out: 'Alas, alas, alas.'

'Why, porter' (quoth the souldiour) 'have you quicke wares in your male? No mervaile you were so daintye in the shewing of it.'

Herewithall the doctor layed doune his male and kneeling doune to the souldiour, saied: 'Ah, sir, for the love of God, bee content, and I will not let to confesse the whole truth unto you. I have a gentlewoman in my male whiche I have stolne from her housebande, and, seing you to be a gentleman but yong in yeres and impossible but that you should love the companye of a faire woman, beholde, I will deliver her unto you to use at your pleasure, and when you shall see time to restore her unto me againe, desiring you, sir, of all courtesye, to seeke no other displeasure against us.'

'You have sayed well' (quoth the souldiour) 'but is she suche a one as is to bee liked, faire, fresh, and yong?'

'Trust me, sir' (quoth the doctor) 'if she bee not as faire and well liking as any dame within the walles of this citye, make me an example to all other how they shall dissemble with a gentleman suche as you are.'

'Thou sayest well' (quoth the souldiour) 'and now I thinke long till I have a sight of this paragon whiche thou haste so praised unto me.'

'You shall see her straight, sir' (quoth the doctor). And herewithall he began to unlase the male with great expedition, whiche, when he had unlosed at the one ende, that he might come to the sight of this gentlewoman's face (as he had thought), he sayed to the soldiour: 'See here the sight whiche you so muche desire.' And pulling the ende of the male open with his handes, the lawyer thruste forthe his hedde and looked with suche a piteous countenaunce, as though he had been readye to bee turned of the ladder.[27] But the doctor, seing a face to appeare with a long beard, was in suche a maze, that he could not tell in the worlde what he might saye.

The souldiour, who had never more adoe then to forbeare laughter to see how these twoo, the one beheld the other, sayed to the doctor: 'And is this the faire gentlewoman whiche thou hast promised me? Haste thou nobodye to mocke but me, that with suche commendations thou givest praise to a woman, whereby to set my teeth an edge, and then in the ende thus to delude me?[28] But I will teache thee how to playe the knave againe while thou liveste.' And herewithall he layed on with his cudgell, sparing neither hedde, shoulders, armes, backe, nor breast. And so he bumbasted the doctor, that for the space of a quarter of a yere after, he was not able to lift ane urinall so hie as his hedde.[29]

The lawyer, who had nothing out of the male but his hedde, seeing this fraye, struggeled so muche as he could to have gotte forthe and to have runne awaye while the porter was a-beating, but it would not bee. His armes were so surely laced doune by his sides that for his life he could not gette them forthe.

The souldiour, when he had throughly requited maister doctour's knaverye that he had used against his beloved mistres in his letter, left him and beganne to bende himself towardes the lawyer. The lawyer, seing the souldiour comming, had thought verely that he had been some good fellowe that was walking there so late to have taken some prey, said: 'O sir, for the love of God, spare my life and take my purse.'

To whom the souldiour aunswered: 'Naye, villaine, my comming is neither to take thy life nor thy purse, but to minister revengemente for thy large speeches, whiche, like a discourteous wretche, thou haste used against a woman.' And therewithall layed upon him so long as he was able to fetch any breath, and then calling the porter unto him, he sayed: 'Let these wordes whiche I minde to speake suffice for a warning to you bothe. If ever I maye learne that any of you, hereafter this, do use any misdemeanure towardes any woman, either by word or writing, assure yourselves, that, although I have but dallied with you at this time, I wil devise some one meane or other to minister revenge, that all suche as you bee shall take an example by you. And thus I leave you', going his waye to his sweeteharte, telling her the whole discourse how he had spedde, by whom he was welcomed with a whole laste of kisses, etc.

And now to retourne to those twoo that were lefte in the feeldes, as you have heard. The doctor, taking good vewe of the lawyer, knewe him verye well, but the doctor was so disguised in his porter's apparrell that the lawyer did not knowe him, but sayed unto him: 'A mischeef light of all suche porters that, when they be put in truste with carriages into the citye, will bring them into the feeldes to such banquettes as these.'

'Marrye,' quoth the doctor, 'a mischeef take all suche bur-thens that when a manne hath almoste broken his backe with bearing them and then shall receive such a recompence for his labour as I have doen.'

'Villaine' (quoth the lawyer) 'why diddest thou not beare me to my chamber, as thou wert willed when thou diddest receive me?'

'I would I had carried thee to the gallowes' (quoth the doctor) 'so I had escaped this scouring. But I perceive this banquette was prepared for us bothe.' And herewithall with much adoe he got of the porter's coate, and, making himself knowne to the lawyer, eache of them conferred with the other how cunningly they had been dealt withall, and did thinke it not beste for them any farther to deale in the matter, for feare of farther mischeef, but with much adoe got them home, where the lawyer kept his bedde very long after. But the doctor tooke sparmaceti and suche like thinges that bee good for a bruse and recovered himself in a shorte space.

Now it fell out afterwardes that this souldiour, who lived in greate credite with mistres Doritye (as he had well deserved), was imployed in the kinge's warres against forraine foes with a greate number of others, where he spent his life in his prince's quarrell. And mistres Doritye, sorrowing a long time the losse of so faithfull a freende, seeing the diversitye of men, that she had made her choise emongst three and had found but one honest, feared to fall into any further infamye, contented herself to live orderly and faithfully with her housband al the rest of her life. And her housebande, who never understoode any of these actions, loved her dearely to his dying daye.

And now to saye something of the other brother and his wife, whiche as you have heard was suche a notable scold that her housebonde could never enjoy good daye nor merye houre. She was suche a devill of her tongue and would so crossebite him with such tauntes and spitefull quippes as, if at any time he had been merrye in her companye, she would tell him his mirthe proceaded rather in the remembraunce of that she had brought

him then for any love that he had to herself. If he were sadde, it
was for greef she was not dedde that he might enjoye that she
had. If he used to goe abroad, then he had been spending of that
he never gotte himself. If he taried at home, she would saye it
was happye he had gotten suche a wife that was able to keepe
him so idelly. If he made any provision for good cheare or to
fare well in his house, she would bid him spende that whiche he
himself had brought. If he shewed himself to bee sparing, then
she would not pinche of that whiche was her owne. Thus, doe
what he could, all that ever he did was taken in the worste parte.
And, seing that by no maner of faire meanes he was able to
reclaime her, in the ende he devised this waye: himself, with a
trustye freend that he made of his counsaill, gotte and pinioned
her armes so faste that she was not able to undoe them, and
then putting her into an old peticoate which he rent and tattered
in peeces of purpose, and shaking her heire loose about her eyes,
tare her smocke sleeves that her armes were all beare, and
scratching them all over with a bramble that the bloud followed,
with a greate chaine about her legge wherewith he tied her in a
darke house that was on his backside.[30] And then, calling his
neibours about her, he woulde seeme with greate sorrowe to
lament his wive's distresse, telling them that she was sodainly
become lunatique, whereas, by his geasture, he tooke so greate
greefe, as though he would likewise have runne madde for
companye.

But his wife (as he had attired her) seemed indeede not to be
well in her wittes. But, seeing her housebande's maners, shewed
herself in her conditions to bee a right bedlem. She used no
other wordes but cursinges and banninges, crying for the plague
and the pestilence, and that the Devill would teare her housbande in peeces. The companye that were about her, they would
exhorte her: 'Good neighbour, forget these idle speeches, which
doeth so muche distemper you, and call upon God, and he will
surely helpe you.'

'Call upon God for help?' (quoth the other) 'Wherein should
he helpe me, unlesse he would consume this wretche with fire
and brimstone? Other helpe I have no need of.'

Her housebande, he desired his neighbours, for God's love,
that they would helpe him to praye for her. And thus, al together
kneeling doune in her presence, he beganne to saye 'Miserere',
whiche all they sayed after him.[31]

But this did so spight and vexe her that she never gave over her railing and raging againste them all. But in the ende, her houseband, who by this shame had thought to have reclaimed her, made her to become from evil to worse and was glad himself, in the ende, cleane to leave and to get himself from her into a straunge countrey, where he consumed the rest of his life.

Thus to conclude, besides the matter that I meane to prove, menne maye gather example here, when they goe a-wiving, not to chose for beautye without vertue, nor for riches without good conditions. There be other examples, if they be well marked, worth the learning, both for men and women, whiche I leave to the discretion of the reader.

OF GONSALES AND HIS VERTUOUS
WIFE AGATHA

The Argument

*Gonsales, pretending to poison his verteous wife for the love
of a courtisane, craved the helpe of Alonso, a scholer something practised in physicke. Who in the steade of poison gave
him a pouder whiche did but bring her in a sounde sleepe
during certaine howers, but Gonsales, judging (indeede) that
his wife had been dedde, caused her immediatly to be buried.
The scholer againe, knowing the operation of his poulder, for
the greate love he bare to Agatha went to the vault where she
was entombed about the hower that he knew she should
awake. When, after some speeches used betweene theim, he
carried her home to his owne house, where she remained for
a space. In the meanetime, Gonsales, being married to his
courtisane, was by her accused to the governour for the
poisoning of his first wife. Whereof being apprehend, he
confessed the facte and was therefore judged to die. Whiche
being knowne to Agatha, she came to the judge, and, clearing
her housbande of the crime, they lived together in perfect
peace and amitye.*

There was sometime in the citye of Siville, in Spaine, a gentilman
named Gonsales, who, though he were a man of yeares sufficient
to be stayed and to give over the wanton pranckes of youthfull
follye, yet was he by nature so enclined to followe his lustes,
and withall so variable and so unconstant, that he suffered
himself to be ruled wholy by his passions and measured all his
doing rather by his delightes and pleasures then by sounde
discourse and rule of reason. This gentleman, falling in love
with a gentlewoman of the sayed citye, whose name was Agatha,
sought all the meanes he could to have her to wife. And her
freendes, although they were well enough enformed of the
disposition of Gonsales, wherby they might have feared the
entreatye of their kinswoman, for that they knewe him very

riche and her dowrye not to be very greate, they were well content to bestowe her uppon him and thought that they had in so doing placed her very well. But, before the first yere after their marriage was fullye expired, Gonsales, following his wonted humour and waxing wearye of love, grewe to desire chaunge, giving thereby a notable example for women to learne how little it is to their commoditye or quiet to matche themselves to suche that be rather riche then wise and how muche it were better for them to bee married to men then to their goodes.

For beeing come to sojourne in that streate wherein he dwelt a notable courtesane, who to the outward shewe was verye faire, though inwardly she was moste foule, as she that under a goodlye personage did cover a wicked and dangerous minde, corrupted with all vices (as for the moste part all suche women doen), it was Gonsales' chaunce to be one of the first that fell into those snares whiche she had sette for suche simple men's mindes as haunte after the exteriour apparance of those thinges whiche their senses make them to delight in and, not considering the daunger whereunto they commit themselves by following of their disordinate appetites, doe suffer themselves to be entrapped by suche leude dames. Emong whiche, this (forsoothe) was one that was of singuler skill to captive men's mindes, whiche by experience and by the naturall disposition of her minde, bent wholye to deceipte and naughtinesse, had learned a thousande giles and artes which waye to allure men with the pleasauntnesse of her baites.[1] Wherefore, after he was once entangled with her snares, he fell so farre beyond all reason and past all beleef to dote upon this strumpet that he could finde no reste, nor no contentment, but so long as he was with her.

But she, beeing as dissolute a dame as any lived in the world and as greedye likewise of gaine as ever any was of her profession, would not content herself with Gonsales alone, but yeelded unto as many as list to enjoye her, if they came with their handes full and spared for no coste to reward her liberallye. Whiche thing was unto him, that was so besotted on her, so greevous and so intollerable that nothing could be more.

There was at that same time a scholer in the citye that studied physicke, with whom Gonsales had familier acquaintaunce, and the scholler, thereby having accesse and conversation in his house, beganne so fervently to be in love with Agatha, his wife, that he desired nothing so earnestly in the worlde as to enjoye her and to winne her goodwill. Wherefore, having (as I have saied) free accesse to her house and to declare his affection unto her without suspition, he ceased not by al the meanes he was able to devise to sollicite and to procure her to yeelde unto his desire, with his endevour and earneste suite, although it were unto Agatha noisome and displeasaunt, as she that was disposed to kepe herself honest. And that she could in that respecte have been very glad that he would forbeare to frequent her house, yet, knowing her housebande to be a man of no verye great substaunce, and but slenderly stuffed in the hedpeece, and that he delighted greatly in the familiarilye of the scholler, she forced herself to endure with pacience the importunate molestation whiche he still wearied her withall, taking from him, neverthelesse, all hope to obtaine at any time any favour at her handes and cutting him shorte from all occasions, as muche as she could, whereby he might have cause either to molest her or to looke for anything to proceade from her that were lesse then honest.

The scholer, perceiving that his owne travaile to win her affection was but labour loste, thought best to trye if by the allurement or perswasion of any other, he might happly move her to shew herself more courteous and favourable unto him. Wherefore, having founde out an olde mother Elenour, a disciple of the Spanishe Celestina,[2] suche a one as was most cunning and skilfull in mollifying of women's mindes to worke them afterwarde to receive the impressions of their lovers, he caused her to take acquaintaunce of Agatha and by degrees (as though she had been moved with pittye and compassion of her case) to declare unto her the love which her housband bare unto the courtisane and to shewe her how unworthye he was that she should be true unto him. And in the end, passing from one speeche to another, she sayed plainly unto her that it was a greate follye, since her housebande did take his pleasures abroade with other women, to stande to his allowances and to take the leaving of his strumpets and therewith to bee content. And that, if she were in her case and had a housebande that would strike with the sworde, she would undoubtedly requite him and strike with the scabberde,[3] so she counselled her to doe likewise.

Agatha, being a very discrete gentlewoman and loving her

housbande as an honest woman ought to doe, sayed to her in aunswere of her talke that she would bee right glad to see her housbande to be suche a man as she wished him to be and as he ought to be. But that, since she sawe it would not be and that he could not frame himself thereto, she would not take from him or barre him of that libertye whiche either the custome of the corrupted worlde or the priveledge that men had usurped unto themselves had given unto them. And that she would never, for her parte, violate or breake that faithe whiche she had given him, nor slacke or neclect that care and regarde of her honour whiche all women by kinde and nature ought to have, as the thing that maketh them to bee moste commended throughout the worlde, let her housbande doe what he list, and like and love as many other women as pleased him. And that she thought herself so muche the rather bounde so to doe because he did not in the rest misuse her any waye or suffer her to want anything that reasonably she could desire or crave at his handes. And for that she had not brought him in effect any other dowrye worthye to bee accompted of then her honestye, wherefore she was fully resolved never to varye from that constant resolution. And, finally, shewing herself somewhat moved and stirred with choler, she tolde her that she marvailed at her not a little that being a woman of those yeres that she should rather reprehend and chide yong folke, if she should see them so bent, then encourage them to evill, and mused much she could finde in her harte to give her suche counsell; whiche she assured her was so displeasant and so ungrateful, as if from henceforthe she durst presume to speake thereof any more, she would make her understande, perchaunce to her smarte, how ill she could awaye with suche pandarly practises.

This olde hag, having had her head washed thus without sope,[4] departed from Agatha and came unto the scholler and tolde him in breefe how ill she had sped and in what sorte the honest gentlewoman had closed her mouth, whereof the scholer was very sory. Yet, for all this, he thought he would not give over his pursute, imagining that there is no harte so harde or flintye, but by long love, by perseverance, prayer and teares, maye in the ende be mollified and wrought to be tender.

In this meane season, Gonsales, still continuing his olde familiaritye with the scholer, and having made him privye of the love he bare unto the courtisane and what a greefe it was unto him to see her enjoyed by any other then by himself, one daye, among other talke betwene them of that matter, he sayed unto the scholer that it never grieved him so muche to have a wife as it did then, for that if he had bin unmaried, he would have taken Aselgia (for so was the courtisane named) to be his wife, without whom he could finde no rest nor quiete in minde. And, so long as every man hath a share with him in her, he accompted himself as ill as if he had had no parte in her at all. And thereto sayed further that assuredly if it were not for feare of the lawe, he would ease himself of that burden by ridding of Agatha out of the worlde.

Thereunto replied the scholer, saying that indeede it was a grievous thing for a gentleman to be combred with a wife whom he could not finde in his harte to love and that, in suche a case, he that did seeke the best waye he could to deliver himself of that yoke was not altogether unexcusable, though the rigor of justice had appoincted severe punishementes for suche as violentlye should attempt or execute any suche thing, but that men that were wise could well enough finde out the meanes whiche waye to woorke their ententes without incurring any daunger of the lawe for the matter.

Whiche language, indeede, he used unto him but to feede his humour and to see whereunto that talke in fine would tende. And, according to his desire, before it was long, Gonsales, having used the like speeches twoo or three times and still finding him to soothe his saying, tooke one daye a good harte unto him and brake his minde unto the scholer at large, and in plaine termes, to this effect:

'Alonso' (for that was the scholer's name) 'I doe assure myself and make full accompt that thou art my faste freende, as I am thine, and I doubte not but that the freendship whiche is betweene us doeth make thee no lesse sorye then myself to see me greeve with this continuall trouble of minde wherein I live, because I cannot compasse to take this woman whom I love so dearely to bee my wife and by that meanes come to have the full possession of her unto myself whiche is the thing I doe desire above all other thinges in the worlde. And forasmuche as I dooe perswade myself that by thy meanes and with the helpe of thy profession I maye happ to finde some remedye for my greef, I have thought good to tell thee a conceit whiche I have thought on oftentimes, wherein I meane to use thee and thy assistance for the better accomplishing of my purpose in that behalfe, assuring myself that thou wilte not refuse or denye me any furtheraunce that thy skill maye aforde me or shrinke and drawe backe from the performing of any freendly offer whereby I maye come by to finde some ease of minde and be delivered of that intollerable torment of spirite wherwith I am oppressed for the love of this Aselgia, in whom I have fixed and sette all my joyes and delightes. Thou shalte, therefore, understande that I am determined, as soone as I can possible, to ridde my handes of Agatha my wife and by one meane or other to cause her to die. And I have been a this good while about the execution of this my entent, but, because I could never yet devise the beste waye to performe it, so that her death might not bee layed unto my charge, I have delayed it hetherto, and, perforce, contente to beare the heavye burthen of my greeved minde till now, whiche henceforwarde I am resolved to beare no longer, if thou wilt, according to my trust in thee and as the freendship whiche is betweene us doeth require, graunt me thy furtherance and helping hande. Wherefore, knowing that through thy long studye in physicke thou haste attained so great knowledge that thou canste devise a noumber of secretes, whereof any one might bee sufficiente to bring my purpose to effecte, I dooe require thee to fulfill my desire in that behalfe and to give me thy helpe to bring this my desire to passe. Whiche if thou doe, I will acknowledge myself, so long as I shall live, to bee so muche bounde unto thee that thou shalt commaunde me and all that I have in any occasion of thine, as freelye and as boldlye as thou mayest now any thing that is thine owne.'

The scholer, when he had heard Gonsales and his demaunde, stoode still awhile, as musing uppon the requeste, and in the meanewhile discoursed with himself how by the occasion of this entente and resolution of Gonsales he might perhappes finde out a waye to come by the possession of Agatha, and to have her in his handes and at his devotion. But, keeping secrete his thoughtes and meaning, he made him aunswere that true it was that he wanted not secrete compositions to make folke die with poison, so as it could never bee discerned by any physition or other whether the cause were violent or no, but that for twoo respectes he thought it not good to yeeled unto his requeste: the one, for that physicke and physitions were appoincted in the worlde not to bereve menne of their lives but to preserve them and to cure them of suche diseases as were daungerous and perillous unto theim; the other, because he did forsee in what jeoperdye he should putte his owne life whensoever he should dispose himself to woorke any suche practise, considering how severely the lawes have prescribed punishementes for suche offences, and that it might fall out, how warely soever the thing were wrought, that by some seldome or unlooked-for accident the matter might be discovered (as for the moste parte it seemeth that God will have it). In whiche case he were like to encurre no lesse daunger then Gonsales, and bothe (assured) without remission to lose their lives. And that, therefore, he would not for the first respect take upon him to doe that whiche was contrarye to his profession, nor for the seconde hazarde his life to so certaine a daunger for so hatefull a thing as those practises are to all the worlde.

Gonsales, verye sorye to heare his deniall, told him that the lawes and dueties of freendship doeth dispense well enough with a manne though for his freende he straine sometime his conscience, and, therefore, he hoped that he would not forsake him in a cause that concerned him so weightilye as that did. And that neither of those twoo respectes (if they were well considered) ought to bee able to remove him from pleasuring of his freende, for that nowadayes as well were they accompted and estemed physitions that killed their pacientes as they that did cure them. And, because the thing being kept secret betweene them twoo alone, he needed not to doubt or feare any daunger of his life by the lawe, for, if it should by any mischaunce happen that he should bee imputed or burthened with poisoning of his wife, he assured him that he would never, whilest he had breathe, confesse of whom he had the poison, but would rather suffer his tongue to be pulled out of his hedde, or endure any torment that might be devised.

The scholler, at the laste, seeming to bee wonne by the earnestnesse of his petition, sayed that, upon that condition and promesse of not revealing him at any time, he would be content rather to shewe himself freendlye unto him then a true professor of his science or an exact regarder of his conscience, and that he would doe as he would have him.

And, having lefte Gonsales verye glad and joyfull for that his promesse, he went home and made a certaine composition or mixture of pouders, the vertue whereof was suche that it would

make them that tooke any quantitye thereof to slepe so soundlye
that they should, for the space of certaine howers, seme unto all
menne to bee starke dedde. And the nexte daye he retourned to
Gonsales, and to deliver it unto him, saying: 'Gonsales, you
have caused me to dooe a thing I proteste I would not dooe it
for my life, but since you maye see thereby that I have regarded
more your freendshippe then my duetye or the consideration of
that whiche is honest and lawfull, I muste require you eftsones
to remember your promesse, and that you will not declare to
any creature living that you have had this poison of me.'

Whiche thinge Gonsales verye constauntlye upon his othe did
promise him againe and, having taken the pouder of him, asked
him in what sorte he was to use it. And he tolde him that if at
supper he did caste it there upon her meate or into her brothe,
she should die that night following, without either paine or
tormente or any greevous accidentes, but goe awaye even as
though she were asleape. That evening at supper time, Gonsales
failed not to put the pouder into his wife's potage. Who having
taken it, as sone as supper was doen, feeling herself verye heavye
and drousye, went to her chamber and gatte her to bedde (for
she laye not with Gonsales but when he liste to call her, whiche
had been verye seldome since he did fall into love with the
strumpet). And, within an hower after, the operation of the
pouder tooke suche force in her bodye, that she laye as though
she had been dedde and altogether sencelesse. Gonsales, in like
sort, when he sawe his time, went to his bed, and, lying all that
night with a troubled minde, thinking what would become of
Agatha and what successe his enterprise would take, the morning came upon him before he could once close his eyes. Whiche
beeing come, he rose, not doubting but that he should assuredlye
finde his wife dedde, as Alonso had promised him.

As soone as he was up he went out of his house, and stayed
but an hower abroade, and then he retourned home again, and
asked his maide whether her mistres were up or no. The maide
made him aunswere that she was yet asleape, and he, making as
though he had marveiled at her long lying in bedde, demaunded
her how it happened that she was so sluggishe that morning,
contrarye to her custome, whiche was to rise every morning by
breake of the daye, and badd her goe and wake her, for he
would have her to give him something that laye under her
keyes.[5] The wenche, according to her maister's commaunde-

ment, went to her mistres' beddeside and, having called her once or twise somewhat softely, when she sawe she waked not, she layed her hand upon her, and giving her a shagge, she sayed withall: 'Mistres, awake! My maister calleth for you.' But she lying still, and not awaking for all that the maide tooke her by the arme and beganne to shake her good and hard – and she, notwithstanding, neither answering nor stirring hande or foote – the maide returned to her maister and tolde him that for aught she could doe she could not gett her mistres to awake. Gonsales, hearing the maide to saye so, was glad in his minde, but faining himself to be busied about somwhat els and that he regarded little her speeche, he bidde her goe againe and shake her till she did waken. The maide did so, and rolled and tumbled her in her bed, and all in vaine. Wherefore, comming againe unto her maister, she sayed unto him that undoubtedly she did beleeve that her mistres, his wife, was dedde, for she had founde her verye colde, and rolled her up and doune the bedde, and that yet she stirred not.

'What! Dedde?' quoth Gonsales, as if he had been all agaste and amazed. And, rising therewithall, he went to her bedde's side, and called her and shaked her and wrong her by the fingers and did all that might bee, as he thought, to see whether she were alive. But she, not feeling anything that he did, laye still like a dedde bodye or, rather, like a stone.

Wherefore, when he sawe his purpose had taken so good effecte, to dissemble the matter he beganne to crye out and to lament and to detest his cruell destinye, that had so sone bereved him of so kind, so honest and so faithfull a wife. And, having in the ende discovered her bodye, and finding no spot or marke whereby any token or signe of poisoning might be gathered, as one that would not seme to omit any office of a loving husband, he sent for the physition to loke upon her. Who, having used some suche meanes as he thought mete to make her come to herself, finally, seing her to remaine unmoveable and without sence, concluded that some sodaine accident had taken her in the night, whereof she had died. And for dedde he left her.

At whiche his resolution, though Gonsales were very glad, yet to the outward shewe declaring himself to be verye sorye and full of woe and heavinesse he behaved himself in suche cunning sorte, as he made all the worlde beleeve that he would not long live after her. And, having called her freendes and lamented with them her sodaine death and his misfortune, in fine he caused her funerall to bee very sumptuouslye and honourably prepared, and buried her in a vaute, whiche served for a toumbe to all his auncestours, in a churche of a frierye that standes without the citye.

Alonso, that was verye well acquainted with the place and had himself a house not verye farre from that frierye, wente his waye that same night unto his sayed house. And when he sawe the time to serve for his purpose, he gatte him to the vaute or toumbe wherein Agatha was layed, with one of these little lanterns that they call blinde lanterns (because they tourne them and hide their light when they liste). And because he was a yong manne of verye good strengthe, and had brought with him instrumentes of iron to open the toumbe and lifte up the stone that covered it, he gatte it open, and, having under-propped it surely, he went into the vaute and toke the woman straightwaye in his armes, minding to bring her out and carrye her awaye so asleape as she was.

But the force and vertue of the pouder beeing finished and spent, as sone as he moved her she awaked out of her sleape, and seing herself clad in that sorte, among ragges and dedde bones, she beganne to tremble, and to crye: 'Alas! Where am I? Or who hath brought me hether, wretche that I am?'

'Marye, that hath your cruell and unfaithfull houseband', aunswered the scholer, 'who, having poisoned you to marrye a common strumpet, hath buried you here, whether I come to trye if by my skill I could revive you, and call back your soule, by those remedies whiche I had devised, unto your bodye again. Whiche if I could not have doen as I entended, I was resolved to have died here by you and to have layed my dedde bodye here by yours to reste until the latter daye, hoping that my spirite should in the meanewhile have come and enjoyed yours, wher-eever it had been. But since the heavens have been so favourable unto me as, in this extreme daunger wherein you were, to graunt suche vertue unto the remedies whiche I have used toward you, as the whiche I have been able to keepe undissolved your gentle spirite with your faire bodye, I hope (my deare) that you wil henceforthe consider what the affection of your wicked hous-bande hath been toward you and how greate goodwill, and, by consideration thereof, discerne and resolve whiche of us twoo hath beste deserved to be beloved of you.'

Agatha, finding herself in that sort buried indeede, did easily beleeve the truthe whiche the scholer told her, and to herself concluded that her housebande had shewed himself, in her behalf, a man of all other moste cruell and disloyall. Wherfore, tourning herself toward the scholer, she sayed unto him: 'Alonso, I cannot deny but that my housebande hath been to me not onely unkinde, but cruell also. Nor I cannot but confesse that you have declared yourself to bee moste loving and affectioned toward me; and, of force, I must acknowledge myself beholding unto you of no lesse then of my life, since (alas) I see myself here among dedde bodies, buried alive. But forasmuche as though my housebande have broken his vowe to me, I have not yet at any time failed my faithe to him, I doe require you that, if you desire that I should esteeme this kind and loving office of yours as it deserveth to bee esteemed or make accompt of this life whiche you have given me, you will have due regarde and consideration of mine honestye and that you will not, by offering me any villanye, (whiche neverthelesse I cannot any waye misdoubte, where I have alwayes founde so muche and so great courtesye) make this your courteous and pitifull acte to bee lesse commendable and praiseworthye then it is. Whiche, if you dooe bridle your unlawfull and sensuall appetite and desire, will remaine the moste vertuous and worthye of honour and fame that ever courteous gentleman hath doen for a miserable woman since the worlde began.'

Alonso failed not with affectuall and manifest argumentes to perswade her that her housband had now no more right or title to her at all, and that although he had,[6] yet, if she were wise, she should not committe herself unto his courtesye againe, since, by this mortall token, he had given her a sufficient testimonye of his ranckor and evill will towardes her, whereby she might well enough bee assured not to escape whensoever she should resolve to putte herself againe into his handes. And that, therefore, she was not to make any accompt of him but to shewe herself thankfull for so great a benefite as she had received and to requite him so with her favour and courtesye as he might now in the ende attaine to gather the fruite of his long and constaunte goodwill and of his travell susteined for the saffegarde of her life.

And with those woordes, bending himself towarde her, he would have taken a kisse of her lippes, but Agatha, thrusting him backe, sayed to him again: 'If my housebande (Alonso) have broken those bandes wherewith I was knit unto him by matrimonye through his wicked and leude demeanour, yet have not I for my parte dissolved theim, neither will I at any time so long as I shall live. As for committing myself unto his courtesye, or going any more into his handes, therein I thinke it good to followe your advise, not that I would bee unwilling to live and dwell with him if I might hope to finde him better disposed, but because I would be lothe to fall eftsones into the like daunger and grevous perill. And as for requiting you for this your commendable travaile in my behalfe, I knowe not what better recompence I am able to give you then to rest bounde unto you for ever and to acknowledge my self beholding unto your courtesye for my life. Whiche obligation, if it maye satisfye you, I will be as glad and as content as I maye bee in this miserable state wherein I am. But if your meaning perchance bee that the losse of mine honestye should bee the rewarde and hire for your paines, I dooe besoche you to departe hence out of this toumbe and to leave me here enclosed, for I had rather die here, thus buried quicke through the crueltye of my houseband, then through any suche compassion or pitye to save my life with the losse of mine honour and good name.'

The scholer by those wordes perceived well enough the honest disposition of Agatha, whiche he wondered at, considering that the terror of death itself was not able once to move her from her faithfulnes and constancye of minde. And though it were grievous unto him to finde her so stedfast, yet hoping that by time in the ende he might overcome her chaste and honest purpose, aunswered that he could not but commende her for her disposition, though he deserved a kinder recompence of his long and fervent love, and she a more loving and faithfull housbande. But since she was so resolved, he would frame himself to be content with what she would, and not crave of her anything that she would not willingly graunt him to have. And therewith helping her out of the sepulcher, he led her home unto his house, and lefte her there with an olde woman that kept his house, to whom he recomended her, and whose helpe he was assured of to dispose the goodwill of Agatha towardes him, and the next morning retourned into the citye.

Gonsales, after a fewe dayes, seeming not to be able to live without a wife to take care of his familye, wedded that honest dame Aselgia and made her mistres of himself and all that he had. This, his newe mariage, so sone contrived, caused the freendes of Agatha to marvaile not a little and to misdoubte that the sodaine death of their kinsewoman had not happened without some misterye. Neverthelesse, having no token nor evidence or profe, they helde their peace. But Gonsales, having his desired purpose and living with his newe wife, it befell unto him (through Godde's just judgement with this his joly dame) as it chaunced to Agatha with him before. For Aselgia, that was never wont to feede with so spare a diet, as she that had never bin contented before without greate chaunge, nor had not bin used to that kinde of straightnes (which Gonsales, growing jelous of her, began to keepe her in) but had alwayes lived at libertye and with suche licentiousnesse as women of her profession are wont to doe, became in shorte space to shewe herself so precise unto him and to hate and abhorre him in suche extreme sorte that she could not abide to see or heare him spoken of. By occasion of whiche her demeanour towardes him, Gonsales, to his greefe, began at last to knowe and to discerne what difference there is betweene the honest and carefull love of an honest wife and the dissembling of an arrant strumpet.

Wherefore one daye, among the rest, complaining of the little love whiche he perceived she bare him, and she aunswering him thawartly, Gonsales, falling into heate of choler, sayed angerly unto her: 'Have I, thou naughtye packe, poisoned Agatha for thy sake, that was the kindest and the lovingest wife that ever man had? And is this the rewarde I have, and the requitall thou yeeldest me, to shewe thyself every daye more despightefull and crabbed then other?'

Aselgia, having heard him and noted well his wordes, tooke holde of them, and straightwaye thought that she had founde the waye to rid herself of Gonsales. Wherefore she reveiled his speeches unto a ribalde of hers, such a one as supplied her want of that which Gonsales alone, nor ten suche as he, were able to satisfye her withall, and induced him to appeache him for that facte, assuring herself that the lawe would punishe him with no lesse then death, and thereby she to remaine at libertye to dooe what she list againe, as she had doen before. This companion accused Gonsales upon his owne wordes unto the frendes of Agatha, who, having had halfe a suspition thereof before, went and accused him likewise before the judge, or hed magistrate of

the citye. Wherupon Gonsales and his woman were both apprehended and put to their examinations to searche out the truthe.
Which Gonsales, being halfe convicted by the confession of the
gentle peate, his newe wife, but chiefly grieved with the worme
of his owne conscience, and to avoide the torment of those
terrors which he knewe were prepared for him, confessed flatly,
affirming that he had poisoned her with a poisone, whiche he
had kept of long time before in his house, perfourming yet
therein the promise whiche he had made unto the scholer. And
upon his owne confession sentence was given against him that
he should loose his hed.

Alonso, when he understoode that Gonsales was condemned
to die, was very glad thereof, supposing that, he beeing once
dead, Agatha (who all this while, for anything that the olde
woman could saye or alledge unto her in the behalfe of Alonso,
would never yeeld or consent to any one poincte wherein her
honour might have beene touched or spotted) should remaine at
his discretion, and that she would no longer refuse to graunt
him her goodwill when she should see her self delivered of
Gonsales.[7] But the daye being come wherein he was to be put to
execution, she, having had inteligence of all that had passed and
knowing that he was appoincted to die that daye, determined
with herself that she would in that extremitye deliver her
disloyall housebande and give him to understande how little she
had deserved to bee so entreated by him as she had been.

Wherefore, having gotten out of Alonso his house, she hied
her unto the citye as fast as she could, and, beeing before the
justice or magistrate, she sayed unto him: 'Sir, Gonsales, whom
you have condemned and commaunded to be put to death this
daye, is wrongfully condemned, for it is not true that he hath
poisoned his wife, but she is yet alive, and I am she. Therefore, I
beseche you, give order that execution maye be stayed, since
that your sentence is grounded upon a false enformation and
confession, is unjust, as you maye plainly discerne by me being
here.'

When the governour heard Agatha speake in this sorte, whom
he had thought to have been deade and buried, he was all
amazed and halfe afrayed to looke upon her, doubting that she
was rather her spirite or ghoste, or some other in her likenesse,
then a lively woman indeede, for she was apparelled in a very
plaine and blacke attire and was very wanne and pale by reason

of the affliction whiche she had indured, first for her owne ill-fortune and then for the mischaunce of her housband.

In this meanewhile the sergantes and officers had brought Gonsales before the justice or magistrate, to the ende that he (according to the custome of the citye) should give them commaundement to leade him to the place of execution, and there to fulfill his sentence upon him, but as sone as Agatha perceived him she ranne unto him and, taking him aboute the necke and kissing him, she said: 'Alas! My deare housebande, whereunto doe I see you brought through your owne folly and disordinate appetite, which blinded your judgement? Beholde here your Agatha alive, and not deade, who even in this extremitye is come to shewe herself that loving and faithfull wife unto you that she was ever.'

The justice or governour, seing this straunge accident, caused execution to be stayed, and signified the whole case unto the lorde of the countrey, who at that time chaunced to bee at Sciville. Who, wondering no lesse then the other at the matter, caused bothe Gonsales and his wife to be brought before him and demaunded of them how it had chaunced that she, having bin buried for deade, was now found alive? Gonsales could saye nothing but that for the love he bare unto Aselgia he had poisoned his wife and that he knewe not how she was revived againe. But Agatha declared how the scholler, with his skill, had delivered her from death and restored her life unto her, but how or by what meanes she could not tell.

The lorde, having sent for Alonso and demaunded him of the truth, was certified by him how that in steede of poison he had given to Gonsales a pouder to make her sleape, affirming likewise that, notwithstanding the long and earneste pursuite whiche he had made to obtaine her love and the crueltye and injurye whiche she sawe her housebande had used towarde her to put her in that daunger and perill of her life out of whiche he had delivered her, yet could he never by any perswasion or entreatye winne her to fulfill his desire or bring her to make breache of her faithe and honestye.[8]

By whiche reporte the lorde knewe verye well that in an honest woman the regarde and respect of her honour and chastitye doeth farre exceade any other passion, for any miserye, be it never so great. And commending highly the love and constancye of the woman towarde her housebande, and praising the pollicye of Alonso, he tourned himself unto Gonsales and sayed unto him: 'Full evill hast thou deserved to have so good and so verteous a gentlewoman to thy wife, and in reason she ought now rather to be Alonso his wife then thine. Neither wert thou worthye of lesse then that punishment which the lawe hath condempned thee unto, though she be yet alive, since thou as much as in thee laye hast doen to bereve her of her life, but I am content that her vertue and goodnesse shal so muche be availeable unto thee that thou shalt have thy life spared unto thee for this time: not for thy owne sake because thou deservest it not, but for hers, and not to give her that sorrowe and greefe whiche I knowe she would feele if thou shouldest die in that sorte. But I sware unto thee that if ever I maye understande that thou dooest use her henceforth otherwise then lovingly and kindely, I will make thee, to thy greevous paine, prove how severely I can punishe suche beastly and heinous factes, to the example of all others.'

Gonsales, imputing his former offence to want of witte and judgemente, made promis unto the lorde that he would always dooe as he had commanded him. And accordinglye, having forsaken cleane that baggage strumpette that he had wedded, he lived al the rest of his dayes in good love and peace with Agatha his wife, whose chaste and constant minde caused Alonso, where before he loved her for her exterior beauty, ever after to reverence her and in maner to worship her as a divine creature, for the excellencye of her vertue, resolving with himself, that a more constaunt faithe and honest disposition could not bee founde in any mortall woman.

TWO TALES FROM WHETSTONE'S

AN HEPTAMERON OF
CIVILL DISCOURSES

The Adventure of Frier Inganno, reported by Mounsier Bergetto

In a little village among the Appenine mountaines, not far from the place where S. Fraunces lieth intombed,[1] there sometimes dwelled a faire younge country woman named Farina. And, for that her house was in the hiewaye to S. Fraunces' holy relikes, she was many times visited with friers of his order; who were intertained rather for their habit than their honestye,[2] for the poore, ignorant people reverenced Sainct Fraunces as a seconde Christe, for whose sake they hould his disciples not inferiour to saincts. Amonge manye that visited Farina's house, Frier Inganno, a smugge chapleine, ever sealed his blessings uppon his dame's lippes, and yet without suspicion of the husband or dishonest intent of the wife, for such greeting was ever taken for a holly favour.

Uppon a time, after Frier Inganno had wel beaked himselfe with a warme fire and a good breakefast, the spirit that Saint Fraunces was driven to conjure downe by tumbling naked in the frost and snowe tempted his disciple with suche sweete motions as he was minded willfully to abjure Heaven rather then to deale so roughly with the devill, and taking advantage of the good opinion the ignoraunt heald of his holines, and was so bould with Saincte Fraunces (his maister) as to make a wanton match in his name. So that, after he had awhile considered of his perswasion, uppon a quiet oportunitye: 'Blessed art thou,' quoth he, 'among the Appenine countreywemen,

It is saide, S. Frances subdued incontinent desires by tumbling naked in frost and snowe.

A premiditated sinne.

The tricke of a knavish servaunt.
A gentle perswasion.

for Sainct Fraunces, from Heaven, hath behelde
thy charitable usage of his disciples.[3] And the last
night, after I had prayed with great devotion
before his image, I behelde him in the majestye of
an angell, faire, yonge, lustye and in every proportion like myselfe, and nothing at all like his meagre
cripple image, so that I was in doubt of beinge
transfourmed out of myselfe. Till, with a meeke
voice, he said: "Be not dismaide. I am thy maister,
Inganno, and am come to bestow my blessinges
upon the good Appenine dames, that for my sake
cherish you, my disciples. But with an especiall
affection I wil visite the good dame Farina. And,
for that her feminine weakenes can not indure my
heavenly presence, I will many times borrowe thy
earthly shape. And in my name go salute Farina
and showe her that this night, in that her husbande
is from home, I meane to visite her. Will her to
leave open the doores, because I purpose to come
as Frier Inganno and not as Saint Fraunces." '

Ignoraunce
heareth every
tale as trueth.

'This is his message; therfore, as I began, I end:
blessed art thou among the Appenine countrye
dames.' The poore woman, as apparant as this
trecherye was, had not the power to mistrust, but
gave the frier a good almes for his newes, and said
she would attende Saint Fraunces' blessed will.

Flatterye
eateth the
bread of the
Just.

Away goeth the frier with a light hart and a
heavy cowle.[4] But God, to punish his lewde intent
and to preserve her from sinning through ignoraunce, so tickled her hart with joy of this bless-
inge at hande as to welcome Saint Fraunces shee
must needes have the belles roonge. The prieste of
the parrishe, hearing the cause, smelt out the
Frier's counning and was glad to take one of those
beggers in a pitfall that with glorious lies had
robbed him of his parishioners' devotions, and,
withall, perswaded her with suche reasons as shee
was fully resolved of the frier's deceite.[5] And, to
bee advenged, by the parson's direction shee
caused Leaida to lie in her bed, a maide so ougly,
sluttish and deformed as thorough the parish shee

A note of litle
secreacy in a
woman.

Envy setteth
hatred
betweene
fellowes of
every
vocation.

was called the Furye of Lothsomnesse.[6] About ten of the clocke, findinge the doores open, Frier Inganno mountes into Farina's chamber and, without light or leave, leaps into her bed. But hee had not blessed Leaidae's lippes before the priest, Farina and others entred with taper and torch-lighte singing 'Salve Saincte Francisce' and, kneeling about his bedsides, sung, 'Sancte Francisce, ora pro nobis.'[7]

An unwelcome salutation.

The poore frier, like a fox in a grin, being both intrapt and imbraste by a hag of Hel, cried from his hart: 'A dolore inferni libera me, Domine.'[8]

After, the prieste and the rest of the companye were wearye of laughinge, and the frier almost dead with weeping. 'It is an office of charitye' (quoth the priest) 'to put Saint Frances againe in his tumbe. For it is so long since hee was in the worlde that he hath forgot the way backe into Heaven.'

Pleasure in others increaseth sorrow in the afflicted.

The frier, learing like the theefe that honge on the left side of Christe, tooke all with patience, for well hee wist, prayer booted not.[9]

Envy and rude people, are not passified with prayers of the afflicted.

Well, for that night they bounde and stript him like a dead coarse and, instead of sweete flowers, laid him in a bundell of nettles.

Rude people extreame revengers.

The next morning, the rude countrye people (who in revenge are without civillitye or order) cruelly scourged the poore frier. And (setting him the forenoone naked in the sunne) annointed his bodye with honey, so that the hornets, waspes and flies tormented him with the paines of Hell.

In the afternoone, with a hundred torches, tapers and other waxen lightes, this rustick multi-tude caried seconde Saint Fraunces unto his tumbe. And had not other friers used milde and plawsible requests in his behalf, they would surely have buried him alive. For threatning increaseth a tumult when faire wordes may peradventure staye it.

The best way to win the communaltye.

The poore frier, discharged from the handes of these ungentle people, learned afterwardes to be more warye but, for all this punishment, was nothinge the honester. For amonge men of his habit remaineth an opinion that the faultes which the worlde seeth not God punnisheth not.

After the company had wel laughed at Frier Inganno's pennaunce, Queene Aurelia axed maister doctor, the archedetracter of women, how many suche stories he had read of the religious dames?[10]

'None' (quoth hee) 'that hath beene so sorely punished, but of an number that have as highly trespassed.'

Men offende subtilly, and women simply.

'What' (quoth Helena Dulce) 'by suche subtill practises?'

'No' (quoth the doctor) 'but through simple affection.'

Wemen's evils are writ in their forheds. Men's faultes, lie hidde in their hartes.

'Well' (quoth Alvisa Vechio) 'their evils are written in their foreheades that slaunderous men's tongues may reade and inlarge them.[11] And your great evils are buried in the bottome of your hartes that, unlesse the devill meane to shame you, the worlde knoweth not how to blame you.'

This was the gentlewomen's day,[12] wherefore the civill gentlemen would not offer to crosse them much. So that, following their advantage,

A civill curtesye in a gentelman.

'Madam' (quoth Isabella) 'with your favour and patience, I will reporte an historye that shall open suche a hainous trecherye done by a man as shall take away all possibilitye from a woman to commit so impious an act.'[13]

Queene Aurelia willed her to proceede, and the whole company seemed to be attentive. Whereupon Isabella reported as followeth.

The Rare historye of Promos and Cassandra, reported by Madam Isabella

At what time Corvinus, the scourge of the Turkes, rained as kinge of Bohemia,[14] for to well governe the free cities of his realme, hee sent divers worthy majestrates. Among the rest, he gave the lorde Promos the lieutennauntship of Julio;[15] who, in the beginning of his government, purged the cittye of many ancient vices and severely punished new offenders.

In this cittye, there was an olde custome (by the suffering of some majestrates growne out of use) that what man soever committed adulterye should lose his head and the woman offender should ever after be infamously noted by the wearing of some disguised apparrell. For the man was helde to bee the greatest offender and, therefore, had the severest punishment.

Lord Promos, with a rough execution, revived this statute and, in the hiest degree of injurye, brake it himselfe, as shall appeare by the sequell of Andrugio's adventures.

This Andrugio, by the yeelding favour of faire Polina, trespassed against this ordinaunce; who, through envye, was accused and by lorde Promos condemned to suffer execution.

The wofull Cassandra, Andrugio's sister, prostrates herselfe at lorde Promos' feete and, with more teares then wordes, thus pleaded for her brother's life: 'Most noble lorde and worthy judge, vouchsafe mee the favour to speake, whose case is so desperate as, unlesse you beholde mee with

This historye, for rarenes therof, is lively set out in a commedye by the reporter of the whole worke, but yet never presented upon stage.[16]

A hard lawe for incontinent persons.

the eyes of mercye, the fraile trespasse of condemned Andrugio, my brother, will bee the death of sorrowfull Cassandra, his innocent sister. I wil not presume to excuse his offence or reproche the lawe of rigor, for, in the generall construction, hee hath done most evill, and the law hath judged but what is right. But (reverent judge, pardon that necessitye maketh mee here tel that your wisdome already knoweth) the most soveraigne Justice is crowned with laurell, although shee bee girt with a sword.[17] And this priveledge shee giveth unto her administrators: that they shall mitigate the severetye of the law according to the quallity of the offence. Then, that Justice bee not robbed of her gratious pitty, listen, good lorde Promos, to the nature of my brother's offence and his able meanes to repaire the injurye. Hee hath defiled no nuptiall bed, the staine whereof dishonoureth the guiltlesse husband. Hee hath committed no violent rape, in which act the injuryed maide can have no amends. But, with yeelding consent of his mistresse, Andrugio hath onlye sinned through love, and never ment but with marriage to make amendes.

'I humbly beseeche you to accept his satisfaction, and, by this example, you shall be as much beloved for your clemencye as feared for your severitye. Andrugio shal be well warned, and hee with his sister, wofull Cassandra shall ever remaine your Lordship's true servantes.'

Promos' eares were not so attentive to heare Cassandras' ruethful tale as his eyes were settled to regarde her excellent beautye. And Love, that was the apoincted headsman of Andrugio, became now the soveraigne of his judge's thought. But, because he would seeme to bridle his passions, he aunswered: 'Faire damsell, have patience. You importune me with an impossibilitye. He is condempned by lawe; then, without injurye to lawe he cannot be saved.'

Lawe adjudgeth by the generall offence.

Justice is more renowned by lenitye, then severitye.

A good cause to moove pitye.

Love favoureth no degre.

'Princes' and their deputies' prerogatives' (quoth she) 'are above the lawe. Besides, lawe, truelye construed, is but the amends of injurye; and where the faulte may bee valued and amendes had, the breache of lawe is sufficiently repaired.'[18]

Quoth lorde Promos: 'Your passions moveth more then your proofes, and, for your sake, I will reprive Andrugio and studye how to do you ease without apparant breache of lawe.'

Cassandra, recomforted, with humble thankes received his favoure, and in great haste goeth too participate this hope with her dying brother. But oh, that aucthoritye should have power to make the vertuous to doo amisse as well as, throughe correction, to enforce the vicious to fall unto goodnesse.

Promos is a witnes of this priviledge. Who, not able to subdue his incontinent love and (withal) resolved that Cassandra would never be overcome with faire wordes, large promises or riche rewardes, demaunded the spoile of her virginitye for raunsome of her brother's libertye.

Cassandra, imagined at the first that lorde Promos used this speache but to trye her behaviour, aunswered him so wisely as, if he had not ben the rivall of vertue, he could not but have suppressed his lewde affection and have subscribed to her just petition. But, to leave circumstaunces, Promos was fiered with a vicious desire which must be quenched with Cassandra's yelding love or Andrugio must die.

Cassandra (mooved with a chaste disdaine) departed with the resolution rather to die herselfe than to staine her honour and, with this heavye newes, greeted her condemned brother. Poore man, alas, what should he do? Life was sweete, but to be redeemed with his sister's infamye could not but be alwayes unsaverye.

To perswade her to consente was unnaturall; too yealde to death was more greevous.

Princes' prerogative are above lawe.
The true intent of the lawe.
A good turne upon an evil cause.

Aucthoritye in evill majestrates is a scourge unto the good.

A monstrous request.

Unlesse they be reprobate, good examples may refourme the wicked.

A hard choice
of two evils.

To choose the leaste of these evilles was difficult; to studye long was daungerous.

Faine would he live, but shame cloased his
mouth when he attempted to perswade his sister.

But Necessitye, that maistereth both shame and
feare, brake a passadge for his imprisoned intent.

'Sweete Cassandra' (quothe he) 'that men love
is usuall, but to subdue affection is impossible,
and so thornye are the motions of incontinent

The force of
necessitye.
The force of
love.

desire as, to finde ease, the tongue is only occupied
to perswade.[19] The purse is ever open to entice,
and, wheare neither words nor giftes can corrupt
(with the mightye) force shall constraine or dispight avenge. That Promos do love is but just; thy
beautye commaundes him. That Promos be
refused is more just, because consent is thy shame.

'Thou mayste refuse and live but, he beinge
rejected, I die. For, wanting his will in thee, he
will wreake his teene on mee.

'This is my hard estate: My life lieth in thy
infamye, and thy honour in my death. Which of
these evilles be leaste I leave for thee to judge.'

A hard
fortune.

The wofull Cassandra answered that death was
the leaste, whose darte we cannot shunne, when
honour, in death's dispight, outliveth time.

Death is to be
preferred
before
dishonorable
life.

'It is true' (quoth Andrugio) 'but thy trespasse
will be in the leaste degree of blame. For in forced
faultes, justice sayth, there is no intent of evill.'

'Oh, Andrugio' (quoth she) 'intent is nowadayes
litle considred. Thou art not condemned by the
intent but by the strickt worde of the law; so shall
my crime bee reproched and the forced cause

The
venemous
nature of
envy.

passe unexcused. And, such is the venome of
Envye, one evill deede shall disgrace ten good
turnes, and in this yeelding so shall I be valued.

The vertuous
are assured of
many
enemies and
incertaine of
any friendes.

Envye, Disdaine, Spight, Mallice, Sclaunder and
many moe furies will endevour to shame mee, and
the meanest vertue will blush to help to support
my honour. So that I see no libertye for thee but
death, nor no ease for mee but to hasten my ende.'

'O yes' (quoth Andrugio) 'for if this offence be

known, thy fame will bee enlarged, because it will likewise bee knowne that thou receavedst dishonor to give thy brother life. If it be secreat, thy conscience wil be without scruple of guiltinesse. Thus, knowne or unknowne, thou shalt be deflowred but not dishonested, and for amends wee both shall live.

A cause that may excuse the breach of honour.

'This further hope remaineth that as the gillyflower both pleaseth the eye and feedeth the sence, even so the vertue of thy chast behaviour may so grace thy bewty as Promos' filthye lust may bee turned into faithfull love and so move him to salve thy honour in making thee his wife or, for conscience, forbeare to doe so heinous an injurye.'

A faint hope.

Soveraigne maddame and you faire gentlewomen (quoth Isabella)[20] entreate you in Cassandra's behalfe, these reasons well wayed, to judge her yeelding a constrainte and no consent. Who, werye of her owne life and tender over her brother's, with the teares of her lovely eyes bathed his cheekes with this comfortable sentence:

'Live, Andrugio and make much of this kisse, which breatheth my honour into thy bowels and draweth the infamye of thy first trespasse into my bosome.'

A loving kis.

The sharpe incounters between life and death so occupied Andrugio's sences that his tongue had not the vertue to bid her farewell. To greeve you with the hearing of Cassandra's secreate plaints were an injurye, vertuous ladies, for they concluded with their good fortune and everlasting fame. But, for that her offence grew neither of frailtye, free wil, or any motion of a woman, but by the meere inforcement of a man, because she would not staine the modest weedes of her kinde, shee attired herselfe in the habit of a page and, with the bashfull grace of a pure virgin, shee presented wicked Promos Andrugio's precious ransome.[21]

A good consideration in Cassandra.

This devill in humaine shape, more vicious then Hyliogabalus of Rome and, withall, as cruell as Denis of Sicill, receaved this juell with a thousande

A damnable offence.

protestations of favour. But what should I say? In
the beginning of his love, Promos was metamor-
phosed into Priapus.[22] And of a feende what may
we expect but vengeaunce heaped upon villany?
And, therefore, let it not seeme straunge that, after
This helhound had dishonoured Cassandra, hee
sent this warrant to the gailer prively to execute
Andrugio and, with his head crowned with these
two breefes, in Promos's name to present
Cassandra:

'Faire Cassandra, as Promos promist thee:
From prison, loe, he sendes thy brother free.'

This was his charge; whose cursed will had ben
executed had not God by an especiall providence,
at the howre of his death, possessed Andrugio
with the vertues of the two brave Romanes
Marcus Crassus and Marius, the one of whiche by
the force of his tongue and the other by the motions
of his eyes caused the axe to fall out of the
headsman's hand and mollified his cruell minde.[23]

With like compassion, the gailer (in hearinge
Andrugio's hard adventure) left his resolution.
And uppon a solempne othe to live unknowne,
yea, to his deare sister, he gave him life, and, in
the dead of the night, betooke him to God and to
good fortune. Which done, this good gailer tooke
the head of a yonge man newe executed who
somewhat resembled Andrugio and, according to
lewde Promos' commaundement, made a present
thereof to Cassandra. How unwelcome this present was the testimonye of her former sorowes
somewhat discover; but to give her present passion
a true grace were the taske of Prometheus, or such
a one as hath had experience of the anguishes of
Hell.[24]

'O' (quoth shee) 'sweete Andrugio, whether
shall I firste lament thy death, exclaime of Promos'
injurye or bemone my owne estate, deprived of
honour? And, which is worse, cannot die, but by
the violence of my owne hands. Alas, the least of

A villanous
ingratitude.

An especiall
providence of
God.

A signe of an
honest
nature.

An
unwelcome
present.

these greefes are to heavye a burden for a man,
then all, joined in one poore woman's hearte
cannot be eased but by death. And to be avenged
of injurious Fortune, I wil forthwith cut my fillet
of life. But so shall Promos' lewdnesse escape
unpunished. What remedye? I am not of power to
revenge. To complaine, I expresse my owne infamye but, withal, proclaime his vilanye. And to
heare his lewdnes reproved woulde take away the
bitternesse of my death. I will goe unto the king,
who is just and mercifull. Hee shall heare the
ruthfull events of Promos' tyrannye. And to give
him example of vengeaunce, I will seale my com-
plaintes with my dearest bloode.'

Continuing this determination, Cassandra
buried her imagined brother's heade and with
speed jornyed unto King Corvinus' court. Before
whose presence when shee arrived, her mourninge
attire,[25] but especially her modest countenance,
moved him to beholde her with an especiall
regarde.

Cassandra (uppon the graunt of audience), with
her eyes overcharged with teares, reported the
alreadye discoursed accidentes with suche an
apparaunce of greefe as the king and his attend-
ants were astonyed to heare her. And, sure, had
shee not been happily prevented, shee had concluded her determination with chast Lucretia's
destiny.[26] The king comforted her with many
gratious words and promised to take such order
that (although he could not be revived) her
brother's death should fully be revenged and her
crased honour repaired withoute blemish of her
former reputation.

A mischiefe
well
prevented.

A noble
favour.

Cassandra, upon these comfortable wordes, a
litell succoured her afflicted hart and with patience
attended the justice of the king. Who, with a
chosen companye, made a progresse to Julio and
entred the town with a semblaunce of great favour
towardes Promos, by that colour to learne what
other corrupte majestrates ruled in the cittye. For

A necessarye
pollicye.

well he knewe that birdes of a feather would flye together, and wicked men would joine in affection to boulster each other's evil.

After this gratious king had by heedfull intelligence understoode the factions of the people, unlooked-for of the magistrates, he caused a proclamation to be published in which was a clause that if anye person coulde charge anye magistrate or officer with anye notable or hainous offence, treason, murder, rape, sedition, or with any such notorious crime, where they were the judges of the multitude, hee woulde himselfe bee the judge of them and doe justice unto the meanest.

A royal grace.

Uppon this proclamation, it was a Hell to heare the exclamations of the poore, and the festered consciences of the rich appeared as lothsome as the river of Styx.[27]

The clamors of the poore and the consciences of the rich like Hell.

Among manye that complained and received judgement of comfort, Cassandra's processe was presented. Who, lead betweene sorrow and shame, accused Promos to his face.

The evidence was so plaine as the horrour of a guiltye conscience reaved Promos of all motions of excuse. So that, holding up his hande among the worst degree of theeves, the litle hope that was leaft moved him to confesse the crime and with repentance to sue for mercy.

Sorrowe and shame, the attendantes of Cassandra.

'O' (quoth the king) 'such espetial mercy were tyrannye to a commonwealth. No, Promos, no. *Hoc facias alteri, quod tibi vis fieri*: you shall be measured with the grace you bestowed on Andrugio.[28]

An unusual place for a judge.

'O God' (quoth hee) 'if men durst bark as dogges, manye a judge in the world would be bewrayed for a theefe. It behoveth a prince to know to whom hee committeth authoritye least the sword of justice, appointed to chasten the lewde, wound the good. And where good subjects are wronged, evill officers receave the benefit, and their soveraignes beareth the blame.

A necessarye regarde in a prince.

Princes bere the blame of evill officers' extortion.

'Well, wicked Promos, to scourge thy impious

offences, I heere give sentence that thou foorthwith marry Cassandra, to repaire her honour by
thee violated, and that the next day thou lose thy
head to make satisfaction for her brother's death.'

A just
judgement.

This just judgement of the good kinge, in the
first point, was foorthwith executed. But sacred is
the authoritye that the vertues of the good are a
sheelde unto the lewde. So sweete Cassandra, who
(simply) by vertue overcame the spight of Fortune,
in this marriadge was charged with a new assault
of sorrow, and, preferring the dutye of a wife
before the naturall zeale of a sister, where she
before prosecuted the revenge of her brother's
death, shee now was an humble suter to the kinge
for her husband's life.

The good
protect the
lewde.

The duetye of
a wife, truely
showen.

The gracious kinge sought to appease her with
good words, but hee could not do her this private
favour without injurye unto the publike weale.
'For though' (quoth he) 'your sute be just and the
bounden dutye of a wife, yet I in fulfilling the
same should do injustly and (generally) injure my
subjects. And therfore, good gentlewoman, have
patience, and no doubt vertue in the ende will give
you power over all your afflictions.'

The comon
weale is to be
regarded
before private
favour.

There was no remedye; Cassandra must
departe, out of hope to obtaine her sute. But as
the experience is in daily use, the dooinges of
princes post through the world on Pegasus' backe,
and as their actions are good or badde, so is their
fame.[29] With the like speede, the kinge's justice
and Promos' execution was spred abroad and, by
the tonge of a clowne, was blowen into Andrugio's
eares, who till then lived like an outlawe in the
desart wooddes.

*Sive bonum,
sive malum,
fama est.*

But upon these newes, covertly, in the habit of
an hermit,[30] by the divine motion of the sowle,
who directes us in thinges that be good (and the
flesshe in actions of evill), Andrugio goes to see
the death of his capitall enemye. But on the other
parte, regarding the sorrow of his sister, he
wisshed him life as a friende.

Good
motions
proceede
from the
soule, and
evill from the
flesh.

268   PROMOS AND CASSANDRA

To conclude, as well to geve terrour to the lewde as comfort to his good subjectes, the king (personallye) came to see the execution of Promos. Who, garded with officers and strengthened with the comfortable perswasions of his ghostly fathers,[31] among whom Andrugio was, meekely offered his life as a satisfaction for his offences, which were many more then the lawe tooke knowledge of. And yet, to say the trueth, suche was his repentance as the multitude did both forgeve and pittye him. Yea, the king wondred that his life was governed with no more vertue, considering the grace he showed at his death.

A gratefull parte.

Andrugio, behoulding this ruethfull spectackle, was so overcome with love towardes his sister, as, to give her comfort, he franckly consented anew to emperill his own life. And, followinge this resolution, in his hermit's weede, upon his knees, he humblye desired the kinge too give him leave to speake. The king (gratiously) graunted him audience. Whereupon quoth he: 'Regarded soveraigne, if lawe may (possibly) be satisfied, Promos' true repentance meritteth pardon.'

'Good father' (quoth the king) 'he cannot live and the lawe satisfied, unlesse (by miracle) Andrugio be revived.'

Murther asketh death and no other satisfaction.

'Then' (quoth the hermit) 'if Andrugio live, the law is satisfied and Promos discharged?'

'I' (quoth the king) 'if your prayer can revive the one, my mercye shall acquite the other.'

'I humbly thanke your majestye' (quoth Andrugio), and, discovering himselfe, shewed the providence of God and the meane of his escape. And, tendringe his sister's comfort above his owne safetye, hee prostrated himselfe at his majestye's feete, humblye to obay the sentence of his pleasure. The kinge, uppon the reporte of this straunge adventure, after good deliberation, pardoned Promos to keepe his worde and, withall, houlding an opinion that it was more benefitiall for the citezens to be ruled by their olde evell

Princes are bounde to their word.

governour, new refourmed, then to adventure uppon an newe whose behaviours were unknowne. And, to perfect Cassandra's joye, he pardoned her brother Andrugio, with condition that he should marrye Polina. Thus, from betweene the teethe of daunger, every partye was preserved and, in the ende, established in their harte's desire.

Of two, the least evill is least daungerous.

'Madam' (quoth Soranso) 'your good conclusion hath likewise preserved us from a great daunger; for had you ended with the sorrow you began, wee had beene all like to have bene drowned in teares.'[32]

Ruthfull tales raiseth remorce in the hearers.

'Indeede' (quoth Katharina Trista) 'you men had cause sufficient of sorrowe by hearing your kinde reproched with such monstrous evils, and we women free passage to lament in behoulding none but crosse fortunes to succeede the good indevours of a vertuous ladye.'

By example of evill, the evill are feared.

'It is true' (quoth Fabritio). 'But to participate of their joye, wee men have learned out of Promos' example of evil, for feare of his likelye punishment of evil, to doo well;[33] and you women, by example of Polina's vice and Cassandra's vertue, are both warned and incouraged to wel-dooing.'

By example of the good, the good are strengthned.

'Indeede' (quoth Queene Aurelia) 'there are many morall precepts in either historye to be considered, whiche I hope the company have so regarded as there needeth no repetition. And further, because I will not be to bould of the victorye over my late distemperature,[34] we will heare ende. And therwith she rose and retired into her chamber, with charge that the company should attende her in the same place until supper. Who, obaying, intertained time, everyone with their special fancy.

Good order is to bee kept among such as have bene late sick.

FOUR TALES FROM

TARLTON'S NEWES OUT
OF PURGATORIE

This group of tales extracted from *Tarlton's Newes out of Purgatorie* is set in a narrative frame: the anonymous author begins by explaining that he had been so saddened by the death of Richard Tarlton, the comic actor, that he did not go to the theatre for a long time, and when he finally decided to go, he 'founde such concourse of unruely people' that he went for a solitary walk in the fields instead. He fell asleep and was visited by the spirit of Dick Tarlton with 'newes out of Purgatorye'. Tarlton recounted to the dreaming author his experiences as a new spirit being initiated into the geography and scheme of punishments of Purgatory; the following stories were told to him in order to explain the presence of some of the inhabitants and the nature of their punishments.

The tale of Friar Onion, why in Purgatorye he was tormented with waspes.

There dwelled a widow in Florence of good parentage and large possessions, more beautifull then she was wealthye, and yet she was the richest widow in al Florence. Hir name was Lisetta. The onely faulte that was found in hir was that hir beautye was more then hir wit, and that such a selfe-love of hir excellencye had made hir overweene hirselfe, that she thought none fit to bee her husband in all Florence. Thus, though she were lookde at for hir outward perfection, yet was she laughde at for hir inward follies. Well, howsoever others censured of her, she thought her peny better silver then the rest and would so strive to excell other gentlewomen in the nicenesse of gesture that ofttimes she marde all, in so much that hir coy quaintnesse was a byword in the citye.

Every weeke forsooth, because she would seeme as vertuous as she was faire, she devoutly went to Friar Onion to be confessed of hir sins. The priest, who was a lusty lubber and a tall swaine, and nurst up lust with idlenesse, began to looke upon hir more narrowlye and to take a particular view of hir perfections; with that, entring with a piercing insight into hir selfe-love, thought that she might quickly be overreacht in hir owne conceipts. For he thought that if the wisest women were wonne with faire praises and large promises, it were more easye to intrap hir with the discourse of her excellencye. Therefore, he laid his plot thus: The next time Lisetta came to shrift, after she had made her confession and had received absolution for hir sinnes, Friar Onion looking earnestlye upon hir, fetch a far sigh and said: 'Ah, madam! If you knew as much as I know, as you are the fairest, so you would thinke yourselfe the happiest of all weomen that are alive.'

'Why sir, I pray you?' quoth Lisetta.

'Ah,' said Friar Onion, 'it is such a secret as may not be revealed. For if I should disclose it to you, and you by any meanes make it manifest, there were no way with me but a most miserable death.'

Lisetta, as all women be desirous of noveltye, was so greedye to heare what good was toward hir that she made a thousand protestations and uttered a thousand oathes never to bewray what her ghostly father should tell her in secret.

'Then madam', quoth Friar Onion, with a grave and a demure countenance, 'know your beautye is so excellent and your perfection so farre beyond the common course of all other women that not onely all men that see you admire you as a miracle but the very angels in heaven are enamored of your proportion.'

'The angels?' quoth she. 'Is that possible?'

'The angels, madam, and not the meanest, but the most beautifull of all the rest. For the angell Gabriel is so far in love with you that the other night he appeared unto me and charged me to do his earnest commendations unto you, with promise that, if hee might be assured of your secrecye, he would at convenient times visit you and interteine you with such love as befitteth such holy spirits.'

This tale so set afire Lisetta that she not onely thanked Friar Onion for his commendations but counted herselfe the most fortunate of all women that she was beloved of so blessed a saint.[1] And, therfore, when and where it pleased him, he should be intertained with as honourable secrecye as a poore dame of her calling might afford. Friar Onion, seeing this geere would worke, prosecuted his purpose then subtilly. He presently fell downe on his knees before hir and desired that for such happye newes as he had brought, she would graunt him a boone. Lisetta, liberall now to performe any demaund, bad him aske. Then he began thus: 'Madam', quoth he, 'for that the angell Gabriell is a spirit, and his brightnesse such as no mortall eye can suffer, and therefore must come unto you in some humane shape, I pray you vouchsafe that my bodye may be the receptacle for him, that while he putteth on my carcasse, my soule may enjoy the sight and pleasures of Paradise. So shall you not hinder yourselfe and do me an unspeakeable benefit.' Lisetta, seeing Friar Onion was a lusty tall fellow, willing in what she might to pleasure him, graunted his request verye willinglye.

Whereupon it was concluded that she should leave the doore open, and about midnight the angel Gabriell should come to visit her.

Upon this resolution, home went Lisetta, as merry as a pie, tricking up hir bedchamber with all braverye and rich perfumes for the interteinment of hir paramour. And Friar Onion, as busye as a bee, was making his winges and his trinckets ready to play the angell. Well, he delt so that he agreed with an old pandor that dwelt opposite to the house, and there made himselfe ready and at the houre appointed went to Lisetta. Where he found the doore open, and so entred up till hee came to her bedchamber, where she sat expecting his comming. As soone as she sawe him with his glorious wings and his white roabes, she rose and fell at his feet, but he lovingly tooke her up, imbracst hir, kist hir and pointed to the bed, whether the angell went after he had laid apart his abiliments, and Lisetta followed with as much speed as might be. *Caetera quis nescit?*[2] Early before breake of the day, Gabriell tooke his leave of his Lisetta and went to his lodging, leaving hir the proudest woman in the world that shee was beloved of an angell.

Friar Onion, hee got him to his cell and there tooke uppe his broaken sleepe hee had lost, till nine of the clocke that hee went into his oratorye. Where hee had not sitten long, but Lisetta, in as great braverye as might, came to the church, and then offerd up in greater devotion a burning taper to the angell Gabriell. Afterwards, hir orisons done, she came to Friar Onion. Who, after some conference, demaunded hir of hir new lover, whom shee highly commended, and he againe gave hir great thanks that shee vouchsaft him to be the receptacle of so holy a saint, for, all the while his bodye was with hir, his soule did tast the joyes of Paradice. These two thus agreed, it so fell out that sundry times, as occasion and opportunity would give leave, the angell Gabriel visited Lisetta.

The friar thus frolicke in this conceited content was thwarted by fortune on this manner. Lisetta, waxing very proud with the remembrance of hir new lover, was so coy and disdainefull as she thought never a dame in Florence fit for hir company, insomuch that many wondred why shee grewe so insolent. But the more they marvailed, the more shee was malapert, conceiving such abundance of selfe-love within hir stomacke that shee was with childe till shee had uttered hir minde to some of hir gossips. On a day, sitting with one in whom shee had most affiance, shee beganne to require secrecy, and shee would unfold unto hir a thing not onely strange but of great import. Hir gossip, as the custome is, began to blame those wives whose secrets lay at their tongue's end, and saide shee was never toucht with any staine of hir tongue, and therefore whatsoever shee told hir should bee buried underfoote and goe no further. Upon this, Lisetta began to rehearse unto hir from point to point the whole discourse of the angell Gabriell, howe hee was in love with hir, and how sundry nights he lay with hir, and many more matters which he told hir of the joyes of Paradise. Hir gossip, being a wily wench, kept hir countenance very demurely, commending the excellencye of hir beauty that did not onely amaze men, but drew even angels to be inamoured of hir, promising to be as secrete in this matter as hirselfe. Shee thought the time long till they might breake off talke, and therefore as soone as shee could finde opportunity, shee tooke hir leave, and hied hir homeward. But to hir house shee coulde not goe, till shee had met with two or three of hir gossips, to whom in a great laughter shee unfolded what madam Lisetta had told hir, how shee was beloved of the angell Gabriell, and how sundry nights he lay with hir, and tould her of the joyes of Paradice. This was worke enough for nine dayes,[3] for the woonder of madame Lisetta's barne went through all Florence, so that at last it came to the eares of Lisetta's friends, who greeved that such a clamor should be raised of their kinswoman. Knowing hir follye, thought to watch neere, but they would take the angell Gabriell and clip his winges from flying.

Well, secret they kept it, and made as though they had not hard of it, yet kept they such diligent watch that they knew the night when the angell would descend to visit Lisetta. Where-upon, they beset the house round, and assoone as Friar Onion was in and had put off his wings and was gone to bed, the rushing-in of the watch wakened him from his rest, and that with such a vengeance that trusting more to his feete then to his fethers, hee left madam Lisetta amazed at the noise. And he himselfe was so sharpely beset and so neere taken that he was faine to leape out of a hie garret windowe, and so almost breake his neck, into a little narrow lane. Well, his best joint scapte, but he was sore brused. Yet feare made him forget his fall, that away hee ran to a poore man's house where he saw light, and there got in, making an excuse how he had fallen among theeves and so desired lodging.

The man, having heard talke of the angell Gabriell, knowing verye well Friar Onion, that knew not him, let him have lodging verye willinglye. But all this while that he escapt were Lisetta's friends seeking for the saint that so tenderlye loved their kinswoman, but they could not finde him, and to Heaven he was not flowne, for they had found his wings. Sorry they were that Gabriell had mist them. But they chid harde, and rebuked the follye of Lisetta's selfe-love that was not onely so credulous, but such a blab as to reveale hir owne secrets. It was late, and, because they had mist of their purpose, they departed, leaving Lisetta a sorrowfull woman, that she was so deceived by the angell Gabriell.

Well, night passed and the morning came, and this poore man Friar Onion's hoast tould him that he knew not how to shift him, for there was that day a great search for one Friar Onion that had escapde naked from Lisetta's house, and who so kept him in secret should have his eares naild on the pillorye.

At this the friar started and said: 'Alas friend, I am the man. And if by any meanes thou canst convay me to the dortor of our friory, I will give thee fortye duckats.'

'If you will', quoth his hoast, 'follow my counsaile, feare not. I will convey you thither safe and unknowne, and thus. This day there is great shewes made before the duke of Florence, and strange sights to be seene, and diverse wilde men disguised in strange attire are brought into the market-place.[4] Now, I will dresse you in some strange order, and, with a maske over your face, lead you amongst the rest, and when the shew is doone, carrying you as though I should carrye you home, I will conveigh you into the dortor backside, secret and unknowne.'

Although this seemed hard to the friar, yet of two evils the least was to be chosen, and he consented to suffer what the hoast would devise. Whereupon he, that was of a pleasant conceipt, used him thus. He annointed him over with barme mixed with hony and stuck him full of feathers and, tying him by the neck with a chaine, put a visor on his face, and on either side tide a great ban dogge. In this *come equipage* marched this poore man with the friar.[5] He was no sooner come into the open streete, but the people, having never seene such a sight before in Florence, did not onely wonder at the strangenesse of his dressing, but marvailed what this novelty should meane. Where-upon an infinit number not onely of the common sort, but of the gravest citizens followed, to see what should be the end of this woonder.

With a solemne pace marched his keeper, till he came to the market-place, where, tying him to a great piller that stoode there, he then let make in all places of the citye solemne proclamation that whoso would see the angell Gabriell should presently come to the market-place and behould him there in that amorous dignitye that he did usually visit the dames of Florence. At this proclamation there was a generall concourse of people, especially of the better sort that had hard of Lisetta's loves, so that the duke himselfe came thither and, amongst the rest, Lisetta's kinsmen. When all the market-place was full of people, the hoast pulled the visor from the friar's face. At which the people gave a great shoute, clapping their hands, and crying: 'The angell Gabriell, the angell Gabriell. He that comes from Heaven to make us weare hornes.'

I need not, I hope, intreate you to beleeve that poore Friar Onion was heavily perplexed, especially when the day grew hot, he naked and anointed with hony, so that all the waspes in the citye, as it were by a miracle, left the grocers' shops and came to visit the friar because his skin was so sweete. But, alas to the poore man's paines, that he was almost stoong to death. Divers of his convent came thither to see the strange apparition of the Angell. Who, when they saw he was Friar Onion, then they covered their shaven crownes with their cooles, and went home with a flea in their eares.[6] Thus, all day stood the poore friar, woondered at of all people of Florence, and tormented with waspes, and at night fetcht home to the dortor by some of his brothers. He was clapt in prison, where for sorrow poore Gabriell died. And because he did so dishonor the other friars he bides this torment in Purgatorye.

A little below I saw a cooke that was a mad merry fellow, and he sate demurely with a crane's leg in his mouth, having no other punishment. At this I smilde and asked the cause, and it was told me thus.

The tale of the Cooke and why he sate in Purgatory with a crane's leg in his mouth

There dwelled in Venice a gentleman called signor Bartolo, who, being one of the *consiliadorie* and greatlye experienced in the civill law,[1] was much frequented of sundry sutors. Amongst the rest there was a gentleman, his neighbour, that by fortune had caught some eight or ten cranes, a fowle in high esteeme in that citye. These, as a thing of great price, hee bestowed on signor Bartolo, who accepted them with that gratefulnes that so good and bountiful a gift merited. Proude forsooth of this present, he fedde them up in one of his yardes, looking with great care to them, because the Venetians hold them so rare.

On a day, desirous to make his neighbours partakers of his dainties, he bad divers of them to supper, and commanded his cooke to provide good cheere and, amongst the rest, chargde him to kill a crane and to see that it were excellently well rosted. The cooke, whose name was Stephano, made all thinges in a readines for supper, and when the time was convenient, laide the crane to the fire.

Now, sir, this Stephano was a fellowe that was somewhat amorous, and excellent at courting of a country wench; insomuch that he was the chief gallant of all the parish for dancing of a Lincolnshire hornepipe in the churchyard on Sondayes. Being thus well qualified, he was generally loved of al the girles thereabout and especially of one in the towne, whom he had so long dallied withall that the maide fell sicke, and hir disease was thought to be a tympany with two heeles.[2] Wel, howsoever, shee was spedde, and Stephano had done the deede.

This maide, hearing what a great feast should be at signor Bartolo's house, hied hir thither, not onely to see the good cheere but that shee must feede her eye with the sight of hir Stephano, who now was ruffling and sweating in the kitchin. She made an excuse and came in for fier, but in an unlucky time for the poore cooke, for shee no sooner sawe the crane but shee longd for a leg and that so sore that there was nothing but that or death. Whereupon shee calde Stephano to hir and told him that shee must needes have a legge of the crane, for shee so deepely longd for it that, if shee had it not, it were able both to cast hir away and that shee went withall.[3] Although poore Stephano alledgde many excuses, as the displeasure of his maister and the feare of the losse of his service, yet no reason could prevaile with hir, who was without reason, and therefore, what for love hee bare hir and for dread of discredite that might ensure if for want of hir longing shee shoulde fall to travell, hee ventred a joint and, when the crane was enough, cut hir off a legge. His wench thus satisfied went home.

And supper time grew on, for all the guests were come and presently, because it was somewhat late, sate downe, where they were served very bountifully. At last, the dainties, the crane forsooth, was brought up, and signior Bartolo commaunded the carver to truncke hir, which when he had done, shee was set upon the table. The gentleman of the house fell to distributing to his guests, and at last mist a legge. With that, looking about, he calde the carver, and askt him where the other leg was.

'Sir', quoth hee, 'your maistership hath all the cooke sent up.'

'Then', quothe Bartolo, 'goe to the cooke and aske him where the other leg is.'

The carver went down and did his maister's commande. The cooke, thinking to face out the matter, began to smile. 'Why', quoth he, 'we may see cranes are dainty in this country when gentlemen cannot tell how many legs they have. Goe tell my maister I sent him up as many legges as shee had.'

The fellow brought this newes to his maister, who in a great chafe called for the cooke and asked of him howe many legs a crane had. 'Marry, sir', quoth he, 'one.'

'Why, malapert villeine', quoth Bartolo, 'mockest thou me before all these gentlemen?'

'Not I, sir', quoth the cooke. 'For I am sure I have drest many in my life, and hitherto yet I never saw a crane have but one leg.'

With this answer Bartolo was throughly inflamed with choller but, that he would shew himselfe to be patient amongst his neighbours, he suppressed his anger with this mild reply: 'Either, gentlemen, you may thinke I or my cooke is drunke, that hold a dispute about a crane's legge. But, for that this night I will not bee impatient, I passe it over. But tomorrow morning all as you are heere, I humbly request you to take so much paines as to rise betimes and to be judges betweene me and my man whether cranes have two legs or no. For I have nine cranes more, and wee will early goe into the yarde where they feede. And this shall be the wager betweene my man and me: if they have but one leg, I will give him twenty duckats and a sute of satten. If they have two, hee shall have twenty blowes with a cudgill, and I will turne him quite out of service.'

With this motion the cooke seemed very wel contented, that all the guests smilde to see poore Stephano so obstinate. Upon this matter they began to descant and fell into pleasant chat, and so passed away the supper time. At last, although loth to depart, yet every man departed with great thanks to signior Bartolo for their good cheere, promising very early in the morning to be with him. Where we leave them, and againe to the cooke, who provided all his trinckets in a readines, to trudge away with bag and baggage the next morning. For he knewe his matter was nought; thus, with a heavy hart he passed away the night and in the morning fell in a slumber. But hee had not long lien in his dreame but Bartolo, accompanied with his neigh-bours, knockt at his man's chamber doore, and bad him rise, that they might end the quarrell. Poore Stephano started up and with a heavy cheere comming out of his chamber, gave his maister and the rest the 'bon joure'.[4]

'Come, sirrah', quoth his maister, 'heere are the gentlemen; my neighbours are come to be equal censors of our controversye. Hold, take the key of the yard, and open you the doore, and then let us see how many legs a crane hath.'

The cooke tooke the key and very easily opened the dore and entred in, and all the cranes, because it was so early, were at strud. As their custome is generally, all stoode upon one leg and held the other under their wing. Stephano, seeing the advantage, not willing to let so fair a ball fall to the ground, began himselfe: 'Now sir' (quoth he) 'I hope yourselfe and the rest of the gentlemen will confesse I have woonne the wager. For you see heere is never a crane that hath more then one legge.' At this, seeing how nimble he was to take the advantage, they all laught.

'Truth, sir', quoth his maister, 'they stand now on one leg, but straight you shall see me make them all have two.' With that signor Bartolo, lifting up his hande, cried: 'So ho.' And with that the cranes let downe their legges, and every one stoode upon two. 'How now, you knave', quoth his maister, 'how many legges hath a crane. Hath shee not two?'

'Yes, marry, sir', quoth hee, 'and so would your other crane have had, if you had done this. For if your worship, when you had seene the crane in the platter had but one legge, had as lowde as you doe now, cried "So ho", why then shee woulde have had two legges as well as these.'

At this jest signor Bartolo fell into such a laughing, and all his guests with him, that he laught away choller and admitted his man into his woonted favour. Whereupon Stephano tolde them the whole discourse, what happened betweene him and his wench, and uppon this merrily they went all to breakfast.

Now, sir, although this fault was forgiven, yet, because hee died not in favour with the priest of the parish, hee was appointed for stealing the crane's leg to stand in Purgatorye with a legge in his mouth for a certaine season.

A little above sat the ghost of a young gentlewoman that had beene false to her husband. Shee shoulde have beene greevously tormented, but that shee bestowed an annuitye for three yeeres' pension upon a morrow masse preeste who so laboured it with dirges, trentals and masses *Ad requiem* that shee had no other punishment but this: that her beautifull haire, wherein shee so much delighted and whose tramels was a traine to intrappe young gentlemen, that nowe was clipt off bare to the scull, and so shee sate ashamde and mourning.[1] The cause, as I learnde, was this.

Why the gentlewoman of Lyons sate with her haire clipt off in Purgatorye

In the cittye of Lyons there dwelt a gentleman of good acount amongst his neighbors called monsieur Perow. This gentleman, having land and revenues sufficient to maintaine his estate, thought fullye to heape to himselfe content and therefore sought out a yong virgin of equall parentage to himselfe, with whom he had a sufficient dowry, and her he loved, and she likte him, and so they maried, living in good estimation amongst their tenants.

As they were thus linked together in wedlock, so it seemde in outward appearance that they were so strictlye tied in affection as no meanes might alienate. But women, whom nature hath framde to be inconstant, cannot be altred by nurture.[1] The palme will grow straite though it be never so depressed, and a wanton will be a wanton were she married to Cupid, and so it provde by Maria (for so was the gentlewoman's name). Who, because she was faire, had many sutors that attempted to bee rivals with her husband in her love. Amongst the rest, as shee resolved to choose one, there was a yong amorous youth of Lyons calde Pier. He sought divers meanes to creep into her favor, past by her house, and cast up looks that pleded for pitty and had handed him again glaunces that foreshewed goodwill. Thus with interchange of favours they lived.

Pier, seeking oportunity how to reveale his minde to Maria, at last as hee walked one day forth the towne he saw where she was walking only with one of her maides. Taking therefore oportunity by the forehead,[2] he stept to her and beganne to court her with sundry protestations of his love, which had been long and so surely set as no dispaire coulde race out, promising not onely to be a faithfull servant in constancye but to be so carefull of her honour as of his own life: 'And for your gravity, think mistres', quoth he, 'that faults in affections are sleight follies, that Venus hath shrines to shade her trewants, and Cupid's winges are shelters for such as venter far to content their thoughts, unseene is halfe pardoned, and love requires not chastity, but that her souldiers be chary.' Maria, hearing the wag thus play the orator, having love in her eyes and desire in hart, after a fewe faint denials, thrusting him away with the little finger and pulling him to her with the whole hande, shee graunted him that favour to be cald hir servant.[3] Graced thus, he grewe in such credite that there was no man with Maria but Pier.

Having thus a love beside her husband, although hee was a faire man and well featured, yet shee found fault with him, because he was a meacocke and a milkesoppe, not daring to drawe his swoorde to revenge hir wrongs. Wherefore shee resolved to entertaine some souldier, and so shee did, for one signior Lamberto, a brave gentleman, but something harde-facde, sought her favour and found it, and him shee intertained for her champion.

Thus had shee a white-liverd Adon to feede her eye with beautye and a stoute Hercules to revenge all her wrongs with his swoorde, and a poore husband to shadowe both with his hornes.[4] Living thus contentedlye in her owne conceite, her husband went into the countrye to a farme of his, and thither with him he carried his wife, where hee passed away many merry dayes in such pleasure as cuntry sports can affoorde. At last, serious affairs forcing him to it, he rid his way for three or four dayes to certaine of his freends there adjoining.

Maria, seeing her husband gone, thought not to let time slip, nor to lose oportunity, and therefore the next day after sent for Pier, who hasted as fast as might be till he came to his mistres, where he had such freendly intertainment as fitted both their humours. Shee caused her maide to make great cheere and, as soone as it was readye, to dinner they went, where they were scarce set but one knocked at the doore. The maide looked out, and it was signior Lamberto. She ran and told hir mistres, who, fearefull that he should see Pier or know of him, hid him under the bed and commanded her maid to bid signior Lamberto come up, she like a cunning curtizan giving him such favourable intertainement as though hee were the man whom above all other shee made account off.

'Faithe sweete' (quoth hee) 'I heard thy husband was from home, and so I took my nag and came gallopping hither.'

'Set him into the stable', quoth the mistres.

'No' (quoth signior Lamberto) 'let him bee there stil and bite of the bridle, for my businesse is such as I will onelye dine with you and then bid you farwell.' With that he sat him downe to dinner, poore Pier lying close under the bed, thinking every minute an houre till he were gone.

As thus they sat in their cuppes and were wantonlye quaffing one to another,[5] came in the maide running and said her maister came riding. At this signior Lamberto started up and was amazed, but the gentlewoman was in a feare that had two lovers at once in her house and yet could have hidden them both had it not beene for the horse that stoode tied in the courtyarde.

Wel, a shift must bee had, and where sooner then out of a woman's head?

'What shall I doe?' quoth signior Lamberto.

'Marry, I pray you, good sweetheart', quoth shee, 'to save your owne credite and mine, drawe your swoorde and goe downe the staires, and as you go, sweare and say that you shall finde a time and place more convenient when you will bee revengde to the uttermost.'

So he did, and by that time was the gentleman of the house come in, who marvailed to see a horse tied in the court, and, therefore, alighting off, came up the staires, and as he came, met Lamberto with his swoorde drawne and his face full of frownes, swearing when fitter time and place woulde serve, hee woulde revenge and that with extremity. 'What is the matter?' quoth the master of the house. He answered nothing, but put up his swoord, took horse and away towards Lyons.

As soon as the gentleman came up, he found his wife amazde,

sitting in the hall in the middest of the flowre, as halfe beside herselfe. 'What is the matter, wife?' (quoth hee) 'that thou art so amazed and that signior Lamberto went downe with his swoorde drawne in such a rage?'

'Ah husband' (quoth shee) 'as I sate heere at my woorke, came running into the courtyarde a proper young man, having throwne awaye his cloake and his hatte, and desired mee, as I tendered the state of a man, to save his life, for signior Lamberto would kill him. I, pittying his case, stept in and hidde him in my bedchamber. With that came signior Lamberto gallopping, dismounted in the court and, drawing his swoorde, came running up and woulde have broken open my chamber dore, but that on my knees I intreated him to the contrary. At my request hee went his way, frowning as you see, and so he is rode to Lyons. The poore young man (alas) husband, lies hid under the bed in great feare.' And this tale shee tolde so lowde that Pier heard every woorde, and, therefore, had his lesson what hee should answere, smiling at the prompt witte of his mistres that had so sodaine a shift.

'Bidde him come out, wife', quoth he. Then shee oapte the doore, and Pier he came (as one greatly affrighted) from under the bed. The gentleman, seeing him a proper young man and weaponlesse, had pittye on him and saide hee was glad that his house was a sanctuarye for him, and greatlye commended his wife that she had saved him from the furye of signior Lamberto, whom all Lyons accounted a most desperate man. Upon this, taking Pier by the hand, they sat downe to dinner, and when they had taken their repast, the gentleman very curteouslye conducted Pier home to Lyons.

Now, for because shee was thus inconstant, shee to qualifye her pride and insolencye sate in Purgatorye with the punishment afore rehearsed.

This tale beeing ended, I looked a little further, and I might see where a young man and a young woman sate together naked from the middle upward, and a very olde man whipping of them with nettles. They, as persons that little regarded his punishment, woulde oftentimes kisse, and then the olde man, as one inwardly vexed, woulde bestirre all his strength to torment them. The reason of this strange shewe was thus discourst unto mee.

The Tale of the two Lovers of Pisa, and why they were whipt in Purgatory with Nettles

In Pisa, a famous cittye of Italye, there lived a gentleman of good linage and landes, feared as well for his wealth as honoured for his vertue, but (indeed) well thought on for both, yet the better for his riches. This gentleman had one onelye daughter, called Margaret, who for her beauty was liked of all and desired of many, but neither might their sutes nor her owne eye prevaile about her father's resolution,[1] who was determined not to marrye her but to such a man as should be able in abundance to maintaine the excellency of her beauty. Divers young gentlemen proffered large feoffments, but in vaine. A maide shee must bee still, till at last an olde doctor in the towne that professed physicke became a sutor to her; who was a welcome man to her father, in that he was one of the welthiest men in all Pisa. A tall stripling he was and a proper youth, his age about fourescore, his heade as white as milke, wherein for offence sake there was left never a tooth.[2] But it is no matter; what he wanted in person he had in the purse, which the poore gentelwoman little regarded, wishing rather to tie herselfe to one that might fit hir content, though they lived meanely, then to him with all the wealth in Italye. But shee was yong and forcst to follow her father's direction; who, upon large covenants, was content his daughter should marry with the doctor, and, whether shee likte

him or no, the match was made up, and in short time shee was
married. The poore wench was bound to the stake and had not
onely an olde impotent man but one that was so jealous as none
might enter into his house without suspition, nor shee doe
anything without blame. The least glance, the smallest countenance, any smile was a manifest instance to him that shee thought
of others better than himselfe. Thus he himselfe lived in a hell
and tormented his wife in as ill perplexitye. At last it chaunced
that a young gentleman of the citye, comming by her house and
seeing her looke out at her window, noting her rare and excellent
proportion, fell in love with her, and that so extreamelye as his
passions had no meanes till her favour might mittigate his
heartsicke discontent. The yong man, that was ignorant in
amorous matters and had never beene used to court anye
gentlewoman, thought to reveale his passions to some one freend
that might give him counsaile for the winning of her love, and
(thinking experience was the surest maister) on a daye seeing
the olde doctor walking in the churche that was Margaret's
husband, little knowing who he was, he thought this the fittest
man to whom he might discover his passions, for that hee was
olde and knewe much and was a physition that with his drugges
might helpe him forward in his purposes. So that, seeing the
olde man walke solitary, he joinde unto him, and, after a
curteous *salute*,[3] tolde him that he was to impart a matter of
great import unto him; wherein if hee would not onely be secrete
but indevour to pleasure him, his paines should bee every way
to the full considered.

'You must imagine, gentleman', quoth Mutio (for so was the
doctor's name) 'that men of our profession are no blabs, but
hold their secrets in their heart's bottome, and, therfore, reveale
what you please, it shall not onely be concealed, but cured, if
either my art or counsail may do it.'

Upon this Lionel (so was the yong gentleman called) tolde
and discourst unto him from point to point howe he was falne
in love with a gentlewoman that was maried to one of his
profession, discovered her dwelling and the house, and for that
hee was unacquainted with the woman and a man little experienced in love matters, he required his favour to further him with
his advise.

Mutio at this motion was stung to the hart, knowing it was
his wife hee was fallen in love withall. Yet, to conceale the

matter and to experience his wive's chastity and that, if shee playd false, he might be revengde on them both, he dissembled the matter and answered that hee knewe the woman very well and commended her highly, but saide shee had a churle to her husbande and, therefore, he thought shee woulde bee the more tractable: 'Trye hir, man', quoth hee, 'fainte heart never woonne faire ladye. And if shee will not be brought to the bent of your bowe, I will provide such a potion as shall dispatch all to your owne content.[4] And to give you further instructions for oportun- itye, knowe that her husband is forth every afternoone from three till sixe. Thus farre I have advised you because I pitty your passions, as myselfe being once a lover, but now I charge thee reveale it to none whomsoever, least it doo disparage my credit to meddle in amorous matters.'

The young gentleman not onely promised all carefull secrecye, but gave him harty thanks for his good counsell, promising to meete him there the next day and tell him what newes. Then hee left the old man, who was almost mad for feare his wife any way should play false. He saw by experience brave men came to besiege the castle, and, seeing it was in a woman's custodye and had so weake a governor as himselfe, he doubted it would in time be delivered up, which feare made him almost franticke. Yet he drivde of the time in great torment, till he might heare from his rival.

Lionello he hastes him home and sutes him in his bravery and goes downe towards the house of Mutio, where he sees her at the windowe; whome he courted with a passionate looke with such an humble *salute* as she might perceive how the gentleman was affectionate. Margaretta, looking earnestlye upon him and noting the perfection of his proportion, accounted him in her eye the flower of all Pisa, thinkte herselfe fortunate if shee might have him for her freend to supply those defaults that she found in Mutio. Sundry times that afternoone he past by her window, and he cast not up more loving lookes then he received gratious favours. Which did so incourage him that the next daye betweene three and sixe hee went to hir house, and, knocking at the doore, desired to speake with the mistris of the house, who hearing by her maid's description what he was, commaunded him to come in, where she interteined him with all curtesye.

The youth (that never before had given the attempt to court a ladye) began his *exordium*[5] with a blushe; and yet went forward so well that hee discourst unto hir howe hee loved her and that if it might please hir so to accept of his service as of a freende ever vowde in all duetye to bee at her commaunde, the care of her honour should bee deerer to him then his life, and hee would bee ready to prise her discontent with his bloud at all times.

The gentlewoman was a little coye, but, before they past, they concluded that the next day at foure of the clock hee should come thither and eate a pounde of cherries, which was resolved on with a *succado des labres*, and so, with a loath to departe, they tooke their leaves.[6]

Lionello, as joyfull a man as might be, hied him to the church to meete his olde doctor, where hee found him in his olde walke.

'What newes, sir?' quoth Mutio, 'How have you sped?'

'Even as I can wishe', quoth Lionello, 'for I have been with my mistresse and have found hir so tractable that I hope to make the olde peasant her husband looke broad headded by a paire of brow antlers.'[7]

How deepe this strooke into Mutio's hart, let them imagine that can conjecture what jelousye is. Insomuch that the olde doctor askte when should be the time. 'Mary', quoth Lionello, 'tomorrow at foure of the clocke in the afternoone, and then, maister doctor', quoth hee, 'will I dub the olde squire knight of the forked order.'

Thus they past on in chat till it grew late, and then Lionello went home to his lodging and Mutio to his house, covering all his sorrowes with a merrye countenaunce, with full resolution to revenge them both the next day with extremetye. He past the night as patiently as he could, and, the next daye after dinner, awaye he went, watching when it should bee foure of the clocke. At the houre justly came Lionello and was intertained with all curtesye. But scarse had they kist ere the maide cried out to her mistresse that her maister was at the doore, for he hasted, knowing that a horne was but a little while on grafting. Margaret at this alarum was amazed, and yet (for a shifte) chopt Lionello into a great driefatte full of feathers and sat hir downe close to her woorke. By that came Mutio in blowing and, as though hee came to looke somewhat in haste, called for the keyes of his chambers and looked in everye place, searching so narrowlye in everye corner of the house that he left not the verye privye unsearcht. Seeing he could not finde him, hee saide nothing, but, faining himselfe not well at ease, stayde at home, so that poore

Lionello was faine to staye in the driefatte till the olde churle was in bed with his wife; and then the maide let him out at a backe doore; who went home with a flea in his eare to his lodging.

Well, the next day, he went againe to meete his doctor, whome hee found in his woonted walke. 'What newes?'quoth Mutio. 'How have you sped?'

'A poxe of the olde slave', quoth Lionello, 'I was no sooner in and had given my mistresse one kisse but the jealous asse was at the doore; the maide spied him and cried her maister, so that the poore gentlewoman for verye shifte was faine to put me in a driefatte of feathers that stoode in an olde chamber. And there I was faine to tarrye while he was in bed and asleepe; and then the maide let me out, and I departed. But it is no matter. 'Twas but a chaunce, and I hope to crye quittance with him ere it be long!'

'As how?' quoth Mutio.

'Marry, thus', quoth Lionello. 'She sent me word by her maide this daye that upon Thursday next the olde churle suppeth with a patient of his a mile out of Pisa, and then I feare not but to quitte him for all.'

'It is well', quoth Mutio. 'Fortune bee your freend.'

'I thank you', quoth Lionello. And so, after a little more prattle, they departed.

To bee shorte, Thursdaye came and, about sixe of the clocke, foorth goes Mutio no further then a freende's house of his, from whence hee might descrye who went into his house. Straight hee sawe Lionello enter in, and after goes hee, insomuche that hee was scarselye sitten downe before the maide cried out againe: 'My maister comes.'

The goodwife, that before had provided for afterclaps, had found out a privye place between two seelings of a plauncher,[8] and there she thrust Lionello; and her husband came sweting. 'What a news', quoth shee, 'drives you home againe so soone, husband?'

'Marrye, sweete wife', quoth he, 'a fearefull dreame that I had this night which came to my remembrance, and that was this: methought there was a villeine that came secretly into my house with a naked poinard in his hand and hid himselfe, but I could not finde the place. With that, mine nose bled, and I came backe;[9] and by the grace of God I will seeke every corner in the house for the quiet of my minde.'

'Marry, I pray you doo, husband', quoth she.

With that he lookt in all the doors and began to search every chamber, every hole, every chest, every tub, the very well. He stabd every fetherbed through and made havocke like a madman, which made him thinke all was in vaine, and hee began to blame his eyes that thought they saw that which they did not. Upon this he rest halfe lunaticke, and all night he was very wakefull, that towards the morning he fell into a dead sleepe. And then was Lionello conveighed away.

In the morning when Mutio wakened, hee thought how by no meanes hee should be able to take Lionello tardy; yet he laid in his head a most dangerous plot, and that was this. 'Wife', quoth he, 'I must the next Monday ride to Vicensa to visit an olde patient of mine. Till my returne, which will be some ten dayes,[10] I will have thee staye at our little graunge house in the countrey.'

'Marry, very well content, husband', quoth she.

With that he kist her and was verye pleasant, as though he had suspected nothing, and away he flinges to the church, where hee meetes Lionello. 'What, sir', quoth he, 'what newes? Is your mistresse yours in possession?'

'No, a plague of the old slave', quoth he. 'I think he is either a witch or els workes by magick, for I can no sooner enter in the doores but he is at my backe, and so he was againe yesternight, for I was not warme in my seate before the maide cried, "My maister comes." And then was the poore soule faine to conveigh me betweene two seelings of a chamber in a fit place for the purpose, wher I laught hartely to myself to see how he sought every corner, ransackt every tub, and stabd every feath-erbed, but in vaine. I was safe enough till the morning, and then, when he was fast a sleepe, I lept out.'

'Fortune frowns on you', quoth Mutio.

'I, but I hope', quoth Lionello, 'this is the last time, and now shee wil begin to smile. For on Monday next he rides to Vicensa, and his wife lies at a grange house a little of the towne, and there, in his absence, I will revenge all forepassed misfortunes.'

'God send it be so', quoth Mutio, and so took his leave.

These two lovers longd for Monday, and at last it came. Early in the morning Mutio horst himselfe, and his wife, his maide and a man, and no more, and away he rides to his grange house, where, after he had brok his fast, he took his leave, and away towards Vicensa. He rode not far ere (by a false way) he returned into a thicket, and there, with a company of cuntry peasants, lay in an ambuscado to take the young gentleman. In the afternoone, comes Lionello gallopping, and, as soon as he came within sight of the house, he sent backe his horse by his boy and went easily afoot, and there, at the very entry, was entertaind by Margaret, who led him up the staires, and convayd him into her bedchamber, saying he was welcome into so mean a cottage. 'But', quoth she, 'now I hope fortun shal not envy the purity of our loves.'

'Alas, alas, mistris', cried the maid, 'heer is my maister, and 100 men with him, with bils and staves.'

'We are betrayd', quoth Lionel, 'and I am but a dead man.'

'Feare not', quoth she, 'but follow me.' And straight she carried him downe into a lowe parlor, where stoode an olde rotten chest full of writings.[11] She put him into that, and covered him with olde papers and evidences, and went to the gate to meet hir husband: 'Why, signior Mutio, what means this hurly-burly?' quoth she.

'Vile and shamelesse strumpet as thou art, thou shalt know by and by', quoth he. 'Where is thy love? All we have watcht him and seen him enter in. Now', quoth he, 'shal neither thy tub of feathers nor thy seeling serve, for perish he shall with fire, or els fall into my hands.'

'Doe thy worst, jealous foole', quoth she. 'I ask thee no favour.' With that, in a rage, he beset the house round and then set fire on it.

Oh, in what a perplexitye was poore Lionello that was shut in a chest, and the fire about his eares? And how was Margaret passionate, that knew her lover in such danger? Yet she made light of the matter, and, as one in a rage, called her maid to her and said: 'Come on, wench, seing thy maister mad with jeal-ousye hath set the house and al my living on fire, I will be revengd upon him; help me heer to lift this olde chest where all his writings and deeds are. Let that burne first, and as soon as I see that one fire I wil walk towards my freends, for the old foole wil be beggard and I wil refuse him.'

Mutio, that knew al his obligations and statutes lay there, puld her backe, and bad two of his men carry the chest into the feeld, and see it were safe, himself standing by and seeing his house burnd downe sticke and stone. Then, quieted in his minde, he went home with his wife, and began to flatter her, thinking assuredly that he had burnd her paramour, causing his chest to be carried in a cart to his house at Pisa.

Margaret, impatient, went to her mother's, and complained to her and to her bretheren of the jealousye of hir husband. Who maintained it to be true, and desired but a daye's respite to proove it. Wel, hee was bidden to supper the next night at her mother's, she thinking to make her daughter and him freends againe. In the meanetime, he to his woonted walke in the church, and there, *praeter expectationem*,[12] he found Lionello walking. Wondring at this, he straight enquires: 'What newes?'

'What newes, maister doctor', quoth he, and he fell in a great laughing. 'In faith, yesterday I scapt a scowring. For, sirrha, I went to the grange house, where I was appointed to come, and I was no sooner gotten up the chamber but the magicall villeine hir husband beset the house with bils and staves and that he might be sure no seeling nor corner should shrowde me, he set the house on fire, and so burnt it down to the ground.'

'Why', quoth Mutio, 'and how did you escape?'

'Alas', quoth he, 'well fare a woman's wit.[13] She conveighed me into an olde chest full of writings, which she knew her husband durst not burne. And so was I saved and brought to Pisa, and yesternight by hir maide let home to my lodging.'

'This', quoth he, 'is the pleasantest jest that ever I heard. And upon this I have a sute to you. I am this night bidden foorth to supper; you shall be my guest, onelye I will crave so much favour as, after supper for a pleasant sporte, to make relation what success you have had in your loves.'

'For that I wil not sticke', quothe he. And so he caried Lionello to his mother-in-lawe's house with him and discovered to his wive's brethren who he was,[14] and how at supper he would disclose the whole matter. 'For', quoth he, 'he knowes not that I am Margaret's husband.' At this, all the brethren bad him welcome, and so did the mother to, and Margaret she was kept out of sight. Supper time being come, they fell to their victals, and Lionello was carrowst unto by Mutio, who was very pleasant to draw him to a merry humor, that he might to the ful discourse the effect and fortunes of his love.

Supper being ended, Mutio requested him to tele to the gentleman what had hapned between him and his mistresse. Lionello with a smiling countenance began to describe his mistresse, the house, and street where she dwelt, how he fell in love with her and how he used the counsell of this doctor, who in al his affaires was his secretarye.

Margaret heard all this with a great feare, and when he came at the last point she caused a cup of wine to be given him by one of her sisters, wherein was a ring that he had given Margaret. As he had told how he escapt burning and was ready to confirme all for a troth, the gentlewoman drunke to him. Who taking the cup and seing the ring, having a quick wit and a reaching head, spide the fetch, and perceived that all this while this was his lover's husband, to whome hee had revealed these escapes.

At this, drinking the wine, and swallowing the ring into his mouth, he went forward. 'Gentlemen', quoth he, 'how like you of my loves and my fortunes?'

'Wel', quoth the gentlemen. 'I pray you, is it true?'

'As true', quoth he, 'as if I would be so simple as to reveal what I did to Margaret's husband. For, know you, gentlemen, that I knew this Mutio to be her husband, whom I notified to be my lover,[15] and for that he was generally known through Pisa to be a jealous fool. Therfore, with these tales I brought him into this paradice, which indeed are follies of mine own braine. For, trust me by the faith of a gentleman, I never spake to the woman, was never in her companye, neither doo I know her if I see her.'

At this they all fell in a laughing at Mutio, who was ashamde that Lionello had so scoft him. But all was well; they were made friends. But the jest went so to his hart that he shortly after died, and Lionello enjoyed the ladye. And, for that they two were the death of the olde man, now are they plagued in Purgatorye, and he whips them with nettles.

As soone as I had passed over these two of Pisa, I looked about and saw many more, as mad and pleasant as the rest; but my time was come that I must to the judge to be censured what punishment I should have myself for al the mad, wanton tricks that I did when I was alive. Faith, at last, because they knew I was a boone companion, they appointed that I should sit and play jigs all day on my taber to the ghosts without cesing, which hath brought me into such use that I now play far better then when I was alive. For proofe thou shalt heare a hornepipe.'

With that, putting his pipe to his mouth, the first stroak he strucke I started, and with that I waked and saw such concourse of people through the fields that I knew the play was doon. Wherupon, rising up and smiling at my dream, and after supper took my pen, and as neer as I could set it down, but not halfe so plesantly as he spoke it; but, howsoever, take it in good part, and so farewell. FINIS

NOTES

Titus and Gisippus

'Titus and Gisippus' appears in book II, chapter 12 of Sir Thomas Elyot's *The Governour* (1531), the book in which Elyot developed his theory and method for providing a humanist education to the sons of the ruling class. The story is based on the eighth story of the tenth day of the *Decameron*; the topic for the tenth day is 'people who freely and generously do something having to do with love or something else'. Elyot probably translated 'Titus and Gisippus' from a Latin translation of Boccaccio's Italian story, but in any case the translation is very free. Elyot leaves out a great number of the details of the two earlier versions: in them we learn, for example, exactly when the events of the story took place (when Octavian was a triumvir) and the name of the philosopher who tutored the two boys. Shakespeare used a version of the story of Titus and Gisippus in *The Two Gentlemen of Verona*; he probably used Elyot's.

1 The Roman nobility had the custom of sending their children to Greece to be educated.
2 'As shulde like him' means 'as he should like'.
3 In the sixteenth century the word 'lover' did not suggest that a sexual relationship existed between two people. That Gisippus was the lady's 'lover' means that he felt friendship for her or loved her.
4 Titus blames his astrological sign for his bad luck.
5 'It lacked but litle that his harte was ne riven in peces' means 'his heart was nearly broken in pieces'.
6 'Bride' refers to the bridegroom. Gisippus is saying that he will perform all the duties of the groom in the formal, public marriage ceremony.
7 Titus is referring to Greek legends and myths. In order to make love to mortal women, Zeus, the king of the gods, transformed himself into animals: a swan to love Leda, and a bull to love Europa. When in servitude to Omphale, Heracles wore woman's clothing and learned to spin. The princes of Asia and Greece

besieged Troy in order to retrieve Helen, the wife of Menelaus, who had been abducted by Paris, a Trojan prince.

8 That good friends were harder to find than good wives was a commonplace.

9 The ancient Romans considered committing suicide a virtuous act, so the notion that an ancient Roman would be glad to avoid suicide is anachronistic. The sentiment is not original with Painter; it is in Boccaccio's story and in the Latin translation.

The Palace of Pleasure

The title-page of the first volume reads: 'The Palace of Pleasure. Beautified, adorned and well furnished, with pleasaunt histories and excellent nouvelles, selected out of divers good and commendable authors. By William Painter Clarke of the Ordinaunce and Armarie. Imprinted at London, by Henry Denham, for Richard Tottell and William Jones. 1566.'

Melchisedech's Tale of Three Kings

The story of 'Melchisedech and Saladine' appears in Painter's Palace of Pleasure (I, 30). It is a close translation of Decameron I.3, a day on which there is no set topic.

1 Saladine (Salah ed-din), sultan of Egypt (Babilon = Cairo), conquered Jerusalem in 1187. He was celebrated in Western medieval literature for his liberality and courtesy.

Ermino Grimaldi

'Ermino Grimaldi' appears in Painter's Palace of Pleasure (I, 31). It is a close translation of Decameron I.8, a day on which there is no set topic.

1 The Grimaldi were one of the oldest and most powerful families in Genoa. Ermino was a common name in the family.

2 Guglielmo Borsieri is mentioned by Dante in Inferno XVI. 70–2; the topic is the contrast between the morals of the recent past and the present, and Borsieri is an example of the courtesy and valour of men of the previous generation. He died at the beginning of the 1300s.

3 'Nesinges' is a form of 'neezing' or 'sneezing', but in this context it may indicate nescience or ignorance.

4 In Boccaccio's story, Guglielmo suggests that the figure of 'la Cortesia' be painted. *Cortesia* is a more general term than liberality; it indicates good manners as well.

Andreuccio of Perugia

'Andreuccio of Perugia' appears in Painter's *Palace of Pleasure* (I, 36). It is a close translation of *Decameron* II.5; on the fifth day the topic is 'people who are harmed by various things and come to a happy end contrary to all expectations'. Boccaccio lived in Naples for a good number of years, and this story shows his familiarity with the city's geography and culture. Painter mistranslates some of the Neopolitan elements and turns them into nonsense. 'Andreuccio' may be a minor source of an episode in Aphra Behn's *The Rover*.

1 Horses bred in the kingdom of Naples were much sought after in the Middle Ages, especially after the Emperor Charles I improved the breed.

2 Painter has translated the Italian literally. The meaning is 'he liked diverse horses very well'.

3 In the Italian story the district is 'Malpertugio', a neighbourhood near the port where foreign merchants lived and in which there were vice districts. Also, a *pertugio* is a narrow passage, and *mal* means bad; the neighbourhood was entered through an archway, so the name gives an indication of its quality.

4 The 'house of Gergenti' is a mistranslation; the Italian says from the neighbourhood of the town of Gergenti (Agrigento in southern Sicily). Painter's translation elevates the social status of the husband.

5 The young woman sets her fictional biography in the context of the famous struggle between the factions of the Guelphs and the Ghibellines. The Guelphs supported the papacy against the emperor, who was supported by the Ghibellines. The pope financed Charles of Anjou's successful attack on Manfred, heir of the Emperor Frederick II and king of Sicily. Charles was thrown out of Sicily after the Sicilian Vespers in 1282; many Sicilians emigrated to Naples at that time. Charles ruled Naples 1289–1309. King Frederick II of Aragon was on the imperial side and was king of Sicily from 1296 to 1337. There were many conspiracies during his reign.

6 Andreuccio is saying that the lady would seem agreeable even if judged by the standards of a person of high social class.

7 The loosening of a floorboard in a privy is a frequent trick for getting rid of unwanted lovers in novelle. See 'Philenio Sisterno' in this volume.

8 La ruga Catellana runs from the archway at Malpertugio to the upper part of Naples.

9 Francesco Buttafuoco was a Sicilian, loyal to Charles of Anjou. He may have been the head of one of the gangs of thieves (*scaraboni* in Sicilian dialect) which are now called the 'Camorra', or the Neapolitan Mafia. Painter clearly did not understand the reference.

10 Archbishop Filippo (Philip) Minutolo died on 24 October 1301, but the story takes place in the heat of the summer. His tomb can still be seen in the Cathedral.

Giletta of Narbona

The story of 'Giletta of Narbona' appears in Painter's *Palace of Pleasure* (I, 38). It is a close translation of *Decameron* III. 9. Painter probably translated directly from the Italian, although a few of his changes suggest he also used Le Macon's French translation. The stories of the third day are about 'people who, through industrious effort, acquire something that they have wanted a great deal, or recover something that they have lost'.

'Giletta of Narbona' is the source of Shakespeare's *All's Well That Ends Well*.

1 Narbona (Narbonne) is in southern France. Rossiglione is in the eastern Pyrenees. All the people named in these lines are fictitious.

2 The chronic state of hostilities between Florence and Siena in the thirteenth century makes it impossible to identify the exact war to which Boccaccio referred.

3 The exact magic power of this ring is never explained.

4 The daughter lacks a dowry.

5 Montpellier is not far from Narbona and is on the road to Rossiglione.

6 All Saints' Day is 1 November.

7 Spouse indicates the formal status of person to whom one has been married; wife indicates the consummated relationship.

Philenio Sisterno

'Philenio Sisterno' occurs in Painter's *Palace of Pleasure* (I, 49). It is a translation of Straparola's *Tredici piacevoli notti* II. 2. It is an analogue of some of the action of *The Merry Wives of Windsor*.

1 Bologna is located on the border of the plain of the River Po and
the Appenines in northern Italy. The University of Bologna was
famed for its law faculty. Crete is the largest of the Greek islands;
it was under Venetian control during this period.

2 The Bentivoglio family was one of the powerful families that fought
over control of Bologna in the fifteenth century. The next two ladies
have invented names. Panthemia may be from the Greek words *pan*
meaning 'all', and *themis* meaning 'justice', and Simphorosia from
symphero meaning 'expedient' or 'good for one'.

3 Philenio's language imitates the aristocratic language of courtly
love, in which the lover reverses the conventional hierarchy which
puts men above women and vows himself his beloved's servant.
The courtly lover also declares that his lady has the power to cause
his death if she scorns him.

4 That is, his understaking was no longer secret.

5 The loosening of a floorboard in a privy, and the consequent
precipitation of the person who steps on the loose board into the
cesspool beneath, is a conventional way of getting rid of unwanted
lovers in novelle. See 'Andreuccio of Perugia' in this volume.
Philenio seems to have had the good fortune to be shown into a
small room which did not have a cesspool beneath it.

6 The reference to the three women as 'goddesses', and the later
reference to them in bed as 'muses', may recall the three Graces.

7 The scholar left the bedroom because he was worried that his
absence would hinder the feast.

King Massinissa and Queen Sophonisba

'Sophonisba' appears in Painter's *Palace of Pleasure* (II, 7). It is a direct
translation of Bandello, 1.41. The brief moralizing opening is Painter's
invention.

'Sophonisba' was the source of Marston's *Wonder of Women*.

1 The events of this story take place during the second Punic War,
the war between Rome and Carthage in which Hannibal crossed
the Alps and invaded Italy. At the end of the war the north African
state of Carthage surrendered its Spanish province and its war fleet.
Hasdrubal, Hannibal's brother, was the Carthaginian commander
in Spain and fought a long campaign against the Romans. Sophonisba was his daughter and the wife of Syphax, who was an ally of
Carthage as a consequence of his marriage. Massinissa was king of
Numidia, a state on the western border of Carthage which was

nearly the geographical equivalent of modern Algeria. He was an ally of Carthage in Spain but went over to the Romans in 206 and defeated Syphax 203 BC.

2 Massinissa was once Carthage's ally; now he stuns and terrifies her. Cirta, a city in north-eastern Algeria, is modern Qacentina, Constantine or Blad el-Hawa.

3 That is, Syphax was in league with the Romans but changed sides at Sophonisba's urging and went to the aid of the Carthaginians.

4 In other words, Sophonisba will accept to die in any way rather than be turned over to the Romans.

5 Gaius Laelius (d. after 160 BC) was a friend of Scipio Africanus. He accompanied Scipio on his Spanish campaign; in Africa he defeated Syphax and commanded the cavalry in Scipio's victory over Hannibal at Zama.

6 According to Greek legend, the Sirens were monstrous women. With their beautiful song, they lured men to their island, where they were shipwrecked; the Sirens sat surrounded by the men's rotting bones. When Odysseus sailed by, he stopped up his crew's ears with wax to prevent their hearing the song, and had them tie him to the mast so that he could listen without danger.

7 After crossing the Alps into Italy, Hannibal remained there for sixteen years campaigning and living off the land. He returned to Africa to defend Carthage against Scipio Africanus.

8 The Pillars of Hercules form the entrance to the Mediterranean Sea. The Fortunate Islands were believed to be islands in the western ocean, home of the blessed dead; the Canaries and Madeira Islands were sometimes identified with them.

9 Painter follows Bandello in representing Sophonisba as blonde, rather than as a north African. The description of her appearance follows the conventions of Petrarchism in which the beloved lady is always fair, has eyes like stars or the sun, etc.

10 Massinissa is comparing his existence without Sophonisba to that of a body without breath; both are dead. She inspired his soul to life as breath inspires the body. She was his breath and inspiration.

11 'What stand I upon these terms?' means 'Why do I insist upon these conditions?'

12 Croesus was a king of Lydia in the sixth century BC; he was vastly wealthy. His name is used to refer to any very rich man and, as in this case, to great wealth.

13 Massinissa questions his positive calculation ('good accompt') of what would happen if Scipio were to see Sophonisba. To reckon

without one's host is to come to conclusions without complete data.

14 The 'armipotent god' is Mars, the god of war.

15 The hero Theseus found his way out of the famous labyrinth on Crete, after killing the Minotaur, with the assistance of the Princess Ariadne, who was in love with him. Thus the labyrinth was often used as an image for the maze of emotions caused by love; although, paradoxically, the woman usually figured as the provoker of the confusion rather than as the rescuer. Boccaccio's antifeminist satire *The Corbaccio* is subtitled *The Labyrinth of Love*.

16 'Whom no misadventure can affray or mislike' means 'who cannot be frightened or discomfited by any misfortune'.

17 The antecedent of 'whereof' is 'wife'; Sophonisba is saying that her immediate obedience to Massinissa will bring about the ceremonies connected with her death.

The Duchess of Malfi

'The Duchess of Malfi' is the twenty-third story in Painter's *Palace of Pleasure*; it is a translation of Belleforest's French translation of Bandello's story (1.26). Bandello prefaced the story with a dedicatory letter in which he complained that in his society women were killed for marrying secretly or committing adultery, whereas men did the same things with impunity. Belleforest prefaced his with very different sentiments: women must be especially careful of their honour because society looks at their conduct so closely. Painter followed Belleforest. Belleforest and, thus, Painter did not translate Bandello's letter, but they integrated some of Bandello's arguments into the duchess's soliloquy in which she debates about marrying Bologna ('Alas ... am I happed into so straunge misery ...'). Most of the other abstract meditations on love and honour are Belleforest's additions to the tale, as are most of the many long speeches.

HISTORICAL BACKGROUND

This story takes place during the first seventeen years of the long struggle between France and Spain for control of Italy. The wars began when Charles VIII of France invaded Italy; he seized Naples in 1495 but was forced to retreat by a coalition of Spain, the Holy Roman Emperor, the pope, Venice and Milan. His successor, Louis XII, occupied Milan and Genoa in 1499, then, with the consent of the pope and in coalition with Spain, conquered Naples in 1501; Frederick, the last Aragonese king of Naples, abdicated his throne in favour of the

French king. The alliance broke down, and France and Spain were at war in 1502. The Treaty of Blois gave Milan and Genoa to France, and Naples to Spain. Trouble began again when Pope Julius II formed an alliance against Venice with France, Spain and the Holy Roman Emperor Maximilian I (1508). Shortly after the French victory over the Venetians, Julius II formed the Holy League, dedicated to expelling the French from Italy. The French temporarily lost when the Swiss stormed Milan (1512), where they restored Maximilian Sforza as nominal duke, and the French were routed at Novara (1513), but they recovered under Francis I at Marignano. The Peace of Noyon (1516) left the Spanish in control of Naples and returned Milan to France.

Bandello offered the story of the duchess of Malfi as a true story (it had not been a year since Antonio Bologna had been brutally murdered in Milan), and there is documentary evidence of the events: Giovanna, duchess of Malfi, was a grand-daughter of Ferrante I, king of Naples, by his illegitimate son Enrico, marchese of Gerace. At a very young age she married Alfonso Piccolomini, duke of Amalfi and, at his death in 1498, she was pregnant with their only son, Alfonso, who succeeded his father as duke. The duchess made her secret marriage with Antonio Bologna public in November 1510; no documentary records of her exist after that date. Bandello's story was the first account of her death. Antonio Bologna was a member of the Neapolitan nobility. He was murdered in October 1513. Carlo, brother of Giovanna, succeeded his father as marchese of Gerace. Luigi, brother of Giovanna, was a cardinal for twenty-two years and died in 1519.

1 Dionysius the younger was tyrant of Syracuse; driven from Syracuse in 357, he returned and was expelled in 344. Titus Annius Milo was a leader of armed gangs organized to oppose Clodius, a demagogic fomenter of civil unrest, and enemy of Pompey. His killing of Clodius early in 52BC precipitated a crisis that led to Pompey's sole consulship. Exiled, he died in an unsuccessful rebellion against Caesar.

2 Semiramis was a mythical Assyrian queen; she was said to have conquered many lands, to have founded Babylon and to have committed incest with her son.

3 Samson was a judge of Israel whose long hair symbolized his covenant with God and gave him great strength. The Philistine woman Delilah seduced him and cut his hair, thus destroying his might. Blinded and chained in a Philistine temple, with his strength restored by his new-grown hair, he pulled down the temple, killing

himself and his enemies. See Judges 13–16. Solomon was a Jewish
king known for his wisdom.

4 The French defeated Spanish and papal forces at Ravenna in 1512.
The French commander Gaston de Foix died in the battle.

5 Painter added this information about Mary Tudor, daughter of
Henry VII of England, in place of the following phrase that his
French source had added to Bandello: 'qui pour sa bonté & amour
envers ses sujects, a esté appellé le Pere du pais e du peuple' ('who
for his goodness and love toward his subjects was called the father
of his country and his people'). English patriotism replaced French
patriotism.

6 The alliance of France and Spain expelled Frederick I from Naples
in 1501. Frederick assigned his claims to the throne of Naples to
Louis XII and retired to France.

7 King Artaxerxes II of Persia (ruled 404–359 BC) governed Persia in
a time of decay and rebellion. Ariobarzanes was the ruler of the
kingdom of Pontus and a prominent rebel against Artaxerxes. His
betrayal by his son led to his execution.

8 'Little' in this case probably means paltry or contemptible; thus she
would rather marry than burn with such a contemptible fire as
passion that must be hidden. This aspect of Painter's story differs
from Bandello's; the duchess in the latter story at first decides to
take a lover because she does not want to give up custody of her
child, as she knows she would have to do if she married. After
falling in love with Bologna, she decides to marry secretly instead
of taking him as a lover so that she will not offend God. Bandello
does not discourse on the importance of not allowing young women
to remain unwedded for long, as Painter, following Belleforest, does
in the next paragraph.

9 Narcissus was a beautiful youth, the son of a river god and a
nymph. He saw his own image reflected in water and fell in love
with it, thinking it was a nymph. His fruitless attempts to approach
her led to despair and death. Pygmalion was a misogynist sculptor
who fell in love with a statue he made and prayed that he might
marry a girl like his statue. Venus granted his wish and brought
the statue to life, and he was happy. The duchess feels sexual desire without having an object for its release; thus nothing can
bring her bloodless passion (without 'one spot of vermilion rud') to
life.

10 The Neapolitan youths rode a colourful variety of horses. The
'gennet' (jennet) is a small Spanish horse. A palfrey is a saddle-

horse for non-military riding; it was especially used by ladies, and in this case is a Turkish horse. A courser is a stallion.

11 Occasion (or opportunity) was often represented in emblem books as a bald woman with a single long lock of hair hanging over her forehead; the person who wants to take advantage of opportunity must grab it quickly when it is first offered.

12 Two men named Baldouine (or Baldwin) of Flaunders were Latin emperors of Constantinople. I have found no record of either one carrying away Judith, the daughter of the French king.

13 Cupid was said to be the son of Venus, the goddess of love. The duchess suggests that he seems more like the son of Saturn, because the planet named after Saturn disposes men to melancholy.

14 Calabria is the toe of the Italian 'boot'; it is across the Strait of Messina from Sicily.

15 According to tradition, unfaithful women blush.

16 Messalina was the wife of the Roman emperor Claudius; she was famed for her profligacy and was put to death in AD 48. Faustina was the wife of Marcus Aurelius (AD 121–81), the philosopher emperor whose *Meditations* are considered a classic work of Stoicism. Ancient sources speak of Faustina's infidelities and her liking for gladiators.

17 This complex sentence seems to mean: 'It is folly to marry a much younger husband because of the daily inconveniences consequent upon such inequality, and also because when child husbands become adults the wives will have lost interest in sex; as a result, the ladies will not be passionate and their husbands, tired of mundane married sexual activity, will have extramarital affairs.'

18 That is, the way she looked at him would have awakened lust even in philosophers engrossed in their work.

19 The division of the story into 'acts' is the contribution of the French translator.

20 According to canon law at the time these events took place, if two people declared themselves to be married in front of a witness and then consummated the union they were considered legally married.

21 The third is the gentlewoman.

22 Rumour is frequently allegorized as a many-tongued being who races around the earth spreading news, and is represented as such in emblem books.

23 Ancona is located in the Marche in central Italy on the Adriatic Sea. It was a semi-independent maritime republic under the nominal rule of the pope.

24 'Of what wood to make her arrows' is a proverbial expression. Different woods had different qualities appropriate to different occasions.

25 In Bandello's story the duchess does not consult her maid; she herself thinks of this plan. Loreto is in the Marche on the Adriatic. According to legend, the Holy House of the Virgin in Nazareth was brought to Loreto through the air by angels in 1294.

26 To paraphrase: the apothecary applies the flesh of the poisonous viper to his patient in order to purge the patient of infected, leprosy-causing blood.

27 For Semiramis, see note 2 above; for Messalina and Faustina, see note 15 above. Pasiphaë was the wife of Minos, king of Crete. When Minos refused to sacrifice a beautiful bull to Poseidon, the god took vengeance by making Pasiphaë fall in love with the bull; she gave birth to the minotaur, half man, half bull.

   Bandello tells the following story about Romilda, the duchess of Friuli (IV.8). When Cancano, king of Bavaria, who had killed her husband, was besieging the city of Foro di Giulio, Romilda fell in love with him. She agreed to give him the city if he would marry her. In order to keep his bargain, he slept with her one night, a night in which she demonstrated an unbridled sexual appetite. He then called twelve of his soldiers and ordered them to take their pleasure of her all that day and the next night without ever letting her rest. Then he had her impaled on a stake and killed, to show women not to privilege lust over reason, and he sacked and burned the city.

28 He who knows the most obscure and hidden secrets of our thoughts is God.

29 In Bandello's story the duchess does not offer a moral justification for her deed but, rather, explains the provisions she has made for the members of her household, whom she expects will return to Malfi. She has deposited dowries for her ladies in waiting at a particular bank and left written instructions with the mother superior at a convent.

30 Pasquile (Pasquino) was an ancient Roman statue in Rome to which satirical verse was often attached in the sixteenth century.

31 The invective against womankind is not present in Bandello; nor is the extended characterization of the brothers. The animalistic descriptions ('yalped', 'snaffle', etc.) are not in Belleforest; they are Painter's own addition. For example, the French text says *vomist* ('vomited') where Painter's says 'yalped'.

32 The animal imagery continues here; the falconer calls his bird back with his lure, a bunch of feathers in which food is hidden during training.

33 When he was crucified Jesus received a spear wound in his side as well as holes in his hands and feet from being nailed to the cross.

34 The correct names are Cardinal Alfonso Pertrucci and Lord Borghese, brother of the cardinal.

35 Acastus' wife lusted after Peleus, a married man. When he refused her advances, she slandered him to Acastus, telling him that Peleus had tried to persuade her to infidelity. Acastus attempted revenge on Peleas, but Peleas slew Acastus and his wife. Oedipus was a legendary hero from Corinth who became king of Thebes after answering the riddle of the Sphinx and marrying Jocasta, the widow of the king. In the course of time, he discovered that Jocasta was his mother and that he had unwittingly killed his father.

36 Ramagna (Romagna) is the Italian province to the north of Tuscany, on the other side of the Apennine mountains. The city surrounded by the Adriatic Sea is Venice, which is built on islands; it can easily be reached by travelling down the wide valley of the river Po, which traverses Romagna.

37 The entire scene recounting the death of the duchess is not present in Bandello's text, which merely says that it was later learned that she, her children and her maid were killed.

38 The duchess's prayer follows the general outline of the act of contrition spoken by Roman Catholics after confession.

39 Euchrates I, king of Bactria (c. 171– c. 154BC), was murdered by one of his sons. Phraates IV, king of Parthia, murdered his father, and his own death was arranged by his wife and son. Timon of Athens (fifth century BC) was a famous misanthropist, who shunned man as a result of his bad experiences. Witowt or Witold (Vitoldus) was duke of Lituania 1401–30.

40 The return of her dowry means that the duchess is no longer a member of her husband's household and has no claims on it.

41 Silvio Savello reconquered Milan for Massimiliano Sforza in 1512. Francesco Acquaviva, marquis of Britone (Bitonto), was taken prisoner by the French in April 1512 at the battle of Ravenna. All these details indicate that Bologna arrived at Milan before April 1512.

42 Hippolita Bentivoglio (1481–1509), grand-daughter of Galeazzo Sforza, duke of Milan, was the wife of Alessandro Bentivoglio. After the expulsion of the Bentivogli from Bologna, she and her

husband lived in Milan. She was a poet and a literary patron. Bandello often eulogized her, and he frequented her house.

43 In Painter's time, the term 'sonnet' primarily referred to the fourteen-line form, but it could also refer to other short poems, especially love-poems. This sonnet is punctuated as it was in the original edition.

44 Delio is a pseudonym for Bandello himself; he used this name for himself in another story (I.28) and in his poetry.

45 A Lombard is a person from Lombardy, the Italian province of which Milan is the capital. Lombards were unpopular in the late Middle Ages and the Renaissance, probably on account of their wealth and consequent influence. They were noted bankers and usurers.

46 The Apostles were the twelve men selected by Jesus to preach his teachings. The pope is said to be in a direct line of succession from the Apostle Peter. All who imitate the mission of the original twelve are also said to be apostles.

Two Gentlewomen of Venice

'Two Gentlewomen of Venice' appears in Painter's *Palace of Pleasure* (II, 26); it is a direct translation of Bandello 1.15. Painter expanded the story slightly with moralistic commentary.

'Two Gentlewomen of Venice' is the source of the subplot of *The Insatiate Countess* by John Marston. Marston based the tragic plot on another story by Bandello, also translated by Painter, 'The Countess of Celant' (Bandello I.4; Painter II, 24), but Painter translated 'The Countess' from Belleforest's French translation, and thus it is not included in this volume.

1 The introductory praise of women is Painter's addition. The stories of these women are all told in Boccaccio's *De mulieribus claris* (*Concerning Famous Women*). Painter tells the essence of the stories of the wives of the Minyae and Hipsicratea, though Boccaccio also relates that in his old age Hipsicratea's husband killed one of her children and then, when his palace was besieged, poisoned her. The rest of the women he names were Roman.

Tertia Aemilia was the wife of Scipio Africanus, the great general. In his old age he was unfaithful to Aemelia with a slave; she hid his fault and after his death freed the slave and married her to a freed slave in order to prevent the woman from being joined with a man entirely unworthy of following the great Scipio. Turia was married to Quintus Lucretius; when her husband was proscribed she persuaded him to hide in their house rather than escape to the wilderness. Sulpitia was selected to dedicate a statue that was set up in order to inspire Roman women to abstain from lust; she was chosen because she was the woman most celebrated for her chastity. Portia was the wife of Brutus; when she learned of his defeat at Philippi, she committed suicide by swallowing burning coals.

2 Painter may be referring to Peter II, king of Aragon from 1196 to 1213, and his wife Mary, Lady of Montpellier. They had a son Giacomo, but I have found no record of Mary's tricking her husband in this way.

3 Francesco Foscari was doge of Venice from 1423 to 1457. Bembo, Barbadico, and Gradenigo are the surnames of noble Venetian families of the period, but Girolamo, Anselmo, Marco and Isotta are probably fictional, as is Gian Francesco Valerio, although a Venetian of that name was a contemporary of Bandello's and a friend of Ariosto. The procurators of San Marco were supervisors of the structure of the main church of Venice.

4 Valerio's title, *cavaliere*, means 'knight'; it is a title of minor nobility.

5 A man whose wife was unfaithful to him was said to be a cuckold and to have horns on his head. To 'send someone to Cornovale' is to make him a cuckold; similarly, 'learn to play of the cornets' and 'castell of Cornetto' refer to a cuckold's horns. These terms are used in the Italian text.

6 The poem is Painter's addition; although Belleforest also added a poem, the text is entirely different. The punctuation is printed as it was in the original edition. It is not clear why Painter calls this 'Italian metre'. The stanza-form of iambic lines organized into a quatrain and a couplet is not particularly Italian. Shakespeare later used it for *Venus and Adonis*.

7 'Dame Kind' is Mother Nature.

8 Both Jerusalem and Constantinople were in the hands of Muslims. European Christians made numerous attempts to regain control but failed. Hence the conquest of these cities stands as a figure for an enterprise impossible to ordinary men.

9 Painter here omits to translate a brief and allusive description of love-making.

10 The mutual satisfaction is Painter's contribution; Bandello says the husband took more pleasure than the wife.

11 Fortune is Painter's addition.

12 The surname Delphino is Venetian, but Niccolò is probably fictional, as are Giovanni Moro and Gismonda. Aloise Foscari, however, really was a nephew of the doge, but this story about him seems to be fictional.

13 The moral is Painter's addition.

14 The stomach was believed to be the seat of the passions, so by speaking of the men's 'cankered stomachs' Painter suggests that their criticism of the women is nastily irrational.

15 San Marco (St Mark's) is the major cathedral of Venice. The palace of the ruler of Venice (the doge) stands next to it.

16 Domenico Mariperto is probably another fictional character.

17 The Counsell of the Dieci (Ten), a body of the Venetian state, investigated and rendered verdicts on all criminal, moral, religious, and political offenses. It also controlled foreign relations.

18 Venice was at war with Milan and its Visconti rulers from 1423 to 1433 and from 1434 to 1442. Doge Foscari won territory from Milan.

19 This praise of marriage is Painter's addition.

20 The avvocatori (avogadori) were the three magistrates who oversaw legal matters in Venice.

21 'Cornetto' refers to the horns (corna) of a cuckold.

22 An 'angel' was an English gold coin.

23 Painter substitutes English 'primme [privet] and roses' for the Italian cannucce marine.

24 The city of Venice was often represented as a woman. Mistress Isotta is speaking of Venice as a mother, the husbands as her children, and their rancour as the enemy that must be exiled.

The Lady of Boeme

'The Lady of Boeme' is the twenty-eighth story in Painter's *Palace of Pleasure*; it is translated from Bandello's story I.21, 'An Amazing Trick that a Gentlewoman Played on Two Hungarian Barons'. Painter translated it directly from Italian.

'The Lady of Boeme' is the source of Massinger's *The Picture*.

1 Penelope is the wife of Ulysses (Odysseus) in Homer's *Odyssey*. She was famed for her faithfulness to him during the ten years of his absence at the Trojan war, and the ten years he spent trying to get home. Wooed by large numbers of suitors who installed themselves in her house in Ulysses' absence, she used her wits to avoid

accepting any one of them as her husband. This preface is original
with Painter.

2 The antecedent of 'his' in 'his prince's court' is unclear, but it seems
likely that the court referred to is that to which the husband goes
in the course of the story. He, like Ulysses, is threatened on the
home front while he is away. But if this is so, the sentence changes
subjects midway through; he is threatened, she gives the repulse.
The barons' attempt to seduce the lady is represented as a war of
the soldiers of Venus, the goddess of love, against the fort of her
chastity; 'encountries' are armed encounters, 'a well-mured rampart' is a defensive mound of earth surmounted by a stone parapet.
Venus' band called on her to surrender (summoned her fort) and
made a night attack (*camisado*) with frequent calls to arms
(*al'armes*).

   Sardanapalus was the last king of the Assyrians, who, on a revolt
against him, burned himself with his harem and all his treasures.

3 The phrase 'for trustlesse faith in the prime conference of his future
porte' is obscure. It may mean 'because he lacked faith in the
chastity of his wife's conversation', that is, her behaviour with
men.

4 The 'infected humour' is jealousy.

5 Mathias Corvinus (Matyas Hunyadi), king of Hungary from 1458
to 1490, elected king of Bohemia in 1469 (until 1478), and ruler of
Austria by conquest in 1485. He was famed for his humanist
learning and frequently praised by Italian writers. Hungary during
the period of his rule is also the setting in Whetstone's *Promos and
Cassandra*.

   Beatrice of Aragon, Corvinus' wife, was the aunt of Giovanna,
the heroine of the story 'The Duchess of Malfi'.

6 A mercer was a dealer in textiles, especially silk, and a draper was
a maker of or dealer in woollen cloth and other textiles. Their
journals were their account books; to have one's name in their
journals was to be in debt to them.

7 During the fifteenth century the Ottoman Turks conquered substantial European territory. Early in his reign Corvinus successfully held
them off and asserted his rights over Bosnia; he died before leading
his planned crusade against the Turks.

8 During the Middle Ages and Renaissance it was commonly believed
that men and women were capable of different kinds of virtues.
Courage was a masculine virtue, as chastity was a feminine one. It
was thus assumed that woman's social role should not demand

courage of her, and her timidity was seen to be a virtue in itself because it made her thrifty.

9 An anchoress was a devout woman who had herself closed into a solitary cell attached to a church in order to withdraw from the world.

10 The phrase 'sending ... into Cornwall' is yet another way of referring to making one's husband a cuckold. The reference is a direct translation of Bandello's Italian, in which 'Cornwall' puns on the Italian word for a cuckold's horns, *corna*.

11 A spiritual court had jurisdiction in ecclesiastical affairs. '*Rem* to be in *re*': *in re* is legal Latin for 'in the matter of, with reference to'; *rem* means 'the thing, the business'. A proctor is a disciplinary officer in a university charged with the discipline of all students and with the summary punishment of minor offences. A civilian is a lawyer who practises civil law. Padua was the most famous college of civil law in Europe.

12 Alba Regale is the modern Szekes Fejervar.

13 Basca is a variant of the Turkish *pasha*.

14 Revenue in fee farm is the rent paid for an estate held subject to a perpetual fixed rent, without any other services.

15 The baron holds the common medieval and Renaissance belief in woman's natural incapacity for fidelity and chastity.

16 Cicero was a Latin orator famous for his eloquent and elegant style.

17 A hawk of the first coat is in its fourth year.

18 'Uppon howe merry a pinne' is an English proverbial expression meaning 'in how merry a humour'.

19 'As the Jewes do for Messias' is an Italian proverb meaning to wait for someone or something that it taking a long time coming.

20 Heroes in epic and romance are often forced or choose to spin, thus showing that love (or lust) makes men effeminate.

The Sack-Full of Newes

The only edition of *The Sack-Full of Newes* still in existence is the following: 'London, Printed by Andrew Clark and to be sold by Thomas Passenger at the Three-Bibles upon London Bridge, 1673.' The style of the writing and a reference to 'the sak full of nuez' in a list of books in a letter written in 1575 probably demonstrate that there was an earlier edition.

The Old Man and His Young Wife

'The Old Man and His Young Wife', from *The Sack-Full of Newes*, is a translation of the second half of *Decameron* VII. 7. The stories of the seventh day are about 'the tricks that women have played on their husbands, either for love or to save themselves, both discovered and undiscovered'. The first half of the story tells how the young couple fell in love. In Boccaccio's story the cross-dressed husband does not reveal his identity to his servant by calling attention to his beard; he merely runs away and returns to his wife and tells her of his experience.

1 The summer's bird is a cuckoo; the servant has made a cuckold of his master.

The Forrest of Fancy

The Forrest of Fancy, 'wherein is conteined very prety Apothegmes and pleasaunt histories, both in meeter and prose, Songes, sonets, epigrams and epistles, of diverse matter and in diverse manner' (London: Thomas Purfoote, 1579).

Seigneor Vergelis and His Wife
'Seigneor Vergelis and His Wife', from *The Forrest of Fancy*, is a translation of *Decameron* III.5. The stories of the third day are about 'people who, through industrious effort, acquire something that they have wanted a great deal or recover something that they have lost'. The spelling of the names in the story suggests that it is translated from Le Macon's French translation rather than directly from the Italian, but both translations are very close to Boccaccio's version.

This story is the source of the plot of Ben Jonson's *The Devil is an Ass*.

1 The Vergellesi were a powerful family in Pistoia (Pistoy). A Francesco de' Vergellesi was sent to Lombardy as *podestà* in 1326. See note 2 below.
2 The Italian word which potentate translates is *podestà*, which means the head of the communal government.
3 *Magnifico* is a term usually applied to princes to suggest their generosity to others, but the word also suggests the more usual senses of 'magnificent'.
4 The exalted and highly literary language of this speech reproduces the tone of the Italian, which is in the tradition of medieval love literature.
5 Magnifico is offering the lady himself, as he is now and as he will be, and all the worldly goods he may ever acquire.

6 The reference to jousts and tournaments is an example of the literalness of this translation. The translator has retained the forms of courtship traditional in medieval literature rather than substituting contemporary English practice.

7 The lady here is speaking of the 'debt of marriage'. The husband owes her satisfaction of her sexual desire.

Riche's 'His Farewell to Militarie Profession'

The title-page of the first edition of Riche's collection reads '*Riche his Farewell to Militarie profession*: conteining verye pleasaunt discourses fit for a peaceable time: Gathered together for the onely delight of the courteous Gentlewomen, bothe of Englande and Irelande, for whose onely pleasure they were collected together, And unto whom they are directed and dedicated by Barnabe Riche Gentleman. Malui me divitem esse quam vocari. Imprinted at London, by Robert Walley, 1581.'

Apolonius and Silla

'Apolonius and Silla' is the second story in Riche's collection. It is not a translation but, rather, a reworking of several Italian tales, primarily Bandello II.36 and Giraldi Cinthio v.viii.

Shakespeare based the main plot of *Twelfth Night* on this story.

1 During the Middle Ages and Renaissance fairs and markets offered the primary opportunity for exchanging merchandise. They occurred in specific places at specific times and some such, located on important trade routes, drew people from all over Europe.

2 Riche is referring to the length of the first story in the collection, 'Sappho, Duke of Mantona', which was twice as long as 'Apolonius and Silla'.

3 During the fifteenth century the Ottoman Turks conquered substantial European territory. They captured Constantinople in 1453. The first major European victory against the empire was in the naval battle of Lepanto in 1571.

4 Cyprus is an island in the eastern Mediterranean Sea. Captured by Richard I of England, it remained in Christian hands until it was conquered by the Turks in 1571. Pontus is a fictional name for the duke of Cyprus.

5 A bird struggling in birdlime, a glutinous substance spread on twigs, gets more and more entangled.

6 Riche frequently addresses himself to female readers as the audience

to whom his text is principally directed. For more on this topic, see the Introduction to this volume.

7 Taking the height of the sun and stars was a means of navigating.

8 'To put romer before the wind' sounds like an authentic nautical expression, but its exact meaning is unclear.

9 Silvio is walking in a garden or on an expanse of lawn.

10 Riche here mixes Greek mythology with biblical legend. The Greek Phaeton was the son of Phoebus Apollo, the sun; his father gave in to his request to drive the chariot of the sun across the sky, but he lost control of the horses and singed the earth, so that Zeus had to kill him with a thunderbolt. In the Old Testament the Hebrew God made the sun stand still while Joshua fought the battle of Jericho.

11 In Italy before the Council of Trent, if two people agreed that they were married, the marriage was valid.

12 In Riche's day in England, widows had the power to choose whom they would marry, whereas the marriage of a woman who never had been married was arranged by those in authority over her.

Of Two Brethren and Their Wives

'Of Two Brethren and Their Wives' is the fifth story in the *Farewell*. It is a composite translation of four stories by Straparola (VIII.2, I.5, II.5, IV.4), although one story (VIII.2) provides the framework on which the others are fastened.

'Of Two Brethren and Their Wives' is the source of Malvolio's imprisonment in the dark room in Shakespeare's *Twelfth Night* and of parts of *The Merry Wives of Windsor*.

1 The phrase 'of light disposition' means 'inclined to be unfaithful'.

2 Xanthippe was the shrewish wife of Socrates.

3 The 'proverbe' is from Matthew 7:7.

4 She committed adultery and made him a cuckold.

5 See Genesis 16 for the story of Sara, the wife of Abraham.

6 'To set his teeth on edge' means 'to make him eager'.

7 These are the medical authorities of antiquity. Galen (c. AD 129–99) was a celebrated physician; over one hundred of his treatises survive. Hippocrates (c. 460–357 BC) was the most famous physician of antiquity. Avicenna (AD 980–1036) was a Persian physician and philosopher. Pliny the Elder (AD 23–79) was the author of the *Historia naturalis*.

8 'Wordes of course' are customary, natural or expected words.

9 'Store was no sore': a proverbial expression meaning it did no harm to have plenty.

10 There is a series of puns here. An 'action' can be a lawsuit as well as just a deed or gesture; to enter an action is to bring a suit in a court of law. The 'commonplace' where he enters his suit could refer to a memorandum book, or to her loose sexual conduct – what ought to be her most private place is common, i.e. free to be used by everyone.

11 On 25 October 1415 King Henry V of England defeated a superior French force at the town of Agincourt in the north of France. This detail places the action of the story in England in 1415 or 1416. The city is probably London. None of the source stories on which Riche drew was set in England.

12 The narrator of the story is suddenly posing as less than omniscient. He has been unable to find out (*understande*) what the soldier and mistres Doritye said in the chamber.

13 In order to retain the differences that changes in punctuation create in the meaning of the letter, I have reproduced the punctuation exactly as it was originally printed both times it appears.

14 Bridewell was a house of correction in London.

15 'Sware by no beggers' is a proverb meaning to take a genuine oath, not a mere pretence of one.

16 Cresside, a Trojan widow who had a love-affair with the Trojan hero Troilus, was sent from Troy to join her father in the Greek camp and there she had an affair with Diomedes. She is famous for her inconstancy. See Chaucer's *Troilus and Criseyde* and Shakespeare's *Troilus and Cressida*.

17 The lawyer here opposes two sets of parallel but morally opposite qualities: a loose woman is *coye*, *nice* (good at making delicate distinctions) and *fine* (handsome or smartly dressed); a good woman is *wise*, *comely* and *honest* (chaste).

18 A man who simply wants a sexual experience with a woman will have more luck than a man who wants to marry her.

19 *Bugges* are imaginary things that cause fear, such as ghosts; here, however, the reference is to the young women's fear of pregnancy.

20 There is no verse of Proverbs that exactly matches this saying, although chapter 5 contains several relevant concepts: 5:3 compares the iips of a harlot to honey; 5:20 warns against adulterous affairs; and 5:22 says that the wicked are snared by their sins.

21 Authors of antifeminist texts frequently protest that they are only reporting what others have said, and that if truth to what happened

had not forced them to include the antifeminism they would never have written it. They often volunteer to write a defence.

22 The argument that woman is superior to man because she was created in a superior place, Paradise, from superior material, man's rib, rather than in an inferior place, outside Paradise, from inferior material, mud, is a commonplace of texts in defence of women.

23 Two places in Proverbs speak of wine as a comfort to the feeble: in 9:5 Wisdom offers it to the unwise; in 31:6 Wisdom advises that wine be given to those who are grieved in mind.

24 This is the punctuation of the original printed text.

25 Judas kissed Christ in order to identify him to the Roman soldiers who were about to arrest him; thus a Judas kiss is a kiss that betrays the relationship it appears to confirm.

26 Mistres Dorityе was already expert at acting; thus she did not have to learn to play her part.

27 Perhaps Riche is employing a variant of the proverbial expression 'to go up the ladder to bed' which means 'to be hanged'.

28 See note 6 above.

29 The urinal, a glass jar for holding a urine specimen, was the trademark of doctors, since a great deal of medical diagnosis depended on analysis of the appearance of urine.

30 Isolating a person in darkness was a treatment for madness in this period. Malvolio in *Twelfth Night*, for which this novella was a source, was put in a dark house.

31 The wife's raging suggests that she is possessed by the Devil; thus the neighbours urge her to pray. *Miserere* is the first word of Psalm 51, *Miserere mei Deus*, 'Have mercy on me, O God'. It is one of the Penitential Psalms.

Of Gonsales and His Vertuous Wife Agatha

'Gonsales and Agatha' is the sixth story in Riche's *Farewell*. It is based on Cinthio's *Hecatommithi* III.5; it is one of the stories that Riche says were translated by L.B. (see the Introduction). It is a fairly close translation, although the translator or Riche added some moralizing passages and added details about some of the material objects in the story. The topic for Giraldi's third day was the infidelity of husbands and wives.

'Gonsales and Agatha' is the source of *How a Man May Choose a Good Wife from a Bad*, an anonymous play, and of the subplot of *The Old Law* by Middleton, Rowley and Massinger.

1 This critique of the male sexual appetite and of the courtesan is not in Giraldi's original.

2 In *La Celestina* (1499), the Spanish novella and play, the title character is a clever old woman who serves a lover as his go-between and corrupts a young woman.

3 The old woman is using the sword and scabbard as analogies to male and female anatomy. If the husband is promiscuous, the wife should be the same.

4 'Having her head washed without soap' is a proverb meaning 'being scolded'.

5 In the sixteenth century, the wife had custody of the household goods and kept the keys to the chests and cupboards in which they were stored.

6 Here *although* means 'even if'.

7 In Giraldi's Italian story the scholar had decided to use force to get his way with Agatha because all means of persuasion had failed him, but Gonsales' confession made him think that force would be unnecessary.

8 Note the legal language used to describe the giving of evidence before the Lord: 'certified', 'affirmed', etc.

Whetstone's 'Heptameron of Civill Discourses'

The title-page of *An Heptameron of Civill Discourses* (London, 1582) gives the following description of the book:

Containing: The Christmasse exercise of sundrye well courted gentlemen and gentlewomen. In whose behaviours the better sort may see a representation of their own vertues and the inferiour may learne such rules of civil government as wil rase out the blemish of their basenesse. Wherin, is Renowned, the vertues, of a most honourable and brave minded gentleman. And herein also (as it were in a mirrour) the unmaried may see the defectes which eclipse the glorye of mariage and the wel maried, as in a table of housholde lawes, may cull out needefull preceptes to establish their good fortune. A worke, intercoursed with civill pleasure, to reave tediousnesse from the reader, and garnished with morall noates to make it profitable to the regarder. The Reporte, of George Whetstone. Gent. Formae, nulla fides. At London. Printed by Richard Jones, at the Signe of the Rose and the Crowne, near Holburne Bridge. 3 Feb. 1582.

Heptameron means 'seven days' or, as Whetstone puts it, 'Seven Days' Pleasure.' The title is an imitation of Boccaccio's *Decameron* and Marguerite de Navarre's *L'Heptaméron*. Each day of the *Heptameron* has a topic. Both of the following stories are taken from the fourth day, on which the topic is 'of divers speciall pointes concerning marriage in generall'.

Frier Inganno

'Frier Inganno' is an adaptation of two stories from the *Decameron*. The friar masquerading as Francis derives from the second story of the fourth day, but Boccaccio's story is set in Venice, and the friar pretends to be the Archangel Gabriel. The location of the story in the territory most closely associated with St Francis, and the friar's choice to appear as Francis, are substantial variants from the original. The stories of the fourth day are about 'those whose loves had unhappy results'. The substitution of the ugly woman for the desired one, and the discovery of them in bed, derives from the fourth story of the eighth day. The topic for that day is 'the tricks that men or men and women play on each other every day'.

A version of *Decameron* IV.2 that is much closer to the original appears in *Tarlton's Newes out of Purgatorye*; it is printed elsewhere in this volume.

1 The Apennines are a mountain chain in the interior of central Italy. Because of their isolation, the mountains were the location of many hermitages and monastries in the Middle Ages. St Francis of Assisi, founder of the Franciscan order, based the order in this region. He is buried in Assisi in the church built in his honour.

2 The rules of the order established by Francis require that the friars take a vow of poverty and chastity and own no property. Friars are mendicants, that is, they beg for their living. This vow was much abused, and medieval and Renaissance literature abounds with antifraternal satire.

3 Friar Inganno is parodying the words of the Archangel Gabriel to Mary when he announced to her that she was to bear a son conceived of the Holy Spirit: 'Blessed art thou among women . . .'

4 Friar Inganno's cowl (hood) is heavy because he has filled it with the food the poor woman gave him as alms.

5 Parish priests often resented friars because friars had the right to preach and collect alms.

6 The Italian word *laida* means 'ugly'.

7 *Salve, Sancte Francisce* are the first words of a Franciscan hymn, now called 'Hail, St Francis, Our Father and Patron'. *Sancte Francisce, ora pro nobis* ('St Francis, pray for us') is from the litany of the Saints, a series of appeals to saints for intercession.

8 'God, free me from the pains of Hell.' This phrase is constructed on the pattern of the invocations in the Litany of the Saints, although they are written in the plural, rather than in the singular as here.

9 Christ was crucified along with two thieves; one abused him and the other rebuked his companion, declaring Jesus' innocence. Jesus told the good thief 'today you will be with me in Paradise' (Luke 23:39–43).

Link

10 Queene Aurelia, maister doctor, Helena Dulce, Alvisa Vechio, and Isabella are characters in Whetstone's frame story. Dialogue such as this links the stories told to the topic set for the day's discussion.

11 Women's evils are written in their foreheads because they blush.

12 In the frame story of the *Heptameron*, the fourth day begins with mirth, because Queen Aurelia, who has been ill, is recovered, but there is no mention of the gentlewomen being in charge of the day's diversions. The day does end with a debate about the nature of womankind, in which Alvisa Vecchia maintains that woman is 'a creature every way as excellent and perfecte as Man'.

Promos and Cassandra

'Promos and Cassandra' is an adaptation of Giraldi Cinthio's *Hecatommithi* VIII. 5. The topic of the eighth day is ingratitude. Whetstone made a great many changes in the story; some examples are as follows. In Giraldi's story the Emperor Maximillian makes his nobleman Juriste the governor of the city of Ispruchi; the story begins with a meeting between Maximillian and Juriste in which the emperor stresses his great interest in justice and offers to let Juriste decline the job if he feels he is not qualified; the young man is accused of rape; his sister is trained in philosophy. Whetstone also wrote a play called *Promos and Cassandra*. Shakespeare seems to have referred to both when writing *Measure for Measure*, but most scholars believe that he made heavier use of the play than of the story.

13 The name Isabella, here given to the narrator of the story, is used by Shakespeare for its heroine in *Measure for Measure*.

14 Mathias Corvinus (Matyas Hunyadi), king of Hungary from 1458 to 1490, elected king of Bohemia in 1469 (until 1478), and ruler of

Austria by conquest in 1485. He was famed for his humanist learning and frequently praised by Italian writers. Hungary during the period of his rule is also the setting in Painter's 'The Lady of Boeme'.

The syntax is difficult here; essentially the sentence means: 'When Corvinus reigned, he sent magistrates to govern the free cities'; *for to* here means 'in order to'.

15 'Julio' may be Jula in eastern Hungary.

16 This note refers to Whetstone's play *Promos and Cassandra*.

17 Justice is often represented as holding a sword in her hand; laurel symbolizes distinction in poetry, or victory. Here it suggests the triumph of justice.

18 'Where the faulte may bee valued and amendes had' means 'When the damage caused by the misdeed can be assessed and compensation given'.

19 Andrugio seems to be saying that incontinent desire pricks men so much that it forces them to attempt to persuade women to satisfy them.

20 Here and in the next few paragraphs Isabella, the narrator of the story, abandons her stance as neutral 'reporter' of events; she addresses her audience directly and urges it to respond to events in a particular way.

21 A page was a boy employed as the personal attendant of a man of rank, so Cassandra dresses in the clothing of a boy. She thus symbolically shields her female sex from the shame of participating in the sexual act demanded by Promos.

22 Heliogabalus was a priest of a local sun god, and when he was made emperor of Rome (AD 218–22), he imported the worship of his god to Rome, where the citizens were shocked by the indecency of the rites and of the emperor's private life. He was murdered in an uprising. Dionysius (Denis) was the name of two Sicilian tyrants; Dionysius the Younger was known for his debauchery and extravagant living. Priapus was the Greek and Roman god of procreation; he was represented with a large phallus.

23 Marcus Crassus, a very rich man and one of the most powerful public speakers in Rome, was the third member of the first triumvirate with Julius Caesar and Pompey. He died defeated in battle. His relevance here is not clear. Marius Gaius (186–57 BC), a Roman general and consul. Overcome in battle and imprisoned by Sulla, by the majesty of his countenance he moved the man sent to execute him to help him to escape.

24 Because he opposed the will of Zeus, Prometheus was bound to a pillar where during the day an eagle consumed his liver, which grew again every night.

25 During the Middle Ages and the Renaissance, women wore black clothes of a design that indicated that they were mourning and how long they had been mourning.

26 The Roman matron Lucretia (Lucrece) committed suicide after being raped in her own home by her husband's military commander, Sextus Tarquinius, the son of the tyrant king Lucius Tarquinius. She did so to retain her honour and prompt her husband to revenge. The Tarquinii were exiled, and the state government changed from kings to consuls.

27 The Styx was the river of the otherworld over which the dead were ferried by Charon.

28 'What you do unto others, so they shall do unto you' is the golden rule given by Christ in the Sermon on the Mount (Matthew 7:12). Whetstone's note, 'An unusual place for a judge', refers to rhetorical theory; a *place* is a topic that a writer or speaker develops. Judges usually talk about laws made by society, not the law made by Christ.

29 In Greek and Roman myth Pegasus was a winged horse; when his hoof struck the side of Mount Helicon, Hippocrene, the spring of the Muses, gushed out. Whetstone's note, *Sive bonum, sive malum, Fama est*, is a Latin translation of the line 'As their actions are good or badde, so is their fame.'

30 Andrugio is disguised in clothing that indicates that he is a hermit, a monk who lives in a cell by himself.

31 His ghostly fathers are the priests assigned to hear his confession and encourage him to repentance before his execution.

32 Soranso is a member of the audience that has been listening to Isabella tell this tale, as are Katharina Trista and Fabritio.

33 'Punishment of' means 'punishment for'.

34 Queen Aurelia has recently been ill.

Tarlton's Newes out of Purgatorie

Tarlton's Newes out of Purgatorie appeared in three editions: 1590, *c.* 1600 and 1630. The version of the tales printed here is a transcription of the second edition, with a few emendations from the first edition. The title-page of the 1590 edition reads: '*Tarltons Newes out of Purgatorie*. Onely such a jest as *his* Jigge, fit for Gentlemen to laugh an houre, &c. Published by an old companion of his, Robin Goodfellow. At London, Printed for T.G. and T.N. 1590.' A *jigge* was a country dance and song included in plays as a concluding number. Tarlton made the jig famous and popular.

Friar Onion

The story of 'Friar Onion' is a loose translation of *Decameron* IV.2, although the name of the friar is taken from the tenth story of the sixth day, 'Frate Cipolla'; Boccaccio's friar in IV.2 is Frate Alberto. The stories of the fourth day are about 'those whose loves had unhappy results'. Boccaccio's story of Frate Alberto takes place in Venice rather than Florence, and the friar jumps into the Grand Canal rather than a street. Boccaccio's Lisetta is not a widow; her husband is away on a business trip.

A version of Decameron IV.2 also appears in Whetstone's *Heptameron*; it is printed elsewhere in this volume.

1 The term 'saint' can be applied to angels to indicate their holiness.
2 *Caetera quis nescit* ('Who does not know the rest?'): Ovid, *Amores* I.v.25. The narrator's citation of a line from Ovid is not in Boccaccio's story.
3 'Work enough for nine days' is a proverbial expression. Lisetta's *barne* is her secret; earlier she has been spoken of as 'with child till shee had uttered hir minde', i.e. pregnant with her secret.
4 The wild man, a man who lived outside the borders of civilization and was associated with the fertility of the earth, was a popular figure in European art, drama and festival in the Middle Ages and Renaissance.
5 The phrase *come equipage* is unclear. In French, *equipage* means the suite of a king or other dignitary, so the author seems to be mocking the friar by putting him in the place of a dignitary and speaking of the poor man and the dogs as his suite.
6 'A flea in one's ear' is a mortifying reproof. The friars are ashamed.

Why the Cook Sat in Purgatory

'Why the Cook Sat in Purgatory' is a translation of *Decameron* VI.4. The stories of the sixth day are about 'those who have gotten even with a witticism directed at them or with a prompt response or shrewdness avoided ruin, danger, or scorn'. While clearly based on Boccaccio's shorter story, the one in *Tarlton's Newes* differs in several ways from it. In the *Decameron* the action takes place in Florence, but the cook is

Venetian; the host kills a single crane himself when hunting; the interchange between the cook and his girl-friend is brief, and she threatens the loss of her sexual favours if he does not give her the desired meat; the host and the cook ride to the riverside in the morning to test the cook's claim.

1 *Consiliadorie* is a misspelling of the Italian *consigliatori*, which means 'advisors'. The author probably intended to use *consiglieri*, members of a council; if so, he was probably indicating the Council of Ten, the governing body of Venice. Civil law is the branch of law devoted to the private rights and remedies of the citizen.

2 *Tympany* means a swelling or pregnancy. The reference to 'two heels' makes it clear that the maid is pregnant.

3 The maid threatens that if the cook does not give her the leg, her unsatisfied longing will destroy her ('cast her away') and her unborn child ('that shee went withall').

4 'Gave . . . the bon joure': said good morning.

Link

1 The author is satirizing the Roman Catholic belief that a person could be released from punishment in Purgatory by providing money for masses and prayers to be said for his or her soul after death. A *morrow masse* is the first mass of the day; a *dirge* is the office for the dead; a *trental* is a set of thirty requiem masses. The shaving of a woman's head was a traditional punishment for adultery.

The Gentlewoman of Lyons

'The Gentlewoman of Lyons' is a translation of *Decameron* VII.6. The stories of the seventh day are about 'the tricks that women have played on their husbands, either for love or to save themselves, both discovered and undiscovered'. 'The Gentlewoman of Lyons' is a possible source of the secondary plot of Tourneur's *The Atheist's Tragedy*.

1 The narrator of this story here casually asserts an attitude towards women that was held by many in his day. In the Middle Ages and Renaissance the belief that women were inconstant by nature, and that this natural tendency could not be modified by education, was used as a justification for placing more restraints on women's behaviour than on men's. The belief was opposed by many who argued that women's natural capacity for virtue was as great as

men's and should be fostered by education. Thomas More, in letters to his daughters, and Thomas Elyot, in his *Defence of Good Women*, made the latter point.

2 See note 11 to 'The Duchess of Malfi'.

3 In this paragraph and the next two, the author uses the language of courtly love to describe Maria's representation of her affairs to herself (*her own conceite*): *servant, graced, favour, champion*. Pier's language of courtship is a set of clichées; thus he 'plays the orator'.

4 Adonis was the beautiful mortal beloved of Venus, the Graeco-Roman goddess of love; he died gored by a boar that he was hunting. A 'white-livered' person is a coward. Heracles was the most famous of Greek heroes, known for his accomplishment of the 'Twelve Labours', feats that would have been impossible to any other man. Maria's husband has horns because he is a cuckold.

5 'As thus they sat in their cuppes': while they were drinking.

The Two Lovers of Pisa

'The Two Lovers of Pisa' uses story IV.4 from Straparola's *Le piacevoli notti* as its base and adds elements from Ser Giovanni's *Il pecorone* I.2. Both are stories in which a young man seeks an older man's advice about wooing and, without either one of them realizing it at first, woos and wins the old man's wife; in both, the husband comes home and madly searches the house. Straparola's story contributed the carrying of the lover from the burning house in a chest and the dinner party denouement. Ser Giovanni's story provided the stabbing of the furnishings.

'The Two Lovers of Pisa' is a source of *The Merry Wives of Windsor*.

1 Both the 1590 and 1630 editions print this sentence as it is here. The 1600 edition says: 'but neither might their sutes, nor her owne prevaile about her father's resolution'.

2 In keeping with the mock-encomiastic tone of the description, the doctor is described as having no teeth with which he could harm anything.

3 *Salute* means 'health' in Italian and was a traditional greeting.

4 If the young woman is not brought within range for successful shooting by Lionel's persuasive words and actions, the doctor will give him a love potion to administer to her.

5 The *exordium* is the beginning of a formal speech.

6 *Succado des labres*: sucking of the lips.

7 Cuckolds were said to have grown horns or antlers. The reference

to a 'knight of the forked order' in the following speech also refers to cuckoldry.

8 She hid Lionello between the two ceilings of an inner wooden roof.

9 The bleeding of one's nose was believed to be a bad omen.

10 Vicenza is a city near Venice, a long distance from Pisa.

11 This chest contains Mutio's important business papers, deeds, loan agreements, etc.

12 *Praeter expectationem*: against expectation.

13 *Well fare* is an expression of good wishes, so Lionello means 'Thank goodness for woman's wit.'

14 I.e. revealed to his wives's brethren who he [Lionello] was.

15 The word 'whom' refers to Margaret.

GLOSSARY

ABODE   *temporary stay*

ACCIDENTE   *occurrence, event; something that happens by chance; non-essential quality*

ACCOMPLISHED   *fulfilled; completed; perfect*

ACCOMPT, ACCOUMPT   *account*

ACCRIVED   *approved*

ACQUITE   *to requite a benefit or injury; to atone for*

ADMIRATION   *puzzled astonishment; wonder mixed with reverence, esteem*

ADVENTURE   n. *chance occurrence, risk;* v. *venture upon, to risk oneself*

ADVENTUROUS   *fortunate*

ADVICE   n. *opinion, judgement;* v. *to take advice; to deliberate*

ADVOUTRY   *adultery*

AFFECTUAL   *earnest*

AFFECTUOUSLYE   *eagerly; lovingly*

AFFIANCE, AFFIAUNCE   n. *confidence, assurance;* v. *trust in, on*

AFFRAY   *disturb, startle; attack with an armed force; frighten* (especially in passive voice: *to be afraid*)

AFTERCLAPS   *unexpected stroke after the recipient has ceased to be on his guard; surprise happening after an affair is supposed to be at an end*

AGAIN(E)   *besides; against; in preparation for the time that something is to happen; in return, in reply; once more*

AGREABLENESSE   *pleasantness; conformity, consistency*

ALBEIT   *although*

ALLOWANCE   *the taking into account of mitigating circumstances; sum allowed in an account*

AMAINE   *vehemently, at full speed*

AMBASSAGE   *message brought by an ambassador*

AMBUSCADO   *ambush*

AMITYE   *friendship*

ANIMOSITY   *spiritedness, courage*

ANON, ANONE *at once*

APPEACHE *charge with a crime, accuse, inform against*

APPERTAIN *belong; be suited, be proper to; befit*

APPOINT *agree, settle; arrange the time of a meeting; determine, decree*

ARERAGES *indebtedness, debt*

ARMIPOTENT *mighty in arms* (originally of Mars)

ARMURE *armour*

ARRANT *public, notorious; unmitigated*

ARRANTE *errand*

ARTIFICIAL *made by art in imitation of what is natural or real; skilful*

ASSAY *try; try by tasting; experience*

ASSURED *secure, pledged*

ASTONISHMENT *loss of sense or wits; dismay, consternation, dread*

ASTONNED *astonished, dismayed, amazed*

ATCHIEVED *brought to an end*

ATTACHED *seized*

ATTEND *listen, consider, look after; wait upon; await; wait to see or learn; expect; tarry*

AVOID *make void; get rid of; depart from, quit*

BACKSIDE *back premises, back yard, outbuildings attached to a dwelling*

BAN DOGGE *mastiff, bloodhound*

BAND *bond, agreement or promise*

BANKET, BANQUETTE *banquet; a dessert, or course of sweetmeats and wine*

BANKETTED *feasted, entertained lavishly*

BARATOUR *barrator, one who deals fraudulently in his business or office, especially a person who buys or sells ecclesiastical preferment; a hired bully; a rowdy person, one who raises discord between neighbours*

BARGENET *bergeret, a pastoral dance*

BARME *froth that forms at the top of fermenting malt liquors*

BARNE *baby*

BARON *the lowest rank or order of nobility*

BAULE *howl or bark like a dog; bellow*

BEAK *strike or seize with the beak*

BEDLAM *lunatic*

BEHALF *matter*

BEHOLDING *under obligation*

BEHOOFE *use, benefit*

BEND   *turn (one's steps)*

BEWRAY   *divulge secrets prejudically, make known*

BICKER   *quarrel, wrangle*

BILL   *weapon carried by soldiers and watchmen; implement having a long blade with a concave edge, used for pruning, cutting wood, etc.*

BLASON   *blazon; describe in proper heraldic language; publish boastfully*

BLOWING   *breathing hard, panting*

BOOT   v. *profit, avail*

BOMBAST   *stuff, inflate*

BOONE COMPANION   *good-fellow, familiar friend*

BOUNSE   *thump, knock loudly*

BRAST   *burst* (past tense)

BRAVERY   *daring, courage; display, show, fine clothes*

BREAK   *reveal one's mind; begin*

BREADE   *breadth*

BRENNETH   *burns*

BROOKE   *possess, hold; put up with*

BRUITE, BRUTE   *noise, din; rumour; fame, renown, reputation*

BRUNT   *shock, violence of an attack*

BUGGE   *bogey, imaginary object of terror*

BULL   *edict*

BUMBASTE   *beat soundly, thrash*

BUSSE   *kiss*

CAITIF   *despicable wretch*

CALLED STATE   *vocation*

CANCRED   *infected with evil; corrupt, depraved*

CARCANET   *necklace*

CARLE   *man of the common people; base fellow, churl*

CARRAIN   *carrion, dead body, putrefying flesh*

CARRIAGE   *load*

CARROWST (caroused)   *caroused, drank a bumper to*

CAVALIERE   *knight* (Italian)

CENSOR   *a person who judges public morals and conduct*

CERTIFY   *declare or attest by a formal or legal certificate*

CHAFE   *heat, rage, passion, fury*

CHALLENGE   *accuse*

CHARGES   *expenses; responsibilities*

CHARLY, CHARELY   *carefully, frugally*

CHARY   *careful, cautious, circumspect*

CHAPLEINE   *priest of a chantry, private or institutional chapel*

CHAUNCE *fortuitous event, accident*

CHEAP *market; goods;* GOOD CHEAP *cheap*

CHECK *hit; stop or retard the motion of; taunt, revile*

CHIMERA(E) *fabled fire-breathing monster of Greek mythology killed by Bellerophon; an unreal creature of the imagination*

CHOLER *anger*

CHOP *cut with quick or heavy blow; thrust with suddenness or force*

CIRCUMSTANCE *state of affairs; ceremony; detail, particular*

CLOTHES *wearing apparel; bedclothes*

CLOUCHES *clutches, grasp (from the claw of a beast, bird of prey or fiend)*

CLOWN *ignorant person; peasant*

COARSE *corpse*

CODGEL *cudgel*

COGITATION *design, plan*

COLOUR *outward appearance*

COLOURABLE *plausible*

COMBERED *encombered, burdened*

COMELYE *fair, pretty; decorous, proper*

COMFIT *sweetemeat, fruit preserved with sugar*

COMFORTABLE *cheerful; cheering*

COMMODITYE *convenience, advantage, profit*

COMPLAIN *bewail, lament; express discontent*

COMPLAINT *action of complaining, grieving; expression of grief*

COMPLEXION, COMPLEXITION *temperament; the mixture of the four humours in a person's body*

COMPOSITION *action of combining; manner in which a thing is composed; state of being composite; contract, treaty*

COMPOUNDED *made up by combination of several elements*

CONCEIPT, CONCEIT *conception, idea; whim, fancy*

CONDIGNE *equal in worth or dignity; worthy*

CONFINE *border on*

CONJURE *conspire; constrain a person to do something by putting him on his oath or appealing to something sacred*

CONNE THANCK *acknowledge one's gratitude*

CONSTRAIN *compel, oppress; compress into a small space*

CONTEMPTNE *condemn*

CONTENTATION *action of satisfying; fact of being satisfied*

CONTRIVE *wear down; pass the time*

CONVENABLE *suitable; consistent*

CONVENIENT *fitting, suitable, appropriate*

CONVERSATION *intimacy*

COOLE *cowl, garment with hood, worn by monks; hood of this garment*

CORNET *wind instrument, horn*; PLAY THE CORNETS *be a cuckold*

CORNOVALE, TO SEND SOMEONE INTO CORNOVALE *to make someone a cuckold*

CORSER *dealer*

COULD *cold*

COUMPT n. *count, estimation, esteem, consideration*; v. *estimate, regard, notice*

COUNTENANCE *comportment, demeanour; appearance, look; expression of a person's face*

COURTESANE *prostitute*

COSIN *cousin, relative*

COUCH *lie; crouch, cower*

COUSONAGE *cozenage, deception*

CRABBED *cross-tempered, irritable*

CRASED *flawed, damaged*

CREDITE *belief, faith, trust*

CROSSEBITE *attack or censure bitterly or bitingly*

CROW *crowbar*

CRUCIATE *torture, torment*

CRUSE *pot, jar, bottle*

CULLINGES *hugs*

DAINTY *handsome, choice, delightful; of delicate taste or beauty; (of persons) nice, fastidious, particular; choice food*

DAMOSELL *young, unmarried woman*

DECOCTION *boiling-down* (also used figuratively)

DEFENDE *ward off, prevent, forbid*

DEPART *share, bestow; go away*

DEPEND *hang down, be suspended; be contingent on, conditioned by*

DESPITEFULL *insulting; cruel, spiteful*

DETECT *expose; accuse*

DETERMINATE *definite, fixed, clearly defined*

DEVISE *design; desire*

DEVOIRE *duty*

DIFFERED *deferred*

DIGESTURE *digestion*

DISCOMFORT *dishearten; distress*

DISCOVER *uncover, reveal, show, display*

DISGUISE   *transform, disfigure; conceal the identity by dressing as or in*

DISPARCLED, DISPERCLED, DISPARPLED   *scattered abroad, dispersed*

DISPENSE WITH   *exempt*

DISPERGEMENT   *disparagement*

DISPIGHT   *despite, scorn; outrage, injury*

DISPORT   *relaxation, amusement*

DISSOLVE   *put asunder the parts of; melt; loosen, release; release from life*

DISTAINE   *tint, stain*

DISTEMPERATURE   *illness*

DOCTRINE   *lesson, body of knowledge*

DORTOR   *dormitory*

DOUBT   *be uncertain in opinion; dread, be afraid of; anticipate with apprehension; suspect*

DOUDYE   *woman shabbily or unattractively dressed*

DRESSER   *sideboard or table in kitchen on which meat was dressed*

DRIVDE   *passed time; caused time to pass*

DRIEFATTE   *large vessel used to hold dry things*

DUCKAT   *ducat: a gold or silver coin of varying value*

DUMPE   *reverie; fit of low spirits*

EARNEST   *money in part payment for binding a bargain*

EASILY   *comfortably; without hurrying*

EFFECTUOUSLY   *earnestly, urgently*

EFTSONES   *again; soon afterwards; repeatedly*

EGREE   *eager, severe; ardent, impetuous, fierce; impatient*

ELYSIAN FIELDS   *abode assigned to the blessed after death in Greek myth*

ENTAILED   *carved, cut into*

ENTERPRISE   *take in hand; attempt; run the risk of*

ENTERTAIN   *support; deal with; occupy (time); amuse; receive*

ENTERTAINMENT   *financial support; amusement; hospitable provision for a guest's needs*

ENTREAT   *treat, deal with*

ESPIALS   *spys*

ESTATE   *condition as regards worldly prosperity, fortune, etc.; status, degree, rank*

EVIDENCE   *one who, or that which, furnishes proof; witness; title-deeds*

EVIDENTLY   *certainly, conclusively*

EXAMPLE   *serve as a warning*

EXPECT *wait, wait for*

EXPEDITION *prompt execution or supply, despatch; warlike enterprise; haste, speed*

EXPERIENCE n. *test*

EXPERIMENTED *experienced*

FACION, FASHION *particular shape; kind; behaviour*

FACT *action, deed*

FACULTYE *art, trade, occupation, profession*

FAMILIAR *affable, courteous, sociable*

FAMILYE *servants of a house, household*

FARE *make one's way; get on; get on with respect to food, feed*

FATIGATE *tired*

FAUGHT *fault*

FAVOUR *exceptional kindness; permission; appearance, aspect*

FEARED *regarded with awe*

FEATE *fitting, apt; neat, elegant*

FEEL *perceive by smell or taste* (in addition to modern senses)

FEERE *companion, mate*

FELONIOUS *wicked, atrociously criminal*

FEOFFMENT *fief, endowment*

FETCH n. *trick*

FILLET *little band, narrow ribbon*

FINE *subtle, capable of fine discriminations; ingenious, cunning;* IN FINE *in the end*

FISTULA *long narrow, suppurating canal of morbid origin in some part of the body*

FLATLY *in a blunt manner; without ambiguity; completely*

FLESH *render an animal eager for prey by the taste of blood; incite an animal to the chase*

FLET *fleet, float, sail, drift*

FLOUT *mocking speech or action*

FOLE *fool*

FONDE *foolish, doting*

FONDLY *foolishly, dotingly*

FOOTEMEN *foot-soldiers*

FORCE n. *strength; physical coercion; mental compulsion; army;* v. *attach force or importance to; care for* (in addition to the many usual senses)

FORFAIT *misdeed or crime*

FOURD *afford; give of what one has*

FOWLE, FOULE *disgraceful, ignominious, shameful*

FRANKLY   *freely*

FRAY   *make afraid, frighten*

FRITH   *wood, wooded country*

FROLICKE   *joyous*

FROWARD   *perverse; naughty*

FURNITURE   *provision of anything, stores*

GABERDINE   *loose upper garment of coarse material*

GAILER   *gaoler, jailer*

GALLANTIES, GALLANTISE   *gallantry; gallant bearing; courtliness*

GALIARD, GALLIARD   adj. *valiant; lively; having a gay appearance;* n. *man of courage and spirit, gay fellow; quick and lively dance in triple time*

GEERE   *goods, household stuff; matter, stuff*

GENTIL   *well-born, noble, generous, courteous*

GENTILITYE   *nobility*

GESTURE   *movement of the body (esp. in oratory); deportment*

GHOST   *soul, spirit*

GIRDE   *sharp blow; sharp or biting remark*

GLASSE   *mirror*

GOBBET   *piece of anything that is divided or cut; piece of raw flesh*

GOSSIP   *female friend*

GRACED   *favoured*

GRAUNGE   *country house*

GRIN   *snare, trap*

GRIPE   *vulture*

GRISTLE   *tender or delicate person*

GUERDON   *reward, recompence*

HABILE   *able, dextrous*

HABIT   *clothing*

HALED   *hauled*

HALF   *one of two equal parts; side; equal partner*

HAP(P)   *come about by chance; chance upon*

HARBINGER   *one sent on before to purvey lodgings for royal train, army, etc.*

HARDLYE   *certainly, assuredly, by all means*

HAULT   *high*

HAUNT   *habit; practice of frequenting a place*

HEAVY   *weighty, grave*

HEDLESSE   *heedless, careless of consequences*

HIE   *hasten, go quickly*

HIERUSALEM   *Jerusalem*

HISTORY   *narrative, tale, story*

HOLPEN   *helped* (past participle)

HOST   v. *play the host; be a guest, put up*

HUSBAND   n. *spouse; steward, household manager*; v. *till the ground, cultivate; manage with thrift and prudence*

IMAGES   *statues*

IMBASSAGE   *see* AMBASSAGE

IMBRAIDE   *upbraid*

IMBROINED   *befouled*

IMBRUE   v. *stain*

IMPAIRE   *make worse, less valuable, weaker*

IMPORTABLE   *unendurable*

INCONTINENTLY   *straightaway, immediately*

INCOUNTREY   *encounter*

INDIFFERENT   *impartial; of medium or moderate extent, size, etc.; of neutral quality, equal, the same, unimportant, non-essential.*

INFANT   *child under 7; person under legal age*

INFER   *bring on, bring about, cause*

INFORCEMENT   *action of overcoming by violence; constraint, compulsion; forcible exaction of a payment, an action, etc.*

INSIGNEMENT   *instruction*

INSOLENCY   *insolence; pride, arrogance*

INSTANT   *pressing, urgent; importunate*

INTERCHANGEABLY   *mutually, reciprocally*

INTERTAIN   *see* ENTERTAIN

IOTE   *iota, jot*

JACKANAPES   *ridiculous upstart, impertinent person* (originally the name for a tame monkey)

JAKES   n. *privy*

JAR   *make harsh, grating sound; sound in discord*

JAWME   *jamb, sidepost of doorway or window on which the lintel rests*

JETTE   *strut; stroll*

JOIN   *attach; put into close contact; unite*

JOURNEY   *military expedition, campaign*

JUSTLY   *in a just manner, properly; exactly, accurately*

KIND(E)   *birth, origin, descent; natural disposition; manner, way, fashion; gender, race, kin, variety*

KNOWLEGE   *acknowledge*

LACIS   *laces*

LARGE   *lavish; copious; comprehensive; spacious, roomy; lax;* AT LARGE   *copiously*

LEASING   n. *lie*

LEAVING   *what is left, remainder*

LEISHE   *leash; set of three hounds, hawks, foxes, deer, etc.*

LENIFYE   *relax, make soft and supple; mitigate, soothe*

LENITYE   *leniency*

LET   n. *hindrance;* v. *hinder, stand in the way of*

LETTERS   *literature*

LEWDE   *unlearned; common, low, vulgar*

LIBERTIES   *privileges, immunities, rights; person's domain or property*

LICENSE   *give someone permission to do something; dismiss, set free*

LIME-TWIGGES   *twigs spread with a glutinous substance to catch birds*

LIST   *please, like, care, desire*

LITTLE   *small; not very*

LIVING   *livelihood, maintenance;* pl. *estates*

LOTH, LOATH   *reluctant*

LOVESOME   *lovely*

LUBBER   *big, clumsy, stupid fellow*

MAAKE   *mate, husband, wife*

MAINE   *strong, vigorous, mighty;* MAINE SEA   *ocean*

MAISTER   *teacher, master (title)*

MALAPERT   *presumptuous, impudent, saucy*

MALE   *travelling-bag*

MAN   *accustom a hawk to the presence of men; tame*

MANIFOLDE   *having various forms or features; numerous*

MANQUELLER   *murderer*

MANURE   *till, cultivate land; cultivate, train the body or mind*

MARMAIDE   *mermaid*

MARYE   *an exclamation sometimes meaning 'why, to be sure'*

MATCH   *matrimonial contract; bargain*

MAZE   *state of bewilderment*

MEACOCKE   *coward, weakling*

MEANE   *common to two or more; of low degree; of little value; inferior*

MEETE, METE   *suitable, fit, proper*

MERELY   *merrily*

MEVE   *move*

MILKESOPPE   *man or youth lacking courage or manliness*

MIND   *remember; bear in mind; intend*

MISCONSTER   *misconstrue*

MISERYE   *miserliness*

MISHAPPE   *bad luck; unhappy accident*

MO *more*

MODESTYE *moderation,   self-control;   womanly   propriety   of
  behaviour*

MOLEST *cause trouble to, put to inconvenience*

MOSEL *muzzle*

MOTHER *term of address for an elderly lower-class woman*

MOUGHT *might*

MOULD *surface soil; earth as material of human body*

MOVEABLES *personal property; portable object belonging to a person;
  property that does not pass by inheritance*

NEIGHBORHOODE *neighbourliness; vicinity, near situation*

NETTIFY *neaten, purify*

NICE *wanton; over-refined; coy; difficult to please or satisfy*

NIP *pinch; vex*

NODGECOCK *simpleton*

NOISOME *harmful; disagreeable, offensive*

NOTIFY *take note of; make known, announce*

NOURSE (NURSE) CHILDREN *foster-children*

NO(U)SLE (NUZZLE) *train, educate a person in some habit; bring up,
  rear*

OBSEQUYE *ready compliance with the will of another; funeral rites*

OBTESTATION *supplication*

OCCASION *opportunity*

OCCURRENTS *news*

ORDER *regulation, control*

ORISONS *prayers*

OUTRAGED *done violence to*

OVERSHOOT *pass over or beyond the mark; utter a word unguard-
  edly or too violently*

OVERTHWART *perverse; testy, unfriendly*

PACKE *applied to a person of worthless character, almost always with
  'naughty'*

PAINTED *adorned with make-up*

PANDARLY *of the nature of or befitting a pander*

PANDOR *pander, go-between in a love-affair*

PARENTS *relatives*

PARSONAGE *person*

PART *portion of a country; region*

PASS (past tense PAST) *go on, make one's way; travel; go away; go
  by;* PASSE NOT *do not care*

PASSABLE *tolerable; presentable*

PASSAGE   *transition from one state to another (esp. from this life to the next)*

PASSETIME, PASTIME   *that which serves to pass the time agreeably; diversion, amusement*

PAST   SEE PASS

PATER-NOSTER   *Latin name for the Lord's Prayer*

PATRON   *pattern*

PEATE   *term of endearment for a girl; term of obloquy for a woman*

PERADVENTURE   *by chance, perhaps*

PERFIT   *perfect*

PERFORCE   *compulsorily;* PERFORCE HER WILL   *under constraint*

PERFOURM   *carry through to completion*

PETTIE FOGGER   *legal practitioner of inferior status who gets up or conducts petty cases (esp. one who employs mean, cavilling practices)*

PHYSICKE   *medicine*

PIE   *magpie*

PIERE   *peer; equal in rank, natural gifts; member of the nobility*

PINNE   *peg;* UPPON HOW MERRY A PINNE: *in what a merry humour*

PLAT   *ground plan; plot*

PLAUSIBLE   *praiseworthy, commendable; acceptable, pleasing*

PLEASANT   *good-humoured; humorous; merry*

PLUMME   *downright, thoroughgoing*

POAST   *post, courier;* IN POAST   *in haste*

POINARD   *poniard, dagger*

POINCTMENTE   *appointment; agreement*

POINT, POINCT   *punctuate*

POISE   *weight*

POLITIKE, POLLITIQUE   *of persons: sagacious, prudent, shrewd; of actions: judicious, expedient, skilfully contrived*

POLITIKELY (POLITICLY)   *prudently, shrewdly*

POLICYE   *policy; conduct of public affairs; political sagacity; prudent or expedient procedure; crafty device*

POLLACO   *native of Poland, Pole*

PONTIFICALLES   *vestments and other insignia of a bishop*

PORT(E)   *style of living; external deportment; harbour*

POSTERNE   *back door; any door or gate distinct from the main entrance*

POTAGE   *soup*

PRACTICE   *to make a practice of; to bring about; to plan; to plot, conspire*

PRACTICING   *frequenting*

PRATYE   *pretty*

PRECISE   *punctillious, particular, fastidious*

PREFER (PREFARRE)   *advance in condition, status, position in life*

PREFERMENT   *advancement in condition, etc.*

PREPARE   *get ready (to go on a journey); go*

PREPOSTERATED   *reversed, overturned; perverted*

PRESENTLY   *at once, immediately, promptly; in a little while, soon*

PRESS   *large cupboard for holding clothes, books, etc*

PRESTE   *ready; willing, eager*

PRETEND   *intend, design, plan*

PRETENCE   *pretended, feigned*

PRIMME   *privet*

PRISE   *pay for*

PRISTINATE   *original, primitive, ancient*

PRIVYE   *intimate, familiar, private*

PRODIGAL   *(wastefully) lavish*

PROFFER   *offer*

PROPONE   *propound as a question or matter for decision*

PROOF   *trial, test*

PROPER, PROPRE   *(one's) own; fit, suitable*

PROVE   v. *test; experience*

PROVENDER   *dry food for horses*

PROVIDENCE   *prudence*

PRYE   *look closely; spy*

PUISSANT   *powerful*

PURCIVANT   *pursuivant, a royal or state messenger with power to execute warrants; messenger*

PURGATION   *the act of clearing someone from an accusation of guilt*

QUARREL   *short, heavy, square-headed arrow or bolt used with a crossbow*

QUICKE   *alive*

RACE   *erase*

RADDE   *past tense of 'read'*

RAMPE   *snatch, tear, pluck*

RECLAIM   *call back a hawk*

RECLINE   *lay down, make lie down; incline*

RECOMMEND   *commit a person to someone's care*

RECOMPTE   *tell*

REEL(E)   *wind thread after it is spun*

REFECTION   *refreshment*

REHEARSE   *recite in a formal manner; say over and over*

RELENT   *melt; yield, give way*

REPAIR *go, make one's way*

RESOLVE *melt, dissolve*

REVE *reave, spoil, rob*

REWE *rue, regret*

RIBALDE *wicked, lewd, licentious person*

RID *rode*

RIGHT *morally fitting; correct, proper; direct*

ROADE *sheltered piece of water near the shore where ships may anchor safely*

ROISTERS *bullies*

ROME *roam*

ROSIALL *rosy*

ROWLING *rolling*

RUDD *red*

RUETHFUL *rueful*

RUFFIAN *man of low and brutal character; keeper of prostitutes*

RUFFLE *swagger, make a great display*

RUMOR *general talk, report, hearsay; clamour, outcry; noise*

SABBATON *broad-toed armoured foot-covering*

SADDE *steadfast; sober; sorrowful*

SAULF *safe*

SAULFTY *safety*

SAULT *leap; copulate*

SAVER *savour*

SCOFF *mock, deride, ridicule*

SCOPE *intention, purpose; room for activity; spaciousness*

SCOWRING *beating, drubbing*

SCRITCH *n. screech, shriek, loud cry; v. utter a screech, etc.*

SECRESYE *concealment; intimate acquaintance*

SECRETARY *confidant*

SEEMING, TO HIS *as he thought*

SEMBLABLE *like, similar*

SEMBLABLY *similarly; in appearance*

SENSIBLE *perceptible to the senses or inward feelings*

SEPARD *separated*

SESSED *assessed*

SHAGGE *shake*

SHAMBLES *slaughterhouse, meat-market*

SHIFT *ingenious device for effecting some purpose, ruse*

SHIRT *undergarment for the upper part of the body, worn by both sexes*

SIMPLICITYE *want of ordinary judgement; ignorance; plainness*

SIRENES *fabulous monsters, part woman, part bird, who were supposed to lure sailors to their destruction by their singing*

SITHES *since*

SMARTE *mental or physical pain*

SMOLDER *smother, suffocate*

SMUGGE, SMOUGUE *trim, neat, spruce, smart*

SNAFFLE, SNAFFELL n. *simple form of bridle bit;* v. *put on such a bridle*

SNARR v. *snarl*

SODEYNLY *suddenly*

SOMETIMES(S) *occasionally; once; in former times; at some future time*

SONNET *short poem or song, esp. about love*

SOOPE *sip*

SOOTHE *verify, support, corroborate; humour*

SORTED OUT *selected from*

SOTTISH *foolish*

SPARMACETI *spermaceti, fatty substance found in the head of the sperm-whale, used in the manufacture of medicinal preparations and in candles*

SPINSTER *woman (or, rarely, man) who spins; unmarried woman*

SPRENT *sprinkled, sprinkled with*

SQUEIMISHE *affected with nausea; reluctant to do something; prudish*

STAND TO *obey, leave oneself dependent on*

STAY n. *prop, support; restraint, hindrance* v. *support, sustain; remain stationary; detain, hold back; strengthen, comfort;* STAY UPON *rely upon, act upon*

STAYED adj. *propped, supported; grave*

STEWS *brothel*

STOMAKE *courage, valour, bravery*

STOUTNESSE *pride; bravery, valour*

STRAIGHT *narrow*

STRAIGHTNES *strictness; want of room*

STRAINT *application of force or pressure*

STRAUNGE *foreign*

STRAUNGER *foreigner; unknown person*

STRUD *not in OED; at rest*

STRUMPET *unchaste woman, prostitute*

STUDYE *apply oneself to learning; think intently, meditate*

STUR(RE)   *stir, disturbance*

SUCCESSE   *that which happens in the future, result; fortune (good or bad)*

SUFFER   *permit, allow*

SUFFRAGES   *prayers (esp. for the souls of the dead)*

SUITE   *train of followers*

SUMPTURE   *sumpter, saddle-bag, pack*

SURPRISED   *captured, taken prisoner*

SUSTEN   *sustain*

SWINGE   n. *sway, power, rule, authority*; v. *singe, scorch*

SWINGING   *scorching*

TABOR   *small drum*

TAKE TARDY   *catch in a crime*

TEENE   *injury; anger*

TEETH   TO ONE'S TEETH   *directly and openly; defiantly*; IN SPITE OF ONE'S TEETH   *notwithstanding one's opposition; in spite of one*

TENDER   v. *feel or act tenderly towards; treat with proper regard*

THAWART   *thwart; speak or act in opposition*

THEN   *then; than*

THOROUGH   *through*

THRILLED   *pierced*

THWIT   *twit; blame; taunt*

TOWARD   *(of young people) promising, hopeful*

TOYES   *trifles*

TRAFIQUE   *trade*

TRAIN   *retinue*

TRAMPE   *temper (of iron or steel); strength, quality*

TRANSFRETE, TRANIFRAIT   *cross over a strait, channel or narrow sea*

TRAUNCE   *trance; state of extreme apprehension or dread*

TRAVAIL, TRAVEL(L)   n. *labour, hardship*; v. *labour; voyage; labour in giving birth*

TRINCKETS   *tools, implements of an occupation*

TROMPERY   *trumpery, deceit*

TROT   *go or move quickly; bustle*

TROUBLE   *disturb, agitate; interrupt, hinder, mar; distress*

TRUMPS   *trumpets*

TRUNCKE   *cut a part off from, carve*

TRUST   *trussed*

TRUSTLESSE   *untrustworthy*

TYMPANY *distension of the abdomen from a variety of causes; pregnancy*

UNACQUAINTED *unfamiliar*

UNDERSTAND *comprehend; know about, learn of*

UNDISSOLVED *see* DISSOLVED

UNETH, UNNETHES *hardly, scarcely, with difficulty*

UNFIT *unsuitable*

UNKINDE *unnatural; cruel*

UNKINDNESS *unnaturalness; lack of fellow feeling*

UNPOINTED *unpunctuated*

UNREADY *unprepared; undressed*

UNWONTED *see* WONTED

USURY *interest on money or goods lent*

VAIVODA *local ruler or official (esp. in Transylvania)*

VALOUR *value*

VAMURE *vaumure, advanced wall or earthwork thrown out in front of main fortification*

VAUTE *vault*

VENTUROUS *adventurous, bold*

VISARDE *mask*

VISOR *mask*

WAG *(mischievous) young man*

WARELY *cautiously*

WAY *weigh*

WAITS *ambushes*

WARE *vigilant; careful, cautious; prudent, sagacious, cunning*

WARES *goods, articles of merchandise*

WEEDE *clothing; garment distinctive of person's sex, profession or state of life*

WHETHER *whither*

WHITHER *whether; whither*

WIFE *woman*

WIGHT *person*

WISE *manner*

WHOREMONGER *one who has dealings with whores, a fornicator*

WITHOUT *outside*

WITNESS *bear witness to; be a sign or mark of; give evidence of by one's behaviour*

WONTED accustomed

WORSHIP *distinguished in respect of character or rank, dignity, importance, high standing*

WRAPPED   *rapt, deeply interested or absorbed in*
WREAKE   v. *vent*
YALP   *yelp; bark shrilly in excitement or distress*
YARDE   *comparatively small uncultivated area attached to a building or enclosed by it*

When translations of novelle were first published, the moralizing passages with which they seem to bristle did not placate English moralists. They associated the books with the evil that they believed Italy to incarnate. In the following passage Roger Ascham in *The Scholemaster* (1570) seems to be referring to Painter's *Palace of Pleasure*; he speaks most eloquently of the damage he fears novelle can do:

These be the inchantements of Circe's,[1] brought out of Italye to marre men's maners in England; much by example of ill life, but more by preceptes of fonde bookes, of late translated out of Italian into English, sold in every shop in London, commended by honest titles the soner to corrupt honest maners, dedicated over boldlye to vertuous and honourable personages, the easyelier to begile simple and innocent wittes. It is pitye that those which have authoritye and charge to allow and dissalow bookes to be printed be no more circumspect herein than they are. Ten sermons at Paule's Crosse do not so moch good for moving men to trewe doctrine, as one of those bookes do harme with inticing men to ill living. Yea, I say farder, those bookes, tend not so moch to corrupt honest living as they do to subvert trewe religion. Mo Papistes be made by your mery bookes of Italye, than by your earnest bookes of Lovain . . .[2]

Therefore, when the busye and open Papistes abroad could not by their contentious bookes turne men in England fast enough from troth and right judgement in doctrine, than the sutle and secrete Papistes at home procured bawdye bookes to be translated out of the Italian tonge, whereby over many yong willes and wittes, allured to wantonnes, do now boldly contemne all severe bookes that sounde to honestye and godlines . . . ten Morte Arthures[3] do not the tenth part so much harme, as one of these bookes made in Italye, and translated in England. They open, not fond and common ways to vice, but such subtle, cunning, new, and diverse

shiftes to cary yong willes to vanitye and yong wittes to mischief,
to teach old bawdes new schole pointes, as the simple head of an
Englishman is not hable to invent, nor never was hard of in
England before, yea, when Papistrye overflowed all. Suffer these
books to be read, and they shall soone displace all bookes of godly
learning ... Then they have in more reverence the triumphes of
Petrarche[4] than the Genesis of Moses. They make more account of
... a tale in Bocace,[5] than a storye of the Bible.

E. Dering in the Epistle prefixed to *A briefe Instruction* (1572), made
the same point more concisely: 'To this purpose we have gotten our
Songs and Sonnets, our Palaces of Pleasure, our unchaste Fables and
Tragedies, and such like sorceries ... O that there were among us some
zealous Ephesian,[6] that books of so great vanity might be burned up.'

After the initial violent response, the novelle translations suffered
from centuries of neglect. Until very recently, critics simply cited them
dismissively as inadequate forerunners of the novel, or sources of
Shakespeare's plays, described them briefly and went on, but in the last
fifty years critics have become more interested in the novella as a genre
and in marginal genres or popular literature as categories of study, and
the novella collections have benefited. Three have recently been freshly
edited: *Tarlton's Newes out of Purgatorie*, *Riche His Farewell to
Militarie Profession*, and Whetstone's *Heptameron* (see Suggestions for
Further Reading for details). Some have received useful and challenging
criticism.

The story of 'Titus and Gisippus' has traditionally been seen as a
'striking illustration of the theme that friendship between men is more
to be honoured than the love of a man for a woman'.[7] Recently,
however, Lorna Hutson has opposed such sentimental readings of the
tale, in an extended study of the economics of friendship. She relates
the text to 'the extensive theorization of friendship in [Cicero's] *De
Amicitia* and the *De Officiis* [which] sets out not to refute the
instrumentality of friendship, but to set it within an ethical and political
context', and she argues:

> The story of 'Titus and Gisippus' is also, of course, about
> communicative action and the persuasive mobilization of texts.
> Indeed, it seems to define the affection arising from the boys'
> 'similitude of studies' as a source of dynastic and political power
> superior to that commanded by the instrumental friendship of kin
> and fictive kin, the *parenti* and *amici* of Boccaccio's text, and the

'frendes, kynne and alyes' of Elyot's rendering. By persuading one another with exemplary 'counsel' to take socially transgressive action to remedy their situation, and by using similar techniques of reasoning to justify the consequences of that action, the friends mark out a new space in which to control the transference of symbolic capital outside of the economy of agnatic kinship, or of lineal inheritance. In the end of Elyot's story, Titus restores Gisippus to his 'landes and substance' in spite of his kindred, while in Boccaccio, he 'first made him joint owner of all his treasure and possessions, and then gave him to wife a young sister of his, called Fulvia'. To read 'Titus and Gisippus' as a story which introduces into early modern culture a new ideal of masculine friendship as 'affective' rather than 'instrumental' is surely to misrecognize as uncalculated the vastly superior instrumentality proved by Titus and Gisippus' version of 'friendship' over that practised by the 'frendes' that found Gisippus his bride. It would seem that, by this history, the cultural instrumentality of friendship – its power to control the transference of wealth and honour – has not been replaced but *displaced* into a new affective medium.[8]

Painter, Riche and Whetstone have all been praised for the verisimilitude of their work:

Painter has actually left little personal imprint upon his work, yet he has imparted to it an indefinably English stamp. He has accomplished this through his choices – selecting for the most part stories of action, bloodshed and adventure – and by his use of local terms and realistic detail.[9]

In execution as well as style Rich shows greater independence than most of his peers. He stresses human frailties as mainsprings of action; he creates homely English environments despite his use of exotic proper names; he dwells occasionally on economic motives.

[Whetstone's] strongest point, at least for a modern reader, is his occasional regard (resembling Barnaby Rich's) for the external economic factors motivating the actions of his characters. The wreck of a marriage as depicted in Day III is clearly related to the lack of the young couple's financial resources.[10]

The main topic discussed by other critics of Painter is how to enjoy the stories:

In many ways, the renaissance of prose fiction in Elizabethan England owes its origins to Painter, simply by dint of the clear break his stories represent with the earlier homily, romance, and fabliau.

One hastens to qualify that Painter also absorbed certain of the practices of his French sources. He too added stylistic embellishments for the sake of copiousness and indulged in his own moral mollifications. That he defends these stories as valuable exempla whereby the reader might learn to imitate virtue and to shun vice, while at the same time passing them off as mere recreations and idle diversions for the refreshment of the mind, hints at the motives behind his modifications. His double position seems to dissociate entirely the didactic from the diversionary in his fiction – the result of advancing two entirely separate rationales for the acceptability of his work. Subsequent writers, including Riche, would perpetuate both formulae. But a reading of Painter – who can still be read with considerable pleasure today – will reveal that his overlay of morals and embellishments do no fundamental damage to his effectiveness as a story teller. That was his principal legacy to an entire generation of writers. With *The Palace* came a vast vocabulary of social motivation and trickery, new styles of greed, revenge, lust, jealousy, anger, as well as idealized devotion and heroic constancy, and an extensive repertoire of intrigue patterns and character types. English society had its moments of drama, but nothing that could give birth to the sustained raciness, passion and cunning of the characters in the novella tradition.[11]

But what kinds of private enterprise might be prepared for that would require the prudential and oratorial readiness demanded by the exigencies of foreign and domestic policy making? As one reads through Painter's fictions, as well as those translated by contemporaries, one is struck by a preference for plots in which extreme situations are brought about and resolved by the exhibition of skill, not only in conceiving a scheme or plot of action, but in reemplotting the circumstances of the problem itself so as to ensure the cooperation of otherwise doubtful or hostile forces. These 'hostile forces', however, are not military but conceptual; they are the customary codes and beliefs that determine (for example) the acquisition of allies and kinsmen through the gift exchange of women . . .

What we seem to be witnessing here is an interest in narrative not as the working out of a solution to satisfy the reader's desire for an 'explanatory effect,' but as a way of alerting the reader to the *uses* of narrative as a method for the emplotment or reinterpretation of circumstances in the interests of a fortunate end. Painter's material looks less heterogeneous if we think of his histories not as tales but as the opening out in discourse of contingent 'states' subject to fortune and to virtuoso emplotment by fortunate travelers . . .

Even the apparently 'romantic' series from day two of the *Decameron*, treating of 'those who after suffering a series of misfortunes are brought to a state of unexpected happiness,' are not actually narratives resolved through the time/space of wandering, or error, but rather allegories of the oratorical and prudential imperative not to overlook 'temporis munera' or the gifts of fortune, even when these are least expected.

I want to turn now to Bandello, the major source for English novellae, whose influence can hardly be overstressed. Here the fascination of the Italian source has generally been ascribed to an Elizabethan taste for elaborate revenges and violent horrors. My thesis that the real attraction lies in the plotted 'order of discourse' seems unlikely, given Bandello's acknowledged inferiority to the eloquent Boccaccio, but, once again, what I am stressing is not so much a structure as a strategy of reading: Bandello offers *the discovery of potential for emplotment*. For, of course, Bandello was mediated – and extensively reemplotted – by the French authors Pierre Boaistuau and Belleforest. Opened up by these authors, Bandello became a treasure trove of 'states' of extremity in the affairs of individuals, kinsfolk, and allies, in which there lay abundant scope for the representation of prudential and oratorical virtue, discovering its occasions in the rapid turns of fortune.

Thus, where other novellae are more clearly structured as plots whose solution lies in the discovery of a 'discrete and wyse invention' of discourse, these mediations of Bandello are overwhelmingly incoherent and discontinuous in tone, overlaid as they are with the contradictory emplotments of rival narratives, competing for the discursive 'occasion' offered by a single set of events. We find them tedious in the first place because of what seems to us a redundant preoccupation with marking at every stage an alteration in the case by the intervention of Fortune, and noting the protagonist's exploitation or otherwise of the aptitude of the time and place (occasion) thus offered to him.[12]

ANTHOLOGY OF CRITICISM

In the last decade several critics have studied Riche's method of composition and his approach to the woman reader:

> Whatever Riche's method of procedure, his blending of various stories into a composite is a characteristic of fiction writers of the period, and a clumsy anticipation of the method employed by dramatists, as in Shakespeare's The Merchant of Venice.[13]

The distance Riche creates between himself and the narratives 'written ... for pleasure by maister L.B. ...' allows Riche to exploit the popularity of translated material and to figure himself (at least superficially) as an editor rather than a writer. This distance is somewhat diminished by Riche's repeated references to himself on his title page and by the stylistic similarities between portions of the text L. B. produced and those from which he makes no pretense of separating himself. Nevertheless, a slight distance remains. Once an ambiguous relationship has been established between himself and portions of his work, Riche is able to present the implicit pessimism of Giraldi Cinthio's novellas as a means of subverting the potential for societal growth and change the other narratives present. In the 'translated' stories he can subvert the implied possibility for widescale social change contained within the Farewell's other tales while diminishing his own personal responsibility for the contents of those translated novellas. The bleak societies they construct are not, he can always assert, his creation, but Giraldi Cinthio's ... or at least L.B.'s[14]

Perhaps with more success than A Petite Palace, the Farewell does pay close attention to the pleasures and concerns of women. This partly because prodigal interests – the interests of younger sons as these are given limited expression before their inevitable repeal – often intersect with those of women, for both parties may stand to gain from a temporary disruption of the patriarchal status quo. Several of Rich's heroines brave the wrath of unsympathetic father figures, and like Valerya (Shakespeare's source for Viola) pledge to follow their lovers 'without any regard to the obedience and duetie that I owe to my parents'. They are often forced to leave their homes and, in the limited time granted them before their readmittance to the world of their fathers, they wander in disguise, facing dangers, initiating courtship, resisting unwelcome advances, adapting to new circumstances, and working to support themselves. Such freedom is of course circumscribed, contained within the logic of an impending restoration of patriarchal order, and in this careful regulation of disobedience the individual tales of the *Farewell* resemble those prodigal narratives which take men as their heroes, and channel their repentance back into the service of the order which they had temporarily disrupted.[15]

I would suggest that Rich's ambivalent attitude towards women sustained throughout the work is a consquence of the dilemma Rich is in: he despises 'women's culture' and at the same time he is dependent on it to make a living. This dual response generates much of the tension within and between his prefaces and his eight tales. It would appear that the motif of men dressing as women or dressing in 'womanish' fashions occurs when the text is most anxious about the decorum of a man writing romances for women. It is a motif which ultimately challenges male authority; for while romance sanctions women dressing as men . . . it becomes far more problematic and worrying when men dress as women. When, for example, in Spenser's *Faerie Queene*, the victorious Radigund dresses Artegall in 'woman's weeds', it is seen as a moment of complete shame and humiliation . . . But while Britomart reads the 'speaking picture' before her of the noble Artegall dressed in women's clothes as an image of disorder and mortification, its literal equivalent for Rich – men writing romances for women – might, in fact, be far less problematic for women readers than for men. Rich's anxiety over 'becoming like a woman' by writing romances for women could generate a similar anxiety in men who might be reading them: a woman reader is far less likely to be faced with this dilemma. Indeed, there is much for women to value in Rich's romances: his fictional women have mostly been characterized by strength, independence, resourcefulness and wit, as well as loyalty, and virtue, and they have acted in a context of freedom which would have been seldom available to Rich's contemporary women readers.[16]

Lorna Hutson responded to Lucas's work as follows:

My own reading of the prose fiction of the 1560s and 1570s as being fundamentally concerned with the definition of *masculinity* rather than femininity does not preclude attention to the position of women as subjects and readers of this fiction. It does, however, aim to revise the impression given by Lucas' (otherwise very helpful) account, that the centrality of women to this form of fiction was motivated by men's desire to anticipate and cater for women's tastes. For if, as I shall argue, this fiction is primarily concerned with the emergence of textual communication as the new medium in which manhood is to be tried, then its preoccupation with lengthy speeches of courtship made to women, rather than lengthy descriptions of combats between men, may have less to do with the anticipated pleasure of women readers than with the displacement of masculine agency from prowess to persuasion.[17]

The centrality of women to such fiction is not, then, necessarily a concession to the tastes of women readers, nor even a concessionary move from the 'public' to the 'private' sphere. Rather it is that fictions of women, focusing men's narratives of persuasive efficiency, become coextensive with the enterprise of authorship itself as the medium of masculine social advancement. For, as humanism relocated the space of trial for masculine *virtus* from battlefield to text, so anthologies (rhetorical 'gatherings' of poetry and fictional history), appearing in print before other men's eyes, became the new place in which men displayed the cerebral equivalent of chivalric prowess, in virtuoso deployments of their skill in probable argument.[18]

References

1 In Homer's *Odyssey*, Circe is a witch who turns many of Odysseus' men into swine. She is often used as a figure for the power of men's appetites to make them like animals.
2 The publishing of Catholic books was illegal in England, so English-language Catholic books were printed in Louvain, Belgium, and distributed in England.
3 Thomas Malory's *Morte Darthur* is a romance about King Arthur's court.
4 Petrarch's *Triumphs* are a series of six philosophical poems on Love, Chastity, Death, Fame, Time and Divinity. They were translated and published by Henry Parker, Lord Morley (1476–1556).
5 Bocace is Boccaccio. Translations of his tales by Painter, which are included in this volume, had appeared in 1566 and 1567.
6 Early Christians, members of a community founded by St Paul, burned books of sorcery at Ephesus.
7 John Major, *Sir Thomas Elyot and Renaissance Humanism* (Lincoln, Nebr.: University of Nebraska Press, 1964), pp. 256–9.

8 Lorna Hutson, *The Usurer's Daughter: Male Friendship and Fictions of Women in Sixteenth-Century England* (London and New York: Routledge, 1994), pp. 63–4.

9 Yvonne Rodax, *The Real and the Ideal in the Novella of Italy, France and England: Four Centuries of Change in the Boccaccian Tale* (Chapel Hill, NC: University of North Carolina Press, 1968), p. 96.

10 Margaret Schlauch, *Antecedents of the English Novel: 1400–1600 (from Chaucer to Deloney)* (Warsaw: PWN; London: Oxford University Press, 1963), pp. 151, 156.

11 Barnabe Riche, *His Farewell to Military Profession*, ed. Donald Beecher, Publications of the Barnabe Riche Society 1 (Ottowa: Dovehouse; Binghamton, NY: Medieval and Renaissance Texts and Studies, 1992), p. 37.

12 Lorna Hutson, 'Fortunate travelers: reading for the plot in sixteenth-century England', *Representations*, 41 (1993), pp. 94, 96–7.

13 D. T. Starnes, 'Barnabe Riche's "Sappho Duke of Mantona": a study in Elizabethan story-making', *Studies in Philology*, 30 (1933), p. 471.

14 Constance C. Relihan, *Fashioning Authority: The Development of Elizabethan Novelistic Discourse* (Kent, Ohio, and London: Kent State University Press, 1994), pp. 52–3.

15 Juliet V. Fleming, 'The ladies' man and the age of Elizabeth', in *Sexuality and Gender in Early Modern Europe*, ed. James Grantham Turner (Cambridge: Cambridge University Press, 1993), p. 172.

16 Caroline Lucas, *Writing for Women: The Example of Woman as Reader in Elizabethan Romance* (Milton Keynes and Philadelphia: Open University Press, 1989), pp. 116–17.

17 Hutson, *The Usurer's Daughter*, p. 89.

18 Ibid., p. 99.

SUGGESTIONS FOR FURTHER READING

Some of the sixteenth-century novella anthologies have been printed in modern editions; all these editions have very thorough introductions which discuss the texts as translations and as influences on later works: *The Cobler of Caunterburie and Tarltons Newes Out of Purgatorie*, ed. Jane Belfield and Geoffrey Creigh (Leiden: Brill, 1987); William Painter, *The Palace of Pleasure*, ed. Joseph Jacobs (1890; repr. New York: Dover, 1966); Barnabe Riche, *His Farewell to Military Profession*, ed. Donald Beecher, Publications of the Barnabe Riche Society 1 (Ottawa: Dovehouse; Binghamton, NY: Medieval and Renaissance Texts and Studies, 1992); and George Whetstone, *An Heptameron of Civill Discourses: A Critical Edition*, ed. Diana Shklanka, The Renaissance Imagination 35 (New York and London: Garland, 1987).

Two general studies of the novella include discussions of the English versions: Robert Clements and Joseph Gibaldi, *Anatomy of the Novella* (New York: New York University Press, 1977); and Yvonne Rodax, *The Real and the Ideal in the Novella of Italy, France and England: Four Centuries of Change in the Boccaccian Tale* (Chapel Hill, NC: University of North Carolina Press, 1968).

Essential for all study of translations of Boccaccio, and their influence, is Herbert G. Wright, *Boccaccio in England from Chaucer to Tennyson* (London: Athlone Press, 1957). Fundamental to all study of Bandello's inflence is René Pruvost, *Matteo Bandello and Elizabethan Fiction* (Paris: 1937).

Three recent books have extensive discussions of novelle and their authors: Lorna Hutson, *The Usurer's Daughter: Male Friendship and Fictions of Women in Sixteenth-Century England* (London: Routledge, 1994); Constance C. Relihan, *Fashioning Authority: The Development of Elizabethan Novelistic Discourse* (Kent, Ohio, and London: Kent State University Press, 1994); Caroline Lucas, *Writing for Women: The Example of Woman as Reader in Elizabethan Romance* (Milton Keynes and Philadelphia: Open University Press, 1989).

A great deal has been written on Shakespeare and his sources. The fundamental work is Geoffrey Bullough, *Narrative and Dramatic*

Sources of Shakespeare (London: Routledge and Kegan Paul; New York: Columbia University Press, 1958). Two more useful books that provide a basic description of how he shaped the material are: Kenneth Muir, *Shakespeare's Sources*, I: *Comedies and Tragedies* (London: Methuen, 1957; repr. with new appendices 1961, 1965); and Max Bluestone, *From Story to Stage: The Dramatic Adaptation of Prose Fiction in the Period of Shakespeare and his Contemporaries* (The Hague and Paris: Mouton, 1974).

A good general guide to the period is *The New Pelican Guide to English Literature* II: *The Age of Shakespeare*, ed. Boris Ford, rev. edn. (Harmondsworth: Penguin, 1982).

ACKNOWLEDGEMENTS

I am grateful to Helen Cooper of University College, Oxford, and to Sister Mary Clemente Davlin, O.P., for the help that they gave me on the notes, to Jenny Fellows for her excellent editing, to the Plattners for their frequent hospitality, to my husband, David, for his encouragement and advice, to Rhode Island College for research funds, and to the many generous and helpful librarians at the following libraries: Bancroft (University of California), Bodleian, British, Cambridge University, Folger Shakespeare, Houghton (Harvard) and Huntington.

The editor and publishers wish to thank the following for permission to use copyright material:

University of California Press for material from Lorna Hutson, 'Fortunate Travelers: Reading for the plot in sixteenth-century England', *Representations*, 41 (1993), pp. 94, 96-7.

SHAKESPEARE
IN EVERYMAN

*Edited by John Andrews, the Everyman Shakespeare is the
most comprehensive, up-to-date paperback edition of
the plays and poems, featuring:*

face-to-face text and notes

chronology of Shakespeare's life and times

a rich selection of **critical and theatrical responses**
to the play over the centuries

foreword by an actor or director describing
the play in performance

up-to-date commentary on the play

Antony and Cleopatra £3.99

Hamlet £2.99

Julius Caesar £3.99

King Lear £2.99

Macbeth £2.99

Measure for Measure £3.99

The Merchant of Venice £2.99

A Midsummer Night's Dream
£1.99

Othello £3.99

Romeo and Juliet £2.99

The Tempest £2.99

Twelfth Night £3.99

The Winter's Tale £3.99

All books are available from your local bookshop or direct from:
Littlehampton Book Services Cash Sales, 14 Eldon Way, Lineside Estate,
Littlehampton, West Sussex BN17 7HE (*prices are subject to change*)

To order any of the books, please enclose a cheque (in sterling) made payable to
Littlehampton Book Services, or phone your order through with credit card details (Access,
Visa or Mastercard) on 01903 721596 (24 hour answering service) stating card number
and expiry date. (*Please add £1.25 for package and postage to the total of your order.*)

In the USA, for further information and a complete catalogue call 1-800-526-2778

FOREIGN LITERATURE IN TRANSLATION IN EVERYMAN

A Hero of Our Time
MIKHAIL LERMONTOV
*The Byronic adventures of
a Russian army officer*
£5.99

L'Assommoir
ÉMILE ZOLA
*One of the most successful novels
of the nineteenth century and one
of the most scandalous*
£6.99

Poor Folk and The Gambler
FYODOR DOSTOYEVSKY
*These two short works of doomed
passion are among Dostoyevsky's
quintessential best. Combination
unique to Everyman*
£4.99

Yevgeny Onegin
ALEXANDER PUSHKIN
*Pushkin's novel in verse is Russia's
best-loved literary work. It contains some of the loveliest Russian
poetry ever written*
£5.99

The Three-Cornered Hat
ANTONIO PEDRO DE ALARCÓN
*A rollicking farce and one of
the world's greatest masterpieces
of humour. Available only in
Everyman*
£4.99

Notes from Underground and A Confession
FYODOR DOSTOYEVSKY *and*
LEV TOLSTOY
*Russia's greatest novelists ruthlessly
tackle the subject of their mid-life
crises. Combination unique to
Everyman*
£4.99

Selected Stories
ANTON CHEKHOV
edited and revised by Donald
Rayfield
*Masterpieces of compression and
precision. Selection unique to
Everyman*
£7.99

Selected Writings
VOLTAIRE
*A comprehensive edition of
Voltaire's best writings. Selection
unique to Everyman*
£6.99

Fontamara
IGNAZIO SILONE
*'A beautifully composed tragedy.
Fontamara is as fresh now, and as
moving, as it must have been when
first published.'* London Standard.
Available only in Everyman
£4.99

All books are available from your local bookshop or direct from:
Littlehampton Book Services Cash Sales, 14 Eldon Way, Lineside Estate,
Littlehampton, West Sussex BN17 7HE (*prices are subject to change*)

To order any of the books, please enclose a cheque (in sterling) made payable to
Littlehampton Book Services, or phone your order through with credit card details (Access,
Visa or Mastercard) on 01903 721596 (24 hour answering service) stating card number
and expiry date. (*Please add £1.25 for package and postage to the total of your order.*)

In the USA, for further information and a complete catalogue call 1-800-526-2778

SHORT STORY COLLECTIONS
IN EVERYMAN

The Strange Case of Dr Jekyll and Mr Hyde and Other Stories
R. L. STEVENSON
An exciting selection of gripping tales from a master of suspense
£1.99

Nineteenth-Century American Short Stories
edited by Christopher Bigsby
A selection of the works of Henry James, Edith Wharton, Mark Twain and many other great American writers
£6.99

The Best of Saki
edited by MARTIN STEPHEN
Includes Tobermory, Gabriel Ernest, Svedni Vashtar, The Interlopers, Birds on the Western Front
£4.99

Souls Belated and Other Stories
EDITH WHARTON
Brief, neatly crafted tales exploring a range of themes from big taboo subjects to the subtlest little ironies of social life
£6.99

The Night of the Iguana and Other Stories
TENNESSEE WILLIAMS
Twelve remarkable short stories, each a compelling drama in miniature
£4.99

Selected Short Stories and Poems
THOMAS HARDY
Hardy's most memorable stories and poetry in one volume
£4.99

Selected Tales
HENRY JAMES
Stories portraying the tensions between private life and the outside world
£5.99

The Best of Sherlock Homes
ARTHUR CONAN DOYLE
All the favourite adventures in one volume
£4.99

The Secret Self 1: *Short Stories by Women*
edited by Hermione Lee
'*A superb collection*' The Guardian
£4.99

All books are available from your local bookshop or direct from:
Littlehampton Book Services Cash Sales, 14 Eldon Way, Lineside Estate,
Littlehampton, West Sussex BN17 7HE (*prices are subject to change*)

To order any of the books, please enclose a cheque (in sterling) made payable to
Littlehampton Book Services, or phone your order through with credit card details (Access,
Visa or Mastercard) on 01903 721596 (24 hour answering service) stating card number
and expiry date. (*Please add £1.25 for package and postage to the total of your order.*)

In the USA, for further information and a complete catalogue call 1-800-526-2778

DRAMA
IN EVERYMAN

The Oresteia
AESCHYLUS
*New translation of one of the
greatest Greek dramatic trilogies
which analyses the plays in
performance*
£5.99

**Everyman and Medieval
Miracle Plays**
edited by A. C. Cawley
*A selection of the most popular
medieval plays*
£4.99

Complete Plays and Poems
CHRISTOPHER MARLOWE
*The complete works of this great
Elizabethan in one volume*
£5.99

Restoration Plays
edited by Robert Lawrence
*Five comedies and two tragedies
representing the best of the
Restoration stage*
£7.99

**Female Playwrights of the
Restoration: Five Comedies**
edited by Paddy Lyons
*Rediscovered literary treasures
in a unique selection*
£5.99

**Plays, Prose Writings
and Poems**
OSCAR WILDE
*The full force of Wilde's wit
in one volume*
£4.99

**A Dolls House/The Lady from
the Sea/The Wild Duck**
HENRIK IBSEN
introduced by Fay Weldon
*A popular selection of Ibsen's
major plays*
£4.99

**The Beggar's Opera and
Other Eighteenth-Century Plays**
JOHN GAY et. al.
Including Goldsmith's She Stoops
To Conquer *and Sheridan's* The
School for Scandal, *this is a volume
which reflects the full scope of the
period's theatre*
£6.99

**Female Playwrights of the
Nineteenth Century**
edited by Adrienne Scullion
*The full range of female nineteenth-
century dramatic development*
£6.99

All books are available from your local bookshop or direct from:
Littlehampton Book Services Cash Sales, 14 Eldon Way, Lineside Estate,
Littlehampton, West Sussex BN17 7HE (*prices are subject to change*)

To order any of the books, please enclose a cheque (in sterling) made payable to
Littlehampton Book Services, or phone your order through with credit card details (Access,
Visa or Mastercard) on 01903 721596 (24 hour answering service) stating card number
and expiry date. (*Please add* £1.25 *for package and postage to the total of your order.*)

In the USA, for further information and a complete catalogue call 1-800-526-2778

POETRY
IN EVERYMAN

Amorous Rites: Elizabethan Erotic Verse
edited by Sandra Clark
Erotic and often comic poems dealing with myths of transformation and erotic interaction between humans and gods
£4.99

Selected Poems
JOHN KEATS
An excellent selection of the poetry of one of the principal figures of the Romantic movement
£6.99

Poems and Prose
CHRISTINA ROSSETTI
A new collection of her writings, poetry and prose, marking the centenary of her death
£5.99

Poems and Prose
P. B. SHELLEY
The essential Shelley in one volume
£5.99

Silver Poets of the Sixteenth Century
edited by Douglas Brooks-Davies
An exciting and comprehensive collection
£6.99

Complete English Poems
JOHN DONNE
The father of metaphysical verse in this highly-acclaimed collection
£6.99

Complete English Poems, Of Education, Areopagitica
JOHN MILTON
An excellent introduction to Milton's poetry and prose
£6.99

Women Romantic Poets
1780–1830: An Anthology
edited by Jennifer Breen
Hidden talent from the Romantic era rediscovered
£5.99

Selected Poems
D. H. LAWRENCE
An authoritative selection spanning the whole of Lawrence's literary career
£4.99

The Poems
W. B. YEATS
Ireland's greatest lyric poet surveyed in this ground-breaking edition
£7.99

All books are available from your local bookshop or direct from:
Littlehampton Book Services Cash Sales, 14 Eldon Way, Lineside Estate,
Littlehampton, West Sussex BN17 7HE (*prices are subject to change*)

To order any of the books, please enclose a cheque (in sterling) made payable to
Littlehampton Book Services, or phone your order through with credit card details (Access,
Visa or Mastercard) on 01903 721596 (24 hour answering service) stating card number
and expiry date. (*Please add £1.25 for package and postage to the total of your order.*)

In the USA, for further information and a complete catalogue call 1-800-526-2778

MEDIEVAL LITERATURE
IN EVERYMAN

The Canterbury Tales
GEOFFREY CHAUCER
*The complete medieval text with
translations*
£4.99

The Vision of Piers Plowman
WILLIAM LANGLAND
edited by A. V. C. Schmidt
*The only complete edition of the
B-Text available*
£6.99

**Sir Gawain and the Green
Knight, Pearl, Cleanness,
Patience**
edited by J. J. Anderson
*Four major English medieval
poems in one volume*
£5.99

Arthurian Romances
CHRÉTIEN DE TROYES
translated by D. D. R. Owen
*Classic tales from the father of
Arthurian romance*
£5.99

**Everyman and Medieval
Miracle Plays**
edited by A. C. Cawley
*A fully representative selection
from the major play cycles*
£4.99

Anglo-Saxon Poetry
edited by S. A. J. Bradley
*An anthology of prose translations
covering most of the surviving
poetry of early medieval literature*
£6.99

Six Middle English Romances
edited by Maldwyn Mills
Tales of heroism and piety
£4.99

**Ywain and Gawain,
Sir Percyvell of Gales,
The Anturs of Arther**
edited by Maldwyn Mills
*Three Middle English romances
portraying the adventures of
Gawain*
£5.99

**The Birth of Romance:
An Anthology**
translated by Judith Weiss
*The first-ever English translation
of fascinating Anglo-Norman
romances*
£4.99

The Piers Plowman Tradition
edited by Helen Barr
*Four medieval poems of political
and religious dissent – available
together for the first time*
£5.99